Emerging Concepts of Alcohol Dependence

E. Mansell Pattison, M.D.

Professor of Psychiatry and Human Behavior, Social Science, and Social Ecology, and Vice-Chairman, Department of Psychiatry and Human Behavior, University of California, Irvine; and Deputy Director, Training, Consultation, and Education Division, Orange County Department of Mental Health, Santa Ana, California

Mark B. Sobell, Ph.D.

Associate Professor, Director of Graduate Studies on Alcohol Dependence, Department of Psychology, Vanderbilt University

Linda C. Sobell, Ph.D.

Director, Alcohol Programs, Dede Wallace Center, Nashville, Tennessee, and Adjunct Assistant Professor, Department of Psychology, Vanderbilt University

E. Mansell Pattison,
Mark B. Sobell, and Linda C. Sobell

Emerging Concepts of Alcohol Dependence

with 22 contributors

Springer Publishing Company

New York

Springer Publishing Company, Inc.
200 Park Avenue South
New York, N.Y. 10003

77 78 79 80 81 / 10 9 8 7 6 5 4 3 2 1

Designed by Patrick Vitacco

Library of Congress Cataloging in Publication Data

Main entry under title:

Emerging concepts of alcohol dependence.

    Bibliography: p.
    Includes index.
    1. Alcoholism.   I.   Pattison, E. Mansell, 1933–
II. Sobell, Mark B.   III.   Sobell, Linda C.
RC562.E46   616.8'61   77–4115
ISBN 0–8261–1950–6

Printed in the United States of America

To the memory of
E. M. Jellinek
for his contributions to
and encouragement of
the scientific study
of alcohol problems

Contents

Part Two

A Revised Model
of Alcohol Dependence

Contents

Contributors

Don Cahalan, Ph.D.
Professor of Behavioral Sciences in Residence, School of Public Health, University of California, Berkeley

Walter B. Clark, M.A.
Assistant Professor of Sociology, Queen's University, Kingston, Ontario

Ronald Coe, M.D.
Private practice of medicine, Seattle, Washington.

Hans O. Doerr, Ph.D.
Associate Professor of Psychiatry (Psychology), University of Washington

G. C. Gleser, Ph.D.
Professor of Psychiatry (Psychology), University of Cincinnati College of Medicine

Maury Gollob, M.D.
Research Assistant, Oklahoma Medical Research Foundation

L. A. Gottschalk, M.D.
Professor and Chairman, Department of Psychiatry and Human Behavior, University of California, Irvine

E. B. Headley, M.D.
Assistant Professor of Preventive Medicine, University of Cincinnati College of Medicine

William R. Hood, Ph.D.
deceased, formerly Associate Professor of Research Psychology, Department of Psychiatry and Behavioral Sciences, College of Medicine, University of Oklahoma, and Associate Professor of Human Ecology, School of Health, University of Oklahoma

Mark Keller
Editor, *Journal of Alcohol Studies*

A. S. Linsky, Ph.D.
Professor of Sociology, University of New Hampshire

Arnold M. Ludwig, M.D.
Professor and Chairman, Department of Psychiatry, University of Kentucky College of Medicine

Marcia K. Moss
Research Assistant, Alcoholism and Drug Addiction Research Foundation, Toronto, Ontario

Jim Orford, Ph.D.
Research Associate, Addiction Research Unit, Institute of Psychiatry, London, England

Alfonso Paredes, M.D.
Professor of Research Psychiatry, Department of Psychiatry and Behavioral Sciences, College of Medicine, University of Oklahoma

Paul M. Roman, Ph.D.
Professor of Human Relations, Tulane University

Wolfgang Schmidt, Ph.D.
Research Associate, Alcoholism and Drug Addiction Research Foundation, Toronto, Ontario

Harry Seymour, B.S.
Research Assistant, Oklahoma Medical Research Foundation

Reginald G. Smart, Ph.D.
Director of Research, Alcoholism and Drug Addiction Research Foundation, Toronto, Ontario

Louis H. Stark, M.D.
Private practice of medicine, San Francisco, California

H. M. Trice, Ph.D.
Professor of Industrial and Labor Relations, Cornell University

Abraham Wikler, M.D.
Professor of Psychiatry, University of Kentucky College of Medicine

Emerging Concepts of Alcohol Dependence

Introduction:
Old and New Views
of Alcohol Dependence

The field of alcoholism is changing rapidly. A scant quarter of a century ago alcohol problems were virtually neglected. At that time, except for a few professionals, the only concerned people were recovered alcoholics who heroically tried to help one another. When the first formal alcoholism programs did develop, there were few recorded clinical and experimental data. Since that time, the situation has dramatically changed. There is now a variety of para-professional and professional training programs. Local, state, and federal alcoholism authorities have been established with at least modest funding. Formal alcoholism treatment programs have mushroomed across the country, while a wealth of clinical data and experimental research has been published.

In 1950 there was a dearth of established clinical and scientific knowledge from which to design treatment programs. Most of the knowledge about alcoholism derived from the personal experiences of recovered alcoholics and rather perfunctory clinical observations. There were numerous unanswered questions about the phenomenon called alcoholism. Yet, there was an exigent need to organize the existing facts and impressions into a working concept of alcoholism. Thus, there developed a tenuously formulated set of concepts that we shall call the traditional model of alcoholism.

The Traditional Model of Alcoholism

Defining traditional concepts of alcoholism is an extraordinarily difficult task, because they derive from multiple sources —Alcoholics Anonymous, books relating individual struggles with alcoholism, the disease concept of alcoholism formulated by E. M. Jellinek, and public interpretations of these ideas. The traditional model, as we shall consider it, can best be described as a "folk science" model. It is an accretion of beliefs, values, and ideologies. In large part, its development was intended to meet sociopolitical needs rather than to synthesize scientific findings. This brief summary of traditional concepts provides a context for understanding

1

why it is necessary to develop new concepts of alcohol dependence. We have identified the following basic elements as comprising the traditional model of alcoholism; we acknowledge that not everyone working in the field of alcoholism will agree with this exact formulation.

1. *There is a unitary phenomenon which can be identified as alcoholism.* Despite its variations, alcoholism can be considered a distinct entity which can be described and recognized.

2. *Alcoholics and prealcoholics are essentially different from nonalcoholics.* Some of those persons who are not already alcoholics are predisposed to develop alcohol problems if they drink at all. The alcoholic reacts differently to alcohol than the nonalcoholic. This difference may be pre-existing or developmental and probably has a physiological basis, perhaps genetically determined. A nonalcoholic may experience drinking problems but does not become a true alcoholic.

3. *Alcoholics may sometimes experience a seemingly irresistible physical craving for alcohol, or a strong psychological compulsion to drink.* They often appear to begin drinking against their own volition.

4. *Alcoholics gradually develop a process called "loss of control" over drinking, and possibly even an inability to stop drinking.* By Jellinek's definition, this "loss of control" happens even when the alcoholic has ingested only a small amount of alcohol; physical dependence on alcohol becomes established and somehow compels the alcoholic to continue drinking. By popular definition, "loss of control" has been extended to mean that once an alcoholic has begun to drink, that person has no voluntary control over further drinking behavior during that episode—"First drink, then drunk." These two versions of "loss of control" should not be confused with one another.

5. *Alcoholism is a permanent and irreversible condition.* As alcoholism develops, permanent biological changes occur in the alcoholic. Even after a number of years, ingestion of only a small quantity of alcohol by a person who was once physically dependent on alcohol will reinitiate physical dependence. Since the physiological consequences of alcoholism are enduring even when the alcoholic is not drinking, alcoholism can be arrested but never cured in the sense of the alcoholic ever being able to drink in a nonproblem manner. "Once an alcoholic, always an alcoholic."

6. *Alcoholism is a progressive disease which follows an inexorable development through a distinct series of phases.* For most alcoholics,

alcoholism is a disease process which develops gradually over a ten-
to fifteen-year period. If the alcoholic's drinking is not arrested, this
progression will lead to ultimate deterioration and death.

The components of the traditional model are not necessarily
interdependent. Some major elements could be modified or omitted without affecting all of the remaining components. Overall,
however, the traditional model has had clear implications for the
design of alcoholism treatment services. Specifically, it dictates that
alcoholism treatment should emphasize making alcoholics aware of
their permanent physiological abnormality and the necessity for
them to be permanently abstinent. Further, it implies that treatment should be largely concerned with problems which result from
learning to live without alcohol.

However, in recent years many fundamental assumptions of the
traditional model of alcoholism have been seriously challenged by
new clinical and experimental evidence. Because these data conflict
with traditional concepts, the evidence has often been ignored or
dismissed by those working in the field. Taken as a whole, this
recent evidence indicates that substantial changes in the heretofore
popularly accepted "facts" about the nature of alcohol dependence
are inevitable. We shall find, for example, that there appears to be
no separately definable entity which can be identified as "alcoholism." Rather there appears to be a variety of situations which
have in common that persons suffer adverse consequences as a
result of using alcohol. Eventually, certain factors—physiological,
psychological, sociocultural, and/or environmental—which increase the susceptibility for persons to incur drinking problems are
likely to be identified. However, the breadth of such determinants
and problems already appears so encompassing that the post hoc
labeling of individuals as "alcoholic" has little utility and may even
precipitate a worsening of some persons' drinking problems. Physical dependence on alcohol has been repeatedly demonstrated not
to occur merely from the ingestion of a few drinks, even by the
most chronic of "alcoholics." Further, the "progressive" nature of
the development of alcohol problems has been seriously challenged by recent epidemiological and longitudinal data. Finally,
there exist a multitude of demonstrations that alcohol problems
are reversible, at least for some individuals. This accumulation of
evidence conflicts with traditional concepts to such a degree that
the two cannot be reconciled. The resulting problems threaten to
restrict the range of available treatment and prevention services,

and to hinder the development of new and more effective treatment methods.

Having recognized the present failings of traditional concepts, we must develop new concepts of alcohol dependence which are more consonant with contemporary research findings. While it would be premature to specify a formal revised model of alcohol dependence, we can suggest the characteristics of such a model based on the present state of knowledge. The sociopolitical objectives of earlier concepts have in large part been satisfactorily achieved, and the need for providing services to individuals who have alcohol problems has been generally accepted and legislated in most cases. It is now time to move in the direction of developing a better quality of service, both in terms of effectiveness and efficiency.

Emerging Concepts of Alcohol Dependence

In outline fashion, we have identified the following probable implications of recent research evidence which form a preview of the emerging concepts of alcohol dependence more completely enumerated in this book.

1. *Alcohol dependence summarizes a variety of syndromes defined by drinking patterns and the adverse physical, psychological, and/or social consequences of such drinking. These syndromes, jointly denoted as "alcohol dependence," are best considered as a serious health problem.* At present, there is no factual basis upon which to categorize alcohol problems unequivocally as either purely biological or purely psychological phenomena, and there are compelling arguments against making such a simple dichotomy. On the other hand, there is ample evidence that alcohol problems can affect the physical and/or mental well-being of individuals and that persons suffering from alcohol problems are often in need of a variety of interdisciplinary services.

2. *An individual's pattern of use of alcohol can be considered as lying on a continuum, ranging from nonpathological to severely pathological.*

3. *Any person who uses alcohol can develop a syndrome of alcohol dependence.* A variety of factors may contribute to differential susceptibility to alcohol problems; however, these factors in and of themselves do not produce alcohol dependence.

4. *The development of alcohol problems follows variable patterns over time and does not necessarily proceed inexorably to severe fatal stages.* A

given set of alcohol problems may progress or reverse through either naturalistic or treatment processes.

5. *Recovery from alcohol dependence bears no necessary relation to abstinence, although such a concurrence is frequently the case.*

6. *The consumption of a small amount of alcohol by an individual once labeled as "alcoholic" does not initiate either physical dependence or a physiological need for more alcohol by that individual.*

7. *Continued drinking of large doses of alcohol over an extended period of time is likely to initiate a process of physical dependence which will eventually be manifested as an alcohol withdrawal syndrome.*

8. *The population of persons with alcohol problems is multivariant. Correspondingly, treatment services should be diverse, emphasizing the development of a variety of services, with determination of which treatments, delivered in which contexts, are most effective for which persons and which types of problems.*

9. *Alcohol problems are typically interrelated with other life problems, especially when alcohol dependence is long established.* Treatment needs should be uniquely assessed for each individual and should address all areas of alcohol-related life and health problems. Similarly, treatment outcome evaluation should measure other areas of life functioning in addition to measuring changes in drinking behavior. Treatment goals should be realistic and consider the individual's potential for change. Degrees of improvement must be recognized as a beneficial outcome.

10. *An emphasis should be placed on dealing with alcohol problems in the environment in which they occur.* This is because of the strong relationships which have been demonstrated between drinking behaviors and environmental variables.

11. *Treatment services should be designed to provide for a continuity of care throughout the lengthy process of recovery from alcohol problems.*

This book is structured so it can be used by a variety of readers, ranging from the interested layman to the research scientist. The text presents a critical analysis of the traditional model of alcoholism, addressing the major issues in a nontechnical manner. Those readers desiring a rapid overview may read only the text and follow the basic lines of evidence to the conclusions presented. For those who wish to examine the original data for themselves, relevant literature is cited for each of the issues discussed and the citations are assembled in a comprehensive reference list.

Finally, each major section includes original source readings which present technical data to support the content of each text section. They also permit the reader to further evaluate the evidence which has been briefly described in the text.

Since there are still several areas where data are too ambiguous and/or insufficient to draw firm conclusions, we believe it is premature to offer an unrelenting set of new concepts of alcohol dependence that brook no equivocation. Rather, we are attempting to set forth the existing evidence as we see it and to present a reformulation of the data as emerging concepts of alcohol dependence.

Part One
Traditional Concepts in Conflict with New Data

1. A Critical Analysis of the Traditional Model

Traditional Concepts

The most profound and pervasive influence in the alcoholism field to date has been the so-called disease model, formulated most completely by E. M. Jellinek in his book *The Disease Concept of Alcoholism* (1960). Jellinek presented his theory as a working hypothesis—a set of ideas proposed as a possible explanation of how persons develop serious drinking problems, but the validity of which needed to be determined by empirical research. His thoughts were presented modestly and cloaked in caution, lest some mistake his speculations for facts. Noting that his concepts were already being misused, he explicitly stated that he had no intention of creating a rigid model. The disease concept proposed by Jellinek served to organize, synthesize, and give medical credence to the scientific and naturalistic observations of his day. However, while his disease concept had theoretical coherence and clinical utility, he also recognized its shortcomings. Relatively little substantive clinical research on the topic of alcohol problems had been conducted during the first half of this century. Jellinek acknowledged that his model lacked a demonstrated foundation in the scientific literature, stating: "For the time being this may suffice, but not indefinitely" (p. 159).

Why, then, was a theory which lacked empirical support advocated by its proponents with such vigor? To answer this question, it is necessary to look beyond the restricted domain of scientific investigation. Jellinek's primary intent in advancing the disease concept of alcoholism was to influence both contemporary medical practices and sociopolitical processes. He noted that some of his psychiatrically and psychologically oriented colleagues had either denied the occurrence of alcohol withdrawal symptoms, or oddly omitted mention of such phenomena (p. 131). One implication of this orientation was that persons would never be in need of medical management merely for the treatment of alcohol withdrawal. During Jellinek's time, persons were routinely incarcerated for public drunkenness and denied appropriate medical services, thereby having to withdraw from alcohol in the drunk tank of local jails (Pittman and Gordon, 1958). Thus, with regard to both legal and medical involvement, Jellinek's disease concept of alcoholism was intended to change public attitudes from blame and punishment of the alcoholic to concern and treatment.

Additional support for traditional concepts derives from their social utility. Labeling alcoholism as a disease was, in part, intended to remove the moral condemnation and stigma which had been attached to alcohol problems by society. Alcoholism was a medical condition which afflicted its victims, not a self-inflicted moral condition. Further, by grounding the disease concept of alcoholism in an alleged physical allergy (presupposed by Alcoholics Anonymous but not by Jellinek) and physical dependence, there could be no equivocation about the fact that alcoholism was truly a disease. Yet, this stance, particularly as adopted by Alcoholics Anonymous, also provided an interesting paradox. While alcoholism was claimed by many to be a physical disease beyond the control of the individual, rehabilitation simultaneously stressed nonmedical methods. Thus, the justification for labeling alcoholism as a disease did not rest on the demonstration of some biological abnormality but rather on the sociopolitical utility which the disease concept served by way of ameliorating the socially deviant position of the alcoholic in society.

The traditional model of alcoholism often bears only a marginal relationship to the tentative ideas proposed by Jellinek. Keller (1972) has discussed many of the misuses and misinterpretations that have been made of Jellinek's formulations and suggested that the major source of misinterpretation was members of Alcoholics Anonymous, which had already formulated a physical allergy theory of alcoholism parallel to but not at all identical with Jellinek's model. Jellinek dispensed with such a conception by stating that it was adequate for the purposes of AA, "as long as they do not wish to foist it upon students of alcoholism" (1960, p. 87). What makes the origins of the traditional model of alcoholism so difficult to specify, however, is public and professional interpretation and misinterpretation of the Jellinek and AA models.

The following traditional concepts of alcoholism cannot be found in a complete form in any single reference. While we recognize that many might not agree with this precise formulation, we believe that it represents the majority range of opinion of those currently working or interested in the field of alcohol dependence. Our considerations are based primarily on three reference sources: (1) the published literature of Alcoholics Anonymous; (2) the published works of E. M. Jellinek, with special attention to *The*

Disease Concept of Alcoholism (1960); and (3) a variety of less formally stated but publicly influential interpretations of both Jellinek's and Alcoholics Anonymous' positions, particularly Marty Mann's *New Primer on Alcoholism* (1958). The second edition of that book (1968), written by the co-founder of the National Council on Alcoholism, is now in its thirteenth printing. The book is often used as a basic training resource and quoted as an authoritative source. Rather than describing each of these sources individually, we will address traditional concepts in order, illustrating various contributions from each of the above orientations.

Proposition 1. There is a unitary phenomenon which can be identified as alcoholism.

The view of alcoholism as a distinct entity has many historical origins related to simplistic disease notions about drinking problems (Jellinek, 1960). This view is perhaps most evident in the works of Alcoholics Anonymous and the theorizing of Dr. William Silkworth, who was closely involved with the founding of AA in the 1930's. In *Alcoholics Anonymous Comes of Age* (1957), Bill W., one of the co-founders of AA, recalls that Dr. Silkworth supplied the tools with which to puncture the toughest alcoholic ego, "those shattering phrases by which he described our illness: the *obsession of the mind* that compels us to drink and the *allergy of the body* that condemns us to go mad or die" (p. 13). In the original edition of the book *Alcoholics Anonymous* (1939), this proposition is expressed by a physician in the initial chapter which is titled "The doctor's opinion": "We believe, and so suggested a few years ago, that the action of alcohol on these chronic alcoholics is a manifestation of an allergy; that the phenomenon of craving is limited to this class and never occurs in the average temperate drinkers. These allergic types can never safely use alcohol in any form at all . . ." (p. 4). In 1950, Dr. Silkworth himself expressed these ideas more strongly: "In very recent years medical science has classified alcoholism as a disease—the manifestation of an allergy—and alcoholics as those persons whose drinking cannot be controlled but who must resort to it compulsively for the scope and relief they crave and which it seems to provide" (in Reilly, 1950, foreword).

Jellinek, on the other hand, did not consider alcohol problems, except in a general sense, to be a singular definable entity. His definition of alcoholism—"any use of alcoholic beverages that causes damage to the individual or society or both" (1960, p. 35)—was purposely vague. He saw the population of individuals described by Alcoholics Anonymous as representing simply one type, or "species," of alcoholism, asserting that: "By adhering strictly to our American ideas about 'alcoholism' and 'alcoholics' (created by Alcoholics Anonymous in their own image) and restricting the term to those ideas, we have been continuing to overlook many other problems of alcohol which need urgent attention" (1960, p. 35). The type of alcoholism which he speculated was most prevalent in the United States and predominant among members of AA, he denoted as *gamma* alcoholism. He defined this type of alcoholism as having the major characteristics of increased tissue tolerance to alcohol, adaptive cell metabolism, withdrawal symptoms, cravings, and loss of control. This was one of only two types of alcoholism for which he believed a "disease" categorization was appropriate. The other disease type, *delta* alcoholism, demonstrated the same first three characteristics as *gamma* alcoholism but substituted an "inability to abstain" for "loss of control." He also discussed two varieties of alcoholism which he felt could *not* be considered as diseases: (1) *alpha* alcoholism was characterized simply by continual use of alcohol to relieve bodily or emotional pain; any dependence which occurred was purely psychological in nature, and the drinking resulted in no serious physical consequences; and (2) *beta* alcoholism was characterized by physical complications presumably resulting from the use of alcohol, but with neither physical nor psychological dependence on alcohol. Finally, he speculated about a less well-defined form of periodic alcoholism designated as *epsilon* alcoholism. He stressed that the listing of only five species of alcoholism was not exhaustive and could be greatly increased. Jellinek recognized that the species he enumerated—and the many other species which could also be described—shared little besides the maladaptive use of alcohol. For this reason, he preferred to talk about "alcoholisms." While it might seem logical to interpret Jellinek as defining *all* of his species of alcoholism as a disease, on pages 39 and 40 of his book he makes clear that his intention is to define *only* the *gamma* and *delta* varieties of alcoholism as a disease.

At a later point in his book, Jellinek specified even more restrictive boundaries to defining alcoholism as a disease:

> The excessive drinker who has been using alcohol intoxication as a means of "problem solution," while still continuing that use is, in addition—and probably more prominently—using alcohol to remedy the psychological, physiological and social stresses and strains

generated by heavy drinking. Only when this occurs in conjunction with acquired increased tolerance, withdrawal symptoms, inability to abstain or loss of control may the excessive user of alcohol be termed an alcohol addict and his drinking behavior regarded as a disease process. (p. 66)

Jellinek's whole thesis was presented as a series of working hypotheses clothed in a suit of caveats. With regard to the status of the disease concept at the time he published his book (in 1956–1957, the American Medical Association had formally recognized the syndrome of alcoholism as an illness), he deliberately noted: "In the introductory parts of this study it was said that *acceptance* of certain formulations on the nature of alcoholism *does not necessarily equal validity.* I am repeating these words at this juncture lest there should be some misunderstanding on this score" (p. 159, italics added).

In a now famous quotation, Jellinek noted that regardless of empirical evidence, "a disease is what the medical profession recognizes as such" (p. 12). Having considered the various advantages and disadvantages of the terms "illness" and "disease," he chose disease as the word most likely to evoke medical and legislative response. Bacon (1973) has recently noted that Jellinek's argument had to be a strong one: "Perhaps one-tenth of one percent of the medical profession fought for medical adoption of the medical definition. Thank God for their dedication. But this adoption was foisted upon the medical profession by others" (p. 23). For the medical profession, the term "disease" can be used to summarize any deviation from a state of health, particularly when there is a characteristic train of symptoms associated with that process. To his credit, Jellinek (1960) recognized the danger that "For the nonmedical man, the word disease conjures up a vision of blood, rashes, emaciation, and generally a horrifying appearance" (p. 12).

Let us now compare the prudent statements by Jellinek with a more dogmatic interpretation of the disease concept contained in a book which is, in fact, dedicated to Jellinek, among others. The *New Primer on Alcoholism* (Mann, 1968) begins as follows:

Alcoholism is a disease which manifests itself chiefly by the uncontrollable drinking of the victim, who is known as an alcoholic. It is a progressive disease, which, if left untreated, grows more virulent year by year, driving its victims further and further from the normal world and deeper and deeper into an abyss which has only two outlets: insanity or death. Alcoholism, therefore, is a progressive, and often fatal disease . . . *if* it is not treated and arrested. But it can be arrested. (p. 3)

Mann's orientation combines a skillful blending of the scientific authority represented by Jellinek with the lay formulations of alcoholism as developed by Alcoholics Anonymous.

In essence, the question of whether alcoholism can be correctly considered a single entity depends upon whether there are shared characteristics of etiology and development among alcoholics, rather than simply common adverse consequences as a result of alcohol use. It is not sufficient to concentrate wholly on the results of excessive drinking in the search for shared components. More recent statements by authorities in the alcohol field continue to present an unequivocal acceptance of the uniformity hypothesis: "There is little question but that the history, symptoms, and signs of alcoholism form a recognizable pattern" (Gitlow, 1973, p. 3). "From the empirical evidence of those with any valid experience in alcoholic research and therapy, I think we can conclude that there is an entity based on more than one trait that has been labeled alcoholism" (Madsen, 1974, p. 23). "The most significant characteristics of the disease *(alcoholism)* are that it is primary, progressive, chronic, and fatal" (Johnson, 1973, p. 1).

Viewing alcoholism as a definable and specific syndrome continues to be rather popular. Many of the proponents of viewing alcoholism as a single syndrome—one which typically manifests itself in a characteristic way—have restricted their considerations to the population Jellinek defined as *gamma* alcoholics. If Jellinek's writings are restricted to the *gamma* alcoholic, he would also qualify as a uniformity theorist, since he did postulate a characteristic development. If we restrict our considerations to *only gamma* alcoholics, it is clear that all major traditional viewpoints have supported the single entity position.

Proposition 2. Alcoholics and prealcoholics are essentially different from nonalcoholics.

Naturally, *post hoc* differentiations based on the occurrence or nonoccurrence of alcohol problems can always be formed; this is a tautology beyond dispute. This differentiation between alcoholics and nonalcoholics, however, is based on predisposing genetic, biological, and/or personality factors which are necessary conditions for a person to develop physical dependence on alcohol.

Simply put, is it appropriate to dichotomize the general population into two rather distinct groups?

While Jellinek noted that only about one person out of ten who uses alcoholic beverages develops an addiction to alcohol (*gamma* or *delta* alcoholism), he generally eschewed the idea of a biological predisposition to alcoholism. He felt that physical dependence was apt to occur in those persons "who have an urgent motivation to take alcohol in the large quantities and with the frequency that is required to bring about physical dependence on alcohol through conditioning of the metabolism of the nervous system" (1960, p. 152). He did speculate that some individuals may have a greater vulnerability for developing alcoholism because of a psychological need for the tension-reducing properties of alcohol, biologically low tolerance for alcohol (i.e., persons who demonstrate intoxicated behavior after ingesting only a small amount of alcohol), or socioeconomic factors conducive to heavy drinking. With reference to *gamma* alcoholism, Jellinek averred that "pre-alcoholic, high psychological vulnerability is essential" (p. 153). Furthermore, because of the different latencies observed for the onset of alcohol addiction, he was "inclined to think that heredity may play a role in the time necessary for alcohol to exert serious stresses on the system to which the anomaly attaches" (p. 155). Thus, for Jellinek, there was no necessary a priori distinction between alcoholics and nonalcoholics. While not ruling out a genetic or maturational biochemical abnormality as a possible contributing factor to the development of drinking problems, he did not believe such factors would be sufficient to explain the development of alcoholism. However, he did speculate that other factors, coupled with physiological sequelae of chronic heavy drinking, might constitute sufficient conditions for the development of physical dependence.

In the book *Alcoholics Anonymous* (1939), in the chapter titled "The doctor's opinion," it is explained that alcoholics "[H]ave one symptom in common: they cannot start drinking without developing the phenomenon of craving. This phenomenon, as we have suggested, may be the manifestation of an allergy which differentiates these people, and sets them apart as a distinct entity" (p. 7). In his book *The Road Back* (1961), Joseph Kessel describes the history of AA and states that the following rationale preceded the founders' hypothesizing that alcoholics have a congenital predisposition to develop an allergy to alcohol: "Since some people apparently blessed with everything that should save them from alcoholism . . .

take to drink uncontrollably, whereas others much less well-endowed by fate can drink without crossing the fatal frontier, a certain conclusion is inevitable: One does not *become an alcoholic.* One is *born* an alcoholic" (p. 128). "It divides the human race into two categories" (p. 129).

The position of AA with regard to the reaction of alcoholics to alcohol is clearly stated and follows logically from their "physical allergy–mental obsession" premise: "We are equally positive that once he [the alcoholic] takes any alcohol whatever into his system, something happens, both in the bodily and mental sense, which maks it virtually impossible for him to stop" (1939, p. 33). Mann (1968), in describing the AA approach (and few in the alcoholism field would deny her authority in doing so), states that new members are generally told that "[A]lcoholics apparently have something in their makeup which causes them to react to alcohol differently than other people, something for which the word allergy is at least an understandable term; and that this condition is what makes it impossible for them ever to drink, since there is no cure known for it" (p. 170). Describing her own philosophy and shirking the question of whether or not the alcoholic has a different physical reaction to alcohol than the nonalcoholic, Mann describes the alcoholic as " . . . a very sick person, victim of an insidious, progressive disease, which all too often ends fatally" (p. 17).

Should such a distinct physiological aberration ever be documented, it would obviously have resounding treatment implications. However, such a finding, if it occurs at all, is not likely to involve a physical allergy to alcohol. Reviewing the state of knowledge to 1960, the usually cautious Jellinek dismissed the Alcoholics Anonymous allergy notion founded on the theorizing of Silkworth, but noted that: "The figurative use of the term 'alcoholism is an allergy' is as good as or better than anything else for their purposes, as long as they do not wish to foist it upon students of alcoholism" (1960, p. 87).

Others have also claimed a specific physiological distinction. Smith (1957), for example, states that: "It seems likely that an individual is an alcoholic before he takes his first drink. . . . It is certain that those poorly defined qualities which make one alcoholic are unchanging, and the adage 'Once an alcoholic, always an alcoholic' is valid" (pp. 174–175). Madsen (1974) has proposed that the term "alcoholic" be used "to refer to individuals who drink in response to a psychobiological drive" (p. 90), and that "the true alcoholic is no more able to metabolize ethanol than a diabetic can handle sugar" (p. 94). Gitlow (1968), considering the present evidence with more caution, has remarked with regard to pre-existing physical abnormalities of alcoholics that: "This may or may not be so, but many people believe that such a biochemical defect does exist" (p. 39).

Often, the proposed dichotomy between alcoholics and nonalcoholics is based on personality traits rather than metabolic abnormalities. Mann, for instance, while not presenting a specific hypothesis, asserts that:

> Alcoholics generally have more in common with each other than just their alcoholism. It has been noted time and again that alcoholism all too frequently strikes the "most promising" member of a family, a school class or a business. . . . the alcoholic very often seems to be a little more alert, a little better at his job, a little more intelligent than his fellows in their particular social, economic or job level. This may well be the result of an unusual sensitivity, also widely noted by students and researchers, a sensitivity similar to that attributed to creative people. (1968, p. 65)

Proposals such as this, which claim unique characteristics of alcoholics, should be distinguished from orientations investigating common personality traits often found in alcoholics but not unique to that group (Blane, 1968).

Proposition 3. Alcoholics may sometimes experience an irresistible physical craving for alcohol, or a strong psychological compulsion to drink.

Nearly all traditional positions attribute the ingestion of an initial drink to some sort of emotional state or compulsion. For AA, it is termed an "obsession." The obsession is not well defined, but seems most nearly explained in a passage from the book *Alcoholics Anonymous* (1939): "The idea that somehow, someday he will control and enjoy his liquor drinking is the great obsession of every abnormal drinker. The persistence of this illusion is astonishing. Many pursue it into the gates of insanity or death" (p. 41). The reasons for the persistence of this obsession are not suggested, but it is stated earlier in the book that: "The fact is that most alcoholics, for reasons yet obscure, have lost the power of choice in drink. Our so-called will power becomes practically nonexistent. We are unable at certain times to bring into our consciousness with sufficient force the memory of the suffering and humiliation of even a week or a month ago. We are without defense against the first drink" (p. 34).

Mann (1968) appears to include the making of initial decisions to drink among the primary characteristics of alcoholism, defining the condition of alcoholism as being one "which manifests itself as the compulsion to drink regardless of the consequences" (p. 144). She equates this condition with loss of control, a topic which will be discussed in the following section. At another point in her book, she describes the phenomenon as follows: "With alcoholics, choice is no longer possible, whether to drink or not to drink, or of the amount consumed, or the effects of that amount upon them, or the occasions upon which drunkenness occurs" (p. 9).

Jellinek (1960) recognized the necessity for drawing a clear distinction between "(a) the mechanism that leads from the completion of one bout to the beginning of another, and (b) the continuation of drinking within a single bout" (p. 140). An extensive consideration of the meaning of the term "craving" for alcohol was presented at a symposium conducted by the World Health Organization (Jellinek et al., 1955). Jellinek's book summarizes those proceedings in large part. While not closing the door entirely on the possibility that evidence for a physiological basis for cravings may someday be forthcoming, Jellinek clearly viewed the onset of drinking by alcoholics as symptomatic of emotional stress, and the acquisition of such drinking as learned. In a seldom-quoted part of his book, he states: "There remains the fact that a learning theory of drinking in the well-defined terms of psychological discipline is essential to all species of alcoholism, including addiction. The learning process so ably described and interpreted by Conger [1956] is a prerequisite to bring about the conditions which are necessary for the development of addiction in the pharmacological sense" (p. 77). He further noted that such a formulation would not be incompatible with his disease concept: "the learning theory . . . does not exclude any other etiological theories; it can be complementary to any of them. Neither would it conflict with a disease conception of one or the other species of alcoholism" (p. 77). His preference was to consider the onset of drinking as resulting from a psychological compulsion for relief from emotional stress. Therefore, in many ways, Jellinek's position on how drinking begins is remarkably similar to that of AA.

However, speculation continues to the effect that the initial onset of drinking is related to biochemical problems akin to a specific hunger. In early investigations, such ideas were typically incorporated into theories postulating a nutritional deficiency etiology for alcoholism (Mardones and Onfray, 1942; Mardones,

1951; Williams, 1947, 1959). More recently, Madsen (1974) has speculated that alcoholics may suffer from a chronic hypoglycemic condition or have "a metabolic system which triggers a drop in blood sugar under any form of stress" (p. 51), concluding that "I am convinced that the craving is real and the alcoholics know that it is" (p. 70). Gitlow (1968) has also cautiously speculated about the possibility that "on a biochemical basis the alcoholic is truly uncomfortable without sedation" (p. 39).

Considering the preponderance of views which favor statements of a compulsion, strong desire, or need as opposed to a conception of physical cravings for an initial drink, it would seem fair to limit the traditional concept to a psychological base. A more important and controversial phenomenon concerns the alcoholic's continuing to drink once a first drink has been ingested and, in some cases, the actual effect of a "first" drink. The term "cravings" has sometimes also been used with reference to this continued drinking.

Proposition 4. Alcoholics gradually develop a process called "loss of control" over drinking, and possibly even an inability to stop drinking.

The statement, "One drink, one drunk," has long been a favorite at AA meetings, and the *Big Book of AA* states that one symptom all alcoholics have in common is that "they cannot start drinking without developing the phenomenon of craving" (1939, p. 7). Yet, this is not meant to be interpreted literally. As Madsen (1974) asserts, a "misinterpretation of the one drink, one drunk hypothesis was [is] probably the product of listening to the formal philosophy of Alcoholics Anonymous rather than to the actual alcoholic experiences of AA's" (p. 68). Keller (1972) has similarly described such confusions. It must be acknowledged, however, that simplistic notions have been suggested. For instance, describing the philosophy of AA, Kessel (1961) noted that for those individuals with a congenital allergy to alcohol: "The predisposition they were born with means that each glass gives them an irrestible longing for another, and then for a third, and so on, until they are insensible" (p. 129). He proceeds to describe this as part of a formulation which is "accepted law among members of Alcoholics Anonymous. . . . In addition, [to which] the number of eminent doctors and psychiatrists in the United States who believe this theory to be the one closest to truth is growing every day" (p. 130).

Jellinek's definition of the phenomenon he called "loss of control" is frequently quoted out of context. The complete passage in his book (1960) reads as follows: *"Recovered alcoholics in Alcoholics*

Anonymous speak of 'loss of control' to denote that stage in the development of their drinking history when the ingestion of one alcoholic drink sets up a chain reaction so that they are unable to adhere to their intention to 'have one or two drinks only' but continue to ingest more and more—often with quite some difficulty and disgust—contrary to their volition" (p. 41, italics added).

Further, it is often overlooked that Jellinek went on to define such a state not only as brought on by one or two drinks but: "[C]*haracterized by minor withdrawal symptoms* in the presence of alcohol in the bloodstream and the failure to achieve the desired euphoria for more than a few minutes. These symptoms explain superficially the behavior observed in the so-called loss of control and they suggest a combination of short-range accommodation of nervous tissue with long-range acquired increased tolerance" (1960, p. 147, italics added).

Therefore, "loss of control," as Jellinek would appear to have defined it, was presumed to have a physiological basis and indicated that a person was physically dependent on alcohol. He further hypothesized that physical dependence would be initiated in a chronic alcoholic by the ingestion of merely one or two drinks. If the alcoholic attempted to stop drinking after having just a few drinks, withdrawal symptoms would soon develop. However, these symptoms could be forestalled by the ingestion of more alcohol. In this sense, the drinker could not simultaneously control his intake and avoid withdrawal symptoms, and was thus experiencing a "loss of control." With regard to this hypothetical explanation, Jellinek offered one of his strongest caveats: *"I repeat that I regard the above merely as a working hypothesis,* but one which can be tested by means of the newer techniques in pharmacology, physiopathy and biochemistry" (p. 155, italics added). Importantly, he also noted that one of the most perplexing and peculiar characteristics of the phenomenon was that "loss of control does not emerge suddenly but rather progressively and that it does not occur inevitably as often as the *gamma* alcoholic takes a drink" (p. 42). This characteristic has led Keller to rephrase the concept as requiring "something more than alcohol" (1972, p. 156). While still allowing that "loss of control" occurs once physical dependence on alcohol has been initiated, Keller broadened the concept to mean that "if an alcoholic takes a drink, he can never be sure he will be able to stop before he loses control and starts on a bout" (p. 160). Keller then postulated that addictive behavior (taking the first drink) is "a form of learned or conditioned response" (p. 160). He further stated that

"His [the alcoholic's] learning to become an alcoholic almost certainly was unconscious" (p. 161), and for some unexplained reason this learning is nearly inaccessible to analysis and reversal. Unfortunately, consideration of whether or not "normal" drinkers can ever specify with total confidence exactly how much alcohol they will ingest on a given occasion is beyond the scope of our present discussion.

There are at least two major ways of defining "loss of control"—one centering on physical reactions to alcohol, and the other focusing on volitional behavior. For both AA and Jellinek, "loss of control" is postulated as the result of a physical mechanism. Jellinek, in fact, could be described as having interpreted and given scientific credence to the AA concept. Keller's extension of the concept is more consistent with a volitional definition of "loss of control." He explains the now-and-then nature of the phenomenon by assuming that the "loss of control" symptom sometimes unpredictably goes into remission. It should be noted that Keller's formulation is merely a description of the unpredictability of the phenomenon, and in no way constitutes an explanation. Ruth Fox (1957) has expressed a similar idea, without commenting on the possible physiological mechanisms which might be involved: "If a patient is *unable* to stop drinking after two or three drinks, he is almost certainly an alcoholic. It is this 'all or none' law which applies. . . . For him, one drink is usually the beginning of a spree" (p. 164). Glatt (1967) accounted for the common episodic drinking by alcoholics which does not occasion "loss of control" by hypothesizing that for each individual there is a critical blood alcohol concentration "threshold" which must be surpassed before "loss of control" (physical dependence) ensues.

Mann (1968), however, does not differentiate between the act of taking a first drink and continuing to drink, equating "the *compulsion* to drink regardless of the consequences" with *"loss of control over drinking"* (p. 144), and describes the alcoholic as having "lost the power of choice in the matter of drinking" (p. 9). In this case, the occasional and possibly even frequent successful excursions by alcoholics into the world of drinking without "loss of control" are accorded a mystical quality: "It is true that many alcoholics . . . [even those far advanced in the disease] . . . have occasions where their power of choice and restraint seems miraculously returned to them (p. 9). . . . This, unfortunately, is one of the least understood peculiarities of the still baffling disease of alcoholism" (p. 10).

At this point, we need only observe the following: "loss of control" concepts based on physiological formulations of physical dependence (i.e., AA, Jellinek, Glatt) are susceptible to empirical test. On the other hand, formulations supposing a restriction of volitional actions are based on a tautology (i.e., "loss of control" can only be demonstrated by the fact that alcoholics sometimes lose control; they become drunk and develop physical dependence on alcohol). In this regard we must seriously question whether such *post hoc* labeling serves much purpose when the phenomenon it seeks to describe occurs so unpredictably.

Proposition 5. Alcoholism is a permanent and irreversible condition.

Jellinek apparently felt that certain changes hypothesized to occur in the nervous system of alcoholics as a result of chronic excessive drinking are permanent. While this topic is not specifically addressed in his major works, he does state that "an 'alcoholic' cannot regain the lost control, as even after years of abstinence the 'compulsion' sets in on resumption of drinking. . . . there must be a grave disease process and at least its arrest to account for these behavior changes" (1960, p. 81). In his earlier work "Phases of alcohol addiction" (1952), he adamantly states that once an individual has entered the "prodromal" phase (earliest symptoms of the disease) in his development of alcoholism, "It goes without saying that even at this stage the only possible modus for this type of drinker is total abstinence" (p. 679). While it is not totally clear from either of these passages whether or not Jellinek meant to assert that irreversible physical changes take place, such a premise follows logically from his hypotheses.

Regardless of the theoretical perspective of various alcohologists, there has been nearly unanimous traditional agreement that once an individual has acquired an alcoholic pattern of drinking, that individual can never again drink in a normal fashion or drink at all without a high probability of losing control. There are three basic premises which underlie such beliefs: (1) for those who believe that alcoholics have a biogenetic defect which makes them react differently to alcohol than nonalcoholics, a logical corollary belief is that the alcoholic will never be able to drink without encountering problems unless scientific research somehow discovers a method of reversing the defect; (2) for those who believe that, regardless of possible predisposing factors, alcoholics undergo a permanent physiological change as a result of chronic ingestion of alcohol, resumed drinking is also seen as logically impossible without discovering a means of identifying and reversing the physiological changes which have occurred; and (3) the belief, which is most represented in traditional notions, that alcoholics are never able to drink again appears to be due to the clinical experience of alcoholics and those in the helping professions who have known or worked with alcoholics.

Irrespective of the theoretical orientation of the protagonist, however, admonitions about the alcoholic ever drinking again are typically phrased in dogmatic and absolute terms. Among the traditionalists, Jellinek far and away demonstrated the least display of emotionalism in making this point. Other traditional positions are more obstreperously pronounced. In an earlier citation from the Big Book (Alcoholics Anonymous, 1939), it was asserted in reference to alcoholics that "these allergic types can never safely use alcohol in any form at all" (p. 4). Two further citations vigorously support this prognosis: "Physicians who are familiar with alcoholism agree there is no such thing as making a normal drinker out of an alcoholic. Science may one day accomplish this, but it evidently hasn't done so yet" (p. 42). "But here is a man who at fifty-five years found he was just where he had left off at thirty [the man having taken his first drink in twenty-five years]. We have seen the truth demonstrated again and again: 'once an alcoholic, always an alcoholic.' Commencing to drink after a period of sobriety, we are in short time as bad as ever" (p. 44). Along the same lines, Mann (1968) asserts that: "No treatment exists which can restore the alcoholic's control so that he may drink normally." She adds that the recovery from alcoholism involves: "[T]he recovery, in short, of every ordinary human function except one: the ability to drink. This the alcoholic can never do again" (p. 144).

More recent proclamations retain this same air of certainty. Johnson (1973) states that: "The progress of alcoholism can be stopped, and the patient can be recovered. Not cured, but recovered. This is a hard-headed, pragmatic statement of fact which has visible proof in the recovery of thousands of alcoholics who are well today" (p. 1). Similarly, Gitlow (1973) asserts that "the only generally accepted and time-tested technique for treatment of this highly recidivistic illness entails achievement of abstinence" (p. 5). Gitlow, as others, considers any views to the contrary to represent the "psychoanalytically inclined" (p. 6), presumably because such positions usually assume that the onset of alcoholism is preceded by drinking for symptomatic reasons. In this sense, it is curious that both Jellinek and the Big Book of Alcoholics Anonymous present a symptom-relief account of the early drinking career of persons destined to become alcoholics. It would seem that a view of irreversibility as based on physiological factors or changes would be much more defensible than one based on polemic. A formulation fitting these criteria was presented by Glatt (1974). He states that: "Alcoholism and drug dependence can therefore be looked at as conditions which, in many (certainly not all) cases, may have started as symptomatic of underlying psychological problems (Jellinek's *alpha* alcoholism) but which in the course of time may have outrun their original purely symptomatic function, and have assumed the extent and the importance of a disease in their own right, e.g., causing in turn physical and mental complications" (p. 222).

We must recognize that an irreversibility notion is not a particularly necessary theoretical element in any of the traditional approaches except those which postulate pre-existing biochemical defects in persons who become alcoholic. Other orientations, such as Jellinek's, could easily incorporate a proposition of reversibility—that biological changes which result from excessive use of alcohol are largely acute in nature and disappear over time. The idea of reversible disease processes (e.g., tuberculosis) is certainly not novel.

Proposition 6. Alcoholism is a progressive disease which follows an inexorable development through a distinct series of phases.

The idea of a characteristic train of symptoms is central to the classification of alcoholism as a disease. Mann (1968) speaks of the reported similarity among symptoms of alcoholism as having "only minor variations in a great variety of individuals" (p. 4), and specifies that: "It is this inevitable progression, along with the striking similarity of the signs and symptoms marking the progression—both of which appear in identical forms in all kinds of highly differentiated individuals—which mark alcoholism for the disease it is" (p. 10). She divides the progression of disease symptoms into early, middle, and late or advanced states, and summarizes the hypothesized stability of the progression as follows: "In spite of the possibilities of deviation from the general pattern, however, experience has shown that most alcoholics fall within it. The time factor, for instance, holds pretty well throughout the great body of alcoholics" (p. 28).

Alcoholics Anonymous does not specify a particular progression in detail, albeit speculating that the real alcoholic "may start off as a moderate drinker; he may or may not become a continuous hard drinker; but at some stage of his drinking career he begins to lose all control of his liquor consumption, once he starts to drink" (1939, p. 31). A progression, typically to almost total social deterioration and the depths of despair, is a general theme, however, in AA stories of individuals' battles with their alcoholism (AA, 1939, 1955).

The postulated progressive nature of the development of alcoholism in *gamma* alcoholics (those Jellinek believed to be the predominant species in the United States and Canada) is perhaps the single greatest point of confluence between the three major sources of traditional views. Jellinek's (1946) original ideas on the phaseology of alcohol addiction (*gamma* and *delta* alcoholism) have become a classic in the alcoholism literature. The origin of this phaseology is described by Jellinek (1946). A questionnaire designed by AA members was distributed to approximately 1,600 members of AA via the *Grapevine,* the official newsletter of the fellowship. After some of the questionnaires were returned, Jellinek was approached and asked to analyze the results. While apologizing for the poor design of the questionnaire and the method of its circulation, he concluded that some information was better than none and proceeded to undertake the compilation and interpretation of results. Of the more than 1,600 questionnaires distributed, only 98 of those returned were sufficiently completed to be useful. This data base served to generate Jellinek's initial progressive schema for the development of alcohol addiction, a basic structure which has endured since 1946. In 1952, Jellinek revised the phaseology, attributing the changes to a more detailed questionnaire administered to an additional 2,000 alcoholics, but he failed to provide statistical documentation.

Briefly, the progression as described by Jellinek was divided into a prealcoholic symptomatic phase and three alcoholic phases. The "prealcoholic" phase consisted of an increasing frequency of relief drinking and lasted from several months to two years. The three phases of addictive alcoholism were composed of 43 discrete symptoms. He designated the earliest phase of alcoholism the "prodromal" phase. This phase was marked by the onset of "alcoholic palimpsests," more commonly known as blackouts. Allowing for individual differences, this phase was postulated to last between six months and five years. The start of the middle, or "crucial," phase of alcoholism was indicated by the onset of "loss of control" when the alcoholic drank. In 1952, Jellinek had not yet presented a formal working hypothesis of physical dependence to explain "loss of control" and simply regarded the phenomenon as being "felt by the drinker as a physical demand for alcohol" (p. 679). With the onset of the symptom of "regular matutinal drinking," the alcoholic then terminated the "crucial" phase and entered the "chronic" phase of his addiction. The onset of the "chronic" phase was marked by "prolonged intoxications," or benders, ending in a state of utter defeat. Jellinek later (1960) cautioned that this progression, derived from the retrospective self-reports of long-time members of AA, might incorporate an ethnocentric bias. Cahalan (1969) has commented that:

> Jellinek's conceptions appear to have been subtly influenced by the Protestant ethic. . . . His phases of alcohol addiction . . . is of a piece with Hogarth's famous illustration of a drunkard's progress on the downward path to perdition. . . . His vivid descriptions of the progress of alcoholism are so well attuned to the values of the middle-class Western physician and welfare worker that his cautions are largely overlooked by those who apply his concepts and by the many writers who repeat his early concepts. (p. 4)

Glatt (1970) synthesized Jellinek's phaseology and his own view of the recovery process into a single U-shaped diagrammatic presentation (1974, pp. 334–335). The inexorable progression is delineated step by step until the alcoholic, whose career started at the left-side peak of the U, has reached the literal "bottom" of the U. There, in a state of chronic alcoholism, he can either recycle to a limit determined only by his physical health, die, or start up the right-hand side of the U, the proverbial road to sobriety. This diagram, used daily in treatment programs around the world, can be considered as the epitome of postulating a rigid structure for the syndrome known as alcoholism. Although space considerations make it impossible to include this diagram, the interested reader will find that an inspection of the diagram demonstrates the peculiar fact that hardly any of the multitudinous symptoms of development and recovery from alcoholism relate to physiological processes. The specificity attributed to the symptoms and phases of alcoholism, however, provide a fertile ground for empirical tests.

Of Straw Men, Stagnant Waters, and Change

It is possible and even likely that many persons will tend to misinterpret our purpose in attempting to summarize traditional concepts of alcoholism. In particular, it may be argued that in doing so we have fabricated a straw man for the purpose of setting it aflame. Glatt (1974), for instance, has commented that:

> In recent years it has become fashionable in certain social and psychological quarters to attack the so-called "medical models" and the "disease concept" of alcoholism and drug dependence. In many ways these attacks seem to be based on misconceptions and misunderstandings, and the setting up of a "straw man." These critics . . . equate "medical" with "physical" or "physiological," and "disease" with a purely physical illness (p. 313). . . . If this were actually the case, such attacks would be correct . . . however, no medical man actively interested in these conditions would define medical model and disease in this way. (p. 314)

There are two major fallacies with such an argument. First, the problems we are discussing relate to the highly sophisticated disease model promulgated by Jellinek and others, not to a theory limited to physical factors. Second, as in the *Wizard of Oz,* straw men sometimes lead quite active lives. Many of those working in the field of alcoholism, "medical men" included, do in fact apply an overly simplified, predominantly physiological model to guide their daily clinical activities. Similarly, a good many programs throughout the world have retained a structure which was avant-garde 25 years ago but is now archaic. Such stagnation is hardly defensible in light of the tremendous gains in knowledge produced by research conducted over the past two decades. Bacon (1973) has recently commented that while the traditional model has been enormously productive in the past, it is now "emerging as the great new copout for avoiding effective response to this problem of alcoholism" (p. 26). Recognizing the static nature of many current programs, he states: "There will still be great cosmetic programs to cover up ineffective activities or promise of activities with sweet-sounding words. But in this as in other social-problem fields there is growing evidence that such programs are being recognized more rapidly, are being subject to massive criticism, and are failing to persist even as cover-up, face-saving, or image-making devices" (p. 29). In the *New Primer on Alcoholism,* Mann (1968) correctly asserts that "one by one the diseases of mankind have been pulled out of the limbo of superstition, fear and ignorance, into the light of modern knowledge and techniques that could deal with them" (p. 233).

We must also briefly consider the traditional view of scientific progress, which has undergone a necessary major reformulation over the past two decades (Brush, 1974). Traditionally, it had been thought that scientific progress resulted from the gradual accretion to new data, resulting in sequential modification and extension of concepts and theories. In other words, theories change as a result of the accumulation of new data inconsistent with the established theory. However, historical considerations appear to indicate that scientific theory does *not* change with new data, for new data are interpreted in accord with the established theory. As the gathering data become more and more difficult to incorporate under traditional concepts, a state of scientific crisis develops, marked by a polarization of views. It is only when a new theoretical model is proposed and adopted that the new data assume relevance. Until such time, new data that do not fit the prevailing theoretical model are rejected. This "paradigm" concept of scientific change is best described by Thomas Kuhn (1970). A new paradigm (scientific theory and associated methods) is not adopted primarily on the basis of new data, but rather on the basis of logic, persuasiveness, elegance, and utility. Ultimately, the fit between data and paradigm is always loose and linked by logic and conviction. The process of "paradigmatic change" appears well exemplified in the issues discussed in this book.

Conceptual Problems of the Traditional Model

Prior to examining that body of data which cannot be adequately explained by the traditional model of alcoholism and which directly contradicts many of the traditional formulations, it is important to consider the general conceptual problems involved in the traditional model.

Extensions of Jellinek's disease concept

Robinson (1972) recently published a trenchant critique of the disease concept as it has been applied in the alcoholism field. He points out that in that field, the concept of disease has often been taken in a most concrete sense, i.e., as an organic disorder of the body. Jellinek had recognized that the definition of "disease" which is operative for the medical profession is often not identical or even necessarily similar to the definition of disease held by the general public. Ultimately, the labeling process of calling a given state a disease is a social process, where it is both useful to the individual and society to consider a person sick and afflicted with a disease. With disorders of human behavior, our society has used the disease label to sanction certain states of behavior or life conditions. Therefore, technically speaking, it is unnecessary to infer some organic process in order to invoke the social process of labeling alcoholism a disease. We wish to emphasize that our argument is unrelated to the well-documented fact that the chronic intake of large amounts of alcohol by an individual may have definite and serious organic consequences. However, it appears that the organic consequences of excessive consumption of alcohol have often been confused with the total life style of persons having *any* problems with alcohol, and this, unfortunately, has led to oversimplified rhetoric and unjustifiable assumptions that are not supported by available scientific evidence. Regarding legislative reform based on judicial acceptance of the "disease" nature of alcoholism, Fingarette (1970) has urged caution: "One tempting road to reform—the building of a new constitutional doctrine on the basis of purported medical knowledge—is also a very dangerous one" (p. 812). The *New Primer on Alcoholism* would seem a fine example of such reification, changing Jellinek's working hypotheses into unassailable facts, a position which he made absolutely clear would be in error.

Gitlow (1973) has undertaken perhaps the most pervasive enlargement of the disease concept beyond the bounds and sociopolitical intentions of Jellinek. Failing to comment about how a given individual may come to drink to excess in the first place, and repeatedly drink to excess in spite of evidence that alcohol is adversely affecting at least some facet of his life, Gitlow simply defines that very pattern as a symptom of the diseased state. In a massive departure from the views of Jellinek, Gitlow claims the strongest foundation for his disease concept to lie in the "specified clinical pattern" which is so well established that "the categories of both therapy and prognosis of alcoholism possess degrees of specificity such as to warrant little nosological difficulty" (p. 6). Surprisingly, for such a strong and unique statement, he presents no evidence to support this extension of the disease concept. The new data summarized in this book are at even greater variance with Gitlow's version of the disease concept than with traditional views.

The assumption of discontinuity

A predominant assumption of traditional concepts is that alcoholics differ from nonalcoholics either physiologically, psychologically, or by some combination of these factors, and that this differentiation may precede the onset of alcoholic drinking. Based on the notion that alcoholism is by nature a progressive disease (Jellinek, 1960), it has usually been assumed that minor drinking problems are probably indicative of impending alcoholism. In fact, this would seem to be a major facet of Jellinek's "phases" of alcohol addiction—the "prealcoholic" phase. Certainly, differential vulnerability to drinking problems, and to what has been termed "alcoholism," appears to be supported by recent research evidence. Current findings (Cahalan, 1970; Room, 1970; Cahalan and Room, 1973; Park, 1973) appear to indicate, however, that for a great many individuals, and perhaps even a majority, the distinct progression formulated by Jellinek and others is not accurate, and often unnecessary. If one postulates a continuum of alcohol problems, rather than an inexorable progression, then one is faced with the clinical and social dilemma of where to draw the line between accepted alcohol use and deviant alcohol use. It is common clinical experience to be faced with questions from clients asking whether or not they are alcoholic, or prealcoholic. Considering the social labeling connotations, it hardly seems appropriate to define such self-questioning as prima facie evidence of an early drinking problem (i.e., "If you wonder whether you have a drinking problem, you probably do have a drinking problem.").

If alcohol problems can be considered as actually falling along a continuum ranging from a total lack of problems to a total deterioration of physical, emotional, and social functioning due to excessive use of alcohol, then the dilemma of what constitutes an alcohol problem is hardly resolved by labeling the extreme end of the continuum "alcoholic" by virtue of a deus-ex-machina explanation. In similar fashion, the species of alcoholism created by Jellinek often appear to be heuristic devices without rational justification other than as a phenomenological nomenclature. In a recent critique, Griffith Edwards (1974) concluded that little gain can be derived from dividing alcoholismic behavior into discrete and discontinuous species, and that a view of alcoholismic behavior as a continuity of multidimensional variables that produce different syndromes of drinking behavior is considerably more plausible.

As a consequence of traditional concepts of alcoholism, and the reification of those concepts, the orientation of most prevention efforts to date has almost unilaterally stressed the identification and avoidance of something bad—alcoholism—with little, if any, instruction in how to avoid being victimized by such problems (Wilkinson, 1970). Current prevention efforts in the alcoholism field present an in vivo demonstration of the extent of reification. There currently exist few, if any, separately identifiable services for individuals who are only experiencing minor drinking problems. As a result, such persons are often referred to programs that are inappropriately intense and are oriented toward treating chronic alcoholics. This is typically based on the assumption that such individuals are probably "early" alcoholics. Given the rapidly accruing evidence, it is reasonable to expect that services different from those which currently exist might be more appropriate and effective for persons with alcohol problems of mild severity. As has been pointed out by Roman and Trice (1968), the social labeling consequences of traditional beliefs about alcoholism offer little reason for problem drinkers to stop drinking and, conversely, may actually provide them with the basis for repeated attempts to prove that they are not "alcoholics." Antiquated concepts portraying alcoholism as an all-or-none phenomenon which strikes only a particular group of persons, have incurred as their legacy a stark deficiency in both research and development of effective primary and secondary prevention services.

The definition of addiction

Traditional concepts of alcoholism are closely tied to the common sense understanding of the term "addiction." A person is said to be addicted when there is development of physiological tolerance and withdrawal symptoms after cessation of drug use. This pharmacologic-physiologic definition does not include any necessary reference to craving, compulsion, or "need." To our knowledge, there is no documented evidence to support the notion that pharmacological addiction produces any necessary or specific state of mind. Yet the traditional concepts of alcoholism repeatedly make reference to metaphysical concepts like "cell hunger," which are metaphors at best.

Freedman and Wilson (1964), for example, find that there is no experimentally verified concept that links the mechanism of tolerance to behavioral phenomena of addictive behavior. They conclude: "The most significant characteristic of addiction is the qualification of harm to oneself or to others produced by the regular or habitual use of any substance. The production of physical dependence, with its concomitants of tolerance and withdrawal symptoms, is often, but not necessarily, present" (p. 430).

Indeed, the promiscuous use of the term "addiction" has muddled rather than clarified our understanding. For these reasons, the World Health Organization Expert Committee on Alcoholism (1965) declared that the term "addiction" had become an unusable omnibus word. They proposed that the term "dependence" be

used, and that a clear distinction be made between psychological
dependence and physical dependence.

> Drug dependence is a state of psychic or physical dependence, or
> both, on a drug, arising in a person following administration of that
> drug on a periodic or continuous basis. . . . All these drugs have one
> effect in common: they are capable of creating, in certain individuals,
> a particular state of mind that is termed "psychic dependence" . . .
> this mental state may be the only factor involved, even in the case of
> the most intense craving and perpetuation of compulsive abuse . . .
> psychic dependence can and does develop . . . without any evidence
> of physical dependence. . . . Physical dependence, too, can be in-
> duced without notable psychic dependence, indeed, physical de-
> pendence is an inevitable result of the pharmacological action of
> some drugs with sufficient amount and time of administration.
> Psychic dependence, while also related to pharmacological action, is
> more particularly a manifestation of the individual's reaction to the
> effects of a specific drug and varies with the individual as well as the
> drug. (p. 722)

It is remarkable that the above definition has received little
attention, since it so clearly demarcates the limits of physical dependence. The notion of alcohol addiction can connote a pattern of
drinking associated with either a state of mind (psychological) or
physical withdrawal symptoms, or both. Thus, a particular pattern
of alcohol use may or may not have a physiologic basis.

Reinforcement of the sick role

When alcoholism is mistakenly inferred to be a disease in simply
the organic sense, then certain role expectations derived from the
cultural expectancies of sick or ill behavior apply to those persons
self-identified or other-identified as alcoholics (Scheff, 1966).
Roman and Trice (1968) caution that such a sick role assignment
may not be efficacious for use with all individuals having alcohol
problems. In particular, they hypothesize that sick roles may inad-
vertently result in legitimizing deviant drinking patterns for individuals labeled as alcoholics, similar in many ways to a self-fulfilling
prophecy (Archibald, 1974). They conclude that the disease model
"has resulted in a labeling process that may in itself set the stage for
the development of true alcohol addiction" (Roman & Trice, 1968,
pp. 250–251). Along similar lines, Warren (1974) has recently

presented cogent arguments that the application of negative social labels (labeling individuals as different or deviant) may actually facilitate further deviant behavior.

Another unintended consequence of the disease model of alcoholism is that it may acculturate and induce people into a self-identified role definition as "alcoholics," which may not be necessary and which may even preclude appropriate analysis of their alcohol problems. Similarly, when persons find sick roles to be distasteful, these roles may serve to hinder their entrance into treatment. Finally, the traditional model of alcoholism has a built-in set of role expectations. The rehabilitated alcoholic must behave in accord with that model, and this, of course, may preclude treatment programs and treatment goals at variance with the traditional model.

Solidification of the role of helper

Gitlow (1973) has remarked that "the disease concept establishes alcoholism as firmly within the province of the medical profession, fixing responsibility for clinical care of the alcoholic and research into the nature of his suffering upon the physician and his paramedical partners" (p. 7). This would appear to be a somewhat extravagant extension of the professionally accepted disease concept as formulated by Jellinek (1960). Undoubtedly the medical assessment and management of organic complications of excessive drinking is essential. Yet, the reinforcement of the helping role to be played by the medical profession has already proceeded to the point where the American Medical Association (1967), in its *Manual on Alcoholism,* encourages internal medicine specialists to feel confident to engage an alcoholic in a protracted course of individual psychotherapy. The internist is cautioned that the leading of "group" therapy is a special skill to be undertaken only by individuals with appropriate training. On the other hand, "individual" psychotherapy is regarded as well within the general competency of internal medicine specialists. Needless to say, such an assertion is not only unreasonable in light of the mental health professions but might also be given serious review in terms of professional ethics.

Bacon (1973) has described the evolution of the disease concept of alcoholism as demonstrating a changing social function: "Twenty-five years ago this belief acted to tear down the walls of avoidance, denial, ignorance, cruelty, and hopelessness. Today, however, I see signs of it being used as a copout. . . . In the past we turned over these problems [social problems] to the churches, to the schools, to legislative sales controls, to policemen and jails. Now it will be medicine's turn" (p. 24).

Reinforcement of the alcoholic's lack of responsibility

Over the past three decades, largely through the efforts of AA and those promoting Jellinek's disease concept of alcoholism, there has been a shift in the societal position of alcoholics. This shift is evident, for instance, in national policy changes toward the decriminalization of public drunkenness, occupational alcohol programs, and massive federal funding for treatment programs. The intended shift in public attitude is one of viewing such deviancy as a nonmoral situation resulting from biological and social forces beyond an individual's control rather than as a display of personal immoral choice; that is, considering alcoholismic behavior as ill or sick rather than sinful.

However, many people either do not accept this shift or demonstrate a confused acceptance at best (Linsky, 1972; Sobell & Sobell, 1975), possibly because they reject the concept of sick behavior and the disease model as presented in traditional concepts of alcoholism. The problem here seems to lie in basic assumptions involved in the social meaning of sin and sickness (Glock, 1964). The crux of the matter is this: If behavior is labeled sinful, then the person is blamed and punished; to avert blame and punishment, behavior can be labeled as reflecting sickness. However, whether socially deviant behavior is labeled as sin or illness is related to a large extent to the degree of perceived personal choice experienced by an individual (Fletcher, 1966). Shapiro (1965) has examined the qualities of the impulsive addictive character style descriptive of many alcohol addicts. Because such individuals frequently exhibit appropriate social behavior in many contexts, the general public as well as many professionals tend to ascribe a high degree of "personal choice" to the alcoholic. However, Shapiro characterizes the predominant life style of such individuals as having "an absence of a sense of having chosen to act in this particular way" (p. 176). Therein lies a crucial paradox whereby the alcoholic is perceived by others to act with intention and choice, while he experiences within himself an explicit lack of a sense of intention and choice. The clinically relevant aspect of this paradox is that the community, friends, family, and even professional treatment staff often do not appreciate this enigma. Therefore, many persons find it hard to accept the concept of a "sick" alcoholic when the alcoholic appears to be suffering from a "chosen" condition.

Although the disease model eliminates blame and punishment, it also largely eliminates personal responsibility. While this is not a necessarily logical inference from the disease model, it is a presumption that determines staff behavior in many treatment settings (Sterne & Pittman, 1965). What is involved here concerns the various possible interpretations of the social meaning of sick roles. In its most extreme form, the sick role dictates that a person is neither blameable nor responsible for his own condition. In certain disease states (i.e., leukemia) that is certainly the case. On the other hand, the sick role does not always pertain for chronic illness, nor for the recuperative stages of illness, nor for conditions where the person is not socially labeled as sick despite defects. The traditional model as formulated by Mann (1968) sustains an extreme interpretation of the sick role, describing the alcoholic as "a very sick person, victim of an insidious, progressive disease" (p. 17). Obviously it is also possible to appreciate various states of personal responsibility, while still avoiding a blame-and-punishment orientation. This would seem especially appropriate in the case of alcohol problems, as traditional treatment resources, including AA, typically emphasize the need for personal responsibility in the recovery process.

A final consideration regarding the issue of personal responsibility concerns the public response to sin and sickness models. Traditional mores generally hold that if a person is sinful, the community bears no responsibility to help him; whereas if the person is sick, there is often a social sanction to provide rehabilitation services. Again, there is a tendency toward a polarization of responsibility; the alcoholic is seen as either totally responsible for himself, or society is seen as totally responsible for the alcoholic. What is lacking is an alternative to the sick model and the sin model for deviant behavior, an alternative having a conceptual basis for shared responsibility (Pattison, 1967).

In summary, in transforming alcoholism from a sin to a sickness model, traditional concepts of alcoholism eliminated blame and punishment for the alcoholic but also deeply confused and distorted the concept of responsibility.

Distortion of treatment outcome evaluation

A perpetual and unfortunate characteristic of alcoholism treatment outcome evaluation studies has been a broad range of methodological and measurement deficiencies. These problems have been enumerated over the years in a series of excellent reviews (Voegtlin & Lemere, 1942; Hill & Blane, 1967; Miller, Pokorny, Valles, & Cleveland, 1970; Crawford, Chalupsky, & Hurley, 1973; Crawford & Chalupsky, 1973) and will not be a central focus here. It is relevant, however, for us to consider how traditional concepts of alcoholism may have influenced treatment outcome evaluation. In brief, a simplification of expected drinking outcomes into a dichotomous classification of either "drunk" or "abstinent (sobriety)" has too frequently led investigators to dismiss or neglect intermediate categories of drinking outcome. Orford (1973) and others have demonstrated that, in practice, actual outcomes include not only total abstinence but a broad array of drinking behaviors ranging from fully controlled drinking through totally uncontrolled drinking. Disregarding the extreme instance of fully controlled drinking for the moment, it should be noted that such a range of drinking outcomes is a conclusion easily derived from Jellinek's formulation—namely, that except in the most chronic cases, loss of control does not occur as an all-or-none phenomenon. When intermediate categories of drinking outcome have been included in evaluation studies, it is frequently as vaguely defined categories such as "drinking," "heavy drinking," "occasional slips," "drunk," "improved drinking," or "relapses" (Walton, Ritson, & Kennedy, 1966; Voegler, Lunde, Johnson, & Martin, 1970; Kish & Hermann, 1971), rather than a consideration of the absolute amount of drinking taking place and the duration of that drinking. Such lack of definition and arbitrary categorization make direct comparisons of outcome results between studies an exercise of dubious value.

Similarly, it has been amply demonstrated (Gerard, Saenger, & Wile, 1962; Pattison, Headley, Gleser, & Gottschalk, 1968; Chandler, Hensman, & Edwards, 1971) that while drinking outcomes generally bear a somewhat positive relationship to other areas of life functioning, this is not always the case. It has been a frequent assumption that unless an alcoholic was abstinent, no rehabilitation could result, and, likewise, that rehabilitation would occur when an alcoholic was abstinent. Contrary to these assumptions, a multitude of follow-up studies have examined alcoholics from a multivariant set of outcome criteria, such as emotional adjustment, interpersonal relations, social adaptation, vocational stability, and physical health (Kissin, Rosenblatt, & Machover, 1968a, b, c; Kissin, Platz, & Su, 1970; Pattison, 1974; Pattison, Coe, & Doerr, 1973; Pattison, Headley, Gleser, & Gottschalk, 1968; Pattison, Coe, & Rhodes, 1969; Sobell & Sobell, 1973a, b, c, 1976; Trice & Roman, 1970; Trice, Roman, & Belasco, 1969). These studies repeatedly demonstrate that abstinent alcoholics sometimes show no reha- bilitation or even deteriorate in their life adjustment *despite* abstinence; conversely, nonabstinent alcoholics may show partial or total rehabilitation in terms of these other life variables. These data attest to the inadequacy of abstinence as a sole criterion of rehabilitation or treatment outcome and the need for multiple measures of treatment outcome. A discussion of other problems with traditional treatment outcome measures and follow-up proce- dures can be found in Sobell and Sobell (1975) and Sobell (1976).

Reactions to the Controversy

While the broad social advantages which have accrued from the traditional model—"alcoholism as a disease"—have been widely emphasized, there have also been resistances to the continuing extension of this model (Knox, 1971, 1973). Physicians resist the concrete analogy of alcoholism as a disease of the same genre as measles, cancer, or diabetes (Robinson & Podnoe, 1966). Mental health professionals resist the concept of alcoholism as a biological state rather than a psychological development (Curlee, 1971). Judges and lawyers resist the concept of alcoholism as determined by immutable forces which exculpate the alcoholic from legal re- sponsibilities. Politicians resist the extension of alcoholism as a disease for which society must assume treatment, compensation, and liability responsibilities. The objections to the so-called disease model appear not to be against the label of alcoholism as a disease per se. Rather, the objections seem to represent reactions to as- sumptions about the alcoholic and alcoholism which, while incor- rect in light of Jellinek's formulation, nevertheless derived their foundation from the model as promulgated by others (i.e., Mann, 1968).

Surveys of alcoholism manpower, such as by Cahn (1970), reveal that many of the professional staff in alcoholism treatment facilities are often marginal to their professions. Alcohol programs often appear to have attracted those who failed to achieve better profes- sional status positions. These professional personnel maintain and perpetuate a model of alcoholism congruent with their clinical style of operation. A new paradigm constitutes a challenge to this accustomed clinical style.

Considered from another orientation, the traditional model reinforces the power and sanction of the professional, particularly the physician. In the traditional model, the alcoholic is considered sick, weak, and helpless. The professional is strong, powerful, and controlling. A change in this paradigm is likely to shift the balance of power between the helper and the helped (Steiner, 1971).

The field of alcoholism treatment has also long been manned by a great number of paraprofessional personnel. Currently, the field is supported primarily by paraprofessional values, attitudes, and concepts (Pattison, 1973). Thus it is hardly surprising that many paraprofessionals should look upon the influx of scientists and professionals with some concern. More recently, however, the field seems to have divided into two distinct groups (professional vs. paraprofessional) with quite divergent points of view. The professional is usually trained in an analytical-objective-inductive style of operation, whereas the paraprofessional is usually dependent upon an intuitive-subjective-deductive style. For paraprofessionals, empirical data are often seen as obscure or irrelevant in contrast to their own personal experiences. Thus, new data emanating from academic science typically encounter major resistance from those paraprofessionals who operate on a basis of folk science. Jerome Ravetz (1971) has analyzed the consequences of such a confrontation:

> A folk science is a body of accepted knowledge whose function is not to provide the basis for further advance, but to offer comfort and reassurance to some body of believers. . . . In an immature field of scientific development there is inevitable conflict which occurs when the result of disciplined scientific inquiry conflicts with the beliefs of a folk science, usually a popular one which is also adopted by the established cultural organs of society. (p. 389)

The self-help movement, best demonstrated in the fellowship of Alcoholics Anonymous and the organization of the National Council on Alcoholism, is consonant with the traditional model. However, it is often overlooked that one characteristic of self-help groups tends to be an antiprofessional bias. In his classic study of self-help groups, Hans Toch (1966) found that loyalty to the group ideology contains an antiprofessional bias: either the professionals have tried and can't help us, or they are not interested in us.

Pattison (1973) has observed that this bias is not necessarily detrimental, noting that "an inherent anti-professional bias contains a self-fulfilling prophecy of success and the validation of its theories is ideological rather than scientific . . . these elements of a self-help group are the 'social glue' that holds a self-help group together, promotes cohesion and integration, validates hope and commitments and in short, makes it work" (p. 27).

Therefore, conceptual changes necessitated by empirical data meet with controversy and conflict from lay and self-help groups. These conflicts are rarely based on reaction to the data but tend to be founded in the perceived challenge to the lay ideology which those data foretell.

2. The Social Interpretation of Alcohol-Dependent Behavior

The literature describing various aspects of traditional concepts of alcoholism is voluminous. The important point we wish to emphasize here is that these traditional concepts have emerged out of popular opinion and conventional wisdom stereotypes. Conversely, these traditional concepts have widely influenced and formed public opinion, social attitudes, and clinical process. So there is a circular reinforcement of unexamined popular notions about the phenomena of alcohol-dependent behavior.

In a large and important paper, "The Alcohologist's Addiction," David Robinson (1972) reviews many of the undesirable consequences of the undisciplined extensions and reifications of the disease concept of alcoholism as formulated by Jellinek. Robinson concludes by quoting D. L. Davies to the effect that "no area of medicine is so bedeviled by semantic confusion as is the field of alcoholism." The public consequence is that "acceptance of ill-defined notions may lead to false expectations about the nature of alcoholism, its treatment and prognosis."

The importance of public conventional wisdom has been strongly underscored by Craig MacAndrew and Robert Edgerton in their book *Drunken Comportment* (1969). They demonstrate that even the definition of simple "drunkenness" is highly dependent upon social and cultural factors. They review the widely held beliefs that alcohol has a specific psycho-physiological effect that makes people act aggressive, silly, etc., in drinking situations. Contrary to popular opinion, they present a well-documented case that there is tremendous diversity in the supposed effects of alcohol on social behavior. Thus, while drinking, people tend to behave in accord with social norms and expectations.

The two articles selected for reading here emphasize the social components of alcohol use and consequences for treatment.

In his article "Theories of Behavior and the Social Control of Alcoholism," Linsky presents evidence that public attitudes and beliefs, and the foundations of those beliefs, can best be described as "confused." He attributes a good deal of this confusion to prevailing beliefs about alcoholism and the great rapidity of change which has occurred in those beliefs. While alcohol specialists may be confident in their beliefs about the facts of alcohol problems, the general public does not share that certitude. Further, public beliefs about the etiology of alcohol problems are often widely divergent from suggested modes of treatment.

In "The Sick Role, Labeling Theory, and the Deviant Drinker," Roman and Trice describe the social consequences of labeling alcoholism a disease and labeling a person an alcoholic. It is not that such labels are always inappropriate but rather that they can be both useful and noxious. Therefore, they caution the use of discretion and care with such social labels.

A. S. Linsky

Theories of Behavior and the Social Control of Alcoholism

Public Views on the Causes and Cures of Alcoholisms

Why do some methods for controlling deviance, such as alcoholism, come to be accepted and favored? Is it because of their demonstrated superiority in comparison with other methods of control? Such claims are unconvincing, since careful evaluation often is not even considered until new treatment programs are well established. Moreover, where scientifically adequate evaluation of the effects of therapeutic or correctional programs has occurred, the results frequently provide little support for the treatment programs or methods evaluated (Powers & Witman, 1951; Eysenk, 1952).

Aubert and Messinger (1958) and Glock (1964) have argued on a general level that preferences for different methods of controlling deviants follow from assumptions made about the determinants of deviant behavior. That is, the strategy of intervention or prevention is governed by the theories of etiology. The authors also suggest that if deviance is viewed as determined largely by forces beyond an individual's control, then one would not be likely to hold the deviant responsible and might advocate treatment rather than punishment. In similar vein, Stoll (1968) has postulated as follows

Reprinted, with permission of the author and publisher, from *Social Psychiatry*, 1972, 7, 47–52.

for social control agents: "1A. To the extent that individuals believe nonconformity to be conscious defiance of rules (or are voluntarists, hold 'wickedness' assumptions), then they will prefer to restrict and castigate deviants," and the corollary: "1B. To the extent that individuals believe nonconformity to be the result of external forces (or are determinists, hold 'sickness' assumptions), they will prefer to treat or cure deviants without accompanying opprobrium."

Empirical studies have tended to support such relationships. In a public opinion survey, Mulford and Miller (1964) found that persons who viewed alcoholism as illness had more faith in the treatment of alcoholism than those who regarded alcoholics as morally weak. Nettler (1959) found that community leaders who held "free-will" assumptions about the causes of deviance tended to favor more punitive methods dealing with juvenile deviants than those who held more deterministic views.

Most of the studies cited above have focused on the voluntary versus involuntary assumptions about the etiology of deviance and their implications for treatment. Such a focus, however, ignores much of the complexity of theories of deviance, which include many varieties of voluntary and involuntary theories. For example, in their recent theoretical essay, Siegler, Osmond and Newel (1968) argue for the existence of at least eight models of alcoholism, each with a separate theory of etiology and a logically related method of handling the disorder.

The present study attempts a more complete examination than has been undertaken previously of the consistency of a wide range of etiological theories held about alcoholism with preferred methods of social control.

Methodology

Two distinct series of data that bore directly on this problem were available from earlier studies by the author on public views on alcoholism: (1) a household probability survey of community attitudes and beliefs on alcoholism (Linsky, 1970) and (2) a survey of articles written in popular magazines on the subject of alcoholism during the twentieth century (Linsky, 1970–71). Although the studies were originally conducted for other purposes, each contained independent data both on the etiological theories of alcoholism held and the method of treatment advocated, making the present investigation possible.

The household survey

The household probability survey was conducted in 1962 in Vancouver, Washington, a small mixed industrial and port city located in the southwestern part of the state. A probability sample of adults stratified by sex, marital status and census tract was drawn from a city directory. One interviewer completed interviews with 305 of an original sample of 415 adults (or 74%) over a 3-month period. No substitutions of the addresses or of the pre-selected respondents within households were permitted and up to four callbacks were made on persons not at home. The main attrition in the sample was from errors in the directory. Only 8% of persons reached refused to be interviewed.

One question asked of respondents in that survey was what they believed to be the major cause of alcoholism. Their responses were recorded verbatim and were later categorized according to the following classification scheme: (1) failure or breakdown of the biological system, (2) moral character of the alcoholic, (3) disorders of the personality system (in psychological terms), (4) psychological reaction to a situational problem, and (5) social drinking and alcohol itself (these two factors were combined because of low frequencies).

At a well-separated point in the interview respondents were asked what they thought was the best way to get alcoholics to stop drinking. They were presented a card with 10 choices from which they were asked to name their first and second choice. (The 10 treatment choices in order of the frequency with which they were chosen by the total sample are: Medical Treatments; Psychological or Psychiatric Help; Use of Will-Power; Religious Help; Tighter Legal Control of Alcohol; Education; Change of Spouse, Job, or Situation; Pressure from Family, Employer, etc.; A Good Swift Kick in the Pants; Fines or Imprisonment. The order of choices on the cards was rotated in successive interviews.) This permitted the cross-tabulation for each respondent of his beliefs concerning the causes of alcoholism and the treatment method which he saw as most effective.

Popular magazine survey

Popularly oriented magazines have long exhorted and advised the public on a variety of social problems including alcoholism. The universe of articles used in the second study consisted of all articles on the subject of alcoholism and alcohol problems listed in *Reader's Guide to Periodic Literature* from 1900–1966. Technical, scientific, and professional journals were excluded. Random samples of thirty articles were drawn from each of the six decades from 1900 through 1959 and 60 articles were drawn for the 7-year period 1960–1966. Each article was rated independently on several dimensions by at least two judges.

Causal theories presented in each article were classified according to two central dimensions: (1) a locational dimension, i.e., whether the causal agent is seen as inside the alcoholic or located in his environment; (2) a moral dimension, i.e., whether the causal is evaluated moralistically in the article or interpreted naturalistically, i.e., in scientific terms.

Most articles on alcoholism include a position both on the location of the causal agent and a moral evaluation of that agent. These two dimensions dichotomously treated result in four possible combinations. Each combination, represented by a cell in Table 1, contains a logically distinct etiological theory of alcoholism.

Cell (a) represents the traditional "free-will" theory which holds that the cause of alcoholism is internal to the alcoholic and that he is morally at fault for his condition. Cell (b) represents the "social criticism" approach which views morally corrupt standards, individuals, groups and institutions in the external social environment of the alcoholic as the cause of alcoholism, such as greed, saloon keepers, or the "insidious" liquor lobby. In Cell (c), psychological and biological theories are represented, which explain alcoholism on the basis of internal but naturalistic factors, such as emotional, genetic or physio-chemical agents, without blaming the alcoholic. Finally, Cell (d) represents "sociological explanation" which like Cell (b) explains alcohol problems as originating in the external

Table 1. Theories of the etiology of alcoholism by moral and locational dimensions

Moral Dimension	Locational Dimension	
	Within the Alcoholic	External to the Alcoholic
Moralistic	(a) Traditional "free-will" position	(b) "Social criticism"
Nonmoralistic (or naturalistic)	(c) Psychological and biological explanation	(d) Sociological explanation

social environment of the alcoholic, but unlike (b) views these environmental factors within a morally neutral, naturalistic framework.

Type of treatment advocated was tabulated independently for each article. Under the major category "rehabilitation-reform," all suggestions are included for intervening or attempting to reverse the process of alcoholism once it becomes established in the individual alcoholic. The category "prevention" here refers to suggestions for changes on a societal or individual basis for preventing the development of the disorder.

With this data, it was possible to cross-tabulate the four types of theoretical approaches to alcoholism with the types of treatment recommendations suggested in each article.

Findings

Community survey

Table 2 compares for each respondent the etiological theory of alcoholism held and the same respondent's two choices of the most effective way to handle problem drinking.

In the last column of Table 2 we see that personality factors and psychological reaction to situational problems were the most frequently accepted theories of the cause of alcoholism among this lay population, with biological theories next. Social drinking, alcohol itself, and the moral character of the alcoholic were cited with decreasing frequency.

Table 2 presents a pattern of control preference fairly consistent with the theories suggested. Respondents who explained alcoholism in terms of biological determinants such as genetic makeup or the peculiar blood chemistry of the alcoholic were more likely to see medical treatment as the most effective way to get alcoholics to stop drinking.

Those who felt that alcoholism was due to moral weakness of the alcoholic, such as hedonism, selfishness or lack of will power, tended to see tighter legal control over the supply of liquor as the most effective means, with the "use of will power" second. Both methods would seem to be logically consistent with a moral character view of alcoholism depending upon whether one saw the alcoholic as morally weak but potentially changeable (use of will power) or as incapable of moral alteration and thereby in need of external regulation (legal control).

Table 2. Theory of the cause of alcoholism and the treatment seen as most effective (community survey, by percent)

Most Important Cause Cited	Most Effective Treatments					All Treatments
	Medical (n = 212)	Psychological (n = 186)	Will Power (n = 112)	Religious Help (n = 98)	Legal Control (n = 94)	(n = 702)
1. Biological	29.2%	10.7%	12.5%	14.3%	25.5%	19.1%
2. Character (in moral terms)	6.1	3.8	16.1	7.1	19.1	9.0
3. Personality (in psychological terms)	27.4	43.0	14.3	32.6	6.4	27.4
4. Psychological reaction to situational problems	25.5	36.6	21.4	18.4	32.4	26.5
5. Alcohol itself and social drinking	11.8	5.9	35.7	27.5	25.5	18.1

Note. There are 234 respondents with two choices of treatment each. First choice was weighted as 2 points, and second choice was weighted as 1 point.
Chi square = 146.31.
df = 16
P ≤ .001

Respondents who saw alcoholism either as a personality problem (phrased in psychological terms) or as a psychological response to problems in the environment were more likely to recommend treatment by psychologists or psychiatrists. If either alcohol itself or social drinking was viewed as the cause of alcoholism, use of will power was the preferred method for controlling the problem, followed by religious help and legal control. [Punitive methods of control such as fines and imprisonment seem to be consistent also with the "free-will" orientation but they were selected by very few respondents regardless of the etiological theory held.]

Popular magazine survey

The causal assumptions of the magazine articles are cross-tabulated in Table 3 with the methods of controlling alcoholism which were advocated. Several relationships are apparent. Articles favoring inside-moralistic explanations ("free will") were somewhat more likely to advocate rehabilitation-reform (56.2%) as compared with prevention (43.8%). Within this first category most of the suggested methods for bringing about rehabilitation or reform of the alcoholic were either traditional (exercise of will power, religious help) or punitive (fines and imprisonment, etc.) rather than falling into the "therapeutic" category. Suggested methods of prevention were for the most part centered on control of the supply of alcohol, such as prohibition, abstinence, moderation, etc.

Articles favoring outside-moralistic or "social-criticism" explanations of alcoholism overwhelmingly advocated preventive measures (90.1%) as compared with rehabilitation-reform (9.8%). Within the category of prevention, interest centered mostly in prohibition of alcohol for this etiological group.

Articles that explained alcoholism in terms of inside-naturalistic assumptions (psychological and biological explanations) took a predominantly rehabilitation or reform stance with regard to treatment, with 71.5% favoring rehabilitation-reform in comparison with 28.6% favoring prevention as a means of combating drinking problems. Within the general category of rehabilitation-reform, the methods suggested were predominantly therapeutic, such as Alcoholics Anonymous, psychiatric counseling, medical treatment and hospitalization. Education and research was the largest category of prevention mentioned.

Finally, those who took an outside-naturalistic or "sociological" viewpoint for explaining alcoholism favored prevention over re-

Table 3. Theory of alcoholism and suggested treatment (popular articles 1900–1966 by percent of treatments)

Method advocated	Theory of alcoholism			
	Inside-moralistic (n = 16)	Outside-moralistic (n = 63)	Inside-naturalistic (n = 106)	Outside-naturalistic (n = 27)
Rehabilitation-Reform	56.2%	9.8%	71.4%	22.7%
Therapeutic (AA, psychiatric, medical, etc.)	12.5	0	66.6	18.2
Traditional and punitive (will-power, religious help, etc.)	43.8	9.8	4.8	4.5
Prevention	43.8	90.1	28.6	77.3
Social and cultural change	6.2	21.3	8.6	18.2
Education and research	6.2	4.9	11.4	27.3
Control of alcohol	31.2	63.9	8.6	31.8
Prohibition	12.5	49.2	2.9	9.1
Other control	18.8	14.8	5.7	22.7
Other	0	3.3	9.5	22.7

Note. The unit is treatments recommended rather than the article. Some articles recommended more than one method of treatment and some did not suggest any treatments.

Chi square (based on rows 1 and 4; rehabilitation-reform vs. prevention) = 64.81.
df = 3
p = .001

habilitation and reform, with control of alcohol and education and research both in prominent categories.

Findings from the two sets of data support the view that attitudes toward deviants constitute a somewhat complete ideology with treatment preferences dependent in part on theories of behavior.

Discussion

The pattern of findings which emerges is that the different etiological theories have correspondingly different treatment implications. However, the logical and empirical correspondence between etiological theories held and treatment method advocated is a rather loose one, making prediction between these variables tenuous. For example, 44% of articles maintaining an inside-moralistic or "free-will" explanation of alcoholism favored traditional (e.g., use of greater will power) or punitive (fines, imprisonment, etc.) methods of reform while 31% favored prevention through control of the alcohol supply. It would be obviously easy to construct a post hoc interpretation showing the logical compatibility of several forms of treatment with a given theory of etiology as in the above case and in several others.

In other cases, there would seem to be no compelling logic connecting a given etiological theory with the methods of treatment advocated. The largest proportion of persons who indicated that alcoholism was related to problems in the personality of the alcoholic (described in psychological terms) recommended psychological or psychiatric treatment (43%) but almost 33% of the same group indicated that religious help would be most beneficial.

It would seem reasonable to conclude that at the present time beliefs about alcoholism are not tightly integrated into consistent ideologies among the public. This may be one source of confusion in public policy with regard to coping with the problem of alcoholism. There are other sources of confusion as well.

At the current time, there are many competing theories of alcoholism subscribed to within the population, as evidenced by the distribution of views on both etiology and treatment. Stoll has pointed out that much difficulty and confusion may occur from competing ideologies for treatment (Stoll, 1968).

Although not apparent from the cross-sectional data presented here, very rapid change has been occurring in regard to the theories of alcoholism held by the public (Linsky, 1970, 1970–1971). As in most rapid cultural changes, elements of new ideologies and belief systems may be adopted before others, or selectively assimilated into already prevailing belief systems.

The current confusion in public policy with regard to coping with problems of alcoholism may well be the product of these several sources of divergence: (a) divergence within individual belief systems because of the "looseness in fit" between theories of etiology held and type of treatment preferred, (b) of the considerable diversity of current belief systems about alcoholism now extant within the public and (c) the very rapidness of change that has been occurring in beliefs about alcoholism.

References

Aubert, V., Messinger, S. The criminal and the sick. *Inquiry,* 1958, *1,* 137–160.

Eyesenk, H. J. The effects of psychotherapy: an evaluation. *J. Cons. Psycho.* 1952, *16,* 319–324.

Glock, C. Y. Images of man and public opinion. *Public Opinion Quarterly,* 1964, *28,* 539–546.

Linsky, A. Changing public views on alcoholism. *Quart. J. Stud. Alcohol,* 1970, 692–704.

———Theories of behavior and the image of the alcoholic in popular magazines. *Public Opinion Quarterly,* 1970–71, *34,* 573–581.

Mulford, H. A., Miller, D. E. Public acceptance of the alcoholic as sick. *Quart. J. Stud. Alcohol,* 1964, *22,* 314–324.

Nettler, G. Cruelty, dignity, and determinism. *Amer. Soc. Rev.,* 1959, 375–384.

Powers, E., Witmer, H. An experiment in the prevention of delinquency: the Cambridge-Somerville Youth Study. New York: Columbia University Press, 1951.

Siegler, M., Osmond, H., Newell, S. Models of alcoholism. *Quart. J. Stud. Alcohol,* 1968, *29,* 571–591.

Stoll, C. S. Images of man and social control. *Social Forces,* 1968, *47,* 119–127.

Paul M. Roman and H. M. Trice

The Sick Role, Labeling Theory, and the Deviant Drinker

Much effort in recent years has been directed toward educating the public in the United States regarding the definition of alcoholism and deviant drinking as medical problems rather than as criminal offenses (12,24). These efforts are reflected in the various publications of the Rutgers (formerly Yale) Center for Alcohol Studies, the U.S. Public Health Service, and the National Council on Alcoholism. Likewise, as the therapeutic effectiveness of Alcoholics Anonymous has become increasingly visible, the public has become aware of the assumption that is held by this organization that a form of physiological allergy leads to alcoholism. The A.A. concept is somewhat different from the traditional medical model, but the two conceptions share a strong tendency to reduce individual responsibility for the genesis of alcoholism.

The effects of this re-definition have been regarded as positive by most, the most prominent impact being that alcoholics are committed to hospitals for treatment rather than being detained in prison(11). Medical treatment is the natural corollary of the medical model and is aimed toward "recovery" rather than toward the "character reform" goal of incarceration. In any event medical treatment is regarded as a more humane reaction to a form of behavior that may not be inherently anti-social or criminal.

However, disease or medical model conception of alcoholism and deviant drinking is not without its adverse consequences. The concerns of this paper are (1) the possible social-psychological consequences of the use of the medical model and (2) the development of a scheme of preventive intervention which is based on the knowledge of these consequences. Lest there be a misunderstanding about the position taken here, we emphasize at the outset that the disease concept of alcoholism is not being repudiated. Research has definitively shown that the chronic intake of large amounts of alcohol may have pathological effects on the human organism; likewise, the pattern of physiological addiction which develops at

Reprinted, with permission of the authors, from Reprint Series No. 266, New York State School of Industrial and Labor Relations, 1968.

the later stages of the alcoholism syndrome may be viewed in itself as a major symptom of disease. Thus, chronic abuse of alcohol may have as one of its consequences organic illness. However, being sociopsychological in orientation, the primary concern of this paper is the nature and consequences of the social labeling process rather than the nature and consequences of the alcohol ingestion processes.

The basic contention of this paper is that the medico-disease concept of alcoholism and deviant drinking has led to the assignment of the labeling function to medical authorities which in turn has led to the placement of alcoholics and deviant drinkers in "sick roles" (10, 17, 18). The expectations surrounding these sick roles serve to further develop, legitimize, and in some cases even perpetuate the abnormal use of alcohol.

There are two basic mechanisms operating through the medical labeling process, which is based on the disease model of deviant drinking, which may serve to reinforce deviant drinking behavior. The first mechanism is assignment to the sick role, this being the consequence of being labeled by a physician as manifesting illness. The sick role assignment may legitimize deviant drinking patterns since these patterns have been labeled results of pathology rather than as inappropriate behavior. This is due to the fact that one of the main characteristics of the sick role is that the individual is not held responsible for his illness; thus, in this case the illness is abnormal drinking behavior and assignment to the sick role removes the individual's responsibility for engaging in this behavior. In his discussion of the relation between temperance movements and the different labels applied to drinking. Gusfield points out that the sick role "renders the behavior of the deviant indifferent to the status of norms enforcing abstinence" (11). This "indifference" likewise applies to the norms calling for "normal" drinking behavior.

There appears to be a significant parallel between the development of the disease model of deviant drinking and the disease model of hysteria, the latter of which developed during the nineteenth century as an early step in a significant expansion of the aegis of psychiatry and medicine. Szasz points out that previous to the labeling of hysteria as a legitimate disease, such behavior was regarded as malingering and was met with social sanctions, the most prominent of which was the physician's refusal to pay any heed to such a patient (23). The "recognition" of hysteria as a "mental disease" changed this picture considerably; unfortunately we have no epidemiological data to indicate historical trends in the comparative incidence of malingering and hysteria, the implication being that the "legitimization" of malingering through labeling it a "real" disease may have led to more people "choosing" this behavioral alternative. The relativity of definitions of deviant and sick behavior to various sociocultural and historical conditions is borne out by the growing literature in transcultural psychiatry which focuses upon epidemiological variations (26). These data likewise augur against the location of explicit genetic or biochemical factors to explain the development of types of disordered behavior which are subject to discrete societal reactions and definitions.

The second mechanism operating through the disease model which may serve to reinforce deviant drinking behavior is that the labeling process may lead to secondary deviance through a change in an individual's self-concept as well as a change in the image or social definition of him by the significant others in his social life space (3, 6, 7, 13, 15, 16, 22). The individual with the medical diagnosis of alcoholic or deviant drinker occupies a social status which has accompanying role expectations, the principal expectation being engagement in deviant drinking practices. This is illustrated by the fact that we are not surprised to see a drunk alcoholic and we marvel with amazement when we see a sober one. Another sociological fact which helps explain the efficacy of the labeling process is that it is executed by the physician, who is a highly respected societal functionary whose authority is rarely questioned. The end result of the labeling process is a structure of role expectations and a set of self-concept changes that eventuate in the individual's performance of the deviant role. The behavior which is assigned is carried out.

A curious "double-bind" results from the dual operation of these mechanisms (2). Deviant drinking behavior is legitimized through the disease label in the sense that the individual is no longer held responsible for this behavior and this behavior is very rewarding to him. He is also assigned a social role which invidiously surrounds him with expectations for deviance as well as resulting in changes in his self-concept. Simultaneously he is expected by significant others in his life space to "shape up," seek treatment, and above all, stop drinking. Both this message and the message of his being "sick" appear legitimate but are contradictory. This double-bind may be an invidious cause of his mobility and differential association with those like himself, these behaviors representing the "escape from the field" that is postulated as a solution to a double-binding situation (2). This double-bind is very reflective of society's ambivalence toward the labeled alcoholic, a sort of half-acceptance of the sick role notion of problem drinking as well as half-acceptance of the criminal, immoral, or "enemy" label of this behavior (11).

There are two other possible consequences of labeling which may occur and serve to further "lock in" deviant drinking patterns. First is the process of rejecting the individual from primary group associations that may result from the presence of the label as well as from intolerance of his deviant drinking. The developing alcoholic seeks out opportunities to affiliate with more tolerant drinking groups (1, 4, 20, 24, 26). The self-concept or personal identification changes that have resulted from labeling may also tend to lead the individual to primary groups composed of other deviant drinkers and alcoholics. This differential association serves to further legitimize, reinforce, and perpetuate deviant drinking and lead further toward true addiction.

A second consequence of labeling may be the functional integration of the labeled individual into social groups which are composed primarily of nondeviants (5). There is a growing amount of research evidence which indicates that certain potentially unstable social groups, such as potentially unstable families or informal friendship groups, may be stabilized by the presence of a deviant member (19, 21, 23, 28, 29). It is possible for the group to do its own labeling of a selected deviant, but labeling will be much more effective if executed by an outsider who has the institutionalized assignment to label and whose authority is not questioned. The presence of a formally and officially labeled deviant assures that it is not necessary to "pass the deviance around" among the members in order to hold the group together. The functions served by the deviant's presence include (1) the definition of other group members as "normal" because they do not share the deviant's symptoms or his label, (2) the presence of a submissive and relatively helpless target for scapegoating, which in turn allows for displacement of intermember tensions onto the weak deviant member and thereby reduces cross-cutting interpersonal conflicts which would weaken the organization of the group, and (3) the presence of a rule breaker may offer the group a ready excuse for its shortcomings in goal attainment activities. These functions serve to lock the deviant member's role behavior into the group's patterns to the extent that his behavior is invidiously rewarded and attempts by outsiders to change his behavior are strongly resisted.

The basic point we are attempting to make is that the mere processes of labeling and sick role assignment may serve to aggravate and perpetuate a condition which is initially under the individual's control. *In other words, the disease label has disease consequences.* We are not arguing that chronic alcoholism is simply behavioral deviance; protracted heavy drinking with its physiological, psychological, and sociological accompaniments has disease consequences in terms of physiological damage as well as in terms of physiological and psychological addiction. The point is that the use of the medical model conception of deviant drinking leads to processes of labeling and sick role assignment at a point previous to true addiction. In other words, something is called a disease or a disorder before it has actually become such. In most cases the behavior may still be under individual control at the time when labeling occurs. Labeling and the disease model do not allow for this fact, and may serve to "lock" the deviant drinker into a nexus of role expectations as well as changing his self-concept. The performance of this role coupled with the self-reaction to this self-image sets up a system of cybernetic action and reaction which may lead in many cases to true alcohol addiction.

Having developed the theoretical dimensions of the outcomes of labeling deviant drinking behavior, let us turn to an example of how these processes work. This example also sets the stage for applying knowledge of the impact of labeling to the development or revision of programs designed to identify and treat "alcoholics" in various stages of development.

We are acquainted with certain procedures of medical referral in work organizations which may serve to "lock in" the deviant role assignment (8). Early identification of the deviant drinker is stressed, and the immediate step following identification is referral to the medical department—in other words, labeling. We would argue that mere *referral* to a physician is a form of labeling, in terms of changing the individual's self-concept by telling him that he "needs professional help" and in terms of changing the role expectations held toward him by those who referred him. Thus, even if the physician does not formally label him as an alcoholic, he and those in his social mileu are "told" that his drinking had led him to require medical attention. In any event, it appears that in sociological terms the stage is set for progression toward true addiction in the sense of sick role occupancy and role expectations which may lead to secondary deviance.

Obviously the labeling of every early stage deviant drinker by a medical authority does not ultimately lead to alcohol addiction. Affiliation with Alcoholics Anonymous, various therapeutic interventions, or simple response to the pressures to cease deviant drinking which are brought to bear by "significant others" may result in the termination of the progression. However, labeling and sick role assignment processes may create unnecessary risks for the individual whose drinking problem has not yet gone beyond his personal control. It is argued that the labeling and sick role assignment create actual pressures toward alcohol addiction rather than halting the progression.

In the light of this conceptual scheme, an attempt has been made to develop a model of intervention in which the risk-laden use of the alcoholic or deviant drinker label is avoided as much as possible. In light of knowledge that the early stage alcoholic or deviant drinker is unable or extremely reluctant to recognize his difficulties and do something about them, we have asked the question of what societal system possesses the institutionalized authority to bring effective pressure to bear upon him. The answer appears to be that this legitimate authority is possessed by the employer. The job is essentially an exchange relationship whereby rewards are given for a certain kind of performance. If the performance is inappropriate or inadequate, rewards may be legitimately withdrawn. This scheme of intervention is built on the assumption that the individual cannot perform a role in the work place adequately if he is impaired, and the consumption of alcohol or the presence of a hangover is defined as impairment. There is no evidence to indicate that alcohol consumption improves overall job performance (with the possibile exception of a few job roles in the arts). There is an impairment in performance brought about by alcohol consumption, whether the individual has a bottle of beer or a quart of whisky.

For the want of a better term, the intervention is labeled "constructive coercion." Constructive coercion is the confrontation of any employee who shows evidence of drinking on the job or who comes to work with a hangover. This is not only the early identification of alcoholics but also covers much broader groups. It is the "early, early" identification of problem drinkers. It is total intolerance of drinking or hangovers when the individual is to be performing his work role. The early stage alcoholic is included under this umbrella, as well as those whose drinking may never eventuate in a problem.

The confrontation of the employee who allows alcohol to enter in any way into his work role involves a simple statement that repetition of this act will lead to termination. There is no referral to a medical department or introduction into therapy because such referrals are not necessary if confrontation occurs at this point. This approach is similar to the "no tolerance for drinking" policy employed in Czechoslovakian work organizations described by Dr. Morris Chafetz.

It should be stressed that this is not a policy where an individual is confronted after alcohol interferes with his work performance; rather, the simple presence of alcohol in the form of drinking on the job or hangover is regarded inherently as impairment of performance. The hard-line norm against the interference of alcohol with job performance must be universalistic if it is to have potency. If it is universalistic, a company policy will encounter fewer difficulties and will be less often accused of inequity. The arbitrary decision of "how much" drinking actually interferes with job performance seems to offer many difficulties, particularly in training of first-line supervisors about when it is appropriate to "confront" an employee who is a problem drinker. Likewise the notion that certain jobs are more or less compatible with the effects of alcohol ingestion seems to lead in the same direction of arbitrary decisions, foggy policies, and the risk of inequity.

It should also be pointed out that the "hard-line" approach in which the individual is held responsible for his behavior rather than being allowed to enter the sick role and the nurturance of a doctor-patient relationship does not tap into the psychic dependency of the deviant drinker. In other words, since psychological dependency has been found to be associated with the personalities of alcoholics, it may be argued that a tendency toward irresponsibility both precedes and accompanies alcoholic development (26). A focus upon individual responsibility for deviant behavior runs contrary to this propensity, and constructive coercion may in this sense help to "break up" the progression toward addiction.

Several intervening factors which may temper the success of constructive coercion should be mentioned. First, it is assumed that the job is the essential nexus of the individual's status set, particularly his status of breadwinner in the family. If he does not have such obligations or is not responsive to such obligations, the effectiveness of constructive coercion may be reduced. This factor may also reduce the potential effectiveness of constructive coercion with female problem drinkers who are not employed or whose employment role is not considered financially essential to the family.

Secondly, it is assumed that the individual has an investment in his job to the extent that quitting and obtaining other employment is too costly for him in terms of time, training, security, and the personal benefits accompanying his present position. Employees who view quitting and obtaining a new job as a worthwhile investment in order to maintain their deviant drinking may well react in this way to the threat contained within the strategy of constructive coercion.

Thirdly, the visibility of employee behavior to the supervisor is assumed in this scheme. Those who go unsupervised for long periods of time may move too far along the alcoholic progression before they come to supervisory attention to be effectively helped by constructive coercion. This is particularly true of occupations which require extensive traveling.

Fourth, it is assumed that there will be supervisory positions in the organizational hierarchy above an individual with adequate power and authority to carry out constructive coercion. The technique may not be effective for those in executive positions or for those in staff positions where lines of authority are unclear. This same problem may occur in small organizations which lack well-defined status hierarchies. Likewise, constructive coercion is not relevant for the self-employed.

Finally, it is assumed that the process will not be disrupted by the employee's total and effective denial of the existence of a deviant drinking pattern. This may present difficulties, particularly in light of anecdotal evidence of the manipulative skills of developing alcoholics.

A final word should be added regarding the relevance of this paper to current programs on the identification and treatment of problem drinking which are in operation or in the process of development in work organizations. These statements should not be interpreted as allegations that these programs are creating more problem drinkers than they are helping. Rather, the programs on the whole operate within a paradigm of problem drinking as a disorder or a disease, which is the rationale for certain characteristics of the programs (14). The purpose of this paper is to offer a supplemental paradigm for the disease model such that the disease label is not applied before the disease has developed.

It is recognized that there may be many instances in which the alcoholism progression moves beyond the point where medical assistance is unnecessary. However, in these cases the assumptions underlying the constructive coercion strategy are not irrelevant, for a policy of emphasizing individual responsibility for deviance will reduce the degree to which the individual is formally placed in the status of an "outsider" and thereby increase rehabilitation opportunities.

In summary, we have argued that the disease model of alcoholism and problem drinking has resulted in a labeling process that may in itself set the stage for the development of true alcohol addiction. We regard it as a risk factor possibly contributing to eventual addiction rather than as a sufficient condition for addiction. Through the examination of the social role dimensions of alcoholism and problem drinking, we have presented a tentative model of preventive intervention in which the disease or disorder label is applied more cautiously.

References

1. Bacon, S. D. Alcoholics do not drink. *Ann. Amer. Acad. Pol. Soc. Sci.,* 1958, *315,* 62.
2. Bateson, G., et al. Toward a theory of schizophrenia. *Behav. Sci.,* 1956, *1,* 251–264.
3. Becker, H. S. *Outsiders: studies in the sociology of deviance.* New York: The Free Press, 1963.
4. Clinard, M. B. The public drinking house and society. In *Society, culture and drinking patterns,* ed. D. Pittman and C. Snyder. New York: John Wiley, 1962.
5. Dentler, R., and Erikson, K. T. The functions of deviance in groups. *Soc. Problems,* 1959, 7, 98–107.
6. Erikson, K. T. Notes on the sociology of deviance. *Soc. Problems,* 1962, 9, 307–314.
7. Erikson, K. T. *Wayward Puritans.* New York: John Wiley, 1966.
8. Franco, S. C. Problem drinking in industry: review of a company program. *Indus. Med. Surg.,* 1957, *26,* 221–228.
9. Gibbs, J. P. Conceptions of deviant behavior: the old and the new. *Pacific Socio. Rev.,* 1966, 9, 9–14.
10. Gordon, G. *Role theory and illness.* New Haven: College University Press, 1965.
11. Gustfield, J. Moral passage: the symbolic process in public designations of deviance. *Soc. Problems,* 1967, *15,* 175–188.
12. Jellinek, E. M. *The disease concept of alcoholism.* New Haven: Hillhouse Press, 1960.

13. Kitsuse, J. Societal reaction to deviant behavior. *Soc. Problems,* 1962, *9,* 247–256.
14. Kuhn, T. S. *The structure of scientific revolutions.* Chicago: University of Chicago Press, 1962.
15. Lemert, E. M. *Social pathology.* New York: McGraw-Hill, 1951.
16. Lemert, E. M. The concept of secondary deviation. In *Human deviance, social problems and social control.* Englewood Cliffs, N.J.: Prentice-Hall, 1967.
17. Parsons, T. *The Social System.* Glencoe, Ill.: The Free Press, 1951, Pp. 428–479.
18. Parsons, T., and Fox R. Illness, therapy and the modern American family. *Jour. Soc. Issues,* 1952, *8,* 31–44.
19. Paul, N. L., and Grosser, G. K. Family resistance to change in schizophrenia. *Family Proc.* 1964, *3,* 377–401.
20. Phillips, D. L. Rejection: a possible consequence of seeking help for mental disorders. *Amer. Socio. Rev.,* 1963, *28,* 963–972.
21. Ryckoff, I., et al. Maintenance of stereotyped roles in families of schizophrenics. *Arch. Gen. Psychiat.,* 1959, *1,* 93–98.
22. Scheff, T. J. *Being mentally ill.* Chicago: Aldine, 1966.
23. Sonne, J. C., et al. The absent member maneuver as a resistance to family therapy in schizophrenia. *Family Proc.,* 1962, *1,* 44–62.
24. Sutherland, E. *Collected papers.* Bloomington: Indiana University Press, 1956.
25. Szasz, T. S. *The myth of mental illness: Foundations of a theory of personal conduct.* New York: Hoeber-Harper, 1961.
26. Trice, H. M. Alcoholics Anonymous. *Ann. Amer. Acad. Pol. Soc. Sci.,* 1958, *315,* 110.
27. Trice, H. M. *Alcoholism in America.* New York: McGraw-Hill, 1966.
28. Vogel, E. F., and Bell, N. W. The emotionally disturbed child as family scapegoat. In *The family,* ed. N. W. Bell and E. F. Vogel. Glencoe, Ill.: The Free Press, 1960.
29. Wynne, L. C., et al. Pseudo-mutuality in the family relations of schizophrenics. *Psychiatry,* 1958, *21,* 205–220.

3. The Uniformity of Alcoholics

The focus here is primarily on the assumption that alcoholics, having certain predispositions toward alcoholism, are different from normal drinkers. Multiple investigations have described psychological and physiological characteristics associated with or resulting from the development of serious drinking problems. Detailed reviews of this literature are available elsewhere; biological concomitants are reviewed in detail in Kissin and Begleiter's *The Biology of Alcoholism,* volume 1 and 2 (1972, 1973), and psychological and psychiatric characteristics are summarized by Wallgren and Barry (1970a, b) and by Barry (1974).

Many investigators have devoted considerable time to pursuing the discovery of predisposing physical or personality factors unique to alcoholics. As noted by Barry (1974), such studies have concentrated almost exclusively on identifying characteristics shared by alcoholics or persons vulnerable to alcoholism, to the extent of neglecting a search for shared characteristics among persons who are seemingly immune to drinking problems. In reviewing studies of possible genetic or constitutional antecedents of alcohol problems, Wallgren and Barry (1970) concluded that no such factors had yet been identified as strong causative elements in alcoholism. More recently, genetic research (reviewed by Goodwin & Guze, 1974) involving Danish adoptees raised apart from alcoholic biological parents has suggested that genetic factors may contribute to one's susceptibility to developing alcohol problems.

It is important to differentiate between attempts to define a uniformity among *all* alcoholics and attempts to define a number of factors whose presence may make an individual more vulnerable to developing alcohol problems. Blane (1968) has considered the concept of "a personality structure *unique* to alcoholics and *to only* alcoholics" (p. 5) as being a straw man. Although theoretically this may be true, the idea of characteristics unique to alcoholics has been frequently espoused in the traditional literature. Searches for the "alcoholic personality," however, have always been fruitless. In past decades, the rationale for such quests probably stemmed from the strong psychological research interest in personality factors (an orientation quite prevalent during the 1940's and 1950's) and the conventional circular wisdom that since all persons suffering from alcoholism share problems with alcohol, they must, ergo, share predisposing characteristics.

Early searches for the "alcoholic personality" have been critically reviewed (Sutherland, Schroeder, & Tordella, 1950; Syme, 1957; Armstrong, 1958), each critique concluding that alcoholics, per se, do not represent a unique personality type. In a more recent editorial, Keller (1972) concluded that "alcoholics are different in so many ways it makes no difference" (p. 1147).

Adopting a different tack, Mogar, Wilson, and Helm (1970) used an empirical base to demonstrate that while unique personality characteristics clearly have not yet been enumerated, the differentiation of individuals into a number of smaller subsets may have practical implications as regards the development of treatment plans. Hurwitz and Lelos (1968) have shown that groups of alcoholics can be clustered according to variables such as definitions of alcoholism, attitudes, role ascriptions, treatment goals, and degrees of dysfunction in different areas of life health, such as social, vocational, interpersonal, emotional, and physical adjustment. Whereas the severity of the actual drinking may be identical, the degree of life dysfunction among these "alcoholics" varies widely, from the "high-bottom" alcoholic with little life dysfunction to the "low-bottom" alcoholic who has never had much competence in any area of life functioning. Further, a number of studies (Trice & Roman, 1970; Trice, Roman, & Belasco, 1969; Kissin, Platz, & Su, 1970; Kissin, Rosenblatt, & Machover, 1968a, b) have demonstrated differential response to various treatment modalities as a function of sociopsychological variables. Finally, Pattison (1974) has reviewed studies demonstrating that different alcohol treatment program populations have distinctly different characteristics. That work (Pattison, Coe, & Doerr, 1973; Pattison, Coe, & Rhodes, 1969) is supported by two independent studies (English & Curtin, 1975; Tomsovic, 1970).

Thus, it seems clear that *except for sharing alcohol problems, all alcoholics are not the same.* The mere definition of a person as "alcoholic" does not necessarily predict treatment response or degree of life dysfunction. While there appear to be a variety of meaningful clinical differences in both drinking patterns and degree of drinking-related dysfunction in other areas of life health, these tend to be obscured by the summary label "alcoholic." Cahalan and Room (1974), reporting on the results of national surveys of over 1,500 males aged 21 to 59, concluded that their "results suggest that those with at least one drinking problem in the general population are in fact a rather diverse and diffuse 'target' population" (p. 222). Blane (1968) asserts that a variety of personality factors "are not centrally present in all alcoholics, but are common enough to merit attention" (p. 7). The identification of such factors is likely to have immediate clinical value.

It would be valuable to consider anyone in the general population as having the potential to develop alcohol problems—defined simply as adverse consequences resulting from the use of alcohol—with various individuals having differing degrees of susceptibility to the development of such problems. While it is quite reasonable to pursue the delineation of a set of variables which might contribute to placing individuals at risk of developing alcohol problems and to use such knowledge to implement preventive approaches for identified high-risk drinkers, such an approach has substantially different clinical implications from concepts based on unique characteristics typical of "the alcoholic." In light of the confusion inherent in traditional concepts, Cahalan (1970) has suggested that it may be more beneficial simply to refer to those individuals who develop alcohol problems as being "problem drinkers." Such a change in terminology would not only avoid certain negative connotations which now apply to use of the term "alcoholic" but would also be important because it incorporates an implication that problem drinkers come in a variety of forms.

Mark Keller

The Oddities of Alcoholics

Summary: *Alcoholics are different in so many ways that it makes no difference.*

A splurge of reports, in the 1940's, of biochemical characteristics purporting to differentiate alcoholics from nonalcoholics stimulated me to review a voluminous related literature, implicating physical, social and psychological demarcators as well. The only conclusion I could derive, from the entirety of the reportage, took a

Reprinted by permission from *Quarterly Journal of Studies on Alcohol*, 1972, *33*, 1147–1148. Copyright by Journal of Studies on Alcohol, Inc., New Brunswick, N.J. 08903.

form that became known, among colleagues, as Keller's Law: *The investigation of any trait in alcoholics will show that they have either more or less of it.* Accordingly, I then predicted that if sexadactyly should be investigated, alcoholics will yield either more or fewer six-toed and six-fingered people than a control population.

Numerous subsequently published studies seem to confirm this law. Compared with other populations, alcoholics are, for example, more allergic, less leptosomic, more pyknotic, less bald, more first-or-last-born, less introverted, more color blind, less socialized, more dependent, less responsible, more Dupuytren's contractured, less frustration tolerant, more alcohol tolerant, less religiously active, more accident-prone, less hypnotizable, more amnesic, less hippurate excretive, more psychopathic, less mother-loved, more hepatitic, less hypertensive, more drug-consuming, less conditionable, more anomalous-alcohol-dehydrogenasic, less bucolic, more suicidal, less married, more enzymatic, less longevous, more incarcerated, less feminine (women), more effeminized (men), less potent (men), more frigid-promiscuous (women), less prosperous, more impulsive, less libidinous, more genetically vitamin-needful, less arteriosclerotic, more rigid, less self-sex-image secure, more cardiomyopathic, less anesthetizable, more depressed, less body-hairy (men), more anxious, less time-sensitive, more sociopathic, less fecund, more risk-taking, more endocrinopathic, more rejected, more charming, more compulsive, more imaginative, less treatable and more thirsty. (This list, compiled from memory, emphasizes traits with implied relevance to the etiology of alcoholism but includes decidedly irrelevant ones as well as some that may be pertinent to diagnosis. Nevertheless it is incomplete. The totality of examples is so numerous, and the bibliography so extensive, that they would occupy more space than the subject can justify. A reference for any putative alcoholismic trait, whether or not listed here, will be supplied, on request, by the Documentation Division, The Center of Alcohol Studies, Rutgers University.)

A search of the *Classified Abstract Archive of the Alcohol Literature* indicates that sexadactyly has not yet been studied. In my opinion, however, additional researches tending to validate this law are not necessary.

4. The Notion of Cravings and Compulsions

Popular Explanations

A major component of traditional concepts of alcoholism has involved explanations of why individuals who have experienced serious adverse consequences as a result of alcohol consumption continue to engage in such drinking. For this purpose, the term "craving" has often been used indiscriminately. In fact, in 1954, a distinguished panel composed of members of the World Health Organization Committees on Mental Health and Alcohol convened in Geneva to discuss whether or not concepts of "craving" had value in the understanding of alcohol problems (Jellinek et al., 1955). They concluded that "the onset of the excessive use of alcohol, the drinking pattern displayed within an acute drinking bout, relapse into a new drinking bout after days or weeks of abstinence, continuous daily excessive drinking and loss of control, are all behaviors which have been claimed to be manifestations of 'craving' of the same order" (p. 63). Here it is essential to distinguish the act of beginning to drink following a period of abstinence from the process of continuing to drink once initial drinking has begun (see Chapter 5, "The Nature of 'Loss of Control' "). This present discussion considers traditional explanations of why an identified "alcoholic" who has been abstinent for some period of time might resume drinking.

Should an identified alcoholic drink again, it is only natural to infer that the onset of drinking has occurred in response to some sort of "need" state. If the attempt at explanation is limited simply to postulating a need state, however, one is trapped within the confines of circular logic: the process of description has been confused with that of explanation. Thus, traditional concepts often postulate that an alcoholic begins to drink because he experiences a need to drink, while the fact that he did drink is simultaneously presented as evidence that he felt a need to drink. More simply put, he drinks because he needs to drink, and we know he needs to drink because he does drink. Mello (1972) has also made this point. It is important to recognize that such a supposed "need" state has potential value only when it is specified to reflect a tangible process, either psychological or physiological, within the individual which is manifested as the felt "need" to drink. For instance, Williams, Berry, and Beerstecher (1949) and Mardones (1951) have postulated a physiopathological origin of "cravings" to drink in alcoholics following a period of abstinence from alcohol. MacLeod (Jellinek et al., 1955) has reviewed various physiopathological approaches to the origins of felt "cravings" but has failed to distinguish when terms apply to phenomena which occur *between* drinking bouts as opposed to *within* drinking bouts.

Jellinek and the majority of members at the World Health Organization Expert Committees agreed that the mechanisms responsible for the onset of drinking following a period of abstinence were most likely to be psychological in origin (1955). While Jellinek preferred to denote these feeling states as "compulsions," which he felt reflected a neurotic condition, the Joint Committees of the World Health Organization recommended that such feeling states be described as a "pathological desire" for alcohol as a means of relieving psychological tension which would sometimes develop in individuals during a period of abstinence (Jellinek et al., 1955). "Pathological desire" was preferred to "compulsion" and "craving" because the term "compulsion" has a variety of technical definitions in the psychiatric literature. Mann (1968) has asserted that alcoholics are essentially in bondage to alcohol and lose the power even to determine when they will begin drinking. She does not clearly speculate about either a physiopathological or psychopathological basis for the existence of this bondage.

Empirical Tests

Few research studies have investigated the determinants of drinking following a period of abstinence. Some investigators (i.e., Ludwig, 1972; Marlatt, 1973) have obtained retrospective self-reports from alcoholics about their reasons for beginning to drink following a period of abstinence, and their emotional and physical feeling states antecedent to that drinking. Ludwig (1972) reported 18-month follow-up data for a sample of 176 alcoholics who had been treated in an inpatient alcoholism program. As part of follow-up procedure, patients were interviewed concerning their reasons for resuming drinking and/or for abstaining throughout the interval. Of the 176 patients, 161 (91%) resumed drinking at least once during the 18-month follow-up period, but only 1% attributed their resumption of drinking to subjective feelings of craving or similar reasons (e.g., "not enough will power to resist"). The most frequently reported determinant of resumed drinking (25% of the cases) was for relief from psychological distress, with other reasons spanning a gamut from curiosity to family problems. The reasons patients offered for times when they had abstained were similarly broad. Ludwig concluded that "the reasons alcoholics give for resuming or stopping drinking after discharge from a hospital showed such broad diversity that no unitary hypothesis could be confirmed—particularly the concept of craving for alcohol" (p. 91). As recognized by Ludwig (1974), these data were based on self-descriptive statements limited by the self-analytic capacities of the alcoholics interviewed. Thus, it is possible that patients experienced physical cravings or felt needs which they were not able to identify accurately.

A similar analysis of 48 cases of relapse has been reported by Marlatt (1973). In his evaluation, the two most common situations giving rise to relapse were a patient's "frustration and inability to express anger" (29% of cases), or an "inability to resist social pressure" (23% of cases). From this report, it is not possible to identify precisely how many patients actually reported experiencing "craving" states. Such responses appear to have been included in a general category denoted as "inability to resist intrapersonal temptation to drink," which accounted for 21% of relapses and also included social temptations to drink. Thus, physical craving states are seldom mentioned among self-reported reasons for relapse. On the other hand, psychological distress is the most frequently reported antecedent of resumed drinking.

Placebo control studies as well have investigated feelings of cravings. Marlatt, Demming, and Reid (1973) reported a study which utilized a taste-rating task as an experimental analogue to "loss of control" drinking in alcoholics. The experimental situation took advantage of the fact that the taste of five parts of tonic to one part of vodka, well-chilled, is indistinguishable from pure tonic. It was explained to subjects that the taste-test task was being used to obtain comparisons of two different types of tonic waters (or vodka and tonic mixtures) although it was actually used to obtain a relatively unobtrusive measure of the subjects' alcohol consumption. Subjects were free to sample as much of each beverage as they wished in order to make their taste comparisons, with the central dependent variable measure being the actual amount of each beverage sampled (consumed). In this study, both nonabstinent alcoholics and social drinkers were used as subjects. Nonabstinent alcoholics were recruited from the local community and defined as identified alcoholics who claimed "no immediate intentions of abstaining from alcohol," but who would abstain from alcohol prior to their experimental session and had to register a Breathalyzer reading of zero immediately prior to the session. Within each group of alcoholic and social drinker subjects, subjects were then randomly assigned to one of four experimental conditions: (1) Told tonic/Given tonic: subjects were presented with three identical containers of tonic and instructed to compare the three "types of tonic" on a number of characteristics (i.e., sweetness); (2) Told alcohol/Given tonic: subjects were presented with the identical tonic solutions but were instructed that they were comparing varieties of vodka and tonic mixed drinks; (3) Told alcohol/Given alcohol: subjects were given three identical decanters of a vodka plus tonic mixture and told that they were comparing three varieties of vodka and tonic mixed drinks; and (4) Told tonic/Given alcohol: subjects were given three identical decanters of vodka and tonic mixture but were told that they were merely comparing three different types of tonic. Postexperimental tests found that subjects had believed the experimental instructions regarding the type of beverages they were comparing. Of relevance for our discussion, the only significant determinant of how much beverage subjects consumed, regardless of the actual beverage used, was the induced instructional set. Thus, both alcoholics and social drinkers who thought they were comparing (and consuming) mixed drinks of vodka plus tonic consumed significantly more beverage during the test than subjects who thought they were merely comparing varieties of tonic water. The actual beverage content was *not related* to the amount consumed. While this study is not directly related to the concept of "cravings" for a first drink, it does elucidate the powerful cognitive determinants of drinking behavior which operate for both alcoholics and social drinkers.

In a powerful experimental test of the notion of physical cravings, Engle and Williams (1972) evaluated the effects of one ounce of vodka on hospitalized chronic alcoholic subjects. For four consecutive days, 40 patients of an inpatient alcoholic rehabilitation program were acclimated to a regime of drinking a strongly flavored vitamin mixture and then completing a questionnaire in which they rated their desire for alcohol. On the fifth day of testing, a randomly selected half of the subjects each received one ounce of vodka, fully disguised in their vitamin mixture, and the remaining 20 subjects received the vitamin mixture alone. A random half (10) of the subjects in each of the two beverage groups (vitamins alone, vitamins plus vodka) were told that they had received a solution containing one ounce of vodka; the remaining subjects were not so instructed. In addition to completing the questionnaire, on this day all subjects were also given an opportunity to request an additional drink if they felt a strong need for alcohol. As in the Marlatt et al. (1973) study, Engle and Williams found that the cognitive variable of instructional set was the significant determinant of behavior: the report of felt cravings was not related to the actual administration of alcohol. They concluded that "an alcoholic's desire for alcohol increases when he has been informed that he has drunk alcohol whether in fact he has or not" (p. 1103). Of further interest, the only subject who requested an additional drink was among the subjects who had received the vitamin mixture only but had been told that they had ingested an ounce of vodka.

"The First Drink: Psychobiological Aspects of Craving," in Ludwig, Wikler, and Stark (1974), presents the results of an initial test of a recently suggested explanation for phenomena which may be interpreted as felt "needs to drink." In their formulation, a craving for alcohol is represented as the cognitive correlate of a subclinical alcohol withdrawal syndrome. They hypothesize that over an alcoholic's history the rather intense experience of alcohol withdrawal syndromes comes to be associated with the use of alcohol to ameliorate those symptoms. Then, presumably through a process of classical conditioning, interoceptive and exteroceptive sensory cues for alcohol elicit some conditioned components of the alcohol withdrawal syndrome (i.e., agitation, feelings of more serious impending symptoms), which consequently induce a felt need to drink (for relief of the "conditioned" withdrawal symptoms). This felt need is hypothesized to be a conditioned (learned) physical state which the individual must then interpret. Ludwig and Wikler hypothesize that the individual may interpret this feeling state in a variety of ways, all of which are simply different types of labels for the felt visceral state. An implication of this formulation is that: "Because alcoholics do not spontaneously report craving or because they offer some other reason for drinking, that does not necessarily mean that they are not experiencing craving or that craving is not an important determinant in the initiation and perpetuation of drinking" (1974, p. 120). Thus, even if alcoholics do not often verbalize a perceived physical need for alcohol, it can be speculated that they initiate drinking in response to physical cues.

Current Status

Unfortunately, little more is known today than was known many years ago about why some individuals with histories of alcohol problems continually choose to consume a "first drink." At this time, the only conclusion which appears justified is that alcoholics do not periodically suffer from an apparent specific appetite for alcohol based on genetic or metabolic deficiency formulations. When alcoholics are asked to evaluate the circumstances leading to their resumption of drinking, the predominant explanation is psychological relief from stress. Interestingly, identical speculation was voiced by Jellinek and others several years ago. Still, we cannot presume simply on the basis of these self-reports that an attempt to reduce psychological stress has been demonstrated as a cause of alcoholic relapse. For now, the evidence regarding the existence of a stress-reduction function of ingested alcohol is ambiguous at best (Cappell & Hermann, 1972).

As an alternative explanation to stress reduction, Ludwig and his colleagues have suggested that self-reports of why drinking recurs may simply represent an individual's interpretation of a visceral state elicited by exposure to alcohol-related cues. It should be cautioned, however, that the formulation of a conditioned craving is based on classical conditioning learning theory which has often been found to have limited explanatory power in laboratory experiments with humans (Evans, in press). There is, however, a critical distinction between the formulation of Ludwig and his colleagues and the classical notion of physical cravings. The conditioned "cravings" referred to by Ludwig et al. represent an acquired, classically conditioned process. If this should be the case, they would be reversible and subject to extinction by well-known procedures. Thus, the conditioned cravings formulation implies no necessary requirement that individuals who today experience a conditioned craving for alcohol will suffer from that condition for the rest of their lives. On the contrary, if conditioned cravings should be demonstrated to be real, specific treatment procedures aimed at extinguishing the conditioned withdrawal syndrome would appear to be indicated.

Arnold M. Ludwig,
Abraham Wikler, and Louis H. Stark

The First Drink:
Psychobiological Aspects of Craving

It is a truism to claim that alcoholics cannot "fall off the wagon" without taking that "first drink." This truism, however, offers no understanding of why alcoholics take that first drink or often continue to drink to the point of intoxication or sustained inebriation.

Although the related phenomena of "craving" and "loss of control" have been invoked as explanations for relapse (1), there is little current agreement among clinicians and scientists about their nature or even existence. Some theorize that these phenomena are produced by the activation of specific brain centers, conditioned alterations in cellular metabolism, alcohol-induced dissociation of control centers in the brain, or represent learned behaviors (2–5). With one notable exception (6), most investigators have either been unable to document the existence of these phenomena or derogate their importance as authentic determinants of drinking bhhavior (7–12). Still others have argued that the construct of craving represents a superfluous logical tautology since it is often defined by subsequent drinking behavior (12).

In a prior theoretical article (13), we have attempted to resolve this conceptual confusion by advancing a thesis concerning the nature of craving and loss-of-control and the role these phenomena play in the drinking behavior of alcoholics. In essence, we postulate that craving for alcohol (during periods of no physical dependence), similar to "narcotic hunger" (14,15), represents the cognitive-symbolic correlate of a *subclinical, conditioned withdrawal syndrome* that can be produced by appropriate interoceptive or exteroceptive stimuli.

Interoceptive stimuli pertain to the actions of alcohol (or pharmacological agents having similar properties) on appropriate visceral and cerebral neuronal receptors. The induced physiological-neurophysiological changes, presumably, should resemble those found during prior alcohol withdrawal syndromes

Reprinted from the *Archives of General Psychiatry,* 1974, *30,* 539–547.
Copyright 1974, American Medical Association.

(or states of central nervous system [CNS]–autonomic nervous system [ANS] "arousal") or the initiation of prior drinking bouts. According to our theory, a small but adequate amount of alcohol should act like hors d'oeuvres or appetizers—i.e., stimulating but not suppressing hunger (craving). Just as this evoked hunger for food has become associated with the later consumption of an entree, the psychobiological effects of the first drink, under "appropriate" conditions, should become chain-conditioned to the entire sequence of responses and behaviors demonstrated in previous drinking episodes.

Exteroceptive stimuli pertain to a variety of environmental situations associated with prior heavy drinking or with the unpleasant effects of prior withdrawal experiences. Just as salivation and increased appetite or hunger can be evoked by the sight of food (16), a conditioned withdrawal syndrome with associated craving may result whenever the alcoholic passes a bar, sees other people drinking, or encounters·cues relevant to previous drinking practices. Also, since anxiety, nervousness, jitteriness, and other types of emotional dysphoria may produce such physiological responses as increased heart rate and respiration, tremulousness, autonomic lability, increased sweating, insomnia, all of which represent changes associated with the alcohol withdrawal syndrome, we should anticipate that these states, induced by either arguments with spouses, employment difficulties, or loneliness, may likewise evoke craving. Tokar et al. (17) report that alcoholics, in comparison to normal controls, are most likely to go to the bar, drink booze, smoke, and take pills whenever they feel helpless, depressed, angry, or anxious. From our thesis, these responses of alcoholics should be readily understandable.

While appropriate interoceptive and exteroceptive stimuli represent necessary conditions for the elicitation of craving and alcohol-seeking behavior, they cannot be regarded as sufficient. It should be noted that the construct of craving refers to a cognitive-symbolic state and, as such, can be highly influenced by mental set and physical setting. In our view, the function of craving (under ordinary circumstances) is to protect the organism against sensed danger, threat, or physical distress by alerting it to a potential source of relief—namely, ethanol. In a sense, craving represents a conditioned "cognitive labeling" process, in response to psychophysiological imbalance, that permits the organism to engage in efficient, goal-directed, appetitive behavior. If, however, the mental set of the alcoholic is manipulated or altered (i.e., false research instructions) or the physical setting is not conducive to the expression of craving (i.e., treatment or experimental ward, research laboratory) or does not provide stimulus configurations reminiscent of prior drinking bouts and relief from withdrawal symptoms, it should not be surprising that the expression of normal craving and drinking behaviors will be grossly altered or distorted. This simple consideration could account for much of the confusion and discrepant findings on craving and loss of control that are reported in the present literature.

From a scientific standpoint, the major advantages of our general thesis are twofold: (1) it permits the conceptualization of craving as a "psychobiological" phenomenon with concomitant subjective, behavioral, and CNS-ANS dimensions; (2) it permits the formulation of testable hypotheses capable of subsequent modification after interpretation of results.

The Study

This study was designed to evaluate the effects of a single "low" and "high" dose of alcohol, administered during different situations, on reported craving and alcohol acquisition behavior. Additional physiological measurements were taken to assess the comparative internal states of persons under the different alcohol doses and situations. The specific hypotheses advanced, based on our theoretical formulation (13), were as follows:

1. A low dose of alcohol (because of "appetizer" effect), compared to a high dose, should produce greater craving and alcohol acquisition behavior.

2. Compared to an inappropriate drinking situation (e.g., "no label"), an appropriate situation (e.g., "label"), conducive to natural cognitive-labeling, should produce greater craving and alcohol acquisition behavior.

3. The conditions and situations above producing greater craving and alcohol acquisition behavior should be associated with a number of physiological effects attributed to the alcohol withdrawal syndrome or related states of CNS-ANS "arousal."

4. Most important, the maximal expression of craving should be elicited by the *combination* of appropriate interoceptive (i.e., low-dose alcohol) conditions and exteroceptive (i.e., "label") situations.

Subjects and criteria

The sample population for the study consisted of 24 Veterans Administration Hospital detoxified alcoholics who were randomly assigned to either the experimental ("label") or control ("nonlabel") groups. Selection criteria pertained to adequate health status, no evidence of organic brain damage, positive history of alcohol withdrawal symptoms, and an age limit of 55 years. Volunteers were informed that the study was designed "to learn more about alcoholism through the administration of sedative, stimulant, and alcohol-like drugs," any of which might be given during any of the three scheduled sessions. Subjects would be paid at a rate of $1.50 per hour (three sessions × six hours per session = $27) but would be expected to remain off all psychotropic medication for at least three days prior to the first session and until completion of all three sessions.

Demographic data and drinking preference information were obtained. Subjects also filled out a Craving Questionnaire that contained scales pertaining to prior craving experiences (PCE scale developed by Drs. L. I. Stein and J. Newton, Mendota State Hospital, Madison, Wis.) and prior alcohol withdrawal symptoms (PAW scale). The Reitan Trail-Making Test (18) was administered to assess organicity. There were no significant differences between the two alcoholic groups on these variables (Table 1).

Independent variables

A 2 × 3 factorial design was employed to assess the effects of two exteroceptive cue situations (i.e., label or nonlabel groups) and three drug-dose conditions (i.e., placebo, low-dose alcohol, high-dose alcohol) on the various dependent measures. The label (L) and nonlabel (NL) situations were designed to maximize and minimize, respectively, exteroceptive cues (e.g., taste, smell, sight) associated with prior drinking. The L subjects received their preferred liquor (amount disguised) and mixer, whereas NL subjects received comparable amounts of ethyl alcohol in a standard artificially sweetened mixer. Also, a quart of each subject's preferred liquor was within easy reach and view (on top of the work panel) throughout the L sessions whereas a quart vial of water was in the exact same location during the NL sessions. Work expended for alcohol during each session entitled both L and NL subjects to payoff with their preferred liquor at the end of each

Table 1. Selected sample characteristics

	Label (n = 12)	Nonlabel (n = 12)	Total (n = 24)
Age $\bar{x}$	45.3	43.5	44.4
σ	8.6	8.3	8.1
No. of Admissions $\bar{x}$	1.8	3.0	2.4
σ	1.2	3.7	2.7
PCE score $\bar{x}$	27.8	24.4	26.1
σ	5.4	7.5	6.5
PAW score $\bar{x}$	18.8	19.6	19.2
σ	4.9	5.1	4.8
Trail-making $\bar{x}$	241.6	249.9	246.0
σ	275.4	135.8	148.8

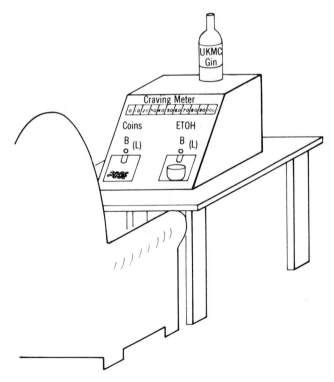

Figure 1. Craving and work panel (label situation). The Craving Meter is on top of the work panel. The letters "B" and "L" on the drawing designate the location of the buttons and light, respectively.

session. The work panel and location of the bottle are depicted in
Figure 1.

Procedures for subjects assigned to either the L or NL groups
were identical. All subjects participated in three separate sessions
scheduled in the morning and spaced at least two days apart. Over
the course of the three sessions, subjects received all three drug
doses but only experienced one of these for any given session
(order of administration random).

The placebo condition (P) corresponded to the equivalent of 5
ml of 100% ethyl alcohol floated on top of 10 ounces of mixer.
The high-dose alcohol condition (Hi) corresponded to the equivalent of 1.2 ml/kg of body weight of 100% ethyl alcohol dissolved in sufficient mixer to make 10 oz. The low-dose alcohol
condition (Lo) corresponded to the equivalent of 0.6 ml/kg of
body weight of 100% ethyl alcohol dissolved in sufficient mixer to
make 10 oz.

Dependent variables

All subjects were seated in a comfortable recliner chair within the
laboratory and were monitored in an adjacent observation-control
room. A 15-minute rest period was then provided before collection of a series of base line (B) measures of the subjective, behavioral, physiological, and neurophysiological variables described below. After this, priming doses of either P, Hi, or Lo
alcohol were administered. Additional series of measures, identical to those collected at B, were then taken 20 minutes (T_1), 80
minutes (T_2), 140 minutes (T_3), and 200 minutes (T_4) later. It took
about 30 minutes to run any given series of measures. The average
low- and high-dose blood alcohol levels (measured by
Breathalyzer) at all five testing periods for the total group of subjects can be noted in Figure 2 (see Comment).

Subjective. A "Craving Meter," with a scale ranging from 0 to
100, was located on the work panel (Figure 1). Appropriate adjec-
tives (determined by a prior pilot study) were assigned to five
levels of this scale (i.e., 0, 25, 50, 75, 100) to designate intensity of
craving.

Behavioral. These measures included two five-minute work
periods (random order)—one for alcohol and one for money. Fif-
teen presses of the button above the alcohol dispenser delivered
0.7 ml of 100 proof alcohol during alcohol work periods, while 15
presses of the button above the coin dispenser resulted in the

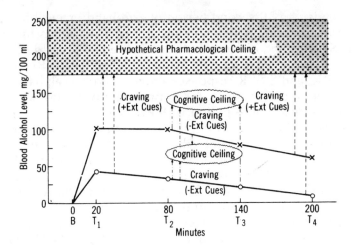

Figure 2. Relationship of interoceptive and exteroceptive cues to craving. The blood alcohol levels (BAL) represent actual mean values for the combined L and NL groups administered either a Hi or Lo dose of alcohol. Under appropriate exteroceptive conditions (+ Ext Cues), craving is a direct function of the distance between the BAL and hypothetical pharmacological ceiling. Under inappropriate exteroceptive conditions (− Ext Cues), craving is a variable function of a lower "cognitive ceiling." For purposes of illustration two ambiguous cognitive ceilings are represented.

delivery of 1¢ during money work periods. A similar number of responses, therefore, had to be emitted to earn either 1 oz of 100 proof alcohol or 43¢. The number of responses for alcohol would serve as a rough indicator for degree of "loss of control." Button presses were recorded automatically on counters, and earnings of money and alcohol could be collected only at the end of the session.

Physiological. An electroencephalogram (Grass Model 78B 12 Channel) and polygraph data recording system were employed to record the following responses: (a) heart rate (HR); (b) respiratory rate (RR) by thermister clipped to nostril; (c) number of spontaneous skin potential responses (S-SPR); (d) number of evoked skin potential responses (E-SPR) during 30-second exposure to strobe light flashes (Grass) at 13 cycles per second; and (e) tremor frequency (T-f) and amplitude (T-a) measured during the middle ten seconds of a 30-second period of arm-hand extension, with a contact microphone on the middle forefinger serving as the transducer. Systolic and diastolic blood pressure (S-BP and D-BP, respectively) were obtained by a manually inflated cuff. Recordings of HR, RR, and S-SPR responses above, as well as alpha activity, were made simultaneously for a two-minute period with eyes open and a two-minute period with eyes closed.

Neurophysiological. Monopolar recordings from scalp electrodes (O_1-A_1) were fed into the polygraph and written out for direct "eyeball" scoring of alpha activity (% time alpha). The signals were fed simultaneously to a voltage integrator via a multipurpose filter set to pass a band from 8 to 13 hertz. The accumulated voltage was recorded as "bins" (alpha bins). (Since product-moment correlations for these two alpha measures proved highly significant both under eyes open [$r = +.92, p <.001$] and eyes closed [$r = +.76, p <.001$] conditions, only the results for the latter measure will be presented.)

A Hewlett-Packard Signal Averager (Model No. 5480-B) was used to record visual average evoked responses (AERs) from scalp electrodes located at C_2-A_1. The stimulus intensity-modulation concept, pertaining to "augmentation-reduction" (19,20), was assessed by employing the method outlined by Buchsbaum and co-workers (21–23). The AERs were produced by 128 light flashes, at 1-second intervals, from a strobe light (10% neutral density filter) for each of four intensities (i.e., 1, 2, 4, 16). The measures collected pertained to (a) the slope of the four amplitudes of the P_{100}-N_{140} and N_{140}-P_{200} waves and (b) the mean of the four latencies for the P_{100} wave ($\bar{x}$ lat P_{100}).

Similar instrumentation and electrode placements were used to obtain the "contingent negative variation" (CNV) or "expectancy wave (24,25). Eight trials were averaged over the 1-second interval separating the warning stimulus (light) from the imperative stimulus (Sonalert tone). Reaction time (RT) was calculated on the basis of the mean length of time (in milliseconds) taken to turn off the tone by pressing a hand button. Measures for the CNV included (a) peak amplitude; (b) amplitudes at 200 msec, 400 msec, 600 msec, 800 msec, and 1,000 msec after the warning stimulus; (c) summed amplitudes of these five time intervals (Σ CNV); and (d) latency of peak amplitude (lat peak CNV) (complete technical and procedural specifications are available on written request to A.M.L.).

Results

Craving and work measures

Because of the highly skewed distribution and wide range of responses for craving and work measures, nonparametric statistics were employed to analyze the data. Wilcoxon Paired Replicates and Mann-Whitney U Tests were run for all intragroup and intergroup comparisons, respectively. In order to evaluate trends for this relatively small sample size (i.e., 12 subjects in each group), p values of .10 or less represented the criteria for statistical significance. When predictions were advanced, one-tailed tests of significance were employed.

Craving

Craving scores for each subject were calculated as percentage change from base line (i.e., $[T_n-B]/B] \times 100$) for each time period. While the distribution of scores tends to be bimodal, the effects of group conditions can be best portrayed by group means for each time period (Figure 3).

Analysis of the data revealed that major differences occurred during T_3 and T_4, with Lo (L) displaying substantially greater craving than all other group conditions except Hi (L). Hi (L) produced greater craving than P (NL) at T_3.

When the three drug conditions were combined (i.e., scores for each subject summed across conditions), the L group displayed greater craving than the NL group during T_3, T_4 and T_{1-4} (average of combined time periods). When the L and NL groups were combined, Lo and Hi alcohol produced greater craving than P at T_3, T_4, and T_4, T_{1-4}, respectively. The significance levels for all these analyses are given in Table 2.

Alcohol acquisition (AA)

Because of the extremely wide range of total button-press responses among subjects (e.g., 0 to 1,374) within any given time period, the inappropriateness of equating change scores without reference to prior base line responses (e.g., a change from 0 to 100 means something clinically different from a change from 1,000 to 1,100 responses), and the conceptual problem of deter-

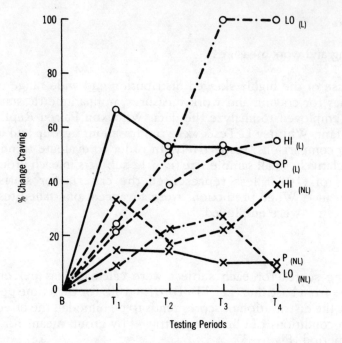

Figure 3. The mean percent change craving scores for the label group (*n* = 12) after administration of placebo (P[L]), high dose (Hi[L]), and low dose (Lo[L]) of alcohol and for the nonlabel group (*n* = 12) after administration of placebo (P[NL]), high dose (Hi[NL]), and low dose (Lo[NL]) of alcohol for each testing period.

Table 2. Summary of craving analyses

	T_1	T_2	T_3	T_4	$T_{1 \text{ to } 4}$
1. LO(L) > P(NL)	ns	ns	.05	.10	ns
> P(L)	ns	ns	.05	.05	ns
> LO(NL)	ns	ns	.10	.05	ns
> HI(NL)	ns	ns	.05	.05	ns
> HI(L)	ns	ns	ns	ns	ns
HI(L) > P(NL)	ns	ns	.10	ns	ns
> P(L)	ns	ns	ns	ns	ns
> LO(NL)	ns	ns	ns	ns	ns
> HI(NL)	ns	ns	ns	ns	ns
2. L > NL	ns	ns	.05	.10	.10
3. LO > P	ns	ns	.10	.10	ns
> HI(?)	ns	ns	ns	ns	ns
HI > (P)	ns	ns	ns	.10	.10

mining percentage change from "0" base line scores, the raw AA response totals for each subject were transformed in each time period to a numeric scale in accordance with the following formula: 1.0 = no increase over base line; 2.0 = 1% to 100% increase; 3.0 = 101% to 200% increase; 4.0 = 201% to 300% increase; 5.0 = infinite increase (e.g., "0" base line score as denominator). As with craving, while the distribution of response scores tends to be bimodal, the effects of the experimental conditions can be best portrayed by group means for each time period (Figure 4).

Results of the analyses revealed substantially greater work output for alcohol for Lo (L) than for all NL conditions during time

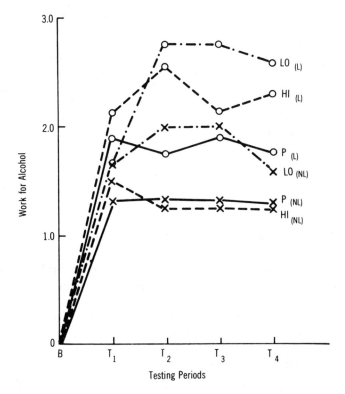

Figure 4. The mean numeric scale scores of alcohol acquisition behavior for the label group ($n = 12$) after administration of placebo (P[L]), high dose (Hi[L]) and low dose (Lo[L]) of alcohol and for the nonlabel group ($n = 12$) after administration of placebo (P[NL]), high dose (Hi[NL]) and low dose (Lo[NL]) of alcohol for each testing period.

periods T_2, T_3, T_4, and T_{1-4}. Hi (L) is distinguished from P (L), P (NL), and H (NL) at T_2 and from both P conditions at T_{1-4}.

When the three drug conditions were combined, the L group displayed greater total AA responses than the NL group at T_2, T_3, and T_{1-4}. When the L and NL groups were combined, Lo alcohol produced more AA behavior than P during all time periods, greater AA behavior than Hi during T_3; and Hi produced greater AA behavior than P at T_2 and T_{1-4}. The significance levels for these analyses are given in Table 3.

Table 3. Summary of alcohol work analyses

	T_1	T_2	T_3	T_4	T_1 to 4
1. LO(L) > P(NL)	ns	.05	.05	.05	.10
> P(L)	. ns	.05	.10	.10	.05
> LO(NL)	ns	ns	ns	ns	ns
> HI(NL)	ns	.05	.05	.10	.10
> H(L)	ns	ns	ns	ns	ns
HI(L) > P(NL)	ns	.10	ns	ns	.10
> P(L)	ns	.10	ns	ns	.10
> LO(NL)	ns	ns	ns	ns	ns
> HI(NL)	ns	.05	ns	ns	ns
2. L > NL	ns	.10	.10	ns	.05
3. LO > P	.10	.05	.05	.05	.05
> HI(?)	ns	ns	.05	ns	ns
HI > (P)	ns	.10	ns	ns	.05

Conversion from abstinence to alcohol acquisition

If we compare the behavior of those members of both groups (L and NL) of subjects who at base line choose "abstinence" (i.e., not work for alcohol) but who, after administration of the priming drug, began to work for alcohol at *any* of the four subsequent testing periods, some very intriguing findings emerge. In the L and NL groups, there were a total of 22 and 23 instances of base line abstinence behavior, respectively, over all three drug dose conditions. The actual numbers and percentages of those who converted in each group for each drug condition are depicted in Figure 5. There was a significantly higher frequency of conversion in the L compared to the NL group ($\chi^2 = 4.57$, $p < .05$). While small n's within each condition do not permit statistical analysis of

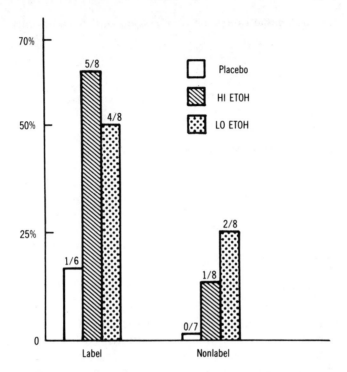

Figure 5. Actual percentage and numbers of alcoholics changing from base line "abstinence" to alcohol acquisition behavior during any subsequent testing period under the L and NL situations and after administration of placebo (P), high-dose (Hi), and low-dose (Lo) alcohol.

drug effects (regardless of group), inspection of the results suggests that such effects likewise contributed to this conversion process—i.e., P = 7.6% (1/13); Hi = 37.5% (6/16); and Lo = 37.5% (6/16).

Relationship of craving to alcohol acquisition

To reduce the number of analyses, the craving and AA scores were separately summed over T_{1-4} and correlated for each of the six group conditions. Rank difference correlations revealed very significant relationships between these variables in five of the six conditions with each of the L conditions displaying higher orders of magnitude than the corresponding NL condition (Table 4).

Table 4. Correlational values between craving and alcohol acquisition

	P	HI	LO
L	.66*	.92†	.90†
NL	.56‡	.43	.69‡

*p <.05   †p <.01   ‡p <.10

Prior craving vs. prior withdrawal experiences

As an incidental analysis, the results of which are relevant to our thesis, a rank difference correlation was run between the PCE and PAW scales of the Craving Questionnaire administered prior to the study. The results revealed a significant relationship between reports of the degree of prior craving when sober and the severity of prior withdrawal symptoms ($r_d = +.59$, p <.01, $n = 24$).

Work for money

In contrast to AA behavior, all but two subjects responded vigorously for money under baseline conditions. Although there were no significant differences in responses for coins as functions of drug conditions and situations, the raw number of button presses for coins was significantly greater than for alcohol over all time periods ($p = .05$ or less).

Physiological and neurophysiological measures

Because all the subsequent data conformed to parametric assumptions, 2 × 3 way analyses of covariance were run for all variables. To reduce the large number of results available for interpretation, the $T_{1-4}/4$ (i.e., mean value of variable over four testing periods) analyses will be primarily presented since, in almost all instances, they reflect similar results obtained for any given time period. However, some selected, statistically significant findings will be reported separately because they appear to be time-dose related and would have been "washed out" or diluted by calculation of the average value over four time periods. Since explicit predictions were not made for these results, two-tailed tests of significance were used.

Table 5 contains the adjusted mean values by condition and situation, as well as their corresponding F values, for each variable

Table 5. Means and F values for psychobiological variables over all testing periods

Variables	Conditions, C			Situations, S		F Values		
	P	Hi	Lo	L	NL	C	S	C×S
HR	83.4	90.5	87.9	84.8	89.8	18.3‡	3.6‡	3.6‡
RR	18.9	20.0	19.3	19.7	19.1	3.5‡	0.7	2.1
T-a	8.7	7.2	9.5	9.2	7.8	5.3†	2.0	0.6
T-f	13.4	14.1	13.8	13.8	13.7	2.0	0.0	0.2
S-BP	134.2	128.4	132.2	132.4	130.8	3.9	0.3	0.4
D-BP	91.5	89.6	91.6	90.6	91.2	0.9	0.0	0.3
S-SPR	1.2	1.3	1.1	1.4	1.0	0.3	1.5	0.3
E-SPR	1.3	1.1	1.2	1.5	0.9	0.8	4.8‡	0.3
No. of Alpha Bins	18.9	27.5	22.4	25.0	20.9	8.7†	4.5‡	1.5
x̄ Lat P_{100}	105.4	108.7	106.8	109.4	105.4	2.2	2.4	1.0
P_{100}-N_{140}	1.5	1.6	1.3	2.0	1.2	0.1	1.3	0.3
N_{140}-P_{200}	0.4	1.0	1.1	0.8	0.8	1.2	0.0	0.4
ΣCNV	29.6	22.8	32.2	24.4	30.8	1.9	0.5	0.5
Lat Peak CNV	782.0	825.4	773.0	793.1	793.0	3.7‡	0.0	0.2
RT	324.1	328.8	316.2	308.3	337.8	0.3	2.3	0.9

Note. All physiological measures and alpha bin values pertain only to "eyes open" testing. Because of temporary difficulties with the Signal Averager, as well as unscorable responses, the total *n*s for the CNV and AER analyses are 20 and 19, respectively..

† $p < .01$ ‡ $p < .05$

Table 6. Means and F values for certain psychobiological variables at specific testing periods

Variables	T_n	Conditions, C			Situations, S		F Values		
		P	Hi	Lo	L	NL	C	S	C×S
x̄ Lat P_{100}	T_4	104.2	107.8	103.8	109.2	102.9	2.2	4.9†	2.3
P_{100}-N_{140}	T_1	1.1	2.2	0.9	1.8	1.2	2.7‡	0.6	0.2
CNV-200	T_1	−0.5	−1.8	0.8	−0.9	−0.3	3.4†	0.2	1.2
CNV-400	T_1	1.6	1.5	4.4	1.1	3.5	3.0‡	1.6	0.6
CNV-600	T_4	9.0	4.6	7.0	5.8	7.5	4.9†	0.5	0.7
RT	T_3	308.3	320.2	319.6	295.9	336.1	0.3	3.9†	0.9
RT	T_4	324.8	314.9	341.8	298.0	356.4	0.3	4.4†	0.6

Note. All physiological measures and alpha bin values pertain only to "eyes open" testing. Because of temporary difficulties with the Signal Averager, as well as unscorable responses, the total *n*s for the CNV and AER analyses are 20 and 19, respectively.

†*p* <.05   ‡*p* <.10

selected for analysis. It appears that the Hi alcohol dose produced the greatest increase in heart rate, respiratory rate, alpha bins, and the greatest decrease in systolic blood pressure; the Lo dose had similar but intermediate effects. The Hi dose was also associated with the greatest delay in latency of peak CNV response and greatest decrease in tremor amplitude; Lo dose had opposite effects.

Situational factors also seemed to exert profound effects on physiological and neurophysiological responses. The L, compared to NL situation, was associated with lower heart rate, greater number of evoked skin potential responses, and larger number of alpha bins.

While there was a trend toward significance (i.e., $<.20$) for certain of the above variables, such as $\bar{x}$ lat P_{100}, slope P_{100}-N_{140}, ΣCNV, and RT, the level of statistical significance became apparently greater at specific testing periods, indicative of time-dose effects. Table 6 contains a summary of significant results with the designated time period. As to drug conditions, the most consistent effects pertain to CNV amplitudes, with Hi dose consistently associated with the greatest "dampening" and Lo dose generally associated with the greatest "enhancement."

As to situational effects, $\bar{x}$ lat P_{100} waves were increased at T_4 and RTs were decreased at both T_3 and T_4 in the L compared to NL situation.

Comment

In general, the results of this study support the hypotheses advanced pertaining to determinants of craving and alcohol-seeking. While alcohol administration and situational variables make separate contributions, their interaction, as exemplified by the Lo (L) condition, seems to exert the most profound effect on the elicitation of these responses, primarily during the descending limb and tail of the blood alcohol curve.

In relation to the above results, it is intriguing to note the essentially "qualitative" conversion from abstinence to alcohol acquisition behavior induced almost equally by the ingestion of both low- and high-dose alcohol administered in the label situation. Though this conversion is not absolute, it does lend qualified credence to the injunction of Alcoholics Anonymous to "avoid the first drink," especially (we could add) in situations or settings associated with prior drinking bouts or conducive to further drinking.

Interpretation of the physiological and neurophysiological results becomes far more speculative since they do not completely support our hypothesis that an "adequate" amount of alcohol, acting much like an hors d'oeuvre, should elicit conditioned withdrawal responses (or comparable states of CNS-ANS "arousal") that, in turn, serve as interoceptive cues for increased craving and alcohol-seeking behavior. Since there is a paucity of data available on the time-dose-situation effects of ethanol administration in chronic alcoholics and since a psychobiological theory of craving must account for the physiological-neurophysiological responses of the organism, our findings warrant some discussion.

While the alcohol-induced increase in alpha activity, a response traditionally ascribed to "inhibitory" cortical function (26), presumably argues against our hypothesis (27), such an interpretation should be made with caution. It is of interest to note that to date no investigators have documented important relationships between alpha activity and ANS measures of "arousal" in groups of subjects (28–30). Moreover, it is possible to administer certain drugs that induce a marked dissociation in animals between EEG activity and general behavior (31). In studies specifically related to alcoholism, Lewis et al. (32) reported that administration of a dose of ethanol producing a blood alcohol level of 30 mg/100 ml in alcoholics greatly raised the critical flicker fusion threshold, a measure associated with "cortical arousal" (33,34). Doctor et al. (35) found that alcoholics given an amount of alcohol comparable to our low dose not only displayed increased alpha activity but performed substantially better than a normal, nonalcoholized control group on a signal detection vigilance task. In our own study, it is interesting that low-dose alcohol, in contrast to high-dose and placebo, tends to increase CNV amplitudes, a measure purportedly related to both attention and arousal (25).

Though the true meaning of alcohol-induced alpha activity will have to be resolved, most of the physiological findings reflecting ANS responses (with the exception of systolic blood pressure) can be assumed to be in general accord with our theory. Not only do low and high doses of alcohol produce increases in heart and respiratory rate compared to placebo, but a low dose of alcohol is associated with the greatest tremor amplitude. All of these responses have been reported to occur during alcohol withdrawal (36,37) and, therefore, should be capable of serving as powerful interoceptive cues for both craving and alcohol acquisition. It is unnecessary to deal with the potential criticism that some of these responses may be attributed to the "peripheral" rather than "central" actions of alcohol. Although the truth of this assumption remains to be demonstrated, it is irrelevant to our theory since all these physiological responses could provide information feedback via the reticular activating system and, hence, provide appropriate cues for conditioning.

From our results, it is apparent that the physiological and neurophysiological responses of alcoholics are not solely determined by pharmacological (i.e., ethanol) factors. Not only may interaction effects between drug condition and situation exist (e.g., heart rate) but situational variables may act independently as well. Most fascinating are the findings that the label situation, in comparison to nonlabel, is associated with slower heart rate, more alpha bins, an increase in evoked skin potential responses, and decreased reaction times at T_3 and T_4. Though there are numerous ways to interpret these results, we are impressed by how well they can be parsimoniously accounted for (with the possible exception of the increase in alpha bins) on the basis of Lacey's concept of "directional fractionation" of response patterns (30). In essence, this concept implies a kind of situational stereotype (i.e., changes in physiological response patterns produced by changes in situational stimuli) that involves alterations in one physiological variable contrary to what may be predicted on the basis of a Cannon-Bard theory of general sympathetic activation by stressors.

Accordingly, a number of replicated studies (38,39) have demonstrated that tasks involving "intake" of pleasant environmental stimuli (externalized attention) are accompanied by heart rate deceleration, while tasks requiring "rejection" of environmental stimuli, such as through the performance of cognitive activity, mental elaboration or the avoidance of noxious stimuli, are accompanied by heart rate acceleration. Skin conductance increases, generally indicative of "arousal" or "activation," are associated with both types of tasks. Also, cardiac deceleration is accompanied by speedier reaction times. "The declerator," according to Lacey, "seems to be wide open to his environment, keyed for reception of input and for release of simple responses to these inputs (30 [p. 36]).

In the present study, it is possible to interpret the label situation as comparable to "environmental intake" and the nonlabel situation as comparable to "environmental rejection." In the label situation, exteroceptive cues are well-defined, relatively nonambiguous, associated with pleasant expectations and behaviors consonant with past alcohol acquisition activities. As a result, minimum mental elaboration or "decoding" of the experimental expectations need occur, thereby allowing the alcoholic to be more attentive to the specific environmental cues. In the nonlabel situation, exteroceptive cues are ill-defined, relatively ambiguous, and associated with uncertain expectations and behaviors. As a result, maximum mental elaboration or "decoding" of the experimental expectations should occur, thereby forcing the alcoholic to be more attentive to his own cognitive activities. To some extent, this interpretation receives support from our findings that correlations between craving scores and alcohol acquisition are of a much higher order of magnitude in label than in nonlabel situations. This would suggest that in the former situation there is much less ambiguity or more correspondence between thought and deed.

With these findings and interpretations as background, we are emboldened both to modify and to elaborate on our original thesis by demonstrating how this composite array of cognitive-symbolic, behavioral, physiological, and neurophysiological responses can be integrated and explained on the basis of a classical conditioning paradigm. Before doing so, it is necessary to introduce our concept of a "hypothetical pharmacological ceiling" as a means of interpreting the differential effects of different doses of alcohol on both craving and alcohol consumption under different exteroceptive situations.

Since the empirical results of other studies (40–42) show that alcoholics in programmed or free drink situations tend to regulate and titrate their drinking to sustain blood alcohol ceilings roughly within the 175-250 mg/100 ml range, we propose that within a physical setting or exteroceptive situation conducive to natural cognitive labeling the degree of craving should be a direct function of the difference between the actual blood alcohol level attained by the first drink and the hypothetical blood alcohol ceiling for each alcoholic. In the presence of inappropriate or incongruous settings, not conducive to natural cognitive labeling, the magnitude of craving should be substantially less than under all appropriate exteroceptive conditions, regardless of actual alcohol dose. This is largely because the hypothetical ceiling for desired blood alcohol levels will more likely be determined by individualized mental constraints (i.e., fluctuating "cognitive ceilings") against the expression of craving and alcohol acquisition in incongruous settings. This concept is illustrated in Figure 2, which also provides the actual mean blood alcohol levels obtained at the different testing periods for the two alcohol doses administered in our study.

As we return to our conditioning paradigm, Figure 6 depicts the sequence of events set in motion by the "first drink" consumed in a situation conducive to appropriate "cognitive-labeling" (i.e., craving) as well as the continuation of further drinking (i.e., loss of control?). Essential to the understanding of this paradigm is the realization that "dried-out" or abstinent alcoholics have had re-peated prior exposures to cycles of heavy drinking, the ap-pearance of withdrawal symptoms and the suppression of these symptoms through alcohol, all in temporal contiguity with specific labels, and therefore, may be regarded as "conditioned." In partial support of this assumption is our finding of the highly statistical significant relationship between reported intensity and range of prior withdrawal experiences and the predilection of sober al-coholics to experience craving.

In brief, our paradigm attributes to alcohol combined proper-ties as an unconditioned stimulus (US_i) and as a conditioned stimulus (CS_e). The US_i, acting interoceptively, produces, in a *nonalcoholic,* certain physiological responses, namely, those charac-teristic of acute alcoholic intoxication. In the *tolerant and physically dependent alcoholic,* however, the initial (intoxicating) effects of alcohol are soon followed by withdrawal phenomena (e.g., tre-mulousness, tachycardia) and, in time, the interoceptive actions of

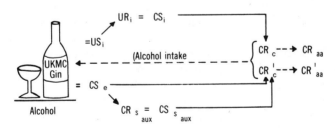

Figure 6. Conditioning paradigm for craving and alcohol acquisition in a previously conditioned "sober" alcoholic. The subnotations above rep-resent the following: i, interoceptive (physiological responses related to direct pharmacological effects of alcohol); e, exteroceptive (taste, odor, color, label); aux, exteroceptive and interoceptive stimuli unrelated to direct pharmacological effects of alcohol but associated with the drinking situation; c, craving (associated with physiological withdrawal changes); aa, alcohol acquisition behavior.

alcohol acquire the properties of a conditioned stimulus (CS_i) that evokes conditioned withdrawal responses, including craving (CR_e) and, because of concomitant operant conditioning (due to suppression of withdrawal phenomena by drinking), conditioned alcohol acquisition (CR_{aa}). As a conditioned stimulus, the interoceptive actions of alcohol can therefore evoke *conditioned* withdrawal phenomena long after cessation of chronic alcoholic intoxication and disappearance of *unconditioned* physical dependence.

The above may be regarded as "necessary" but not "sufficient" conditions for continued drinking. It is the other property of alcohol as a conditioned stimulus (CS_e) that strengthens this response tendency further. The CS_e properties not only pertain to the taste, color, and odor of both alcohol and mixer but to the visual presence of the bottle of liquor and other exteroceptive cues associated with prior drinking bouts. This CS_e acts through two routes to enhance craving and alcohol acquisition. One, it leads to auxiliary CRs, such as the physiological and neurophysiological responses found in the label condition. These CR_{saux} are equivalent to conditional stimuli (CS_{saux}) that, in turn, evoke craving ($CR'c$). Two, the CS_e can lead directly to $CR'c$.

The $CR_{aa} + CR'_{aa}$, acting in concert, should heighten the proclivity for further drinking that, in turn, would reinitiate the same sequence of responses, and so on—behaviors typical of loss of control. As blood alcohol levels rise and approach the alcoholic's hypothetical pharmacological ceiling, inhibitory feedback could be expected to diminish the strength of these response sequences until a dynamic rate-limiting equilibrium is established between frequency and amount of alcohol consumed and its metabolism. The strength of the resultant craving and alcohol acquisition behavior would be a constant function of the discrepancy between the actual and hypothetical blood alcohol ceilings. It should be anticipated that such drinking behavior would continue until a substantial disruption in this dynamic equilibrium occurred either through interoceptive factors (e.g., stupor, coma, liver failure, gastritis, avitaminosis) or exteroceptive factors (e.g., incarceration, family crisis, financial threat).

Despite the thrust of the present findings and their interpretations, there are several notable limitations and qualifications to this study. The subjects selected are hardcore, multiadmission, hospitalized alcoholics with many prior withdrawal experiences and may not be representative of other subgroups or populations.

The number of subjects is not sufficient to permit sophisticated statistical analyses between craving and alcohol acquisition responses and concurrent physiological and neurophysiological measures or to distinguish among response style patterns. The label situation, while sufficient to produce significant results, is still highly artificial: perhaps a more realistic setting could produce even more profound effects. All of these issues, as well as those pertaining to the role of arousal and activation, will require further study.

For the present, however, if we can assume the results of the study to be valid and our interpretations of them to be reasonable, then this should have important implications for the treatment of alcoholics and the prevention of relapse. Obviously, any therapeutic approach, whether it be insight, behaviorally or pharmacologically oriented, that does not recognize the powerful, evocative effects of interoceptive and exteroceptive stimuli on craving and alcohol acquisition behavior and that neglects to provide techniques for modifying the strength of these effects will likely be destined to failure.

References

1. World Health Organization. Symposium on "craving" for alcohol. *Quart. J. Stud. Alcohol,* 1955, *16,* 34–66.
2. Storm, T., Smart, R. G. Dissociation: A possible explanation of some features of alcoholism and implications for its treatment. *Quart. J. Stud. Alcohol,* 1965, *2,* 111–115.
3. Marconi, J., et al. Role of the dorsomedial thalamic nucleus in "loss of control" and "inability to abstain" during ethanol ingestion. In Popham, R. E. (ed.), *Alcohol and alcoholism.* Toronto: University of Toronto Press, 1970.
4. Macleod, L. D. The "craving" for alcohol: symposium. *Quart. J. Stud. Alcohol,* 1955, *16,* 34–66.
5. Jellinek, E. M. *The disease concept of alcoholism.* Highland Park, N.J.: Hillhouse, 1960.
6. Marconi, J., et al. Experimental study on alcoholics with an "inability to stop." *Br. J. Psychiatry,* 1967, *113,* 543–545.
7. Merry, J. The "loss of control" myth. *Lancet,* 1966, *1,* 1257–1258.
8. Ludwig, A. M. On and off the wagon: reasons for drinking and abstaining by alcoholics. *Quart. J. Stud. Alcohol,* 1972, *23,* 91–96.
9. Cutter, H. S. G., et al. Effects of alcohol on its utility for alcoholics and non-alcoholics. *Quart. J. Stud. Alcohol,* 1970, *31,* 369–378.
10. Gottheil, E., et al. Alcoholics' patterns of controlled drinking. *Am. J. Psychiatry,* 1973, *130,* 418–422.

11. Engle, K. B., Williams, T. K. Effect of an ounce of vodka on alcoholics' desire for alcohol. *Quart. J. Stud. Alcohol,* 1972, *33,* 1099–1105.
12. Mello, N. K. Behavioral studies of alcoholism. In Kissen, B., Begleiter, H. (eds.), *Biology of alcoholism.* Vol. 2. New York: Plenum Press, 1972.
13. Ludwig, A. M., Wikler, A. Craving and relapse to drink. *Quart. J. Stud. Alcohol,* to be published.
14. Wikler, A. On the nature of addiction and habituation. *Br. J. Addict.,* 1967, *57,* 73–80.
15. Wikler, A. Dynamics of drug dependence: implications of a conditioning theory for research and treatment. *Arch. Gen. Psychiatry,* 1973, *28,* 611–616.
16. Wooley, S. C., Wooley, O. W. Salivation to the sight and thought of food: a new measure of appetite. *Psychosom. Med.,* 1973, *35,* 136–142.
17. Tokar, J. T., et al. Emotional states and behavioral patterns in alcoholics and nonalcoholics. *Quart. J. Stud. Alcohol,* 1973, *34,* 133–143.
18. Reitan, R. Validity of the trail-making test as an indication of organic brain damage. *Percept. Mot. Skills,* 1958, *8,* 217–276.
19. Petrie, A. *Individuality in pain and suffering.* Chicago: University of Chicago Press, 1967.
20. Petrie, A., et al. Pain sensitivity, sensory deprivation and susceptability to satiation. *Science,* 1958, *128,* 1431–1433.
21. Buchsbaum, M., Pfefferbaum, A. Individual differences in stimulus intensity response. *Psychophysiology,* 1971, *8,* 600–611.
22. Buchsbaum, M., Silverman, J. Stimulus intensity control and the cortical evoked response. *Psychosom. Med.,* 1968, *30,* 12–22.
23. Silverman, J. Stimulus intensity modulation and psychological disease. *Psychopharmacologia,* 1972, *24,* 42–80 (part 1).
24. Cohen, J. Very slow brain potentials relating to expectancy: the CNV. In Donchin, E., Lindsley, D. B. (eds.), *Average evoked potentials: methods, results and evaluations.* U.S. Government Printing Office, 1969.
25. Tecce, J. J. Contingent negative variation and individual differences: a new approach in brain research. *Arch. Gen. Psychiatry,* 1971, *24,* 1–16.
26. Lindsley, D. B. Psychological phenomena and the electroencephalogram. *Electroencephalogr. Clin. Neurophysiol.,* 1952, *4,* 443–456.
27. Wikler, A., et al. Electroencephalographic changes associated with chronic alcoholic intoxication and the alcohol withdrawal syndrome. *Am. J. Psychiatry,* 1956, *113,* 106–114.
28. Sternbach, R. A. Two independent indices of activation. *Electroencephalogr. Clin. Neurophysiol.,* 1960, *12,* 609–611.
29. Elliott, R. Physiological activity and performance: a comparison of kindergarten children with young adults. *Psychol. Monogr.,* 1964, *78* (whole No. 587, No. 10).

30. Lacey, J. I. Somatic response patterning and stress: some revisions of activation theory. In Appley, M. H., Trumbull, R. (eds.), *Psychological stress*. New York: Appleton-Century-Crofts, 1967.
31. Wikler, A. Pharmacologic dissociation of behavior and EEG "sleep patterns" in dogs: morphine, N-allylnormorphine, and atropine. *Proc. Soc. Exp. Biol. Med.*, 1952, *79*, 261–265.
32. Lewis, E. G., et al. The effect of alcohol on sensory phenomena and cognitive and motor tasks. *Quart. J. Stud. Alcohol*, 1969, *30*, 618–633.
33. Venables, P. H., Wing, J. K. Level of arousal and the subclassification of schizophrenia. *Arch. Gen. Psychiatry*, 1962, *7*, 114–119.
34. Tomkiewicz, R. L., Cohen, W. The effects of changes of arousal level on critical flicker fusion frequency and figure reversal tasks. *Psychophysiology*, 1970, *6*, 421–428.
35. Doctor, R. F., et al. EEG changes and vigilance behavior during experimentally induced intoxication with alcoholic subjects. *Psychosom. Med.*, 1966, *28*, 605–615.
36. Isbell, H., et al. An experimental study of the etiology of "rum fits" and delirium tremens. *Quart. J. Stud. Alcohol*, 1955, *16*, 1–33.
37. Mendelson, J. H., LaDou, J. Experimentally induced chronic intoxication and withdrawal in alcoholics: Pt. 2. Psychophysiological findings. *Quart. J. Stud. Alcohol*, 1964, *25*, (suppl. 2), 14–39.
38. Obrist, P. A. Cardiovascular differentiation of sensory stimuli. *Psychosom. Med.*, 1963, *25*, 450–458.
39. Blaylock, B. Some antecedents of directional fractionation: effects of "intake-rejection," verbalization requirements, and threat of shock on heart rate and skin conductance. *Psychophysiology*, 1972, *9*, 40–52.
40. Mello, N. K., Mendelson, J. H. Experimentally induced intoxication in alcoholics: a comparison between programmed and spontaneous drinking. *J. Pharmacol. Exp. Ther.*, 1970, *173*, 101–116.
41. Nathan, P. E., et al. Behavioral analysis of chronic alcoholism. *Arch. Gen. Psychiatry*, 1970, *22*, 419–430.
42. Mello, N. K., Mendelson, J. H. Drinking patterns during work-contingent alcohol acquisition. In Mello, N. K., Mendelson, J. H. (eds.), *Recent advances in studies of alcoholism*. U.S. Government Printing Office, 1971.

5. The Nature of "Loss of Control"

Tests of Physically Based Definitions

The origin of the physically based concept of "loss of control" can be found in Jellinek's work (1946, 1952, 1960). His use of the formulation was tied to a "working hypothesis" that, at some point in the alcoholic's drinking career, he/she would undergo some sort of biological transformation such that from then on, the mere ingestion of small amounts (i.e., one or two drinks) of alcohol would initiate a full-scale process of physical dependence. A corollary of this hypothesis was that alcoholics who did dare to consume even small amounts of alcohol would then experience an alcohol withdrawal syndrome when they stopped drinking. Thus, these alcoholics (*gamma* type) would demonstrate an "inability to stop" drinking once they had begun. It is important to recall that this entire formulation was not founded in empirical study but was generated from interviews with recovered alcoholics (primarily members of Alcoholics Anonymous) who recalled what they believed to have been their experiences. An extension of this biological change was incorporated in Jellinek's classification of *delta* alcoholics, who were postulated to have not only experienced loss of control but also an "inability to abstain" from drinking at all. Marconi (1959) espoused a similar view and speculated about possible physiological mechanisms for this phenomenon.

Marconi and his colleagues (Marconi, Fink, & Moya, 1967) have attempted to provide experimental evidence for the *gamma-delta* distinction. They described an experimental procedure intended "to reproduce the 'inability to stop' and measure it by means of objective and quantitative indexes"(p. 543). Seven *gamma* and six *delta* alcoholics (procedures for diagnosing subjects as either *gamma* or *delta* were not presented) were separately seated at a table on which a glass and a bottle containing a 20% ethanol solution were placed. "The patient was told that his manner of drinking was to be studied and that the entire contents of the bottle was at his disposal for this purpose. He could drink freely in the manner and quantities he desired; his only obligation was to start drinking the amount he wished and to report any physical and psychic changes he might experience" (p. 543).

The authors found that the *delta* subjects consumed relatively more alcohol in this test than the *gamma* subjects. Further, *delta* subjects experienced "a dryness of the mouth, the desire for more ethanol and psychomotor restlessness" (p. 545). While the authors suggested that their results provided an experimental demonstration of "inability to abstain," there are an abundance of alternative, more plausible explanations. For instance, the only subject characteristics reported in the study are age, years of illness, and days of abstinence prior to the experimental session, none of which was significantly different between groups. Demonstrating that diagnosed *delta* alcoholics consumed more alcohol than *gamma* alcoholics in this task constitutes the full extent of the results. The experimental procedures used by Marconi et al. did not include an empirical test of "inability to abstain."

A number of studies have demonstrated beyond reasonable doubt that persons with alcohol problems of varying severity do not experience physical dependence merely from consuming small amounts of alcohol following a period of abstinence (see chapter 4, "The Notion of Cravings and Compulsions"). Engle and Williams (1972) and Marlatt et al. (1973) found that alcoholics from an alcoholism hospital or recruited from the local community did not demonstrate physical dependence based on limited drinking. Merry (1966) reported a study which used nine alcohol addicts as subjects. Using a within-subject experimental design, subjects were sometimes administered a vitamin mixture solution containing certain amounts of alcohol, and at other times were administered the same solution containing water in place of the alcohol. Both the subjects and the hospital staff were blind to the nature of the experiment. No subject developed physical dependence, there were no differences in reported cravings when subjects had received an alcohol mixture versus a control mixture, and the classical "loss of control" hypothesis was therefore not confirmed. Similar findings have been demonstrated with different subject populations: (1) skid-row alcoholics (Cutter, Schwab, & Nathan, 1970; Mello & Mendelson, 1965, 1971, 1972; Mendelson, 1964; Mendelson, LaDou, & Solomon, 1964); (2) veterans (Gottheil, Crawford, & Cornelison, 1973); and (3) state hospital alcoholics (Paredes, Ludwig, Hassenfeld, & Cornelison, 1971; Sobell, Sobell, & Christelman, 1972). In fact, more than 70 references cited later in this chapter all disconfirm a concept of "loss of control" based on early onset of physical dependence.

Glatt (1967) proposed a revision of Jellinek's definition of "loss of control," suggesting that "loss of control" would not be initiated until a critical blood alcohol concentration threshold had been exceeded. Several studies have demonstrated that persons who have been repeatedly addicted to alcohol can consume enough alcohol to obtain a blood alcohol concentration of 140 mg/100 ml on two consecutive days without developing physical dependence (Paredes, Hood, Seymour, & Gollob, 1973, this section) or consume 16 ounces of 86-proof alcohol within a three- to four-hour period without initiating physical dependence (Sobell, Schaefer, Mills, 1972; Sobell & Sobell, 1972, 1973a). While blood alcohol concentrations were not routinely monitored during the latter studies, one blood alcohol test indicated that a subject had a blood alcohol level of 350 mg/100 ml at the conclusion of drinking. These and similar findings seriously challenge the notion of a critical blood alcohol concentration threshold for initiating physical dependence. It may well be the case that physical dependence is initiated by drinking over a sufficient length of time *and* maintaining a sufficiently high blood alcohol concentration. In fact, many of the studies used to refute the notion of early onset of physical dependence (i.e., Mendelson, 1964) are the same studies which have experimentally demonstrated that continuous sufficient drinking does initiate a physical dependence process followed by a withdrawal syndrome (for ethical reasons, no such studies have been conducted using normal drinkers).

Tests of Volitionally Based Definitions

The more popular concept of "loss of control" is not founded in physical dependence but rather postulates that "alcoholics" cannot exert voluntary control over their drinking behavior once they have begun to drink—they are in "bondage." Unfortunately, this version is most often favored in traditional concepts of alcoholism. At this time, a massive number of studies have unanimously refuted such an interpretation. This remains true even if one accepts Keller's (1972) revision of this concept, specifying that even this type of "loss of control" (not based on physical dependence) simply occurs most of the time but not all of the time for "alcoholic" individuals.

Our present concern with a volitional definition of "loss of control" involves whether or not such a characteristic actually exists among individuals who either have serious alcohol problems or have previously been addicted to alcohol. When an "alcoholic" appears to drink contrary to his/her own volition, is this because of internal processes which operate as a "strange obsession" to direct the person's behavior, or does the drinking behavior serve a particular function which is determined largely by factors external to the individual? More concisely, is the drinking of an alcoholic generally "uncontrollable," as inferred by many popular definitions?

Over the past 15 years, an impressive number of studies have robustly demonstrated that even the drinking of chronic, skid-row alcoholics is subject to their precise control under appropriate environmental circumstances. Control, used in this sense, refers to the individual choosing to engage in limited, nonproblem drinking, even though substantial opportunity for uncontrolled drinking exists. An excellent example of such findings has been reported by Oki (1974) for 80 consecutive admissions to the Bon Accord program in Ontario, Canada. The subjects, all male alcoholics, were skid-row chronic drunkenness offenders who had suffered severe social and economic dysfunction. During their residential stay with the program, these chronic alcoholics were given the opportunity to choose either abstinence or controlled drinking as their drinking behavior objective. Further, residents could change their drinking objective at any time by appealing to an evaluation committee composed of both residents and staff. Daily drinking data were collected for all subjects throughout their stay. Results indicated that these men were able to demonstrate good control over their drinking. Uncontrolled drinking, when it did occur, was "minimal and proportionately somewhat less frequent than during enforced abstinence" (p. 31). More important, a sequential analysis was performed to determine whether controlled drinking by these alcoholics led to uncontrolled drinking. Of 372 paired sequences involving "beginning with controlled drinking, only 34 (9.14%) resulted in uncontrolled drinking" (p. 16). Similarly, 51 (12.09%) of 422 sequences beginning with abstinence resulted in uncontrolled drinking. This is important, because many traditional concepts of volitional "loss of control" speculate that while an alcoholic may not demonstrate explicit "loss of control" on a given day, such drinking will eventually lead to uncontrolled drinking.

Other studies have also demonstrated that chronic alcoholics can and do engage in limited, nonproblem drinking without encountering deleterious consequences (Allman, 1972; Allman, Taylor, & Nathan, 1972; Alterman, Gottheil, Skoloda, & Grasberger, 1974; Bigelow, Cohen, Liebson, & Faillace, 1972; Bigelow & Liebson, 1972; Bigelow, Liebson, & Griffiths, 1974; Cannon, Ross, & Snyder, 1973; Cohen, Liebson, & Faillace, 1971a, 1973; Cohen, Liebson, Faillace, & Allen, 1971; Cohen, Liebson, Faillace, & Speers, 1971; Faillace, Flamer, Imber, & Ward, 1972; Goldman, 1974; Gottheil, Alterman, Skolda, & Murphy, 1973; Gottheil, Corbett, Grasberger, & Cornelison, 1972, 1974; Gottheil, Murphy, Skoloda, & Corbett, 1972; Griffith, 1974; Griffith, Bigelow, & Liebson, 1974, 1975; Higgins & Marlatt, 1973; Martorano, 1974; McNamee, Mello, & Mendelson, 1968; Mello, McNamee, & Mendelson, 1968; Mello & Mendelson, 1965, 1970, 1971, 1972; Mendelson & Mello, 1966; Miller, 1972; Miller, Hersen, & Eisler, 1974; Miller, Hersen, Eisler, Epstein, & Wooten, 1974; Miller, Hersen, Eisler, & Hemphill, 1973; Miller, Hersen, Eisler, & Hilsman, 1974; Mills, Sobell, & Schaefer, 1971; Nathan, Goldman, Lisman, & Taylor, 1972; Nathan & O'Brien, 1971; Nathan, O'Brien, & Norton, 1971; Nathan, Silverstein, & Taylor, 1973; Nathan, Titler, Lowenstein, Solomon, & Rossi, 1970; Nathan, Wilson, Steffen, & Silverstein, 1973; O'Brien, 1972; Oki, 1975; Orford, 1974; Paredes, Hood, Seymour, & Gollob, 1973; Paredes, Jones, & Gregory, 1974; Pikens, Bigelow, & Griffith, 1973; Schaefer, Sobell, & Mills, 1971a, b; Silverstein, Nathan, & Taylor, 1974; Steffen, 1975; Steffen, Nathan, & Taylor, 1974; Tamerin & Mendelson, 1969; Tamerin, Weiner, & Mendelson, 1970; Tracey, Karlin, & Nathan, 1974; Vogler, Compton, & Weissbach, 1975; Williams & Brown, 1974; Wilson, Leaf, & Nathan, 1975).

These studies all demonstrate that, within a hospital or laboratory environment, the drinking of chronic alcoholics is explicitly a function of environmental contingencies. Such drinking has been found to occur both naturally and as a product of experimental procedures where limited drinking could result in special privileges, opportunities for socialization, or money. Certain studies have also found that some alcoholics can taper off their drinking within an experimental situation and thereby avoid the severe consequences of abrupt withdrawal, a characteristic sometimes anecdotally reported when chronic alcoholics are interviewed.

In chapter 6, "Reversing Irreversibility," another impressive body of evidence is reviewed which demonstrates that alcoholics can control their drinking for protracted periods of time in their natural environment. In summary, therefore, it appears that traditional notions considering "loss of control" as an essential characteristic of drinking by alcoholics (even if it is postulated only to occur *most* of the time) are not congruent with the empirical evidence. Instead, it appears that the drinking of alcoholics is "controllable" under some circumstances. This leads us to recognize a necessity to reformulate traditional ideas about the nature of "alcoholismic" drinking.

A Reconceptualization

When interpreted within the context of the large amount of empirical data now available, both traditional concepts of "loss of control" are found to need serious modification. While physical dependence on alcohol does occur, it is not initiated by consumption of one or two drinks, or even initial alcohol intoxication. Rather, depending on the individual and the drinking pattern, consumption must occur in relatively large quantities over a substantial period of time, usually a few days (i.e., Gross, 1974, 1975). At any time prior to the onset of physical dependence, the drinking individual can discontinue drinking without experiencing physical withdrawal symptoms.

The volitional version of "loss of control" has similarly been demonstrated to be inadequate. No doubt many individuals commonly referred to as "alcoholic" subjectively experience a feeling of powerlessness over their drinking behavior once they begin in the natural environment. The experimental demonstrations referred to here and in Chapter 4, "The Notion of Cravings and Compulsions," testify that this subjective impression is highly dependent upon the setting and circumstances in which drinking occurs. In a controlled environment, usually quite different from the individual's natural environment, the subjective "loss of control" state is not experienced. Indeed, in some cases it is no longer experienced in the natural environment (see Chapter 6, "Reversing Irreversibility"). The available evidence suggests that subjectively perceived uncontrolled drinking appears to be much more a function of environmental determinants than internal physiological mechanisms.

If the concept of "loss of control" is retained at all, then motivational and environmental variables must be incorporated in its definitions to be consistent with objective findings. Unfortunately, at this time the reasons why individuals repeatedly engage in self-damaging drinking are not clear. The fact that a number of broad-spectrum behavioral treatment approaches have had very promising results in the treatment of persons with drinking problems, including successful drinking outcomes, seems to indicate that treatment interventions based on an assumption that heavy drinking is a functional behavior are likely to have at least some validity. In a comprehensive treatment approach to alcohol problems, it would be ludicrous to ignore *any* factors of demonstrated importance. Traditional concepts sometimes produce treatment outcomes of abstinence maintained by a strong fear that drinking will trigger unknown processes likely to result in undesirable long-term consequences. Such a fear is a realistic response by any individual who has suffered serious alcohol problems and is again confronted with an opportunity to drink. However, abstinence based on rational considerations that drinking in certain or all circumstances is unwise could be expected to better maintain abstinence than would a fear that alcohol will come to control one's behavior.

Orford (1973) analyzed the drinking patterns of 77 male alcoholics over a period of 12 months following their participation in a traditional inpatient treatment program. While all the men engaged in some drinking during the 12 months of follow-up, their demonstrated degree of control over drinking was variable. An assessment of their sentiments toward drinking, self-defined personal diagnosis, and preferred future drinking behavior was gathered at the time of intake and one year subsequent to that time. It was found that "mainly controlled drinkers [at follow-up] were more likely to think that they had no drinking problem or that their problem was of very recent origin, reported significantly fewer symptoms, were much less likely to be institutionalized during the twelve-month follow-up period, were less likely to think of themselves as alcoholics and were less likely to express a preference for abstinence as a target" (p. 565). These findings suggest that uncontrolled drinking and what has been thought of as "alcoholismic" drinking patterns are actually relative phenomena. Such drinking is accompanied by a number of correlates which are currently in need of intensive investigation.

In summary, then, the degree of control that one demonstrates with respect to drinking behavior is likely to be situation-dependent and individual-specific, even if that individual has had drinking problems in the past. If "loss of control" is retained as a concept at all, it should not be regarded as a mysterious phenomenon. It is simply a concise way of summarizing the prediction that if an individual engages in drinking within a context similar to the one in which drinking has previously resulted in undesirable consequences, such a pattern is likely to be repeated in the future unless substantial changes occur in either the environment or the individual's manner of interacting with that environment.

Alfonso Paredes, William R. Hood,
Harry Seymour, and Maury Gollob

Loss of Control in Alcoholism: An Investigation of the Hypothesis, with Experimental Findings

The loss of control over drinking is generally regarded as an important clinical feature of alcoholism (e.g., 1). It suggests that once an alcoholic starts drinking he is almost always unable to stop, and that controlled drinking becomes a practical impossibility. For example, Fox (2) reports that none of the 3,000 alcoholic patients she observed was able to return to moderate social drinking.

Cahalan (3), whose data are based on the findings of a national survey, has proposed that sociological factors play a more conspicuous role among the correlates of problem drinking than do psychological factors. MacAndrew and Edgerton (4) have suggested that drunken behavior follows cultural prescriptions which are different from those applicable during the nondrinking state. Within a society the prescriptions vary according to the social setting. Drunken comportment varies as much in each setting as do the social mores. In their opinion, social prescriptions also influence the behavior of groups conspicuous for problem drinking.

Deviant drinking is not an asocial act, but requires an organization to promote and support it. Some of these social systems have been identified—for example, the "revolving door" of the chronic drunkenness offender (5), the contrastatus Skid Row community (6), the matriarchal alcoholic marriage (7, 8) and several other supportive and concealing social stances (9).

Reprinted by permission from *Quarterly Journal of Studies on Alcohol,* 1973, *34,* 1146–1161. Copyright by Journal of Studies on Alcohol, Inc., New Brunswick, N.J. 08903.

If sociocultural and sociopsychological variables are important, manipulations of the social setting should influence drinking behavior. This report presents evidence demonstrating that alcoholics can control their drinking if permitted to drink in a milieu in which certain social variables are regulated. The results suggest that the loss-of-control hypothesis needs to be reformulated. Drinking paradigms such as the one implemented in this investigation have potential applications in the development of techniques to change attitudes and drinking patterns in alcoholics.

Methods

The research was conducted in a large psychiatric service housing chronic schizophrenic men and women. These patients are representative of the residual "hard core" schizophrenics who through the years have failed to respond to conventional therapies (10). Since these patients are unable to code verbal and nonverbal communication in congruence with conventional culturally attuned behavior, they are not accessible to the communicative styles of alcoholics.

Twelve beds in the service were reserved for groups of alcoholics who were brought to this unfamiliar social milieu in which their typical manipulative behavior and rationalizations were not operative. The situation was expected to encourage alcoholics to reach out to each other and form a cohesive group.

Alcoholics recruited from the detoxification unit of the hospital were asked to stay 5 weeks in the research program. The men were accepted on a voluntary basis and could leave the program whenever they chose. All were told that some would be selected at random to receive alcohol at one point in the study. An informed consent for this and other experimental procedures was obtained on admission. The alcoholics were allowed open-ward privileges throughout their period in the hospital including the days when drinking was scheduled.

A treatment program for the alcoholics included daily group meetings, weekly role-playing sessions and occupational and recreational activities. The patients were expected to attend these activities and to be on time at the dining hall for meals. They were free to ambulate in the hospital grounds until 7:30 p.m. Completion of the program required attendance at the scheduled activities and compliance with hospital rules. Patients not present in the ward at 7:30 p.m. were discharged from the hospital the following day.

Drinking schedule

Every 2 weeks an alcoholic who had been 1 week in the program was randomly selected to receive alcohol. Patients knew 1 week in advance who had been selected. The drinking experience exposed the patient to relatively large amounts of alcohol for 2 consecutive days. This drinking paradigm was favored over others in which drinking is permitted for long periods of time (11–14) since prolonged drinking can induce hallucinosis, memory disturbances and disorientation (15) which may prevent the patient from making therapeutic use of the experience. Sufficient alcohol was given to stimulate thoughts and feelings associated with drinking and yet maintain a level of awareness which could allow the patient to examine these effects and discuss them.

Procedure.   Drinks of alcohol (the beverage was 95% ethanol mixed with ginger ale [1:4]), ginger ale and ice were offered on the hour from 1:30 to 10 p.m. for 2 consecutive days. Blood alcohol concentration (BAC) was monitored every hour with a Breathalyzer. Once a BAC peak of 0.10% was reached, the size of the drinks was decreased to maintain BAC below 0.14%. The patient drank alone in a small room furnished with an easy chair. A research assistant monitored the procedure in an adjacent room which had an impressive array of electronic devices to provide a "scientific" atmosphere. Electroencephalographic sleep recordings and other physiological measures were obtained from the subjects on the nights after drinking had been discontinued and during those preceding and following the 2 days of scheduled drinking (these measurements were part of a parallel study on the effects of alcohol on sleep). The laboratory where the patients drank had direct access to the street. The research assistants were instructed to behave toward the alcoholics as they would toward any nonalcoholic voluntary research subject. The patients were not physically restrained if they wished to leave the laboratory.

In the daily morning group meetings the drinking subject discussed his experiences with the other men. The group and the group leader were available as a source of support to cope with the crisis induced by the "artificial" drinking episode.

Other data collected during the study included demographic information, drinking experience, sociometric measures, a measure of attitudes toward alcoholics and a battery of psychological tests administered at the beginning, the middle and the end of the 5 weeks of participation. The data from these tests will be reported elsewhere.

Social milieu

The important features of the research setting were: (1) drinking was programmed by the experimenters; (2) conditions were created to promote strong group affiliation; (3) the usual risks of drinking were minimal or not present (risks such as disapproval from a wife, possibility of losing a job, being picked up by the police or getting sick or hurt without immediate help available); (4) drinking within the experimental schedule was declared permissible and was presented as a technique to help the patients learn about the effects of alcohol; (5) the environmental cues of the customary drinking places were not present (for example, absent were the drinking buddies, the bar atmosphere, or the familiar home and neighborhood surroundings).

The following guiding principles were made explicit during the group meetings and remained central to the structure and function of all activities. The patient was encouraged to improve his "self-image" by being given considerable responsibility for his behavior in the hospital. Outside the hospital many are no longer respected, trusted or treated as adults, and not welcome in the established institutional structure of society. The program offered a transitional social organization where the patient once again could feel welcome, trusted and treated as an adult in a relationship in which he was not forced to compromise his integrity in order to be received in treatment. We hoped that this experience would help him to return from a deviant-drinking subculture to the dominant culture of society.

We made no claims that we had an answer to the patients' problem, a point which was repeatedly explained. Alcoholics are not likely to be deceived by even implied promises to "cure" their problem. Most of the men (86%) had sought help before and therefore knew what is available to them.

Perhaps the most important point in the treatment philosophy was that we did not try to persuade the men to stop drinking. Drinking on the ward without supervision was not condoned, but if the rule was challenged, the patient was expected to discuss his behavior in the group sessions. The focus throughout the program was not on abstinence but on how alcohol could damage a man's life and why some should choose to do that. The structured drinking was offered as a technique to help him learn something about himself and his problem. It was clearly explained that we did not imply that they could become social drinkers.

Patient characteristics

The 131 subjects were drawn from a population of middle-aged men who at various points in their lives had reached a reasonable level of social functioning and who had become disabled by problems associated with excessive drinking. The group closely conformed to the gamma-alcoholism criteria of Jellinek (16). None was psychotic; their mean age was 43 years, two-thirds being between 35 and 51; 89% were white, 7% American Indian and 2% of Mexican descent; 33% were currently married, 40% had been divorced at least once and 13% had never been married. The mean years of school completed was 9.53; 48% were high-school graduates and 30% had attended college. Their current occupations were concentrated at the labor and semiskilled level (51%); 6% were in management or sales work and 20% in skilled jobs.

The mean number of arrests in the total sample was 12.25 (SD = 20.74); most were for public drunkenness. The subjects reported a mean of 12.67 years of heavy drinking; 81% stated that they had never been able to control it; 18% reported never having had a blackout and 48% that they had never had delirium tremens. Half (48%) of the men had sought help from Alcoholics Anonymous. The typical Minnesota Multiphasic Personality Inventory profile had peaks in the Depression and Sociopathic Scales.

Controlled drinking

For purposes of the study, controlled drinking was behavior which met the following criteria: (1) Drinking was done in a predesignated area; (2) the beginning and the end of the drinking period coincided with the times given by the investigators; (3) drinking was done without a display of disruptive or provocative behavior; (4) the period of drinking was preceded by 2 weeks of abstinence and followed by at least 2 weaks during which the patient maintained his behavior within defined limits.

Results

Of the 131 patients who participated in the program, 101 completed the full 5 weeks in the hospital. All 30 dropouts left of their own accord except one who was referred elsewhere. From the total group, 30 patients were assigned to the drinking schedule, of whom 3 failed to meet the criteria of controlled drinking since they left the program 1, 2 and 6 days after completion of the scheduled drinking. The risk of dropping out was not related to length of time spent in the hospital. The 27 nondrinkers who dropped out of the study left in the third, fourth and fifth weeks. The difference in the number of dropouts between the drinkers and nondrinkers approached significance (chi square = 3.10, 1 df, $p < .10$).

Because of the statistical unreliability of comparing a smaller, randomly selected sample of scheduled drinkers ($n = 30$) with a much larger sample of nondrinkers ($n = 101$), the scheduled drinkers were matched with a nondrinker most like them. It was possible to match 29 of the 30 scheduled drinkers with a nondrinker on 8 variables. The results of 5 matches are shown in Table 1; in addition the men did not differ on race, religious denomination or religious activity. There were no significant differences between the groups on 6 of the variables. The difference in reported years of heavy drinking could be important, but the reliability of this measure has been questioned (17).

In the matched sample of 29 pairs, 3 scheduled drinkers and 3 nondrinkers were lost to attrition. Clearly, in a carefully matched sample, scheduled drinking had no effects on the dropout rate.

Behavior during scheduled drinking

Good cooperation was obtained during the scheduled drinking from all the patients except one. The men read, some watched

Table 1. Characteristics of matched groups (n = 29) of scheduled drinkers and nondrinkers

| | Scheduled Drinkers | | Nondrinkers | | |
	Mean	SD	Mean	SD	t
Age in years	39.07	8.650	39.45	8.509	1.1879
Years formal education	11.55	2.280	11.14	2.232	1.0222
Years heavy drinking	11.93	8.040	9.72	6.304	2.1586*
Locus of Control[1]	5.69	3.318	6.69	3.328	1.0927
Attitudes toward Alcoholics[2]					
Position	4.23	2.118	5.52	2.350	2.0432*
Intensity	63.43	63.558	53.16	46.878	0.6787

[1]Rotter's Internal-External Locus of Control Scale as modified for this study.

[2]A disguised-structured scale specially constructed for this study. The smaller the position number, the more "antialcoholic" the subject. The larger the intensity number, the greater the intensity with which the position is held.

*.10 > p > .05.

television and occasionally conversed with the research assistant. Most became more talkative. Only one man made threats and demanded more alcohol; however, he was easily persuaded to desist. Almost unanimously the patients declared that drinking in the experimental situation was not enjoyable.

Figure 1 shows the mean BAC and the average length of time

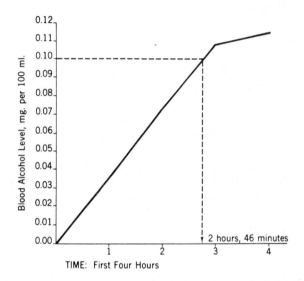

Figure 1. Mean BAC during the first 4 hours of drinking.

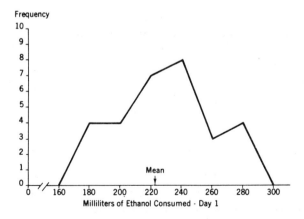

Figure 2. Distribution of ethanol consumption by scheduled drinkers on day 1.

taken by the group to bring their BACs to 0.10%. Measurements were discontinued at 10 p.m. when the drinks ceased to be available. The mean peak BAC reached by the subjects was 0.14% and the mean consumption per subject per day was 222.8 ml of ethanol (SD = 31.78).

Figure 2 shows the distribution of total ethanol consumption on the first day of scheduled drinking. The distribution on the second day was essentially the same.

Self-initiated drinking

Unscheduled drinking occurred during participation in the program. The accessibility of the street and 2 liquor stores about a mile from the hospital grounds made this possible. The total number of men who were suspected of or engaged in unscheduled drinking was 25; 6 acknowledged drinking and 1 was suspected by the staff but clear signs were not detected. In 18 cases, the smell of alcohol on the breath was noted as well as signs of intoxication.

Of the 25 who drank, 6 participated in the scheduled drinking, 2 of whom failed to complete the program. In the other 4, alcohol on the breath without signs of intoxication was detected. Of 19 subjects who did not participate in scheduled drinking, and who initiated drinking on their own, 8 left the hospital without completing the program. A comparison of the probability of attrition following self-initiated drinking was found not to be significantly different between scheduled and nonscheduled drinkers (chi square = 0.3750, 1 df, $p < .5$).

Among the patients who completed the program, self-initiated drinking was limited to isolated episodes. The nursing staff would not have permitted keeping patients who drank continuously or who were drunk or belligerent.

It is possible that other patients drank and were not detected. If this was the case, they attended and participated in ward activities for 5 weeks, skillfully concealing their drinking.

Discussion

We induced periods of controlled drinking in 27 alcoholics, of a total of 30 who received alcohol experimentally. The men received substantial amounts of alcohol, drank in a predesignated area, initiated and stopped drinking on request and did not display provocative behavior while drinking. The periods of induced drinking were preceded and followed by at least 2 weeks of abstinence. An objective sign of their ability to control their behavior was that they remained voluntarily in the hospital to complete the program after being challenged with alcohol. The findings indicate that alcohol can be given to alcoholics without necessarily triggering alcohol-seeking behavior. The stated belief of most of our subjects that once they had a drink they could not stop did not interfere with the outcome of our experiment. The conspicuous absence of pro-vocative or obstinate behavior during drinking might be explained by the theory of MacAndrew and Edgerton (4) who suggest that drunken behavior follows specific social prescriptions that vary with the social situation. We modified temporarily the expected social prescriptions by having the patient drink in an unfamiliar setting. In the absence of conventional expectations, the patients did not become drunk.

The problems of clinical management of patients who drank alcohol as part of the treatment were few. The attrition rate from the program was no greater among the scheduled drinkers. We did not have a control group of patients in a program oriented toward total abstinence. However, the dropout rate (24%) is comparable to that of other programs emphasizing total abstinence (e.g., 18, 19, 20).

During the period in the hospital 19% of all patients engaged in unscheduled drinking. In most cases these were isolated occur-rences which did not lead to continued drinking. The frequency of these incidents is similar to that in other programs (e.g., 21). At least half of the patients who drank complied with most of the hospital rules and completed the 5-week program. Moralistic and punitive attitudes toward drinking promote or at least do not inhibit drinking, yet many treatment programs adopt a more or less subtle punitive attitude toward drinking. For example, patients are summarily dismissed from the program if they are found drinking, and in one program, urine specimens can be demanded by the staff and, if the patient refuses, he can be summarily dismissed. Our study has shown that many of these "unmotivated" patients do not have to be expelled from a therapeutic program.

The loss-of-control hypothesis

The acceptance or rejection of the loss-of-control hypothesis in alcoholism has implications for therapeutic models and research strategies. It is therefore important to examine the concept in some

detail. In the literature on alcoholism, where many terms are used
with dismaying vagueness, "loss of control" is not an exception
(22). Jellinek (16) defined it with relative precision: loss of control
means that "any drink of alcohol starts a chain reaction which is felt
by the drinker as a physical demand for alcohol. The alcoholic is one
who has lost the ability to control the quantity of alcohol ingested
once he has started." The definition has been paraphrased by other
authors. Bacon (23) states that the alcoholic, after the first drink,
shows a loss of rational control over further consumption. Hoff
(24) observes that a definitive element of alcoholism is that "the
victim finds himself drinking when he intended not to drink and
drinking more than he planned." In the terminology of addiction,
loss of control implies "an overpowering desire or need to continue
taking the drug and obtain it by any means" (25).

An early critique and experimental test of the hypothesis was
conducted by Merry (26) who found that there were no differences
in the intensity of reported craving between patients who unknowingly received alcohol and those who received a placebo. Two
related studies have confirmed Merry's impressions. Engle and
Williams (27) demonstrated that informing alcoholics that there
was alcohol in a drink had a greater effect in their stated desire to
imbibe than the actual presence of alcohol in the beverage. Marlatt,
Demming and Reid (28) have shown that the instructional set is a
significant determinant of the amount drunk by nonabstinent alcoholics. The presence of alcohol in the beverage had no effects on
drinking rates, while the amount of beverage consumed—whether
it had alcohol or not—was greater when the subject was told that
there was alcohol in the drink.

In previous studies we noted that 180 ml of 80-proof vodka
administered experimentally did not precipitate "bender" drinking
in inpatient or outpatient alcoholics (29, 30). Cutter, Schwab and
Nathan (31) also failed to induce greater alcohol consumption in
alcoholics who received a priming dose of alcohol. Gottheil et al.
(13) observed that a significant number of patients who had alcohol
available in a closed-ward setting were able to initiate and discontinue drinking "at will." Mello and Mendelson (15) demonstrated
that alcoholics placed in a situation with unrestricted access to
alcohol do not drink all the alcohol available, and challenged most
convincingly the conceptual and empirical bases of the loss-of-
control idea. In the present study alcoholics exposed to substantial
amounts of alcohol in an open institutional setting were not driven
to seek more in the environment surrounding the hospital. The

loss-of-control hypothesis as it is commonly understood is not supported by empirical evidence.

The issue has far-reaching social consequences. In an opinion of the U.S. Supreme Court (*Powell v. Texas,* 392 U.S. 514 [1968]), a person accused of prohibited conduct before the criminal courts can use alcoholism as a defense provided that the accused demonstrates "an inability to abstain" and a "total loss of control" over his behavior once he commenced to drink. The Courts do review the medical literature in their decisions. Scientific support for the loss-of-control hypothesis could accelerate the transition of penal measures to therapeutic programs in the public handling of alcohol-associated problems (32). It is therefore necessary to examine the implications of the empirical findings to the clinical situation.

Variables that affect drinking

Experimental studies of drinking patterns have identified specific conditions, in the laboratory or hospital, under which drinking can be controlled. The investigations have included in their designs variables that influence various parameters of drinking behavior. It has been found, for instance, that programmed and spontaneous drinking differentially affect the behavioral and biological concomitants of drinking; subjects exposed to "spontaneous" or free-access drinking drank more, achieved higher BACs and tolerated alcohol better than did those who drank following a programmed schedule (11), and withdrawal signs were more frequent and severe. Apparently, the compulsive element of drinking is more prominent in a "spontaneous" or "free-access" situation, and probably contributes to higher ingestion. Gottheil et al. (33) noted that in a free-decision situation, 60% of the patients who chose to drink continued to do so throughout the period of 4 weeks when alcohol was available. In the present experiment, drinking was programmed and the compulsive element was not conspicuous.

Another variable considered is social affiliation. Alcohol encourages socialization, a common observation documented experimentally by McNamee, Mello and Mendelson (34) and by Nathan et al. (12). Cohen et al. (35) have shown that an "enriched" environment, which, among other things, offers greater opportunities for socialization, can be used to control the drinking level in alcoholics. Encouragement of socialization may possibly decrease the need for alcohol. The group solidarity induced by the conditions of our ward and the concomitant satisfaction of affiliative needs might have made the alcoholics temporarily less dependent on the "socializing" drug.

The role of risk taking as a positive reinforcer of drinking behavior has not been explored systematically (36). Alcoholics place themselves in considerable jeopardy when they drink, and the risk may increase the appeal of alcohol. On the other hand, when the risks of drinking were considerably decreased, as in the present study, drinking loss much of its appeal.

Alcoholics have considerable ambivalence and conflict about drinking, which has acquired both positive and negative reinforcement properties for them (31, 37–40). An alcoholic can reduce the experienced inconsistency by drinking; if he then stops drinking, the inconsistency reappears. Drinking functions like a device that reduces cognitive dissonance (41). In our experiment the alcoholics did not have to reduce this inconsistency since drinking was declared permissible.

Other variables which have been shown to affect drinking behavior in experimental settings include the amount of work required to obtain alcohol, aversiveness of the task and delay of reinforcement (11). Cohen et al. (35) regulated the amount of drinking by using money as a reinforcement contingency.

Social and sociocultural factors have received limited attention as independent variables in studies of experimental drinking. This neglect contrasts with the importance given to these variables by some social scientists (e.g., 3, 4). Living within the matrix of society entails meeting role expectations ascribed according to age, sex, kinship, education and training (42). The apparent triviality of these culturally defined expectations (e.g., to be at work on time, to discipline a young son, to pay an insurance premium, to supervise a group of workers) is misleading. Many such commonplace social demands involve considerable psychological and psychophysiological stress (43, 44). It may well be that many alcoholics knowingly or unknowingly use alcohol to avoid coping with assigned expectations, expectations that are temporarily suspended when they are admitted to a hospital and assume the patient role (45). Within the institutional setting, away from social stresses, alcoholics can be exposed to alcohol with relative impunity since the critical variables that induce deviant drinking, making it compulsive, redundant and provocative, and just not there.

Those who have challenged the loss-of-control phenomenon might have erected a straw man. Keller (46) in a recent review indicates that it is erroneous to view loss of control as an invariable occurrence following alcohol ingestion. The concept, in his opinion, implies that if an alcoholic takes a drink he cannot be sure he will be able to stop. On occasion an alcoholic is able to drink without continuing to the point of drunkenness, when he is not exposed to the cues or variables critical for him. Such cues might be absent in some settings. Social and environmental contingencies are incorporated in the definition of alcoholism (47). Without these contingencies we can study drinking but not "alcoholic" behavior. We can expect success in controlling drinking patterns of alcoholics in the laboratory. If we wish to have a more accurate idea of the power of manipulations intended to influence drinking patterns of alcoholics, the patients will have to be studied under conventional social demands. The study reported here, by allowing the patient access to his social environment, is a step in this direction.

While we cannot agree with Kalin's (48) contention that "an antiseptic laboratory in a hospital full of scientific gadgets has limited appropriateness for the study of the experiential effects of alcohol," his position contains a warning to those attempting to extrapolate the findings of laboratory studies to the behavior of the alcoholics in the community.

Therapeutic possibilities

The finding that alcohol alone does not trigger a desire for more opens therapeutic possibilities for the controlled drinking paradigm described here. After completion of the controlled drinking experience, an alcoholic will find it more difficult to attribute his desire to drink to a mysterious overpowering force. Drinking becomes only one of the options available to him to cope with social demands. The hospital experience can thus be used to help him formulate more adaptive strategies to meet his commitments in society. This is a change in attitude frequently verbalized by our patients. A follow-up study in progress, which measures the level of social competence achieved by the patient in the community, is testing the validity of this position. Early emerging trends suggest that men who participated in the experimental drinking showed more social stability, had fewer problems with drinking and better attendance at follow-up meetings than those who were not assigned to drinking. Some may argue that the experimental procedure reinforces the rationalizations that patients use to justify drinking, thus encouraging the men to imbibe more. Two studies in the literature indicate that this is probably not the case. Alcoholics who received alcohol experimentally were not more likely to drink within 6 months to 1 year after discharge from the hospital than patients who did not receive it (49, 50).

Several investigators have found that 86% of patients treated for alcoholism drink alcohol within a year after completion of treatment (51, 52). Total and uninterrupted abstinence is a utopian goal for a substantial number of alcoholics. The old dictum *similia similibus curantur* may be applicable to our clinical endeavors. Abstinence does not have to be a keystone in alcoholism therapy.

References

1. Chafetz, M. E. Alcoholism. In: Freedman, A. M., and Kaplan, H. I. (eds.) *Comprehensive textbook of psychiatry.* Baltimore: Williams & Wilkins, 1967. Pp. 1011–1026.
2. Fox, R. A multidisciplinary approach to the treatment of alcoholism. *Amer. J. Psychiat.,* 1957, *123,* 769–778.
3. Cahalan, D. *Problem drinkers: a national survey.* San Francisco; Jossey-Bass, 1970.
4. MacAndrew, C., and Edgerton, R. B. *Drunken comportment: a social explanation.* Chicago: Aldine, 1969.
5. Pittman, D. J., and Gordon, C. W. Revolving door; a study of the chronic police case inebriate. (Rutgers Center of Alcohol Studies, Monogr. No. 2.) New Brunswick, N.J.: 1958.
6. Blumberg, L. U., Shipley, T. E., Jr., and Moore, J. O., Jr. The Skid Row man and the Skid Row status community; with perspectives on their future. *Quart. J. Stud. Alc.,* 1971, *32,* 909–941.
7. Jackson, J. K. The adjustment of the family to the crisis of alcoholism. *Quart. J. Stud. Alc.,* 1954, *15,* 562–586.
8. Paredes, A. Marital-sexual factors in alcoholism. *Med. Aspects Hum. Sexuality,* 1973, *7,* 98–114.
9. Lovald, K., and Neuwirth, G. Exposed and shielded drinking: drinking as role behavior and some consequences for social control and self-concept. *Arch. Gen. Psychiat.,* 1968, *19,* 95–103.
10. Kraft, A. M., Binner, P. R., and Dickey, B. A. The community mental health program and the longer-stay patient. *Arch. Gen. Psychiat.,* 1967, *16,* 64–70.
11. Mello, N. K., and Mendelson, J. H. Experimentally induced intoxication in alcoholics; a comparison between programmed and spontaneous drinking. *J. Pharmacol.,* 1970, *173,* 101–116.
12. Nathan, P. E., Titler, N. A., Lowenstein, L. M., Solomon, P., and Rossi, A. M. Behavioral analysis of chronic alcoholism: interaction of alcohol and human contact. *Arch. Gen. Psychiat.,* 1970, *22,* 419–430.

13. Gottheil, E., Corbett, L. O., Grasberger, J. C., and Cornelison, F. S., Jr. Treating the alcoholic in the presence of alcohol. *Amer. J. Psychiat.*, 1971, *128*, 475–480.

14. Cohen, M., Liebson, I. A., Faillace, L. A., and Allen, R. P. Moderate drinking by chronic alcoholics: a schedule dependent phenomenon. *J. Nerv. Ment. Dis.*, 1971, *153*, 434–444.

15. Mello, N. K., and Mendelson, J. H. Drinking patterns during work-contingent and non-contingent alcohol acquisition. *Psychosom. Med.*, 1972, *34*, 139–164.

16. Jellinek, E. M. *The disease concept of alcoholism.* Highland Park, N.J.: Hillhouse Press, 1960.

17. Summers, T. Validity of alcoholics' self-reported drinking history. *Quart. J. Stud. Alc.*, 1970, *31*, 972–974.

18. Miller, B. A., Pokorny, A. D., Valles, J., and Cleveland, S. E. Biased sampling in alcoholism treatment research. *Quart. J. Stud. Alc.*, 1970, *31*, 97–107.

19. Fitzgerald, B. J., Pasewark, R. A., and Clark, R. Four-year follow-up of alcoholics treated at a rural state hospital. *Quart. J. Stud. Alc.*, 1971, *32*, 636–642.

20. Rohan, W. P. A follow-up study of hospitalized problem drinkers. *Dis. Nerv. Syst.*, 1970, *31*, 259–265.

21. Rathod, N. H., Gregory, E., Blows, D., and Thomas, G. H. A two-year follow-up study of alcoholic patients. *Brit. J. Psychiat.*, 1966, *112*, 683–692.

22. Redlich, F. C., and Freedman, D. X. Alcoholism. In: *The theory and practice of psychiatry.* New York: Basic Books, 1966.

23. Bacon, S. D. Social settings conducive to alcoholism. *J. Amer. Med. Ass.*, 1957, *164*, 177–181.

24. Hoff, E. C. The etiology of alcoholism. *Quart. J. Stud. Alc.*, Suppl. No. 1, 1961, 57–65.

25. Eddy, N. B., Halbach, H., Isbell, H., and Seevers, M. H. Drug dependence; its significance and characteristics. *Bull. World Hlth-Org.*, 1965, *32*, 721–733.

26. Merry, J. The "loss of control" myth. *Lancet*, 1966, *1*, 1257–1258.

27. Engle, K. B., and Williams, T. K. Effect of an ounce of vodka on alcoholics' desire for alcohol. *Quart. J. Stud. Alc.*, 1972, *33*, 1099–1105.

28. Marlatt, G. A., Demming, B., and Reid, J. B. Loss of control in alcoholics; an experimental analogue. *J. Abnorm. Psychol.*, 1973, *81*, 233–241.

29. Paredes, A., and Cornelison, F. S., Jr. Development of an audiovisual technique for the rehabilitation of alcoholics: preliminary report. *Quart. J. Stud. Alc.*, 1968, *29*, 84–92.

30. Paredes, A., Ludwig, K. D., Hassenfeld, I. N., and Cornelison, F. S., Jr. Filmed representations of behavior and responses to self-

observation in alcoholics. In: Mello, N. K., and Mendelson, J. H. (eds), *Recent advances in studies of alcoholism; an interdisciplinary symposium*. Rockville, Md.: U.S. National Institute on Alcohol Abuse and Alcoholism, 1971. Pp. 709–729.

31. Cutter, H. S. G., Schwab, E. L., Jr., and Nathan, P. E. Effects of alcohol on its utility for alcoholics and nonalcoholics. *Quart. J. Stud. Alc.*, 1970, *31*, 369–378.

32. Kittrie, N. N. *The right to be different: deviance and enforced therapy*. Baltimore: Johns Hopkins Press, 1971.

33. Gottheil, E., Corbett, L. O., Grasberger, J. C., and Cornelison, F. S., Jr. Fixed interval drinking decisions. I. A research and treatment model. *Quart. J. Stud. Alc.*, 1972, *33*, 311–324.

34. McNamee, H. B., Mello, N. K., and Mendelson, J. H. Experimental analysis of drinking patterns of alcoholics: concurrent psychiatric observations. *Amer. J. Psychiat.*, 1968, *124*, 1063–1069.

35. Cohen, M., Liebson, I. A.. Faillace, L. A., and Speers, W. Alcoholism: controlled drinking and incentives for abstinence. *Psychol. Rep.*, 1971, *28*, 575–580.

36. Kogan, N., and Wallach, M. A. Risk taking as a function of the situation, the person, and the group. In: Newcomb, T. M. (ed.) *New directions in psychology, vol. 3.* New York: Holt, Rinehart & Winston, 1967. Pp. 111–266.

37. Ullman, A. D. The psychological mechanisms of alcohol addiction. *Quart. J. Stud. Alc.*, 1952, *13*, 602–608.

38. Ullman, A. D. The first drinking experience of addictive and of "normal" drinkers. *Quart. J. Stud. Alc.*, 1953, *14*, 181–191.

39. Menaker, T. Anxiety about drinking in alcoholics. *J. Abnorm. Psychol.*, 1967, *72*, 43–49.

40. Cutter, H. S. G. Alcohol, drinking patterns, and the psychological probability of success. *Behav. Sci.*, 1969, *14*, 19–27.

41. Festinger, L. *The theory of cognitive dissonance.* New York: Harper & Row, 1957.

42. David, K. Status and related concepts. In: Biddle, B. J., and Thomas, E. J. (eds.); *Role theory concepts and research.* New York: Wiley, 1966.

43. Holmes, T. H., and Rahe, R. H. The social readjustment rating scale. *J. Psychosom. Res.*, 1967, *11*, 213–218.

44. Paykel, E. S., Prusoff, B. A., and Uhlenhuth, E. H. Scaling of life events. *Arch. Gen. Psychiat.*, 1971, *25*, 340–347.

45. Parsons, T. Illness and the role of a physician; a sociological perspective. *Amer. J. Orthopsychiat.*, 1951, *21*, 452–460.

46. Keller, M. On the loss-of-control phenomenon in alcoholism. *Brit. J. Addict.*, 1972, *67*, 153–166.

47. Mendelson, J. H. Biologic concomitants of alcoholism. *New Engl. J. Med.*, 1970, *283*, 24–32, 71–81.

48. Kalin, R. Social drinking in different settings. In: McClelland, D. C., Davis, W. M., Kalin, R., and Wanner, E. (eds.), *The drinking man:*

alcohol and human motivation. New York: Free Press, 1972. Pp. 21–44.

49. Gottheil, E., Murphy, B. F., Skoloda, T. E., and Corbett, L. O. Fixed interval drinking decisions. II. Drinking and discomfort in 25 alcoholics. *Quart. J. Stud. Alc.,* 1972, *33,* 325–340.

50. Faillace, L. A., Flamer, R. N., Imber, S. C., and Ward, R. F. Giving alcohol to alcoholics; an evaluation. *Quart. J. Stud. Alc.,* 1972, *33,* 85–90.

51. Ritson, B. The prognosis of alcohol addicts treated by a specialized unit. *Brit. J. Psychiat.,* 1968, *114,* 1019–1029.

52. Rohan, W. P. MMPI changes in hospitalized alcoholics; a second study. *Quart. J. Stud. Alc.,* 1972, *33,* 65–76.

6. Reversing Irreversibility

Studies of Nonproblem Drinking by Former Alcoholics

As a result of rigid adherence to generally accepted although unsupported positions, many subject areas, especially the treatment and evaluation of alcohol problems, have been seriously neglected. Perhaps the most neglected area involves reports of resumed nonproblem drinking by individuals who were previously identified as alcoholics.

One of the most entrenched beliefs in the field is the idea that alcoholism is irreversible: "Once an alcoholic, always an alcoholic!" Essentially, it is believed that once a person who has been physically dependent on alcohol stops drinking, any further drinking by that person can only lead to increasingly worse consequences. A major implication of this belief is that complete abstinence is the only feasible and ethical treatment objective for both alcoholics and anyone considered to be en route to becoming an alcoholic. Yet, evidence contradicting this belief has been rapidly accumulating.

Two lines of evidence support the contention that some former identified "alcoholics" can drink alcohol without incurring problems. First, considerable evidence from experimental investigations of intoxication (see Chapter 5, "The Nature of 'Loss of Control' ") has ubiquitously demonstrated that even persons diagnosed as chronic or *gamma* alcoholics are capable of consuming moderate amounts of alcohol without experiencing a "loss of control." Second, an impressive number of studies have reported that former alcoholics have successfully resumed nonproblem drinking, sometimes referred to as "social," "limited," "moderate," "controlled," or even "normal" drinking.

Data on alcoholics who returned to nonproblem drinking

Table 1 (pp. 130–141) presents a review of 74 references which report that *some* identified alcoholics have successfully demonstrated an ability to resume nonproblem drinking. This review documents that the existing body of evidence is not only substantial but includes a large number of reports about individuals who by the traditional disease taxonomy were definitely diagnosed as "alcoholic," often *gamma* type (Jellinek, 1960). Rather than attempting a detailed analysis of these studies, attention will be focused on certain major characteristics germane to the present discussion. Since the listing in Table 1 is not exhaustive, it is conceivable that a number of similar studies exist or are in preparation and have not been included. In fact, because we have purposefully used conservative inclusion criteria, a number of studies which have reported resumed nonproblem drinking by former alcoholics were specifically not cited in Table 1 because they either lacked sufficient descriptive detail or contained contradictory or ambiguous evidence.

The studies in Table 1 are summarized in terms of (1) the investigator(s), years of publication, and country where the study was conducted; (2) whether or not controlled drinking (CD) was the prescribed treatment goal (Rx); (3) the number of subjects in the original study; (4) the number of subjects (N) found in each study for follow-up (sample size found for follow-up, N, refers to subjects for whom complete follow-up data was reported, as well as deceased subjects and subjects incarcerated in jails and/or hospitals; subjects who refused to be interviewed are not included); (5) the duration, in months, of the follow-up interval reported; (6) the number of subjects (*n*) found for follow-up who were practicing controlled drinking; (7) the percentage of subjects found for follow-up who were practicing controlled drinking; (8) the number of subjects (*n*) found to be totally abstinent throughout the entire follow-up interval; (9) the percentage of subjects found to be totally abstinent throughout the entire follow-up interval; (10) a brief description of how each study defined controlled drinking; and (11) a brief description of the treatment setting and modality for each study.

The studies listed in Table 1 are trichotomized according to how the authors diagnosed or labeled their subject populations. The first category includes studies which identified their subjects as chronic or *gamma* alcoholics. In most cases, sufficient information was provided so the subjects could be described as meeting Jellinek's (1960) criteria for *gamma* alcoholics (primary symptoms for this classification were reports of "loss of control," physiological withdrawal symptoms, or explicit reference to the subjects as *gamma* type). The second category includes studies which simply identified subjects as "alcoholics" but did not provide descriptions of how that diagnosis was derived. The third group of studies identified subjects only as "problem drinkers."

More than half the studies ($n = 38$) in Table 1 reported that their subjects were chronic or *gamma* alcoholics. Furthermore, it is reasonable to expect that some studies listed under the category of subjects "identified as 'alcoholic,' but with no supporting evidence," also dealt with *gamma* alcoholics. On the other hand, subjects in some of the studies using "alcoholics," particularly those studies with a small number of subjects, might certainly be more appropriately diagnosed as "problem drinkers." It is interesting to note that two studies in the table have specifically identified their treatment population as "problem drinkers" and presented very strong evidence for such subjects being able to return to some form of nonproblem drinking.

Seventy of the 74 studies indicated the specific follow-up interval over which data was collected. Since some studies indicated that the follow-up interval varied between subjects, the interval used in Table 1 applies to the majority of subjects followed up in each study. While follow-up intervals ranged from 1½ months to as long as 27 years, 64% ($n = 45$) of the studies which indicated a specific follow-up interval followed subjects for a minimum of 12 months. Further, 33% ($n = 23$) of these studies reported follow-up data for a minimum of 24 months. Current research data suggest that a follow-up interval of 12 to 24 months is adequate for drawing reliable outcome conclusions (Davies, Shepard, & Myers, 1956; Gerard & Saenger, 1966; Gibbins & Armstrong, 1957; Selzer & Holloway, 1957).

The number of subjects for whom data was reported varies from single case reports to a study using an explicit treatment goal of controlled drinking for 893 subjects (Arikawa, Kotorii, & Musaka, 1971). While all attempts were made to gather complete data for each study listed in Table 1, one study did not indicate the number of subjects in the original study, another did not report the number of subjects practicing controlled drinking, and 10 studies did not specify the number of subjects who were totally abstinent throughout the entire follow-up interval. Taken collectively, 11,817 subjects were found for follow-up in the 73 studies for which the number of subjects was known. Of these 11,817 subjects, 18.25% ($n = 2,157+$) were actually practicing controlled drinking. Interestingly, only 10.48% ($n = 1,239$) of the 11,817 subjects were reported as totally abstinent throughout the entire follow-up interval.

While the item of major importance in Table 1 is the reported incidence of controlled drinking, a number of qualifications are in order when interpreting these data. First, the criteria used to determine the number of subjects practicing controlled drinking for each study were purposely conservative. If a study included information from collateral sources or any data which appeared to contradict a report of controlled drinking, those subjects were not included among controlled drinking data. Second, most studies did not provide substantial data about the longitudinal patterns of controlled drinking. The frequency of occasions during follow-up when the subjects practiced controlled drinking is provided in the table for each study; whenever possible the definition of controlled drinking was taken directly from the original report. While the operational definitions of controlled drinking varied from study to study, the authors specifically indicated in their papers that they thought some of their subjects had returned to some form of nonproblem drinking.

A little over half ($n = 40$) the studies were conducted in the United States; the remaining 34 studies were conducted in a variety of other countries. It is interesting to note that prior to 1960 only seven studies had been published reporting some alcoholics returning to some form of nonproblem drinking. In the next ten years, from 1960 through 1969, 32 studies were published reporting some form of nonproblem drinking by former alcoholics. Of special interest, only three of those studies actually used an explicit treatment goal of controlled drinking. In the first published study reported in 1964 by Mukasa, Ichihara, and Eto and subsequent studies by Mukasa and his colleagues, the drug Calcium Cyanamide was used on an outpatient basis to enable subjects to consume moderate doses of saké. In the six years since 1970, an additional 35 studies have been published which report some alcoholics resuming nonproblem drinking. Of these 35 studies, 14 had an explicit treatment goal of controlled drinking.

Thus, of the 74 studies reported in Table 1, 57 (77%) did not have an explicit treatment goal of controlled drinking. Finally, 23% ($n = 17$) of the studies explicitly specified "controlled drinking" as a treatment objective for some alcoholics. It would appear from these figures that studies with explicit treatment goals of controlled drinking and follow-up studies of alcoholics in traditional abstinence-oriented treatment programs have been proliferating in recent years. Such a proliferation may reflect both a dissatisfaction with and failure of traditional concepts of alcoholism.

One-half ($n = 37$) of the studies listed in Table 1 were conducted in an inpatient treatment setting. Of the remaining 37 studies, 22 were conducted in outpatient settings, 5 used both an inpatient and outpatient setting, 8 were simply follow-up reports of subjects who had not received formal treatment, and for 2 studies it was impossible to determine the treatment setting. The specific therapeutic modality used for each study is indicated in Table 1.

While 74 studies are listed, a total of 86 types of treatment modalities were described, as eight studies included multiple treatment groups for comparative evaluation. The predominant treatment modality associated with controlled drinking outcomes was behavior therapy; 18 (20.93%) studies reported using this orientation. The following categories accounted for the remaining treatment modalities: (a) multimodality (a variety of treatment elements): 17.44%, $n = 15$; (b) follow-up, survey, no treatment: 9.30%, $n = 8$; (c) aversive conditioning: 6.98%, $n = 6$; (d) treatment modality not specified: 6.98%, $n = 6$; (e) state hospital program: 6.98%, $n = 6$; (f) drug therapy: 6.98%, $n = 6$; (g) group therapy: 4.65%, $n = 4$; (h) experimental drinking programs: 3.49%, $n = 3$; (i) group and individual therapy: 2.32%, $n = 2$; and (j) unique therapeutic orientations: 13.95%, $n = 12$.

Follow-up studies

It is important to recognize that the vast majority of the studies (64.76%, $n = 48$) in Table 1 were follow-up reports of treatment programs with a specified treatment goal of total abstinence. In all of those studies, the finding of controlled drinking was serendipitous. Thus, the authors of those studies can hardly be accused of finding treatment outcomes to match their expectations or preconceptions. Perhaps the best-known of the studies was published in 1962 by D. L. Davies, who innocently reported the results of a follow-up assessment of alcoholics who had been treated at the Maudsley Hospital in London. He noted that 7 of 93 (7%) former "alcoholic addicts," followed up 7 to 11 years after discharge from treatment, were found to have been drinking "normally" for the better part of those years. An unprecedented barrage of commentary, mostly critical, was directed at his article and eventually appeared as a separate supplement to the *Quarterly Journal of Studies on Alcohol* (Davies, 1963). Most of the critiques made it appear as if Davies had committed an act of heresy rather than objectively reporting the findings of a scientific investigation of treatment outcome. It is now apparent, however, that controlled drinking outcomes in traditional abstinence-oriented treatment programs are not as rare as was once thought. For instance, in a recent review of 265 follow-up studies of psychological treatment programs, Emrick (1974) noted 40 studies that reported controlled drinking results.

Survey or follow-up studies of untreated alcoholics

Seven studies in Table 1 were surveys or follow-up studies of individuals who had not been specifically treated for alcoholism, yet without treatment changed their drinking patterns from alcoholic to nonproblem drinking (Bailey & Stewart, 1967; Barchha, 1968; Glatt, 1967; James & Goldman, 1971; Kendall, 1965; Lemere, 1953; Rakkolainen & Turnen, 1969). In a community health survey, Bailey and Stewart (1967) found that 12 of 91 subjects who reported having a prior alcoholism problem claimed to be moderate drinkers at the time of the study. They reinterviewed these subjects and classified six of them as controlled drinkers. Barchha (1968), in a survey of general hospital patients, found that approximately 33 percent of those patients who reported once having a serious drinking problem demonstrated a marked reduction in both drinking and drinking-related problems. The remaining five studies reported smaller samples of individuals who, without treatment, changed their alcoholic drinking patterns to nonproblem drinking patterns.

Several case studies have been published reporting controlled drinking by alcoholics even though it was not used as an explicit goal of treatment (Shea, 1954; Kraft & Al-Issa, 1967, 1968; Guirk, 1968). Goodwin (1973) has also reported a single case study involving the retrospective report of a man who described his return to moderate drinking from alcoholism.

Controlled drinking as a treatment goal

Of the studies in Table 1 reporting alcoholics successfully returning to nonproblem drinking, a few report very high success rates. Most of these, however, were research investigations specifically designed to explore the use of controlled drinking as a viable treatment goal for some alcoholics. Seventeen (22.97%) of the 74 studies in Table 1 used an explicit treatment goal of controlled drinking (Mukasa et al., 1964; Lazarus, 1965; Mukasa & Arikawa, 1968;

Arikawa et al., 1971; Baker, et al., 1972; Caddy, 1972a; Miller, 1972; Schaefer, 1972; Sobell & Sobell, 1973b; Hedberg & Campbell, 1974; Silverstein et al., 1974; Gibbins, 1975; Miller, 1975; Sobell & Sobell, 1975; Vogler, et al., 1975; Popham & Schmidt, 1976, unpublished manuscript; and Caddy & Lovibond, 1976). In addition to using a controlled drinking treatment goal, four of these studies also used an abstinence treatment goal. Perhaps the most significant aspect of the 17 studies which used an explicit treatment goal of controlled drinking is that 12 (17.59%) also used a treatment modality of behavior therapy. Of the remaining five studies, three were performed in Japan by Mukasa and his colleagues (1964, 1968, 1971) using the drug Calcium Cyanamide, and the other two had multimodality treatment orientations (Vogler et al., 1975; Popham & Schmidt, unpublished manuscript, 1976). The advent of treatment programs based on principles of behavioral analysis and using broad-spectrum behavior therapy appears to have resulted in the use of the treatment goal of controlled drinking as a major component of some alcohol treatment programs. These studies, taken in concert, provide strong preliminary data that some alcoholics treated in behavioral programs can learn to drink in a nonproblem fashion.

At the present time, the issue of controlled drinking is debated in the alcoholism field with great emotional volatility. The current vociferous reaction by some individuals to evidence of controlled drinking outcomes is not a new phenomenon; similar reactions resulted in 1962 when D. L. Davies reported the results of a follow-up study. However, there is now strong evidence from 17 major clinical ventures suggesting that controlled drinking can sometimes be used as a successful and legitimate goal of treatment. Surprisingly, some of the strongest findings among those studies are from a population of alcoholics—chronic, *gamma*, state hospitalized alcoholics—who typically have the poorest prognoses and usually demonstrate the worst treatment outcome results.

Data limitations

In summary, the clinical data just reviewed constitute a substantial body of evidence indicating that with or without treatment, and under various treatment conditions, some proportion of alcoholics do change their drinking behavior from a pathological alcoholic drinking pattern to some type of nonproblem drinking. Unfortunately, the reports do not systematically define the population of alcoholics under observation. To allege that the individuals who became controlled drinkers were never "true" alcoholics or actually were "pseudoalcoholics" is to engage in specious and tautological reasoning. This line of argument merely says that if individuals meet all the criteria of being "alcoholic" but fail to meet the theoretical prediction of never being able to drink again, ergo, they cannot be alcoholics. It seems more plausible, however, that the original theoretical prediction was wrong. In general, the clinical reports cited in this chapter do not give a precise definition of their alcoholic subjects, but as a whole, they incorporate no less precision than is typical of the vast majority of studies in the alcoholism literature. Also, the definition of controlled drinking for the 74 studies in Table 1 is neither uniform nor precise. Therefore, at this time it is not possible to state precisely what types of changes in alcoholic drinking have occurred. Further, since follow-up reports are also lacking in precision, it is difficult to tell over what period of time such drinking occurred. Finally, because the reports derive from diverse treatment modalities and settings, one cannot yet draw any firm conclusions about what types of alcoholic patterns may predispose individuals to acquire and maintain nonproblem drinking behavior, for which populations nonproblem drinking is a reasonable treatment objective, or which treatment methodologies might be most efficacious in achieving such a goal.

At this time, a modest generalization is warranted. These 74 studies strongly contradict the traditional concept that an alcoholic can never drink again. Given the large body of empirical data just reviewed, it is suggested that it is now both justifiable and appropriate to recognize "alternatives to abstinence" as legitimate treatment objectives for some individuals with alcohol problems.

Conclusions

Table 1 contains 74 literature references which have often been neglected or ignored by researchers, clinicians, and others working in the field of alcoholism. The implications of this evidence seem clear.

First, a realistic perspective requires an acceptance that at least some of these findings, especially those arising from controlled experimental studies, have a certain amount of validity. Given the fact that some "alcoholics" do learn to drink in a controlled fashion, rather than denying the existence of this phenomenon, our efforts might be better spent in generating information which would help predict which kinds of treatment objectives might be more appropriate for certain individuals.

Second, this evidence is directly relevant to the construction of alcohol treatment programs. In the past, a lack of recognition of alternative treatment objectives to abstinence may have resulted in some alcohol-dependent individuals being denied efficacious treatment. This limited array of treatment approaches may also have resulted in some individuals being reluctant to become labeled as "alcoholic," and, more importantly, may have served as a powerful deterrent to treatment for individuals with developing drinking problems. With regard to individuals with developing drinking problems, more appropriate treatment might be offered if they were not confronted with a single a priori treatment goal of lifelong abstinence.

Taken collectively, the results of the 74 studies reported here contradict the traditional belief that "once an alcoholic, always an alcoholic." We can, therefore, no longer afford to ignore alternatives to abstinence. However, this is not to suggest that these alternatives constitute a panacea, for there are several accompanying problems. Treatment providers in the alcoholism field often seem to pursue a "cure" for "alcoholics." Part of resultant frustration appears to stem from repeated treatment failures and a lack of permanent success. Thus, as controlled drinking has emerged as a documented successful treatment goal for some alcoholics, it has also been viewed by some eager alcoholism workers as being the answer to all their clients' problems. It takes but a short step, after agreeing that the pursuit of controlled drinking is a legitimate enterprise, to refer to such an outcome as a "cure." Arguments might be made that either outcome—abstinence or controlled drinking—might be an easier long-term behavior to maintain. However, the relative efficacy of various treatment objectives will only be determined by clinical research and will, very probably, be found to be a function of individual case histories and circumstances.

It is cautioned that controlled or nonproblem drinking is probably no more or less likely than abstinence to be obtained simply through self-commitment. Also, the concept of striving toward controlled drinking could be highly detrimental should an individual use this to justify continued excessive drinking. Therefore, for the present time, such a treatment goal should only be pursued as the target of a specifically designed treatment program.

A final caveat is in order. We must urge a serious caution that controlled drinking, like any other therapeutic procedure or goal, should only be used by trained, knowledgeable individuals who are aware of the methodology, benefits, dangers, and limitations inherent in such an approach. If used carelessly and without regard for clients' welfare, controlled drinking, like any other treatment procedure, can probably do more harm than if not used at all.

Table 1. Summary of studies reporting controlled drinking (CD)

Investigator(s), year, country	CD[a] Rx[b] (Yes/No)	Subjects in original study	Subjects found for follow-up (N)[c]	Follow-up length (mos.)	Practicing CD — n	Practicing CD — % of N	Totally abstinent — n	Totally abstinent — % of N	Brief description of CD	Treatment setting; modality
					Subjects identified as chronic or *gamma* alcoholics[d]					
Bailey & Stewart, 1967, U.S.A.	No	13	12	30–60	6	50	1	8	Quant.-freq. index 2–3 drinks twice/week	None; community health survey
Baker et al., 1972, U.S.A.	Yes	20	19	1½	3	16	4	21	12 oz. 86-proof liquor/2 days	IP[e]; behavior therapy
	No	10	9	1½	0	0	0	0		IP; state hospital
Barchha, 1968, U.S.A.	No	82	82	12	27	33	9	11	Marked reduction & no associated problems	Survey of general hospital patients
Barr et al., 1973, U.S.A.	No	503	456	11–34	14	3	68	15	A beer every week or so	IP; therapeutic community
Bhakta, 1971, Australia	No	20	20	12	7	35	1	5	Moderate drinking with no adverse effects	IP; behavior therapy
Blake, 1965, Scotland	No	37	34	6	1	3	18	53	"Drinking in a controlled manner"	IP; behavior therapy
Bolman, 1965, U.S.A.	No	14	14	12–84	2	14	2	14	1–2 glasses beer less than once/month	OP[f]; psychotherapy

Study									Outcome criterion	Treatment
Cain, 1964, U.S.A.	No	36	36	36+	19+	53+	n.d.[g]	n.d.	1–2 drinks after work or at parties	OP; group therapy
Davies, 1962, G.B.	No	93	93	84–132	7	7	n.d.	n.d.	Maximum 3 pints beer/day	IP; multimodal
Davies et al., 1969, G.B.	No	4	4	60–324	4	100	0	0	1–2 pints beer or 1–2 shots whiskey/weekend	IP; multimodal
deMorsier & Feldman, 1952, France	No	500	430	17–64	76	18	155	36	Occasional glass beer or wine with meals	IP; aversion conditioning, 1/3 had psychotherapy
Dubourg, 1969, G.B.	No	79	76	16–26	3	4	n.d.	n.d.	"Resumed controlled social drinking"	IP; group & individual therapy
Faillace et al., 1972, U.S.A.	No	14	13	6	2	15	7	54	Global adjustment rating of 7	IP; experimental drinking program & multimodal
Faillace et al., unpub., U.S.A. (cited in Faillace et al., 1972)	No	14	11	6	2	18	2	18		IP; multimodal
	No	24	20	6	3	15	1	5	Global adjustment rating of 7	IP; experimental drinking program
Gibbins,[b] 1975, unpub., Canada	Yes	5	4	7	3	75	1	25	4 oz. 86-proof liquor or equivalent in alcoholic content/day	OP; Temposil & behavior therapy
Glatt, 1967, G.B.	No	30	30	24	1	3	n.d.	n.d.	1–2 beers/day	n.d.

Table 1. (*continued*)

Investigator(s), year, country	CD[a] Rx[b] (Yes/No)	Subjects in original study	Subjects found for follow-up (N)[c]	Follow-up length (mos.)	Practicing CD n	% of N	Totally abstinent n	% of N	Brief description of CD	Treatment setting; modality
Goodwin et al., 1971, U.S.A.	No	93	93	96	17	18	7	8	Drinking 1–10 times/month & rarely intoxicated	Follow-up of alcoholic felons
Harper & Hickson, 1951, G.B.	No	84	80	24–60	16[i]	20	16[i]	20	Consumed small quantity or only 1 relapse	IP; multimodal
Kendall, 1965, U.S.A. (also, Kendall & Stanton, 1966)	No	62	62	36–96	4	6	9[j]	14	1 glass sherry to 2 pints beer/day	Follow-up only, no treatment
Lazarus, 1965, S. Africa	Yes	1	1	14	1	100	0	0	2 glasses beer, wine, or hard liquor/day	OP; behavior therapy
Levinson, 1975, Canada	No	154	138	60	11	8	29	21	"Drinking significantly reduced.... improved life style"	IP; group therapy
Lundquist, 1973, Sweden	No	200	200	108	40[k]	20	17[k]	8	Occasionally consumed small quantity of alc.	IP; treatment not specified
Moore & Ramseur, 1960, U.S.A.	No	100	91	3–144	5	6	15	16	"Well-controlled social drinkers"	IP; multimodal

Study										Setting
Orford, 1973, G.B.	No	100	89	24	9	10	10	11	8–10 oz. 86-proof liquor/day	OP; individual therapy
Pattison et al., 1968, U.S.A.	No	46	37	18–24	8	22	11	30	Drinking status scale; CD=1–6	OP; multimodal
Pokorny et al., 1968, U.S.A.	No	113	93	12	23	25	22	24	"Resumed controlled social drinking"	IP; group therapy
Quinn & Henbest, 1967, Ireland	No	10	10	1–204[1]	3	30	0	0	"Beer not to excess; improved social efficiency"	IP; aversion conditioning
Rakkolainen & Turunen, 1969, Finland	No	71	71	12–240	6	8	2	3	Reduction & less potent drinks	Follow-up of deceased alcoholics; no treatment
Reinert & Bowen, 1968, U.S.A.	No	156	156	12	4	3	31	20	Drinking with others & no loss of control	IP; treatment not specified
Schaefer, 1972, U.S.A. (follow-up of Mills et al., 1971)	Yes	E[m]=13	10	12	4 ″	40	3 ″	30	6 oz. 86-proof liquor or equivalent in alcoholic content/day	IP; behavior therapy
	No	C[o]=13	11	12	0	0	2 ″	18		IP; state hospital
Schaefer et al., 1972, U.S.A. (follow-up of Schaefer et al., 1971)	No	26	26	12	1 ″	4	12 ″	46	"Drinking in a socially acceptable manner"	IP; video tape self-confrontation
	No	10	9	12	0	0	1 ″	11		IP; "sham treatment"
	No	16	16	12	0	0	4 ″	25		IP; state hospital
Selzer & Holloway, 1957, U.S.A.	No	98	83	72	13	16	18	22	From 1–2 beers/day to 6–12 beers/weekend	IP; state hospital

Table 1. (*continued*)

Investigator(s), year, country	CD Rx (Yes/No)[a][b]	Subjects in original study	Subjects found for follow-up (N)[c]	Follow-up length (mos.)	Practicing CD		Totally abstinent		Brief description of CD	Treatment setting; modality
					n	% of N	n	% of N		
Silverstein et al., 1974 U.S.A.	Yes	3	3	3	1	33	0	0	BAL of 0.08% (8 or less beers/day)	IP; behavior therapy
Skoloda et al., 1975, U.S.A.	No	98	91	6	44	48	14	15	Drink within moderate/socially acceptable limits	IP; experimental drinking program
Sobell & Sobell, 1976, U.S.A. (also see Sobell & Sobell, 1973a, 1st yr. results)	CD-E[b]	Yes	20	20	24	10	50	0	0	6 oz. 86-proof liquor or equivalent in alcoholic content /day; abstinent or controlled drinking 95% of 2nd year of follow-up & no binge drinking[q]	IP; behavior therapy
	CD-C[b]	No	20	19	24	1	5	0	0		IP; state hospital
	ND-E[b]	No	15	15	24	1	7	1	7		IP; behavior therapy
	ND-C[b]	No	15	15	24	1	7	0	0		IP; state hospital
Tomsovic, 1970, U.S.A.	No	266	200	12	13	6	49	24	Drunk occasionally with no associated problems	IP; multimodal
van Dijk & van Dijk-Koffeman, 1973, Netherlands	No	211	200	30–66	20	10	45	22	Intake minimal with no drunkenness	IP; multimodal

Vogler et al., 1975, U.S.A.	Yes	59	43	12	12	28	14	33	Average 50 oz. absolute alcohol/month & 1 episode of 0.08% BAL	IP; multimodal

Subjects identified as "alcoholics" but no supporting evidence provided

Anant, 1968, Canada	No	25	n.d.	24+	1	n.d.	n.d.	n.d.	Able to "take alcohol occasionally; stop at will"	OP; aversion conditioning
Arikawa et al., 1971, Japan	Yes	893	893	12	611	68	45	5	180 ml. 15% saké or 1 bottle beer/day	OP; drug (Cyanamide)
Caddy, 1972a, Australia (follow-up of Lovibond & Caddy, 1970)	Yes	28	27	18	10	37	0	0	Rarely exceeding BAL of 0.07%	OP; behavior therapy
Caddy & Lovibond, 1976, Australia	Yes	60	37[r]	12	10	27	0	0	Exceeding BAL of 0.07% less than once/month	OP; behavior therapy
Evans, 1967, G.B.	No	100	100	3–43	6	6	14	14	Managed to control their drinking	OP; milieu therapy
Gallen et al., 1973, U.S.A.	No	27	27	3	3[s]	11	12	44	Drinking 1–16 days; 1–4 beers/day[s]	IP; behavior therapy
Gerard et al., 1962, U.S.A.	No	21	21	3	4[s]	19	9	43	2–3 beers/day or on rare occasions	IP; group therapy
	No	400	299	24–96	41	14	55[j]	18		1 IP & 5 OP programs; multimodal

Table 1. (continued)

Investigator(s), year, country	CD[a] Rx[b] (Yes/No)	Subjects in original study	Subjects found for follow-up (N)[c]	Follow-up length (mos.)	Practicing CD — n	% of N	Totally abstinent — n	% of N	Brief description of CD	Treatment setting; modality
Gerard & Saenger, 1966, U.S.A.	No	798	618	12	35	6	78'	13	2–3 beers/day, or at social functions	OP; 8 programs, different therapy orientations
Goodwin, 1973, France	No	1	1	n.d.	1	100	0	0	"Had a drink now & then"	None; retrospective report
Hacquard et al., 1960, France	No	160	124	24+	18	15	36	29	Drank alcohol moderately with meals	IP; drug (Antabuse) & multimodal
Hedberg & Campbell, 1974, U.S.A.	Yes	13	13	6"	8	62	n.d.	n.d.	"Controlled drinking"	OP; behavior therapy
Hyman, 1975, U.S.A.	No	54	44	180	5	11	5	11	Sharply reduced daily drinking without any problems	OP; multimodal
James & Goldman, 1971, U.S.A.	No	85	85	1–36	2	2	26	31	Wives stated husbands returned to social drinking	Follow-up; no" treatment

Study		N							Resumed drinking criterion	Treatment
Knott et al., 1972, U.S.A. (see "One of seven ...)"	No	4,000+	4,000+	n.d.	400	10	n.d.	n.d.	Resumed drinking with controlling imbibing	IP; treatment not specified
Kraft & Al-Issa, 1967, G.B.	No	1	1	15	1	100	0	0	Occasional half pint beer	IP; behavior therapy
Kraft & Al-Issa, 1968, G.B.	No	2	2	6–9	2	100	0	0	Occasional half pint beer	IP; behavior therapy
Lambert, 1964, Sweden	No	100	100	n.d.	9	9	n.d	n.d.	Able to drink liquor in moderation	Care at public receiving center
Lemere, 1953, U.S.A.	No	500	500	n.d.	14	3	53	11	Amount & degree abated to normal drinking	Follow-up of deceased alcoholics; no treatment
Marlatt, 1973, U.S.A.	No	E=52	52	3	9	17	10	19	Alcohol intake 50 mg./week	IP; aversion conditioning
	No	C=13	13	3	1	8	4	31		IP; no treatment
Miller, 1972, U.S.A.	Yes	1	1	6	1	100	0	0	"Moderate drinking pattern established"	OP; behavior therapy
Monnerot, 1963, France	No	n.d.	338	6–12	56	17	80	24	"Ingesting drinks but moderately"	IP; multimodal
Mukasa et al., 1964, Japan	Yes	110	110	3–48	96	87	n.d.	n.d.	100–200 ml. saké (30 proof)/day	OP; drug (Cyanamide)

Table 1. *(continued)*

Investigator(s), year, country	CD[a] Rx[b] (Yes/No)	Subjects in original study	Subjects found for follow-up (N)[c]	Follow-up length (mos.)	Practicing CD n	% of N	Totally abstinent n	% of N	Brief description of CD	Treatment setting; modality
Mukasa & Arikawa, 1968, Japan	Yes	330	330	1–72	220	67	40	12	100–200 ml. saké (30 proof)/day	OP; drug (Cyanamide)
Nørvig & Nielsen, 1956, Denmark	No	221	181	33–63	57	32	37	20	"Moderate drinking (with) no overindulgence"	IP; drug (Antabuse) & occupational therapy
Pattison, et al.,[w] 1969, U.S.A.	No No No	12 19 14	12 19 14	36–75 13–35 12–200	2 2 0	17 10 0	10 17 14	83 90 100	"Limited drinking ... maintaining control"	OP; multimodal Halfway House, AA IP; aversion conditioning
Pfeffer & Bergen, 1957, U.S.A.	No	60	60	12	7	12	48[j]	80	Fewer binges & less daily drinking	IP; group & individual psychotherapy
Popham & Schmidt,[x] 1976, Canada	Yes	150	99	12	18	18	9	9	"Average consumption 2.5 oz. alcohol/day"	OP; multimodal

138

Study							Outcome description	Treatment
Quirk, 1968, Canada	No	2	2	24+	2 100	0 0	"Taking occasional social drinks"	IP & OP; behavior therapy
Robson et al., 1965, Canada	No	214	163	10–46	n.d. n.d.	n.d. n.d.	A large number … "managed to control their drinking"	OP; multimodal
Rohan, 1970, U.S.A.	No	178	108	2–30	1–23 1–21	31 31	"May have been improved or practicing controlled drinking"	IP; treatment not specified
Rosengren, 1966, Sweden	No	106	105	1–12+	23 22	4 4	Moderate liquor intake without relapsing	IP & OP; drug (Amtriptylin)
Schuckit & Winokur, 1972, U.S.A.	No	45	45	25–50	11 24	0 0	Drank moderate amounts socially with no associated problems	IP; treatment not specified
Shea, 1954, U.S.A.	No	1	1	60	1 100	0 0	2 bottles beer or 2 glasses wine/day	OP; psychoanalysis
Sobell & Sobell, 1973b, U.S.A.	Yes / No	3 / 3	3 / 3	5+ " / 5+ "	3 100 / 1 33	0 0 / 1 33	6 oz. 86-proof liquor or equivalent in alcoholic content/day	OP; behavior (group) therapy

Table 1. (*continued*)

Investigator(s), year, country	CD[a] Rx[b] (Yes/No)	Subjects in original study	Subjects found for follow-up (N)[c]	Follow-up length (mos.)	Practicing CD n	% of N	Totally abstinent n	% of N	Brief description of CD	Treatment setting; modality
					Subjects identified only as "problem drinkers"					
Kohrs, 1974, U.S.A.	No	20	20	6+–12	16	80	0	0	Moderate drinkers; no alcohol-related arrests	OP; aversion conditioning
Miller, 1975, U.S.A.	Yes	1	1	4	1	100	0	0	2 16 oz. beers/day	IP & OP; behavior therapy

[a] CD: controlled drinking is a summary term used to describe what has also been referred to as "limited drinking," "moderate drinking," "social drinking," or "normal drinking." The specific definitions of such drinking vary from author to author.

[b] Rx: treatment of controlled drinking (CD) prescribed.

[c] N: the sample size found for follow-up refers to subjects for whom complete follow-up data was reported, as well as deceased subjects and subjects incarcerated in jails and/or hospitals. Subjects who refused to be interviewed are not included.

[d] Subjects either met Jellinek's (1960) criteria as *gamma* alcoholics or closely paralleled the chronicity of *gamma* alcoholics.

[e] IP: inpatient treatment setting.

[f] OP: outpatient treatment setting.

[g] n.d.: not determinable from evidence reviewed.

[h] Gibbins, personal communication, 1975.

[i] This is a combined figure for both abstinent subjects and those who consumed only small amounts of alcohol.

[j] Totally abstinent for minimum of 12 months prior to follow-up.

[k] Lundquist, personal communication, 1973.

[l] Of the 3 CD subjects, 2 were followed for 8 years and 1 for 4 years.

[m] E: experimental subjects.

[n] Drinking disposition is for the majority of the 12-month follow-up interval.

[o] C: control subjects.

[p] CD-E = controlled drinker, experimental subjects; CD-C = controlled drinker, control subjects; ND-E = nondrinker, experimental subjects; ND-C = nondrinker, control subjects.

[q] Binge drinking defined as continuous drunk days. See Sobell & Sobell (1975) for individual subject drinking outcome profiles.

[r] 23 subjects had not completed 12 months posttreatment at the time of this report.

[s] Gallen, personal communication, 1974.

[t] Totally abstinent for minimum of 6 months prior to follow-up.

[u] Follow-up was conducted while subjects were in outpatient therapy.

[v] Wives of alcoholics had contacted outpatient family service agency for help with an alcoholic spouse and then were followed up.

[w] Patients in this study were all selected for successful functioning.

[x] Popham & Schmidt, personal communication, 1975.

E. Mansell Pattison, E. B. Headley,
G. C. Gleser, and L. A. Gottschalk

Abstinence and Normal Drinking: An Assessment of Changes in Drinking Patterns in Alcoholics after Treatment

Evaluation of treatment programs for alcoholics has been hampered by the lack of well-defined criteria of what constitutes cure, recovery or successful treatment. One such criterion has been abstinence—the alcoholic is defined as cured or recovered or successfully treated if he no longer drinks any alcoholic beverages at all. But this criterion may be seriously misleading, as Pattison (42, 45) has outlined in previous papers. Abstinence is only one of several variables to be taken into account in defining cure, success or improvement; and the criterion of abstinence can only be adequately evaluated in relation to other variables such as physical health and social, psychological and vocational functioning.

One aspect of the criterion problem has been that use of abstinence by itself has led to the assumption that "addictive alcoholics," by definition, could not develop the capacity to drink normally. In 1962, however, Davies (11) reported on seven alcohol addicts found to be drinking normally after 5 or more years of follow-up. His report was followed by a many-authored discussion of the validity of his findings (12). Yet other clinical reports soon followed corroborating the observation that some addictive alcoholics do change their pattern of drinking from a pathological to a normal one. Subsequently Pattison (42, 45) documented a series of clinical reports which indicate that some addictive alcoholics develop the capacity to drink normally.

The present study was designed to approach some of the questions about abstinence as a research problem, to complement the clinical observational approach. A sample drawn from an alcoholism treatment clinic was chosen for examination with the intent to determine whether (1) any addictive alcoholics might meet predetermined criteria of normal drinking, and (2) if such were found, to determine whether they were as healthy mentally,

Reprinted by permission from *Quarterly Journal of Studies on Alcohol*, 1968, *29*, 610–633. Copyright by Journal of Studies on Alcohol, Inc., New Brunswick, N.J. 08903.

socially, vocationally and physically as those in the sample who were abstinent.

Methods

The study was conducted at the Cincinnati Alcoholism Clinic, an outpatient facility which serves the medically indigent. The majority of referrals came from the psychiatric court clinic, and welfare and social agencies. Individual, conjoint and group psychotherapies are provided along with drugs as indicated.

The sample was drawn from all male patients discharged as improved from July 1962 to June 1963 and who had been seen in the Clinic for 10 or more visits. Patients were chosen who had been defined as "improved" on the assumption that this would maximize the probability of a sample that might contain both abstinent and normal drinkers. The discharge definition of improvement was not at issue in this study because we were interested in the status of the patients at a subsequent time. (The criteria which clinicians use for defining improvement are dealt with in the discussion.) In addition, patients were not included who were discharged from treatment less than a year prior to the follow-up study because several reports indicate that the probability of loss of abstinence is highest during the first 6 months after discharge, and that after the first year adjustment appears fairly well stabilized (17, 19, 60).

Out of 252 discharged patients, 46 men met all of the above criteria but 14 of them were not available for study: 4 were dead, 1 had been in prison, 3 were in distant cities, 2 refused to be interviewed and 4 could not be located. The final sample thus consisted of 32 male alcoholics, seen for 10 or more therapy sessions, and discharged at least 1 year before.

The alcoholism follow-up schedule developed and standardized by Gerard et al. (20, 21) was employed for the scales assessing physical health (PH), interpersonal health (IH) and vocational health (VH). The sum of subscale scores yielded a total score in each of these areas for purposes of statistical analysis. Mental health (MH) was assessed using the total score on the Spitzer Mental Status Schedule (55). A drinking scale score (DSS) was devised to reflect drinking quantity, behavior and sequels (Chart 1). All the scales were ordinal, the scores increasing with pathology. The ranges of the health scales were PH 0–6, IH 0–16, VH 0–12, and MH 0–248. The drinking scale range was 0–15, zero indicating abstinence, 1–6 normal drinking and 7–15 pathological drinking.

Chart 1. *Drinking status scale*

The range is 0–15: abstinent, 0; normal drinking, 1–6; pathological drinking, 7–15.

1. Usual Frequency Pattern of Drinking
   a. Voluntarily, has not taken a drink for at least a year
   b. Voluntarily, has not taken a drink in the past 6 months but has within a year
   c. Drinks only on specific occasions
   d. Drinks about once a week or less
   e. Drinks more than once a week but not daily
   f. Drinks daily

2. Usual Intensity of Drinking
   a. Stops short of intoxication
   b. Stops drinking when intoxicated
   c. Drinks beyond intoxication for a day or more of binge-type drinking

3. Usual Compulsivity of Drinking
   a. Limits drinking at will; no compulsion experienced
   b. Feels a compulsion to continue, although he can still limit his drinking
   c. Has compulsive episodes of drinking to intoxication, although not binges; frequency
   d. Has compulsive episodes of binge drinking lasting more than a day; frequency

4. Social Pattern of Drinking
   a. Drinks only in social situations
   b. Drinks only alone or when socially isolated
   c. Drinks alone and socially

5. CNS Sequels of Drinking
   a. None
   b. One or more blackouts; memory lapses; tremors and shakes; delirium tremens

6. Physical Sequels of Drinking
   a. None
   b. One or more recurrent nausea and vomiting; recurrent diarrhea; neuropathy; cirrhotic symptoms; poor visual-motor coordination

7. Psychosocial Sequels of Drinking
   a. None
   b. One or more episodes of depression; suicidal tendencies or attempts; overt physical aggression when drinking; used narcotics or other drugs in connection with drinking; motor vehicle accidents related to drinking; hospitalized for alcoholism; arrested or jailed in relation to drinking; placed on probation in relation to drinking; sustained physical injury as a result of drinking

8. Summary of Drinking Sequels
   a. No sequels
   b. Sequels in one category
   c. Sequels in two categories
   d. Sequels in three categories

Note. In sections of the chart numbered 1, 2, 3, 4 and 8, the scale weights were 0 for item a, 1 for item b, 2 for item c, 3 for item d, 4 for item e, and 5 for item f.

As it is an ordinal scale, score ranges represent categories, not sequential intervals. (A standard definition of an ordinal scale is given by Hilgard: "An ordinal scale is a scale in which items are placed in order of size but without equal units or a true [absolute] zero." [E. R. Hilgard, *Introduction to Psychology*, 2d ed. New York: Harcourt, Brace, 1957.] No assumptions are made in such a scale about the distance between points, i.e., the distance between points 2 and 3 may be infinitesimal, while the distance between points 3 and 4 may be huge. The advantage of such a scale, one of the most common among psychological scales, is that it allows for the statistical treatment of qualitative data for which linear scales are not representative. For a discussion of the statistical treatment of ordinal scales see: S. S. Stevens, *Handbook of Experimental Psychology*. New York: Wiley, 1951.) Thus a normal drinking score (1–6) could only be achieved by a person whose drinking was less than once a week, without episodes of intoxication, without experiencing compulsivity to continue drinking, without loss of control and without adverse psychological, physical or social sequels. (This definition of normal drinking was made with the rigor of operational criteria having behavioral components. It still does not totally comprehend a crucial component, namely the motivation for and meaning of drinking. Thus, as noted later, three men in our sample met the above operational criteria but on clinical grounds their motivation for drinking had to be considered pathological. We have just concluded a study, to be published soon, in which five patients were found to be drinking "normally" according to the above operational criteria, but were in fact "controlled" drinkers who had not changed their motivation but were merely controlling their impulses. We do not think that the concept of "controlled" drinking is the same as "normal" drinking. This point is elaborated in the discussion. Further, we set no lower limit to our definition of normal drinking, other than that we did not consider "slips" as normal drinking. We are aware that there are numerous discussions of "slips" in the literature, and that alcoholics with "occasional slips" are often rated in follow-up studies as improved. However, the alcoholic who is trying to maintain abstinence and occasionally experiences a slip is very different phenomenologically from the normal drinker, i.e., one who on occasion chooses to use alcohol in an appropriate fashion and can do so without difficulty. The range of DSS scores is as follows: Pretreatment, 7–15, mode 13, mean 13.2 [$n = 32$]. Follow-up, abstinent, 0 [$n = 11$]; normal, 4–6 mode

6, mean 5.5 [$n = 11$]; pathological, 7–11, mode 11, mean 10.1 [$n = 10$].)

Two independent judges (E. M. P. and E. B. H.) reviewed each admission record and rated each patient for health (PH, IH, VH) and alcoholism (DSS) prior to treatment. Reconciliation of scoring was made by joint review in several instances, although the disagreement was only one point apart.

Each ex-patient was interviewed in his own home by a psychiatrist experienced in the field of alcoholism (E. M. P.), without recourse to the initial records. The interview began with the Spitzer Mental Status Schedule administered according to the prescribed routine. (Interviewer reliability was checked against eight standardized protocols. Standard error of measurement = .76, reliability coefficient = .70 [16].) The rest of the interview was unstructured, but specific data were elicited for the PH, IH, VH and DSS scales, as were data on age, education, marital status, the use of other treatment resources, medications, attendance at Alcoholics Anonymous and the motivation for drinking and abstinence. Finally the interviewer and the ex-patient each independently rated the current drinking status on a separate categorical scale (Chart 2). All items on the scales were rated in terms of the characteristics of the past 6 months.

Results

The mean values of our sample describe a 41-year-old man, with 2 years of high school, who had had 40 therapy sessions (SD = 3.2)

Chart 2. Patient self-evaluation and interviewer evaluation of drinking status

---

Self-Evaluation
  a. Abstinent
  b. Does not claim abstinence but has no drinking problems nor trouble related to drinking either within or outside the family
  c. Has a drinking problem but no trouble related to drinking within or outside the family
  d. Has a drinking problem and trouble related to drinking
Interviewer Evaluation
  a. Abstinent
  b. Drinking without difficulty
  c. Has a drinking problem but no trouble related to drinking
  d. Has a drinking problem and trouble related to drinking

---

and was discharged 20 months previously. There were high correlations (.88, $p = .01$) between the patients' self-ratings and interviewer ratings of drinking status: self-ratings and the follow-up DSS (.86), and interviewer ratings and DSS (.90).

The patient, interviewer and follow-up DSS ratings were not correlated with any of the intake health scores or with drinking status then. The patient, interviewer and follow-up DSS ratings, however, had high correlations ($p = .01$) with IH, VH and MH scores, but not with PH. (The correlations were: DSS patient ratings, IH .61, VH .47, MH .53; interviewer ratings, IH .75, VH .60, MH .66; follow-up DSS, IH .64, VH .52, MH .51.) This suggests that current drinking status is not a direct consequence of pretreatment status but is associated with current health status.

Table 1 compares three groups of alcoholics as determined by the follow-up DSS scores: 11 patients were abstinent (DSS score = 0), 11 were scored as nonpathological normal drinkers (DSS score = 1–6) and 10 were scored as pathological drinkers (DSS score = 7–15). The normal-drinking group at follow-up had had a statistically significant lower drinking score at intake (DSS = 10.8) than did the pathological drinkers. This difference, however, is an artifact of ordinal scale construction. All three groups were drinking to a severe pathological degree at that time and presented comparable clinical symptoms, so that scores at the top end of the scale do not reflect a clinical difference in drinking symptomatology. The majority of abstainers and normal drinkers reported that the crucial change in their drinking behavior occurred during therapy. This represents their recall. Review of the records of those who recalled a change before therapy indicates that they were still engaged in severe pathological drinking at the time of intake.

The number of therapy hours did not vary significantly between the three groups, nor did the correlations of therapy hours to individual health and drinking scores reach levels of significance.

Table 2 compares the intake and follow-up scores of the three follow-up DSS groups on the health scales. The three intake scores, PH, VH and IH, were derived from the clinic record, and the follow-up scores from the home interview. The follow-up scores were treated statistically to account for differences in intake values so that the follow-up score represents a comparable degree of change. The PH, VH and IH intake scores of the three groups do not differ significantly at the time of intake. All three demonstrated improvement on these health scales. Nor did the three groups differ on the PH scale at follow-up. However, on the VH and IH

Table 1. Drinking scores at intake and at follow-up, time at which current drinking pattern began and number of therapy hours of 11 abstainers and 11 normal and 10 pathological drinkers

Group	Drinking Scores		When Current Drinking Pattern Began			Therapy Hours
	Intake	Follow-Up	Before Therapy	During Therapy	After Therapy	
Abstainers	12.9	0	1	7	3	35
Normal drinkers	10.8	1-6	2	9	0	46
Pathological drinkers	13.2	7-15	8	1	1	40
	$F=5.05, p=.05$		df=2, $\chi^2=13.33, p=.01$			

Table 2. Health scores at intake and follow-up of 11 abstainers and 11 normal and 10 pathological drinkers

Group	Physical Health		Vocational Health		Interpersonal Health		Mental Health
	Intake	Follow-up	Intake	Follow-up	Intake	Follow-up	Follow-up
Abstainers	6.36	2.50	4.0	0.06	7.36	1.85	9.7
Normal drinkers	5.55	2.84	2.91	0.42	8.73	3.79	16.9
Pathological drinkers	6.90	3.83	4.10	1.96	10.00	7.00	32.3
	$F=0.43$, n.s.		$F=9.04, p=.01$		$F=8.56, p=.01$		$F=7.12, p=.01$

scales the abstainers and normal drinkers improved relatively more than the pathological drinkers. The abstainers and normal drinkers show the same relative improvement. The three DSS groups all differ significantly from each other on the mental health scale. In summary, the data in Table 2 indicate that the patient sample was homogeneous in "life health" at the time of intake. At follow-up there had been some improvement in all three DSS groups, but the abstainers and normal drinkers had improved approximately to the same extent and both had improved more than the pathological drinkers. At follow-up the three groups did not differ in physical health (PH), but in vocational health (VH) and interpersonal health (IH) the abstainers and normal drinkers now had virtually identical low scores (healthy), and on these scales and the mental health scale they scored significantly lower than did the pathological drinkers.

Table 3 compares four groups of alcoholics, as defined by the patients' self-rating of drinking status, in terms of the four follow-up health scale scores. The pattern is similar to that in Table 2 where the DSS scale was used to define drinking status. The abstainers and normal drinkers have low (healthy) scores on three scales (VH, IH, MH); the two groups of pathological drinkers have significantly higher (unhealthy) scores. The four groups do not differ significantly in physical health (PH).

Table 3 also compares 4 groups of alcoholics, as defined by the interviewer ratings of drinking status, in terms of the 4 follow-up health scale scores. The pattern is again similar: the abstainers and normal drinkers have virtually the same low scores on VH, IH and MH, while the pathological drinkers have significantly higher scores. The only difference was that the interviewer rated only 8 patients as normal drinkers, instead of 11 as in the other 2 ratings. This affected the average scores only on the MH scale, the normal drinkers as defined by the interviewer having an almost identical average with the abstainers. It should be noted, however, that the interview data used in the MH scale and other follow-up ratings were all available to the interviewer when he made his ratings on drinking status.

Comparison of the DSS ratings of patients and interviewer revealed that those who had high pathological drinking scores tended to underestimate their own drinking; whereas the interviewer rated three drinkers as pathological although their drinking scores fell within the normal range, these men reported a better adjustment than appeared clinically justified.

Variables not found to be significant included marital status, age,

Table 3. Health scores by patient and interviewer evaluations at follow-up

Evaluation	n	Physical Health	Vocational Health	Interpersonal Health	Mental Health
Patient Evaluation					
Abstainers	11	2.5	0.1	i.4	9.7
Drinking without difficulty	11	2.5	0.6	4.1	17.8
Drinking problem alone	3	6.3	2.0	7.3	36.0
Drinking problem and psychosocial problems	7	3.3	1.6	7.1	29.9
		$F=1.01$, n.s.	$F=3.20$, $p=.05$	$F=6.26$, $p=.01$	$F=4.34$, $p=.05$
Interviewer Evaluation					
Abstainers	11	2.5	0.1	1.4	9.7
Drinking without difficulty	8	0.9	0.0	2.3	9.1
Drinking problem alone	3	6.3	2.0	7.3	36.0
Drinking problem and psychosocial problems	10	4.3	1.8	7.7	32.3
		$F=2.61$, n.s.	$F=7.55$, $p=.01$	$F=14.55$, $p=.01$	$F=9.89$, $p=.01$

race, current employment status, type of vocation, living arrangements, expressed motivation for drinking or abstinence, attitude toward treatment at the time of intake, the use of other treatment resources, the use of disulfiram or other medications and attendance at Alcoholics Anonymous. Four of the pathological drinkers sporadically used disulfiram. Three of the abstainers attended A.A. regularly; one of them also took disulfiram regularly. None of the normal drinkers had attempted to remain abstinent.

Discussion

Methodology

Our sample is a very specific one, not necessarily generalizable to the whole population of alcoholics. This presents an important problem in alcoholism research since there appear to be subpopulations of alcoholism syndromes. For example, Seiden (50) noted that

A.A. may represent a highly selected population; this has been documented by the comparison of successful "takes" to A.A. and to treatment clinics by Trice and Belasco (57) and by Canter (7). Further, Gerard and Saenger (19) have demonstrated marked differences in clinical outcome among alcoholics treated in different clinics. Interestingly, they found that in some clinics no patients became normal drinkers after treatment while in others a consistent percentage did.

The adequacy of self-reporting by the alcoholic ex-patient can only be clinically estimated. However, Guze et al. (22) reported that alcoholics gave more accurate data on their drinking than did their own families. We received excellent cooperation in every obtained interview and we were considerably aided by holding the interviews in the patients' homes. (The research team had had no treatment contact with the sample.) Although we tried to interview every alcoholic alone, the wife or other family members often wanted to make comments about the patient's improvement or lack of it. Some of the men expressed strong negative feelings about the Clinic and their treatment despite the fact that they were clinically much improved. Others feared that we had heard that they were drinking and that we had come to check up on them. Most of the latter were men who were now normal drinkers, leading us to suspect that follow-up studies which rely on impersonal mail contacts or a return interview at the treatment facility obtain a strongly biased sample of their results. Particularly, they may not contact ex-patients who are negativistic about the treatment program or who have returned to some type of drinking. This may explain the paucity of reported clinical experiences with alcoholics who have developed normal drinking patterns. Other factors may include clinical and cultural biases which Pattison (42–45) has discussed elsewhere.

Another issue concerns the definition of "alcoholic" used in this study. In the construction of the drinking scale (DSS) the clinical characteristics of Jellinek's (26) *gamma*-type of alcoholic were used. Thus, if a subject scored in the pathological end of the scale, he would meet the criteria for that type of addictive alcoholism. Conversely, the criteria of normal drinking could only be met if none of the criteria for *gamma* alcoholism and none of the criteria in the Keller (28) and World Health Organization (62) definitions of alcoholism was present. Our definition of normal drinking has been given in the Methods section.

In addition, we reviewed the intake clinical descriptions of each patient who was rated as a normal drinker. At intake these 11 men had reported an inability to control their drinking, with compulsive episodes of drinking occurring several times a week; 8 reported binge-type drinking of several days' duration, including blackout episodes and other medical complications. The other 3 reported uncontrolled drinking which inevitably led to marked intoxication accompanied by violent aggressive episodes, although these did not lead to extensive binges. The latter 3 had been arrested repeatedly for drunkenness. All of them had experienced disruption of home life and none had been able to function vocationally at the time of intake. Thus their clinical picture corresponds to the Jellinek, Keller and WHO formulations of addictive alcoholism.

A final issue concerns the adequacy of the follow-up interval after discharge. A minimum of 1 year was the criterion for inclusion. It turned out, however, that 18 months was the minimum time since discharge of any subject and the mean was 20 months. The mean time since discharge of the normal drinkers was 22 months. As noted in the Methods section, several studies have suggested that 1 year is a minimal follow-up interval, with the probability that by the time an 18-month interval has elapsed there will be little further significant change in the patterns of drinking. In a recent large-scale study Gerard and Saenger (21) cite further evidence from their data to support this conclusion. They believe that after 18 months "the time interval does not influence that statistical patterning of the patients' status at follow-up." This does not mean that there may not be changes in individual cases but rather that the pattern of groups of cases is unlikely to be affected.

To further extend the study because of the limitations of the time interval, one member of the team made an attempt to locate each of the normal drinkers 2 years after the original interviews. (The original follow-up interviews were done in the fall of 1964 and the second interviews in the fall of 1966). Although the additional data were not analyzed statistically, the follow-up interview schedules were completed for comparison with the original ones.

In the resurvey we were able to locate and interview 5 of the 11 normal drinkers. In each instance the subject and his family indicated a normal pattern of drinking. Likewise, the scores on the interview schedule were similar to those on the original schedules of these subjects. This evidence is corollary, rather than substantive, but it does lend credence to the validity of the original evaluations.

Clinical implications

Abstinence has been a traditional criterion in the conduct of treatment and in the assessment of success. In the present study we set
out to test one aspect of that tradition, namely, whether abstinence
is an adequate criterion of successful treatment.

Clinical reports have questioned the criterion; the reports have
been discussed by Pattison (42, 45). In 1962 Davies (11) reported
that 7 of 93 alcohol addicts had returned to normal drinking after a
period of abstinence. Fox and Smith (17) compared first- and
second-year follow-up and reported that 24% of their total group
had improved in the second year and were drinking to some extent.
Moore and Ramseur (36) found that 5 of 14 most improved patients were well-controlled social drinkers, whereas 6 of 15 abstinent patients were only slightly improved. Nørvig and Nielsen
(40) reported that 74% of 57 patients who sometimes drank were
doing well. Pfeffer and Berger (46) found that 7 of 60 patients had
changed their pattern of drinking to normal drinking and that 3 of
the 7 were free of psychological symptoms. Selzer and Holloway
(51) reported that 16% of 83 patients had returned to successful
social drinking. Lemere (32) reported that 3% of problem drinkers
returned to normal drinking, and Shea (52) described a
psychoanalytic case of an addictive alcoholic who resumed normal
drinking. Lambert (31) found 25 of 100 alcoholic patients who
claimed the ability to drink in moderation, although he thought that
only 9 of them were truly able to do so. Robson, Paulus and Clarke
(47) stated after a large follow-up study that "a surprisingly large
number seemed to have managed to control their drinking . . .
while not completely abstaining." In a group of 62 untreated alcoholics Kendell (29) found 3 men and 1 woman who had resumed
normal social drinking for 3 to 8 years. From a visit to Japan,
Lemere (33) reported a treatment plan by Dr. H. Mukasa who gives
alcoholics a small daily dose of calcium cyanamide which allows the
patient to take 1 or 2 drinks although he will become ill if he drinks
more; thus these alcoholics are treated as continued moderate
drinkers. Hacquard et al. (23) reported that 18 of 100 patients
returned to moderated drinking after disulfiram therapy. Bailey
and Stewart (1) reinterviewed 12 subjects they had classified as
alcoholics who reported reduced moderated drinking. They concluded that 6 of the 12 were normal drinkers; this was 7% of their
original sample of 91 cases of alcoholism. Cain (6) reported that 4 of
7 successfully treated alcoholics and over half of 29 other cases had

developed the ability to drink in normal fashion. In two careful methodological studies of alcoholic patients Gerard and Saenger reported a substantial number who had become "controlled drinkers." In their first study (20) this was 41 out of 300 patients, and in their second study (21), 35 out of 797 patients. Further, they note that in their second study, which included 8 different treatment agencies, the proportion of controlled drinkers "turned out" by the 8 clinics varied widely from one-third of all patients in one clinic to only an occasional patient in another clinic. They suggest that the clinical outcome of "controlled drinkers" may reflect the treatment philosophy of different clinics. And finally, a highly relevant report was published in the French literature back in 1952. De Morsier and Feldmann (37) prospectively followed 500 patients in whom they made a distinction between social cures and abstinence cures. Of the 500, 76 (15%) were classified as social cures, while 155 (31%) were abstinence cures. They commented that the social cures were noticeably superior in their adjustment, did not want to present themselves socially as abstainers and so learned to avoid the psychological bad effects of alcohol, and now drank only in a family and social context.

Since these reports were essentially clinical follow-up studies they were not designed specifically to test the relationship between drinking and healthful adaptation. This sequence of clinical reports, however, does support the hypothesis that some treated alcoholics do change to normal drinking with good life adaptation,

Our findings are in accord with other reports. Sikes, Faibish and Valles (53) found no relation between follow-up drinking behavior and improvement in MMPI profile, and concluded that there was relative independence of personality changes and changes in drinking behavior after treatment. Negrete, MacPherson and Dancey (39) found that the social adaptation of alcoholics improved with abstinence, but that personality variables and personality problems showed little change. Clancy, Vornbrock and Vanderhoff (9) found that improvement in drinking behavior and improvement in other variables of personality and adaptation were separable variables not closely related. In the reports of Bailey and Stewart (1) and Kendell (29) the subjects who changed to normal drinking had apparently received no treatment, although there had been significant changes in their social relationships. Chein et al. (8, p. 234) have noted that some narcotic addicts and some alcoholics spontaneously revert from their addictive life, which illustrates the fact that the pharmacology of drug use is determined by social and cultural factors.

They conclude, "Such behavior is not random but shows a remarkable precision of aim and aptness to life situations and relationships." The same concept is found in the observations on "maturing out of narcotic addiction" (61) and in the concept of "social addicts" by Brotman, Meyer and Freedman (5).

The importance of these observations on normal drinkers may not bear so much on clinical treatment policies as it does on our theories of addiction.

The commonly held concept of addiction is based on the development of physiological tolerance to a drug, withdrawal symptoms and physiological and psychological dependence on the drug. This concept of addiction is a pharmacological one, giving rise to the assumption that once addicted the addict is saddled with irreversible pharmacological and physiological changes. Hence an addict must maintain abstinence. All this is based on a particular concept of addiction that constricts the definition incorrectly. For example, Freedman and Wilson (18) note that no experimentally verifiable concept has emerged clarifying the mechanism of tolerance or relating it to physical dependence or addiction. They conclude, "The most significant characteristic of addiction is the qualification of harm to oneself or to others produced by the regular or habitual use of any substance. The production of physical dependence, with its concomitants of tolerance and withdrawal symptoms, is often, but not necessarily, present."

Narcotic addicts vary in their pattern and degree of addiction. Some use narcotics in an addictive fashion for a period but later use the same narcotic in a nonaddictive fashion. The same observations have been made in alcoholics. All addictive alcoholics do not always drink in an uncontrolled fashion. Indeed at times they may drink in a fashion that superficially might be considered normal.

Recently the World Health Organization Expert Committee on Addiction-Producing Drugs (13) has issued a position statement which makes some very helpful clarifications. They observe that the term "addiction" has become an unsusable omnibus word and they propose that the term "drug dependence" be substituted, with specification of the specific nature of the dependency. Further, they distinguish between psychic dependence and physical dependence:

Drug dependence is a state of psychic or physical dependence, or both, on a drug, arising in a person following administration of that drug on a periodic or continuous basis. . . . Individuals may become dependent upon a wide variety of chemical substances that produce central nervous system effects ranging from stimulation to depression. All of these drugs have one effect in common: They are capable of creating, in certain individuals, a particular state of mind that is termed "psychic dependence." In this situation, there is a feeling of satisfaction and a psychic drive that require periodic or continuous administration of the drug to produce pleasure or to avoid discomfort. Indeed, this mental state is the most powerful of all of the factors involved in chronic intoxication with psychotropic drugs, and with certain drugs it may be the only factor involved, even in the case of the most intense craving and perpetuation of compulsive abuse. ... Psychic dependence can and does develop ... without any evidence of physical dependence, and therefore, without an abstinence syndrome developing after drug withdrawal. Physical dependence, too, can be induced without notable psychic dependence; indeed, physical dependence is an inevitable result of the pharmacological action of some drugs with sufficient amount and time of administration. Psychic dependence, while also related to pharmacological action, is more particularly a manifestation of the individual's reaction to the effects of a specific drug and varies with the individual as well as with the drug.

We may conclude that the observed phenomenon of addictive behavior is not identical with or dependent upon phenomena of pharmacological or physiological dependence, tolerance and withdrawal symptoms. Rather, addiction is a psychosocial behavior syndrome, involving physiological factors but not as the primary determinants of addiction. Indeed, addiction appears better conceptualized as behavior based on the use of drugs as the central integrative symbol around which the person organizes his life. (This is a very cursory statement referring to the "symbolic-interactional" theory of behavior. For extended discussion of the application of this theory to alcoholism behavior see: Cutter [10], Fallding [14], Heilizer [24], Jackson & Connor [25], Jones [27], Kinsey [30], Mulford & Miller [38] and Pattison [45].) If this be so, we may assume that a person who has changed his pattern of living could use (without harm) a drug to which he had previously been "addicted."

The concept of psychosocial equilibrium as a determinant of behavior has been described by Berne (2) as an interpersonal game. Despite some misgivings about the philosophical underpinnings of "gamesmanship," the emphasis on the multiperson network that characterizes alcoholism is worth noting. Alcoholism cannot be adequately conceptualized as solely a phenomenon of the individual alcoholic. Thus Berne is helpful when he observes that a number of people in the interpersonal network of the alcoholic play into the perpetuation of alcoholic behavior. Berne then concludes: "the criterion of a true cure is that the former alcoholic should be able to drink socially without putting himself into jeopardy. . . . The psychological cure of an alcoholic also lies in getting him to stop playing the game altogether. . . . The usual total abstinence cure will not satisfy the game analyst" (p. 77). Berne goes on to point out that the same alcoholism game can continue as "dry alcoholism."

Cain (6) has noted that the "recovered" alcoholic does not drink primarily because he does not want to drink, whereas the "arrested" alcoholic still has the desire to drink but knows that he cannot and tries to avoid doing so. Cain states, "The recovered alcoholic, by definition, does not care whether he can drink normally, and he definitely does not want to become intoxicated again"; and he points out further that "most alcoholics do not want to return to normal drinking; rather by normal drinking they (the alcoholics) mean the intoxication they were once able to control—which is nothing like our definition of normal drinking. . . . The arrested alcoholic never really loses his desire to become intoxicated with alcohol. He learns to control his desire (he learns to live with his disease) but he never learns to transcend his desire." Cain suggests that such arrested alcoholics could never return to normal drinking because their pattern of life still revolves around alcohol even though they do not drink. He concludes, "The fact that normal drinking has been achieved is a dramatic indication of one's successful effort to attain social, intellectual, and religious maturity."

If this be the case, then the addictive alcoholic does not "return to normal drinking" but rather learns for the first time a new attitude toward alcohol. His pattern and motivation for living have been reintegrated around healthy symbols, and alcohol is no longer a central symbol of his life. The alcoholic who would like to "return" to normal drinking cannot; the alcoholic who no longer cares whether he ever drinks or not may no longer abuse alcohol.

The change from addictive drinking to normal drinking may then reflect a shift in psychosocial equilibrium. Until recently, mental health workers have been wont to conceptualize psychopathology in terms of individual pathology. But recent work in family therapy has provided strong evidence that social gestalt, whether it be nuclear family or other "significant others," may be determinative in both the development and perpetuation of psychopathological behavior (4, 49). Studies on the psychosocial characteristics of alcoholics also support the hypothesis that patterns of drinking are less a reflection of individual pathology than of psychosocial gestalt (34, 35, 54). Mendelson and Mello (35) conclude that their data "strongly support the notion that the perpetuation of drinking behavior is related to a variety of complex social-environmental factors rather than alcohol dosage per se."

If we may conclude that addictive drinking behavior represents a particular gestalt—a particular combination of cultural norms, character structure and social-familial context—then a person may behave in a pattern of addictive drinking only so long as that particular combination obtains. It may be that if any one of those factors is changed, or the relationships between the factors are changed, i.e., the psychosocial gestalt for addictive drinking is changed to a psychosocial gestalt for abstinence or normal drinking, then the alcoholic living and behaving in the altered gestalt (Kurt Lewin's "field") can change from his addictive drinking to a different pattern of drinking.

This hypothesis is illustrated when alcoholism develops from family disequilibrium in response to crisis, which Pattison (43) has outlined in detail elsewhere. Briefly, if a family is subjected to stress, it may no longer be able to use its old adaptive maneuvers and must seek new patterns to achieve equilibrium. If the new patterns are unsuccessful, the family members may exhibit social dysfunction, such as alcoholism in one of its members. Restoration or reformation of a stable family equilibrium, however, may replace the dysfunctional adaptive manuevers which supported the alcoholism. What has been changed then is not the basic personality structure but rather the psychosocial equilibrium involving and including the personality of the alcoholic. This may explain why seemingly minor intervention may effect a dramatic change in member behavior: the dysfunctional equilibrium is broken up and the family and person are afforded an opportunity to weld a more stable adaptive equilibrium in which alcohol is no longer a necessary functional component.

Returning now to the question of abstinence as a criterion of assessment of successful treatment, numerous clinical reports indicate that abstinence may be misleading.

Bolman (3) has observed that abstinence may not necessarily indicate an improvement in overall health or total life adjustment. In 1962, Gerard, Saenger and Wile (20) reported a study of "successfully" treated abstinent alcoholics: 43% were overtly disturbed, 24% inconspicuously inadequate, 12% A.A. "addicts" and only 10% independently making a successful adjustment. Moore and Ramseur (36) reported that 6 of 15 abstinent patients were only slightly improved. Wilby and Jones (60) found that overall improvement declined in a group of abstinent patients assessed at 18- and 24-month intervals. Pfeffer and Berger (46) observed that 30% of their abstinent patients still had significant psychological symptoms and difficulties, and Flaherty, McGuire and Gatski (15) and Wellman (59) have described the symptoms of depression and anxiety that may occur many months after remaining abstinent. Among others, Wallerstein (58) has noted that enforced sobriety can be disastrous to personality integration, particularly when alcohol is the mechanism by which people with borderline characters or psychotic personality structures maintain ego integration, diminish hallucinations or allay overwhelming anxiety.

From our own research sample we observed that several of our abstinent patients were not "healthy." This is not to say that their abstinence necessarily caused a deterioration in their life, since they had made poor adjustments previously. But the outcomes in some of our patients indicate that abstinence and healthy life adjustment are two different dimensions. The following are illustrative cases.

Case 1. This 56-year-old white salesman had been a compulsive drinker since age 18. He had asthma and stuttered. Although deeply attached to his mother, he was very angry with her for her overconscientious religious scruples. He was continually plagued by guilt feelings and still had difficulty expressing his anger. He was treated in the Clinic for about 5 years with both individual and group psychotherapy. Although he had been abstinent for 2 years, he continually feared a relapse. He believed the Clinic was of tremendous value in helping him to understand himself. However, he believed that his very active participation in A.A. was the main thing that kept him sober. His wife was a leader in the local Al-Anon movement. Although he enjoyed his sobriety, he was plagued by many neurotic traits which interfered with effective social functioning and his wife sheltered him. He remained very dependent and could neither assert himself nor handle rage without developing psychosomatic symptoms.

Case 2. This 39-year-old white technician had always felt inadequate and yet angry that superiors did not give him adequate recognition. He had started drinking 5 years previously over difficulties on the job. As the drinking increased he almost had a nervous breakdown, but instead drank himself to oblivion. He was on the verge of losing his job and was in legal difficulties when he came to the Clinic. He tested the therapist several times by coming to the Clinic drunk. When he found that he was still accepted, he stopped drinking and had been abstinent for 2 years. At follow-up 19 months after discharge he was working steadily and his family adjustment was good. But he had many anxiety attacks and psychosomatic symptoms. He frequently felt depressed and asked the interviewer directly for help. He had intense feelings of inadequacy and although he was performing well on the job, he had continuing difficulties with his supervisors.

Case 3. This 38-year-old white government employee had been drinking at an increasing rate over the past 5 years until he drank continually on the job. He was on suspension when he came to the Clinic. He was seen for 12 interviews during which he stopped drinking and he remained abstinent for 19 months. He felt that the Clinic sessions were of some help, but that the most important factor was that he wanted to stop drinking. On interview 14 months after discharge he was highly defensive and used overt paranoid defenses. He emphatically denied any difficulties in any sector of his life, yet his defensive needs led to a furtive type of existence, continually covering the tracks of his past difficulties and maintaining a rigid self-concealment which left little room for any social interaction.

We conclude that the two groups of clinical reports and the research data reported here indicate that abstinence per se is only one of several variables which are relevant in assessing the outcome of treatment of alcoholics. The presence of drinking subsequent to therapy may not imply that the patients are less well adjusted or less successfully treated than patients who are abstinent. Nor does the fact that a patient has successfully achieved abstinence necessarily indicate that he has also achieved a healthy life adaptation.

The present research was not designed to evaluate the efficacy of treatment, but rather to clarify the relationship between the parameters of drinking and life adjustment as outcome criteria in the treatment of alcoholics. In spite of the methodological limitations of this study, the evidence corroborates other published reports on the change to normal drinking among addictive alcoholics. The characteristics of these alcoholics remain to be more clearly determined. Studies on social competence have demonstrated that essential alcoholics possess less of this trait than reactive alcoholics, and that the alcoholics endowed with higher social competence may have significantly different treatment outcomes (48, 54, 56). The importance of social variables in the lives of alcoholics who change to normal drinking has been commented upon in a number of the studies cited and in our data.

We have no reliable estimate of the incidence of change to normal drinking among treated or untreated alcoholics, nor under which conditions of treatment such a change may occur. Most random samples thus far report an incidence of 4 to 10%. The variable of sample selection may play a crucial role here. For example, in our study, one-third of our highly selected sample became normal drinkers, but if we had defined our sample as the original 252 men seen at least once in our clinic, we would have an incidence of only 4%. Thus the findings do not necessarily call for a basic change in clinical treatment philosophy. The data from the Gerard and Saenger study (21), however, do indicate that the type of change in drinking pattern produced by a clinic may be significantly determined by the philosophy of the clinic.

The most relevant implications of our data and of the studies cited may be for our conception of the nature of addiction. As suggested above, addiction has been frequently conceptualized with primary emphasis on the qualities of physiological dependence, whereas the emphasis should perhaps focus on the qualities of psychic dependence. Alcoholism may be best described as a psychosocial behavior syndrome which is dependent on a variety of social and cultural variables. Changes in patterns of drinking behavior may result not so much from changes in personality variables as from changes in social and cultural variables.

Bibliography

1. Bailey, M. B., and Stewart, J. Normal drinking by persons reporting previous problem drinking. *Quart J. Stud. Alc.,* 1967, *28,* 305–315.
2. Berne, E. *Games people play; the psychology of human relationships.* New York: Grove Press, 1964.
3. Bolman, W. M. Abstinence versus permissiveness in the psychotherapy of alcoholism; a pilot study and review of some relevant literature. *A.M.A. Arch. Gen. Psychiat.,* 12, 456–463, 1965.
4. Boszormenyi-Nagy, I. A theory of relationships; experience and transaction. In: Boszormenyi-Nagy, I., and Frame, J. L. (eds.)*Intensive family therapy, theoretical and practical aspects.* New York: Harper & Row, 1965.
5. Brotman, R., Meyer, A. S., and Freedman, A. F. An approach to treating narcotic addicts based on a community mental health diagnosis. *Compr. Psychiat.,* 1965, *6,* 104–118.
6. Cain, A. C. *The cured alcoholic.* New York: John Day, 1964.
7. Canter, F. Personality factors related to participation in treatment of hospitalized male alcoholics. *J. Clin. Psychol.,* 1966, *22,* 114–116.

8. Chein, I., Gerard, D. L., Lee, R. S., and Rosenfeld, E. *The road to H: narcotics, delinquency, and social policy.* New York: Basic Books, 1964.
9. Clancy, J., Vornbrock, R., and Vanderhoof, E. Treatment of alcoholics: a follow-up study. *Dis. Nerv. Syst.,* 1965, *26,* 555–561.
10. Cutter, H. S. G. Conflict models, games, and drinking patterns. *J. Psychol.,* 1964, *58,* 361–367.
11. Davies, D. L. Normal drinking in recovered alcohol addicts. *Quart J. Stud. Alc.,* 1962, *23,* 94–104.
12. Davies, D. L. Normal drinking in recovered alcohol addicts. (Comment by various correspondents.) *Quart. J. Stud. Alc.,* 1963, *24,* 109–121, 321–332.
13. Eddy, N. B., Halbach, H., Isbell, H., and Seevers, M. H. Drug dependence: its significance and characteristics. *Bull. World Hlth. Org.,* 1965, *32,* 721–733.
14. Fallding, H. The source and burden of civilization illustrated in the use of alcohol. *Quart. J. Stud. Alc.,* 1964, *25,* 714–724.
15. Flaherty, J. A., McGuire, H. T., and Catski, R. L. The psychodynamics of the "dry drunk." *Amer. J. Psychiat.,* 1955, *112,* 460–464.
16. Fleiss, J. L., Spitzer, R. L., and Burdock, E. I. Estimating accuracy of judgment using recorded interviews. *A.M.A. Arch. Gen. Psychiat.,* 1965, *12,* 562–567.
17. Fox, V., and Smith, M. A. Evaluation of a chemopsychotherapeutic program for the rehabilitation of alcoholics: observations over a two-year period. *Quart. J. Stud. Alc.,* 1959, *20,* 767–780.
18. Freedman, A. M., and Wilson, E. A. Childhood and adolescent addictive disorders. *Pediatrics,* Springfield, 1964, *34,* 283–292.
19. Gerard, D. L., and Saenger, G. Interval between intake and follow-up as a factor in the evaluation of patients with a drinking problem. *Quart. J. Stud. Alc.,* 1959, *20,* 620–630.
20. Gerard, D. L., Saenger, G., and Wile, R. The abstinent alcoholic. *A.M.A. Arch. Gen. Psychiat.,* 1962, *6,* 83–95.
21. Gerard, D. L., and Saenger, G. *Outpatient treatment of alcoholics: a study of outcome and determinants.* Toronto: University of Toronto Press, 1966.
22. Guze, S. B., Tuason, V. B., Stewart, M. A., and Picken, B. The drinking history: a comparison of reports by subjects and their relatives. *Quart. J. Stud. Alc.,* 1963, *24,* 249–260.
23. Hacquard, M., Beaudoin, M., Derby, G., and Berger, H. Contribution à l'étude des résultats éloignés des cures de désintoxication éthylique. *Rev. Hyg. Méd. Soc.,* 1960, *8,* 686–709.
24. Heilizer, F. Conflict models, alcohol and drinking patterns. *J. Psychol.,* 1964, *57,* 457–473.
25. Jackson, J. K., and Connor, R. Attitudes of the parents of alcoholics, moderate drinkers and nondrinkers toward drinking. *Quart. J. Stud. Alc.,* 1953, *14,* 596–613.

26. Jellinek, E. M. *The disease concept of alcoholism.* Highland Park, N.J.: Hillhouse, 1960.
27. Jones, H. *Alcoholic addiction: a psycho-social approach to abnormal drinking.* London: Tavistock, 1963.
28. Keller, M. Definition of alcoholism. *Quart. J. Stud. Alc.,* 1960, *21,* 125–134.
29. Kendell, R. E. Normal drinking by former alcohol addicts. *Quart. J. Stud. Alc.,* 1965, *26,* 247–257.
30. Kinsey, B. A. *The female alcoholic: a social psychological study.* Springfield, Ill.: Thomas, 1966.
31. Lambert, B. E. V. "Social" drinking by the alcohol-damaged. *Svenska Läkartidn.,* 1964, *61,* 315–318.
32. Lemere, F. What happens to alcoholics. *Amer. J. Psychiat.,* 1953, *109,* 674–676.
33. Lemere, F. Comment on "Normal drinking in recovered alcohol addicts." *Quart. J. Stud. Alc.,* 1963, *24,* 727–728.
34. McGuire, M. T., Stein, S., and Mendelson, J. H. Comparative psychosocial studies of alcoholic and nonalcoholic subjects undergoing experimentally induced ethanol intoxication. *Psychosom. Med.,* 1966, *28,* 13–26.
35. Mendelson, J. H., and Mello, N. K. Experimental analysis of drinking behavior of chronic alcoholics. *Ann. N.Y. Acad. Sci.,* 1966, *133,* 828–845.
36. Moore, R. A., and Ramseur, F. Effects of psychotherapy in an openward hospital on patients with alcoholism. *Quart. J. Stud. Alc.,* 1960, *21,* 233–252.
37. Morsier, G. de, and Feldmann, H. Le traitement de l'alcoolisme per l'apomorphine; étude de 500 cas. *Schweiz. Arch. Neurol. Psychiat.,* 1952, *70,* 434–440.
38. Mulford, H. A., and Miller, D. E. An index of alcoholic drinking behavior related to the meanings of alcohol. *J. Hlth. Hum. Behav.,* 1961, *2,* 26–31.
39. Negrete, J. C., MacPherson, A. S., and Dancey, T. E. A comparative study on the emotional and social problems of active and arrested alcoholics. *Laval méd.,* 1966, *27,* 162–167.
40. Norvig, J., and Nielsen, B. A follow-up study of 221 alcohol addicts in Denmark, *Quart. J. Stud. Alc.,* 1956, *17,* 633–642.
41. Ornstein, P. H., and Wilitman, R. M. On the metapharmacology of psychotropic drugs. *Compr. Psychiat.,* 1965, *6,* 166–175.
42. Pattison, E. M. A critique of alcoholism treatment concepts: with special reference to abstinence. *Quart. J. Stud. Alc.,* 1966, *27,* 49–71.
43. Pattison, E. M. Treatment of alcoholic families with nurse home visits. *Fam. Process,* Baltimore, 1965, *4* (No. 1), 75–94.
44. Pattison, E. M. The differential diagnosis of alcoholism. *Postgrad. Med.,* 1967, *41,* A–127–132.

45. Pattison, E. M. Abstinence criteria: a critique of abstinence criteria in the treatment of alcoholism. *Int. J. Soc. Psychiat.*, 1968, *14*, 260–267.

46. Pfeffer, A. Z., and Berger, S. A follow-up study of treated alcoholics. *Quart. J. Stud. Alc.*, 1957, *18*, 624–648.

47. Robson, R. A. H., Paulus, I., and Clarke, G. G. An evaluation of the effect of a clinic treatment program on the rehabilitation of alcoholic patients. *Quart. J. Stud. Alc.*, 1965, *26*, 264–278.

48. Rudie, R. R., and McGaughran, L. S. Differences in developmental experience, defensiveness, and personality organization between two classes of problem drinkers. *J. Abnorm. Soc. Psychol.*, 1961, *62*, 659–665.

49. Seeley, J. R. *The Americanization of the unconscious.* New York: International Science, 1967.

50. Seiden, R. H. The use of Alcoholics Anonymous members in research on alcoholism. *Quart. J. Stud. Alc.*, 1960, *21*, 506–509.

51. Selzer, M. L., and Holloway, W. H. A follow-up of alcoholics committed to a state hospital. *Quart. J. Stud. Alc.*, 1957, *18*, 98–120.

52. Shea, J. E. Psychoanalytic therapy and alcoholism. *Quart. J. Stud. Alc.*, 1954, *15*, 595–605.

53. Sikes, M. P., Faibish, G., and Valles, J. Evaluation of an intensive alcoholic treatment program. *Amer. Psychologist,* 1965, *20*, 574–580.

54. Singer, E., Blane, H. T., and Kasschau, R. Alcoholism and social isolation. *J. Abnorm. Soc. Psychol.*, 1964, *69*, 681–685.

55. Spitzer, R. L., Fleiss, J. L., Bundock, E. I., and Hardesty, A. S. The mental status schedule: rationale, reliability and validity. *Compr. Psychiat.*, 1964, *5*, 384–395.

56. Sugerman, A. A., Reilly, D., and Albahary, R. S. Social competence and the essential-reactive distinction in alcoholism. *A.M.A. Arch. Gen. Psychiat.*, 1965, *12*, 552–556.

57. Trice, H. M., and Belasco, J. A. A selective approach to the improvement of treatment for alcoholics. Paper read at the annual meeting of the National Council on Alcoholism, New York, 13 April 1966.

58. Wallerstein, R. S., et al. *Hospital treatment of alcoholism: a comparative, experimental study.* New York: Basic Books, 1957.

59. Wellman, M. Fatigue during the second six months of abstinence. *Canad. Med. Ass. J.*, 1955, *72*, 338–342.

60. Wilby, W. E., and Jones, R. W. Assessing patient response following treatment. *Quart. J. Stud. Alc.*, 1962, *23*, 325.

61. Winick, C. Maturing out of narcotics addiction. *Bull. Narcotics,* 1962, *14*, 1–7.

62. World Health Organization. Expert Committee on Mental Health, Alcoholism Subcommittee. Second Report. *World Hlth. Org. Techn. Rep. Ser.*, No. 48, Aug. 1952.

7. The Progressive Development of Alcohol Problems

Jellinek's Data Base

The idea that alcohol problems characteristically have a slow, progressive development most likely has its roots in the observed outcome of highly conspicuous "skid-row" alcoholics and individuals who suffer from organic brain syndromes due to heavy consumption of alcohol. There can be little doubt that prior to reaching a state of personal devastation these individuals probably experienced a variety of less serious alcohol-related problems.

The formal concept of an inexorable progression of alcohol problems is based on Jellinek's work. His phases of alcohol addiction have their origins both in his interpretation of responses to an open-ended questionnaire developed by Alcoholics Anonymous and in his later clinical experiences (1946, 1952, 1960). He postulated a sequence of 43 specific symptoms of alcoholism, with three symptoms—blackouts, loss of control, and prolonged intoxication (binges)—serving as phase markers to identify the onset of each major phase—the prodromal phase, the crucial phase, and the chronic phase, respectively. Jellinek cautioned that: "Not all symptoms . . . occur necessarily in all alcohol addicts, nor do they occur in every addict in the same sequence," even though he viewed the sequence as characteristic "of the great majority of alcohol addicts and to represent what may be called the average trend" (1952, p. 676). As so often has been the case, his caveats have been repeatedly overlooked by those using his disease concept. Nevertheless, it is Jellinek's work which has most singularly influenced the concept of a progression of symptoms of alcoholism.

The data base for Jellinek's model of progression suffers from multiple methodological problems. First, the individuals represented in his data were a highly selected group. Approximately 1,600 questionnaires were distributed only to AA members via their in-house newsletter, the *Grapevine.* Of those questionnaires returned, only 98 (6.13%) were sufficiently completed for statistical analysis. Thus, the sample consisted of a small group of self-identified recovered alcoholics, AA members who were willing to complete the questionnaire. Seiden (1960) and others have

165

pointed out that AA members tend to be atypical of the general population of persons who have alcohol problems.

Second, the technique used involved retrospective reconstruction and self-report. It is likely that the ideology of AA greatly influenced the nature of reconstructed symptom development. This would have provided the data with an unduly limited amount of variance.

Third, the questions were open-ended, and the data were coded by Jellinek in a post hoc manner. When he presented the results, he apologized for these problems but asserted that some data were better than none. Other serious problems with Jellinek's methodology have been discussed at length by Clark and Cahalan (1973), Orford and Hawker (1974), Park (1973), and Trice and Wahl (1958).

Retrospective Studies

One way of empirically testing Jellinek's phaseology is to collect similar retrospective data for different populations. Park (1962, 1973) interviewed or administered a supervised questionnaire to 686 Finnish alcohol addicts and tested three hypotheses derived from Jellinek's phaseology: (1) that Jellinek's phase-marking symptoms of blackouts, loss of control, and binge drinking should occur in sequential order; (2) that a phase marker should occur before all other items within that phase; and (3) that all of the experiences associated with a given phase should follow the events of an earlier phase. A substantial incidence of order reversals were found for all three hypotheses, forcing Park to conclude: "If there be three phases in the development of alcohol addiction such as Jellinek postulated, a sizable proportion of the experiences do not occur in the phases to which they are assigned, at least in the present study sample. That is, the presumed manifestations of alcoholism do not necessarily develop in the order given by Jellinek" (1973, p. 483).

Park then developed a new ordering based on the Finnish data, arranged so that order reversals only occurred 1% of the time. Comparing this empirically derived ordering of symptoms with Jellinek's phaseology, he concluded that there was "little agreement between Jellinek's assignment of the symptoms and the empirically determined allocation of the same symptoms among the three phases" (1973, p. 485). It should be recognized that Park's empirically determined ordering of symptoms is appropriately considered as a hypothesized sequence rather than as a proven ordering. As with Jellinek's data analysis, Park's new ordering was based on a post hoc statistical procedure which may have some empirical validity but which is also apt to capitalize on chance orderings in the data. A formal empirical test of this ordering can only be performed by gathering similar data for yet another sample and evaluating how well it follows Park's hypothesized sequence.

In another retrospective study, Orford and Hawker (1974) gathered structured interview information from 59 male alcoholic Halfway House residents. Their interview items were in large part limited to questions concerning drinking behavior and adverse physical consequences of drinking. They found that there were a small number of clusters of items which seemed to be ordered in a fairly definite sequence. These clusters were "firstly, the onset of psychological dependence; secondly, tremor, morning drinking and amnesia; and, thirdly, aspects of alcoholic psychosis" (p. 281). Rephrased, this developmental sequence would include awareness of drinking problems, followed by physical dependence, then followed by consequences of physical dependence. They concluded that: "There *is* a characteristic ordering of new events or symptoms in the development of alcoholism but we would argue strongly that the extensions of this notion to include a wide range of events encompassing psychophysiological, social and treatment events is not feasible and has served only to obscure a number of more basic and relatively circumscribed processes which are related but require separate study" (p. 287). While this sequence seems likely to be supported in future studies, one must question whether such a limited progression has much utility, other than technically specifying deterioration due to alcohol consumption as a disease process. Finally, it must be constantly borne in mind that the studies by Jellinek, Park, Orford and Hawker, and others have been limited in their application to persons who have become physically dependent on alcohol. Currently, there is no empirical basis for assuming that any progression necessarily applies in a predictive fashion to the drinking careers of individuals who have not yet evinced physical dependence on alcohol.

Longitudinal Studies

Cahalan and his colleagues (Cahalan, Cissin, & Crossley, 1969; Cahalan, 1970; Cahalan & Room, 1974) have conducted a series of national and regional epidemiological surveys of drinking practices which have longitudinally followed individuals with varying degrees of drinking problems. Of major importance, their subjects were members of the general population and not selected from among patients in alcoholism treatment programs. Thus, to some extent, the reported drinking histories of these individuals should be more representative of individuals with alcohol problems in the general population than are data derived from the reports of self-identified alcoholics.

In one such study, reprinted here, Clark and Cahalan (1973) discussed changes in problem drinking among a representative sample of 615 males over a four-year period. Rather than a unilinear progression of alcohol problems, studies of the general population indicate a considerable turnover in problem drinkers, with a sizable proportion of persons moving into and out of the problem-drinker category. They consistently found a substantial frequency of problem remissions, over a span of only four years. They argue that the empirical data encourage a concentration on particular drinking problems rather than on an underlying unitary and always progressive phenomenon located within the individual, i.e., "alcoholism."

Chandler, Hensman, and Edwards (1971) suggest a similar strategy after comparing the questionnaire results of life history, socioeconomic, and personality factors for several groups of alcoholics. They concluded that: "It may be useful to call alcoholism a disease,' but the notion is simplistic in the extreme if it ignores the probably vital influence of social circumstances and personality in patterning the consequences of abnormal drinking" (p. 362).

Evidence of nonprogressivity of alcohol problems has similarly been reported in other longitudinal studies. Fillmore (1974) gathered information about problem drinking and the quantity and frequency of drinking from a stratified sample of 109 men and 97 women ($n = 206$) who had 20 years earlier been studied as college students (Strauss & Bacon, 1953). As expected, it was found that early problem drinking bore a significant relationship to the existence of problem drinking 20 years later. However, Fillmore also reported a high incidence of remission of problems. Of those who had been classified as problem drinkers in the initial study, 68% of the males and 67% of the females had become nonproblem drinkers 20 years later. It was further determined that 10% of the abstainers and nonproblem drinkers in the initial study had become problem drinkers by the time of the second interview. Finally, Goodwin, Davis, and Robins (1975) reported a study of the drinking patterns and problems of 451 United States Army enlisted men following their return from Vietnam. They concluded that: "Apparently many young men drink heavily and have problems with drinking during a period in their life, only later to reduce the drinking and hence the problem" (p. 233).

Implications

The accumulating evidence suggests that a major reevaluation is needed concerning the idea that alcohol problems by nature become progressively more severe. To be sure, drinking problems and other maladaptive behaviors can easily lead to increasingly adverse consequences. However, traditional concepts of alcoholism have incorporated descriptions of progressions which specify a sequence of maladies which are purported to befall individuals experiencing drinking problems, unless they reform, recognize their standing on the continuum and the horrors which lie ahead, and refrain from drinking for the rest of their lives. The major disadvantage of such an orientation is that prophecies delivered with eloquence by persons "who should know" are likely to be fulfilled, although in some cases this fulfillment may reflect a congruence with personal expectations more than with a progressive disorder. That is, they may become self-fulfilling prophecies. The data are clear: While alcohol problems may sometimes develop as a series of increasingly serious consequences, this is not always the case. A preoccupation with the supposedly progressive nature of the disorder, when substantial demonstrations to the contrary exist, may hinder or preclude research investigations into the situational, personal, and periodic determinants of alcohol problems. In accordance with the evidence, clinical practitioners should be prepared to deal with "persons having alcohol problems." Clinical interventions are apt to be more efficacious if they address the problems which exist rather than consider all persons with serious alcohol problems as traveling down a one-way road to oblivion. As of now, the clinical and empirical data suggest that it is a person who has a problem, and not vice versa.

Walter B. Clark and Don Cahalan

Changes in Problem Drinking Over a Four-Year Span

Introduction

In this paper we will discuss some of the implications of the disease conception of alcoholism in the light of findings from a longitudinal study. We will suggest that the common conception of alcoholism as a disease fails to cover a large part of the domain of alcohol problems and that a more useful model would place greater emphasis on the development and correlates of *particular problems* related to drinking, rather than assuming that alcoholism as an underlying and unitary progressive disease is the source of most alcohol problems.

In terms of popular imagery, the conception of alcoholism was born on skid row and in the drunk tank. There, miserable circumstances and the excessive use of alcohol were interpreted as causally related, and the evidence for the involuntariness of the drinking was more or less obvious in the bad circumstances these men endured. The prognosis was downward mobility, declining health and increasing problems due to drinking.

The classic exemplar of this model is of course Jellinek's *gamma* species of alcoholism, which was regarded as " . . . apparently (but not with certainty) the predominating species of alcoholism in the United States and Canada as well as in other Anglo-Saxon countries" (Jellinek, 1960, p. 38).

Alcoholism and Loss of Control

In terms of the social consequences of the Jellinek formulation, the most important implication was that alcoholics could not themselves control their drinking. But "loss of control" is particularly difficult to subject to empirical test. At least two factors seem to be implied: first, a will or volition which would conform to drinking customs if left to its own devices; and second, an overriding craving for alcohol which nullifies the power of the will.

This subjective "craving" for alcohol is presumed to arise at the same time as the onset of withdrawal symptoms. But there is a problem in specifying what the term refers to in one's subjective experience. Not that it is difficult to detect impulses to do things that one should not do, but here the subjective impulse is to be taken as evidence of a tissue need that was not there prior to experiencing the withdrawal symptoms and which is essentially different from simple appetite. In the absence of a means of external validation, how can one know whether one craves a thing or merely desires it? Is it, for example, craving to give in to the impulse to smoke a cigarette years after having quit smoking, but appetite when one gives in to the impulse to have a second serving of cake while on a diet? The subjective feelings may be indistinguishable, but it is on the differentiation of the two that the disease model of alcoholism has been based.

Jellinek's (1952) publication concerning phases of alcohol addiction provided a possible way around this problem. His description of a defined syndrome which unfolded in a prescribed way seemed to be evidence of the irrelevance of the individual drinker's volition.

This orientation to research on alcohol problems is still ubiquitous in the literature. In general it has emphasized the commonalities peculiar to alcoholics in order both to establish the integrity of the concept of alcoholism (and by extension, loss of control) and to seek etiological or therapeutic generalizations.

Researchers have asked, for example, not only if the characteristics of alcoholics formed a sequential syndrome as Jellinek contended, but whether the characteristics scaled (Jackson, 1957; Mulford & Miller, 1960), clustered together (Trice & Wahl, 1958), would correlate highly and factor analyze into an alcoholic factor (Park, 1967) or whether this would be the case if the alcoholics were first divided into a number of differing groups (Horn & Wanberg, 1969).

The same research agenda has also given rise to a legion of papers in which the characteristics of some sample of alcoholics are simply described and summarized. The sparse utility of this kind of research in the search for an adequate theoretical picture of alcohol problems has been parodied in Keller's "Law" that on any given characteristic, alcoholics are different from nonalcoholics (Keller, 1972). The impetus for clinically based typologies is, however, the same as that evidenced in Jellinek's papers on the phases of alcoholism.

The finding of etiologically and therapeutically significant commonalities peculiar to alcoholics has been beset by a number of serious methodological weaknesses. In the first place, this research has been conducted primarily among clinical samples of analogous criterion groups which present a wide variety of inherent sampling difficulties (Miller et al., 1970). In the second place, researchers have run the risk that the responses of the patient were influenced by the ideology of the staff—Jellinek (1960), for example, cautioned that Alcoholics Anonymous has created alcoholism in its own image. Thirdly, the commonalities that have turned up in these studies often suggested long-term consequences of drinking, or of the label of alcoholism, rather than causal factors.

Besides the methodological weaknesses, such studies frequently fail to confirm the typicality of phases of alcoholism. Peter Park (1973), for example, reported that Jellinek's ordering of symptoms could not be confirmed in his sample, and in fact a strong ordering could be achieved " . . . only for a small number of characteristic experiences, and then only by subdividing the alcoholics into more homogeneous groups" (p. 486).

Alcoholism and General Population Studies

Epidemiological studies of the distribution and correlates of drinking practices and drinking problems in the general population have provided a new avenue for the empirical evaluation of the alcoholism paradigm of drinking problems.

Some methodological difficulties were side-stepped in general population studies (Cahalan, 1970). Then, too, longitudinal studies had the promise of reducing the contribution of retrospective contruction and ideology to an understanding of the unfolding of an alcoholism syndrome. As in most survey research, we included in the questionnaire a wide variety of items drawn from several perspectives on alcoholism. However, the general features of the alcoholism paradigm are not easily tested.

Consider the problems associated with identifying loss of control in respondents. In Jellinek's (1960) terms, loss of control referred to the inability to drink in moderation once the first drink had been taken, and it was the central characteristic of *gamma* alcoholism. But one cannot infer loss of control from the amount a respondent drinks. Heavy drinking is often the product of conforming to the requirements of a heavy drinking subculture or social position. Then, too, the situations of some genuine loss-of-control drinkers might be such that their drinking is, after all, not particularly heavy even though it is damaging to the drinker or to others. And, of course, a long period of heavy drinking is thought to be a necessary precursor to loss of control. Finally, the use of compulsive or undisciplined drinking to indicate loss of control was discouraged by Jellinek's warning that: "Paradoxically enough, after the establishment of loss of control, deliberate, undisciplined drinking greatly diminishes in the *gamma* alcoholic as he knows or is afraid that the loss of control might bring about serious consequences in situations where that behavior would be most dangerous" (p. 42).

Perhaps because of the difficulties of linking the amount of drinking directly to loss of control, some definitions (Keller, 1962) of alcoholism have taken the existence of problems associated with drinking as indications of loss of control. While this measurement of many drinking problems quite naturally adjusts for the standards of the drinker's associates and circumstances, it is seriously flawed. It uses drinking problems as the indicator for the loss of control which was formerly seen as a cause and effect relationship. Thus loss of control is bound together with drinking problems in language rather than by empirical demonstration that loss of control and drinking problems are causally related.

An alternative—the one used here—is to infer loss of control by asking whether "unplanned" episodes of drinking and drunkenness have occurred. Whether, for instance, the respondent had difficulty in his attempts to quit drinking or cut down on the amount of drinking in the past 12 months is one such item. A second asks whether the respondent got drunk at inappropriate places or times, while another item concerns whether or not the respondent *almost always* drank to unconsciousness on those occasions during the past year when he had anything to drink. (Details on the construction and scoring of this and other scales are available from the authors on request.)

The inductive approach in our surveys has afforded the opportunity to question respondents on several important aspects relating to the development of drinking problems. Earlier work has already pointed to some difficulties in the alcoholism paradigm. Clark (1966) showed that the overlap of different problems was not as high as might be expected on the basis of the classical model of alcoholism. Cahalan (1970) reported that the intercorrelations among drinking problems were relatively low and the external correlates of drinking problems were sometimes different from problem to problem. Cahalan and Room (1974) have also shown that alcohol problems do not often follow the progression of worsening problems that Jellinek's model suggests is typical.

The present paper briefly reports the fit of our latest data to the alcoholism paradigm and the proportion of drinking problems that are comfortably accounted for by that paradigm.

Sample and Data Collection

Data were collected by means of personal interviews on the first wave, and by personal or mail-form interviews on the second wave. The two waves of interviews were conducted approximately four years apart. The strict probability sample was designed to be representative of white males aged 21 through 59 years living in San Francisco at the time of the first interview. Transients, institutionalized men and those living on college campuses or military bases were excluded. Males in this age range were selected because this segment of the population has by far the highest rates of drinking problems (Cahalan, 1970). Others, e.g., women and nonwhites, were excluded because these groups are sufficiently different to require separate consideration.

The Polk City Directory was used as a sampling base, supplemented and checked by area-probability sampling methods. Approximately 80% ($n = 786$) of the sample were interviewed on the first wave of intereviews, which were conducted in late 1967. (The analysis of this 1967 cross-sectional data is reported elsewhere, Cahalan & Room, 1974.)

Reinterviews with the original respondents took place approximately four years later during the early months of 1972. The completion rate for this second wave of interviews was approximately 80% of those interviewed on the first wave (or 615 of 786). Thus this analysis is based on 615 respondents who were interviewed on two occasions approximately four years apart. This is sufficient time, it turns out, for drinking problems to emerge or to subside.

Bias of nonresponse was minimized in the first wave of interviews by making every effort to achieve a high completion rate. Both past and present experience with surveys of this sort indicates that there is no reason to think that those lost to the survey include an especially high proportion of problem drinkers. Of the 786 respondents interviewed at Time 1, about 20% ($n = 171$) were *not* reinterviewed again at Time 2. These losses include respondents who died, refused cooperation, could not be found—losses from all causes. For these, of course, we have the Time 1 data, and thus the means of seeing whether these losses are directly related to alcohol problems. In general they are not. For instance, a comparison of Time 1 rates of drinking problems to the same Time 1 rates *minus* the contribution of cases lost to the second wave of interviews shows little of significance. In general, those who were not reinterviewed were more apt to be hard to find than they were apt to be problem drinkers. More of the unmarried, for instance, and more of those with manual occupations were in this group of respondents.

Of course it is possible that those who were not reinterviewed at Time 2 were those who had developed drinking problems in the time between interviews, but there is no reason to think that this is the case.

As noted above, all Time 1 interviews were obtained in personal form; Time 2 data came largely from mail questionnaires. Those who failed to mail back the questionnaire were contacted in person and an effort was made to persuade them to cooperate. Finally, some were interviewed in person if all else had failed. The same mail-form questionnaire was used for personal interviews as for those contacted by mail. This raises a question of comparability between the instruments used. In our experience, as in that of others, this is not a serious problem. Comparison of cases that were personally interviewed to those who returned mail questionnaires does show some differences, but again these are not generally related either to the use of alcohol or to problems due to drinking. A working paper (Shanks, 1975), *Biases in Longitudinal Surveys,* contains an analysis of these and related points. Similarly, J. Hochstim's (1967) excellent study which compares data obtained by personal interviews, telephone interviews and mail questionnaires found few differences; the substantive findings from the three methods were virtually interchangeable.

Alcoholism and Drinking Problems

Four tables are presented here that touch on several empirical implications of the alcoholism paradigm of drinking problems. Table 1 concerns the cross-tabulation of drinking problems and reported loss of control. In Table 2 is presented the cross-sectional correlations among drinking problems. In Table 3 longitudinal data

Table 1. Drinking problems and loss of control scales

A. Current drinking problems[a] by current loss of control score

At least one point on the loss of control scale [b]	At least one minimum-severity current drinking problem (1972)		
	Yes	No	Total
Yes (1+)	50	19	69
No (0)	110	436	546
	160	455	615

B. Current drinking problems by current loss of control score

At least one point on the loss of control scale	At least one relatively severe current drinking problem (1972)		
	Yes	No	Total
Yes (1+)	44	25	69
No (0)	83	463	546
	127	488	615

Current drinking problems occurring during the 12 months prior to the interview included financial problems (spending too much money on drinks), accidents or injuries related to drinking, problems with police (being stopped and talked to or sent home, or arrested, in connection with one's drinking), problems with spouse (respondent's drinking made wife unhappy, or resulted in her leaving or threatening to leave the respondent), and job problems (fired or laid off or failed to be hired or advanced because of drinking, or quit a job because of drinking). The columns in Table 1A are presented in terms of minimum-severity drinking problems; Table 1B is presented in terms of having at least one problem in relatively severe form.

[b] Current loss of control was measured by items indicating that respondent had difficulty during the last 12 months in cutting down or stopping drinking, sometimes got drunk at inappropriate times or places and almost always drank to unconsciousness when drinking. For present purposes the scale was dichotomized, one or more positive answers to the above being counted as an indication of loss of control. (Details of these scorings are available from the authors upon request.)

are used to show the persistence of drinking problems over time. Finally, in Table 4 the longitudinal data are used to examine the relative chronicity and remission in drinking problems.

The alcoholism paradigm implies a close association between problems and loss of control. Table 1 shows the association between these two. Respondents have been split into those who reported at least one *current problem* associated with drinking and split again according to whether or not they gave any indication of current loss of control at the same time. At least three observations can be made here. Loss of control predicts drinking problems rather well; among 69 respondents who reported current loss of control, 50 (or 73%) also reported drinking problems. Among respondents who did not report loss of control, only 20% reported a drinking problem.

If now we ask how well the drinking problem scale predicts loss of control, the result is contrary. One hundred sixty respondents reported at least one problem associated with drinking. Among this group, only 31% also reported any indication of loss of control. If by following the alcoholism paradigm we were to concentrate upon that group that had *both* drinking problems and some indication of loss of control (50 persons), then the other 129 respondents would be conceptually marginal to the scheme—although they would account for almost 70% of the observed problems and about 27% of the reported instances of loss of control.

We should point out that this table might be interpreted differently by different analysts. For instance, the research tradition of sociological survey research leans toward the face-value interpretation of responses; some clinical traditions include strong presumptions of defense mechanisms and denial in response to questions. The respondents who did not report loss of control, but who did report problems (as well as respondents who reported neither problems nor lost control) may have been gilding the truth. But, here denial is to some extent controlled in Table 1 since those respondents *have* reported drinking problems; thus they give indirect evidence of having eschewed at least one opportunity to deny or to distort. Yet most of them still do not report loss of control.

It might also be objected that the drinking problems of a general population sample are too ephemeral to be thought of as effects of loss of control. In Table 1B, therefore, the cutting point for drinking problems has been raised somewhat to a more severe level, while the cutting point for loss of control is left low. This has the result of examining the loss-of-control variable in the most favorable light. Even so, the results of this table are substantially the same as those in Table 1A.

Association among Problems – Cross-sectional Data

Table 2 presents zero order correlations among the various drinking problems at Time 1 and Time 2 (above and below the diagonal, respectively). The computations are based *only* on those respon-

Table 2. Correlations among problem scales at Time 1 (1967) and Time 2 (1972)

Problems or potential problems (dichotomized at indicated level):	1	2	3	4	5	6	7	8	9	10	11
1. Binge drinking (any)		0.24	0.19	0.18	0.19	0.30	0.27	0.11	0.17	0.20	0.44
2. Symptomatic drinking (3+)	0.53		0.20	0.19	0.18	0.09	0.15	0.15	0.12	0.08	0.22
3. Psychological dependence (4+)	0.14	0.23		0.20	0.07	0.06	0.03	0.12	0.11	0.06	0.08
4. Loss of control (2+)	0.31	0.33	0.29		0.07	0.06	0.12	0.10	0.05	0.11	0.07
5. Police problems (any)	0.19	0.29	0.06	0.24		0.10	0.11	0.04	0.09	0.09	0.09
6. Job problems (any)	0.34	0.13	0.17	0.17	0.21		0.12	0.07	0.05	0.11	0.21
7. Problems with relatives or friends (3+)	0.14	0.20	0.24	0.17	0.17	0.07		0.28	0.15	0.12	0.29
8. Accidents (any)	0.19	0.29	0.16	0.29	0.34	0.21	0.31		0.12	0.01	0.13
9. Financial problems (any)	0.22	0.21	0.01	0.24	0.17	0.19	0.26	0.20		0.01	0.18
10. Problems with wife (3+)	0.03	0.06	0.02	0.09	0.06	0.16	0.19	0.06	0.00		0.10
11. High current intake of alcohol (2+)	0.41	0.42	0.10	0.27	0.26	0.25	0.24	0.19	0.18	0.11	

Above the diagonal are the correlations of the problem scales at Time 1. The Time 2 figures are below. Instances of no problem at either Time 1 or Time 2 are excluded here; accordingly, this table is based on 228 interviews.

dents who had one or more problems at either Time 1 or Time 2, since we are interested in the process of adding drinking problems, keeping them or losing them over the 4-year span. The large number of cases with no problems at either time, if included, would artifactually change the correlations among the drinking problem scales and obscure the relationships we are interested in. What we are concerned with here is the likelihood that those who have one problem will also have others. A glance at Table 2 indicates that low- to moderate-sized coefficients are the rule. (The interpretation and analysis of these intercorrelations is obviously of importance in its own right. See Cahalan, 1970; Cahalan & Room, 1974.) There is, in short, a tendency for problems to occur together, but that tendency is never sufficient to explain more than a small fraction of the variance in any of the problem scales. It is clear from this that all drinking problems are not alike, and therefore one may not use different drinking problems as more or less equivalent indicators of an underlying alcoholism.

Associations among Problem Drinking Scales Over Time

Table 3 presents the correlations among the various problem scales over the 4-year span of the study. This was a true two-stage longitudinal study of the relationship of the same problem scales applied four years apart, with each measurement referring to problems occurring during the year prior to the interview. Again, only those cases that had one or more problems at either Time 1 or Time 2 were included. There is a weak tendency for problem scales to be more highly correlated with the corresponding scale at Time 2 than with other scales, but even here there are exceptions. Note also that those problems such as binge drinking which are regarded as being rather advanced signs of troubles due to drinking to have comparatively high associations with other problems over time when compared to problems such as accidents due to drinking or financial or job problems, which did not correlate at all highly with other problems and did not tend to repeat themselves in both measurements.

In general it may be said that the various drinking problems studied are significantly correlated over time and cross-sectionally, but that, again, the strengths of those correlations do not warrant the assumptions of a single underlying entity such as it suggested by the disease concept of alcoholism.

Table 3. Correlations among problem scales at Time 1

Time 1 (1967)

Problems or potential problems (dichotomized at indicated level):	x̄	Time 2 (1972)										
		1	2	3	4	5	6	7	8	9	10	11
1. Binge drinking (any)	0.20	0.43	0.32	0.08	0.08	0.25	0.14	0.30	0.08	0.12	0.13	0.32
2. Symptomatic drinking (3+)	0.14	0.22	0.30	0.06	0.04	0.14	0.05	0.14	0.18	0.03	0.13	0.30
3. Psychological dependence (4+)	0.09	0.18	0.21	0.14	0.09	0.02	0.02	0.03	0.15	0.05	0.03	0.08
4. Loss of control (2+)	0.12	0.14	0.36	0.11	0.13	0.05	0.02	0.04	0.15	0.02	0.17	0.10
5. Police problems (any)	0.08	0.04	0.19	0.03	0.10	0.14	0.10	0.04	0.10	0.06	0.05	0.01
6. Job problems (any)	0.12	0.17	0.23	0.10	0.15	0.06	0.05	0.16	0.01	0.04	0.10	0.21
7. Problems with relatives or friends (3+)	0.10	0.08	0.10	0.04	0.17	0.04	0.01	0.25	0.17	0.10	0.07	0.08
8. Accidents (any)	0.08	0.04	0.19	0.11	0.10	0.14	0.06	0.04	0.10	0.01	0.05	0.05
9. Financial problems (any)	0.07	0.03	0.13	0.03	0.17	0.06	0.00	0.13	0.03	0.05	0.05	0.06
10. Problems with wife (3+)	0.07	0.03	0.04	0.06	0.14	0.05	0.10	0.02	0.02	0.06	0.19	0.10
11. High current intake of alcohol (2+)	0.14	0.15	0.22	0.15	0.12	0.04	0.05	0.16	0.04	0.13	0.13	0.37

Instances of no problem at either Time 1 or Time 2 are excluded here; accordingly, this table is based on 228 interviews.
x̄: The mean correlation for each problem scale at Time 1 (positive or negative sign omitted).

Problem Remission and Continuity Over Time

Table 4 presents more data bearing on the progressiveness of alcoholism, or rather, the typicality of that progress into more, and more severe, problems. A collateral implication of the alcoholism paradigm is the expectation that alcoholics will accumulate increasing numbers of problems over time, and the "early symptoms" of progressive alcoholism are not thought to be replaced by the later ones, but rather the later ones are added to those that came before. (For a detailed critique of this view, see Robin Room, "Assumptions and Implications of Disease Concepts of Alcoholism," a paper presented to the 29th International Congress on Alcoholism and Drug Dependence, Sydney, Australia, Feb. 2–14, 1970. "Accretionality" as an assumption of studies in the "*Grapevine* tradition" is discussed.) The result is supposed to be a snowballing of drinking problems which come to include more and more areas of the individual's life. In the first two columns of Table 4 are data bearing on that aspect of the disease model of alcoholism. For each individual problem at Time 1, the proportion of individuals who still have that identical problem at Time 2 is found to be quite low on the average. Of course, the extremely small n's in some scales indicate that the values need to be interpreted with caution. However, the figures obtained by Cahalan and Room (1974), which are based on a national sample and which were obtained by using the same research methods, are very similar indeed. In general it may be safe to conclude that even over as short a span as four years, our expectations should be that particular problems will tend not to persist in severe form.

However, the last three columns of Table 4 make it clear that drinkers with drinking problems at Time 1 are not apt to be completely free of problems at Time 2. In general, many of those with problems when first interviewed tend to be still at risk of problems due to drinking at Time 2. Moreover, substantial numbers of those same individuals report having gone on binges in the 12 months prior to the second interview. Binge drinking (here defined as staying high or drunk for more than one day at a time) is reported by only 3% of the total study population; the corresponding figures for those with problems at Time 1 are enormously higher. Finally, the proportion of respondents with at least one problem of any of those inquired into at Time 2 is also very substantial.

It may be fair to conclude from these data that continuity of

Table 4. Drinking problems at Time 1 (1967) by selected outcomes at Time 2 (1972)

Time 1 problems or potential problems	(n)	(1) Remission of problem by Time 2	(2) Comparable figures from national study[a]	(3) Heavy intake at Time 2	(4) Binge drinking at Time 2	(5) One or more drinking problems at Time 2[b]
		%	%	%	%	%
Binge drinking	(29)	59	66	48	41	55
Symptomatic drinking	(21)	51	63	62	38	76
Psychological dependence	(42)	50	50	48	14	48
Loss of control	(18)	78	46	67	17	78
Police problems	(13)	77	72	23	38	61
Job problems	(24)	96	58	37	21	50
Problems with relatives or friends	(23)	61	53	56	35	70
Accidents	(10)	80	—	50	20	50
Financial problems	(98)	63	58	42	13	50
Problems with wife	(25)	52	45	52	20	64

[a] National figures, presented for comparison, are from Cahalan & Room, op. cit., 1974, Table 7, in which the numerical bases for problems ranged from 48 to 171.

[b] Problems here include only the following current (Time 2) problems (at levels of severity specified in Table 2 above): police problems, job problems, spouse problems, other interpersonal problems, accidents, and financial problems.

particular problems over time is low but that continued involvement in *some* alcohol problems is the rule rather than the exception for those with drinking problems at Time 1. Too much can be made of even this, however; substantial proportions of drinkers with problems at Time 1 report a complete absence of problems at Time 2 (see Table 4, column 5). None of this fits well with the disease model of alcoholism insofar as that model implies keeping "early symptoms" and early problems and adding others as time passes. The progressiveness of the model of alcoholism is thus open to question. The apparent rapidity with which particular problems arise and subside suggests the possibility that situational factors may have a strong bearing on the problem drinker's behavior. That is, the drinker with problems is not, typically, welded into a milieu where his behavior remains constant or gets more serious as do the reactions of others to that behavior.

Summary

To sum up, the dominant conceptualization of alcohol problems in the U.S. tends to picture alcohol problems as springing from particular persons who have a progressive disease, which is thought to be a unitary phenomenon, pushing alcoholics in a drunkard's progress toward ruin. There is a growing body of information to suggest that a more useful model of alcohol problems would place greater emphasis on the development and correlates of *particular* problems related to drinking, rather than assuming an underlying disease process.

Drinking problems do not typically appear to be unilinear, with progression from less severe to more severe problems and from single problems to many problems. Rather we have observed great flux and turnover in alcohol problems, both in terms of numbers of problems and types of problems, over the short span of four years. Many drinkers with numerous and severe problems are found to have gotten out of trouble at a later time. These findings are in keeping with recent findings that it is among young males rather than older men that the highest rates of almost all types of drinking problems are to be found.

It should be pointed out that these distinctions between the concept of alcoholism as a disease and the concept of problems-related-to-drinking are not mere quibbles. If an alcoholism-as-disease model is emphasized, public policy tends to be oriented around the *individual* as the locus of the disease; and alcoholism research and treatment accordingly take on a clinical and pathological emphasis. If instead the "problems" approach is emphasized, there are fewer conceptual barriers to viewing the drinking problems as associated with disjunctions in the interactions between the individual and his environment—with considerably different implications for research and remedial measures.

Perhaps one of the least-mentioned side effects of a disease model is the search for a heroic solution, a breakthrough, a final solution. If it may be suggested, however, that alcohol problems are not one, but many, then rather different and diverse conceptualizations are invited.

Taken together these (and earlier) findings suggest that the alcoholism paradigm does not fit well the life experiences of the general population. By extension it seems wrong to assume that an alcoholism paradigm should structure either research directions toward a comprehensive understanding of alcohol problems or a national policy toward them. In a sense, the territory of alcohol problems has been viewed through bifocals; up close are the clinical cases which pose the immediate management and care problems of detoxification centers, clinics and so forth. Farther out are the dimly seen diffuse alcohol problems of the larger community and its nonclinical citizens. To project too readily the paradigm of the former on the latter is faulty, we have argued, and misses much that is important, and conceptualizes it ineptly.

Several consequences flow from the conceptual reform we have suggested. At the least it suggests that we have become more critical of the elements of what has been called "disease ideology" (Taber et al., 1969) in the organization of alcohol problems research. Perhaps the problems of nosology, pathology, etiology and therapy—which define the major orientations of research conducted from within a disease ideology—are only a part of a comprehensive picture.

References

Cahalan, D. *Problem drinkers.* San Francisco: Jossey-Bass, 1970.

Cahalan, D., and Room, R. *Problem drinking among American men.* New Brunswick; N.J.: Rutgers Center of Alcohol Studies, 1974.

Clark, W. Operational definitions of drinking problems and associated prevalence rates. *Quarterly Journal of Studies on Alcohol,* 1966, 27, 648–668.

Hochstim, J. R. A critical comparison of three strategies of collecting data. *Journal of the American Statistical Association,* 1967, *62,* 976–989.

Horn, J. L., and Wanberg, K. W. Symptom patterns related to excessive use of alcohol. *Quarterly Journal of Studies on Alcohol,* 1969, *30,* 35–58.

Jackson, J. K. The definition and measurement of alcoholism: H-technique scales of preoccupation with alcohol and psychological involvement. *Quarterly Journal of Studies on Alcohol,* 1957, *18,* 240–262.

Jellinek, E. M. Phases of alcohol addiction. *Quarterly Journal of Studies on Alcohol,* 1952, *13,* 673–684.

Jellinek, E. M. *The disease concept of alcoholism.* New Brunswick, N.J.: Hillhouse Press, 1960.

Keller, M. The definition of alcoholism and the estimation of its prevalence. In: David J. Pittman and Charles R. Snyder (eds.), *Society, culture, and drinking patterns.* New York: Wiley, 1962.

Keller, M. The oddities of alcoholics. *Quarterly Journal of Studies on Alcohol,* 1972, *33,* 1147–1148.

Miller, B. A., Pokorny, A. D., Valles, J., and Cleveland, S. E. Biased sampling in alcoholism treatment research. *Quarterly Journal of Studies on Alcohol,* 1970, *31,* 97–101.

Mulford, H. A., and Miller, D. E. Drinking in Iowa. IV. Preoccupation with alcohol, and definitions of alcohol, heavy drinking and trouble due to drinking. *Quarterly Journal of Studies on Alcohol,* 1960, *21,* 279–291.

Park, P. Dimensions of drinking among male college students. *Social Problems,* 1967, *14,* 473–482.

Park, P. Developmental ordering of experiences in alcoholism. *Quarterly Journal of Studies on Alcohol,* 1973, *34,* 473–488.

Shanks, P. Biases in longitudinal surveys. Working paper, Social Research Group, U. C. Berkeley, School of Public Health, 1975.

Trice, H. M., and Wahl, J. R. A rank analysis of the symptoms of alcoholism. *Quarterly Journal of Studies on Alcohol,* 1958, *19,* 636–648.

Taber, M., Quay, H. C., Mark, J., and Nealey, V. Disease ideology and mental health research. *Social Problems,* 1969, *16,* 349–357.

Part Two

A Revised Model
of Alcohol Dependence

8. Toward an Emergent Model

Conclusions Consonant with the New Data

On the basis of the reviewed data, it now appears necessary to reformulate concepts of alcohol dependence to be consonant with the available data. The empirical studies in the literature suggest the following conclusions:

1. *There is no single entity which can be defined as alcoholism.* Alcoholism is not a thing but a collection of various symptoms and behaviors that collectively comprise different types of syndromes. There appears to be a broad array of life situations—dependent upon psychological disposition, past learning, sociocultural influences, and physiological states—that lead to inappropriate use of alcohol, which in turn leads to deleterious physical, psychological, and social consequences for the individual. These consequences are manifested in different patterns. Alcohol dependence is a health problem that may involve various organ systems of the body and affect one's personal and social well-being.

2. *There is no clear dichotomy between either alcoholics and nonalcoholics, or between prealcoholics and nonprealcoholics* even though individuals may have differing susceptibility to both the use of alcohol and the development of alcohol problems as a result of genetic, physiological, psychological, and sociocultural factors. Accurate assessment of alcohol problems is best achieved through operational descriptions of the pattern of alcohol use and the consequences of such use for an individual, which could range from no adverse effects to severe or even fatal consequences.

3. *The developmental sequence of adverse consequences appears to be highly variable,* ranging from an almost immediate and rapid progression to a slow progressive development. The alcohol problem may also remain static or even become less severe. Further, with or without treatment, various types of alcohol problems may moderate or simply desist. Such remission bears no necessary relationship to abstinence, for it may accompany a change in patterns of drinking and the consequences thereof.

4. *There is no evidence to date for a basic biological process that predisposes an individual toward dysfunctional use of alcohol.* That is, there is no mysterious "cell hunger" or metabolic "need." However, there is evidence that physical dependence is established after

189

the consumption of large amounts of alcohol. This condition may activate psychophysiological response patterns, which in turn serve as stimuli to engage in further drinking.

5. *The empirical evidence suggests that alcohol problems are reversible.* It would appear that the more severe and long-term patterns of alcohol dependence are more resistant to change than less entrenched patterns. The potential for reversibility may lie along a continuum, so that theoretically, except for irreversible cellular damage, it might be possible to reverse any drinking pattern. More practically, it is likely that for some individuals with alcohol problems, abstinence would be both an easier and a more appropriate treatment goal, with less danger to their ongoing stability. For others, it may be more judicious and appropriate to change their patterns of alcohol use rather than to insist on abstinence. Further clinical research on drinking goals is needed to clarify the most efficacious and appropriate long-term clinical options.

6. *Alcohol problems are typically interrelated with other life problems.* Therefore, treatment plans and goals should be determined on an individual basis, with specific assessment of dysfunction in each major area of life function. This is necessary to evaluate treatment effectiveness and to assess unintended or detrimental side effects. Abstinence should not be the only criterion used for assessing changes in drinking behavior nor the only criterion for assessing the effectiveness of treatment.

7. *It may be clinically useful to develop typologies of subpopulations for administrative program development* since people with alcohol problems characteristically differ from one another in many respects, yet may share common treatment problems. Efficient treatment, from the recipient's viewpoint, is that strategy which includes the minimal necessary changes in life function to obtain amelioration of alcohol-related life problems.

Formal Propositions for an Emergent Model

Except for Jellinek's preliminary formulations, there has never been any formal or salient definition of the concepts of alcohol dependence. Nevertheless, a set of loosely organized concepts has haphazardly developed, which were collected and arranged in logical sequence for discussion in Part I. Here we will organize the emerging concepts of alcohol dependence into formal statements in order to (1) clarify the conceptual issues, (2) offer a framework for logical critique by others, and (3) provide a set of concepts that may guide further experimental and clinical research to clarify each proposition.

Proposition 1. *Alcohol dependence subsumes a variety of syndromes defined by drinking patterns and the adverse consequences of such drinking.*

    Corollary A. These syndromes are defined as any combination of deleterious physical, psychological, or social consequences that follow the use of alcohol by an individual.

    Corollary B. These syndromes can vary along a continuum from minimal consequences to severe and even fatal consequences.

    Corollary C. These syndromes, jointly denoted as "alcohol dependence," are best considered as serious health problems.

    Corollary D. In specific circumstances it may be desirable for sociocultural, legal, political, and therapeutic goals to label alcohol dependence as a "disease," perhaps especially at the time of acute physical symptomatology. At the same time, the alcohol-dependent person may appropriately be labeled as "sick." Such circumstances should be carefully delineated and limited in application to specific situations.

Proposition 2. *An individual's use of alcohol can be considered as a point on a continuum from nonuse, to nonproblem drinking, to various degrees of deleterious drinking.*

    Corollary A. There may be preexisting differences between individual reactions to alcohol or vulnerability to adverse consequences of alcohol use, as a function of genetic, biological, psychological, and sociocultural factors. Such factors may increase or decrease the possibility that one may encounter problems in the use of alcohol.

    Corollary B. Differing susceptibility to alcohol problems does not in and of itself produce alcohol dependence. Any person who uses alcohol can develop a syndrome of alcohol dependence.

    Corollary C. There is no natural dichotomy between alcoholic and nonalcoholic but rather a continuous spectrum of drinking patterns that may result in different combinations of deleterious consequences.

Proposition 3. *The development of alcohol problems follows variable patterns over time.*

    Corollary A. Alcohol problems may develop gradually over time, leading to increasingly severe consequences, or such problems may develop rapidly.

    Corollary B. Alcohol problems do not necessarily proceed inexorably to severe fatal stages but may remain static at any level of severity.

Corollary C. Alcohol problems may follow a cyclic course of exacerbation and remission without progression beyond a limiting level of severity.

Corollary D. Alcohol problems may be partially or completely reversed through either a naturalistic process or a treatment program.

Proposition 4. *Abstinence bears no necessary relation to rehabilitation.*

Corollary A. A person may be totally abstinent without improvement in other areas of life function which were related to deleterious use of alcohol.

Corollary B. A person may demonstrate little change in his patterns of alcohol use, yet make major improvements in other areas of life function which were related to his use of alcohol.

Corollary C. A person may change his patterns of alcohol use so that his drinking no longer constitutes a problem in and of itself.

Proposition 5. *Psychological dependence and physical dependence on alcohol are separate and not necessarily related phenomena.*

Corollary A. Psychological dependence on alcohol is a syndrome of learned patterns of alcohol use.

Corollary B. Genetic, biological, psychological, and sociocultural factors may increase or decrease a person's vulnerability to develop a pattern of psychological dependence. None of these factors in isolation is necessarily sufficient to cause psychological dependence.

Corollary C. The consumption of a small amount of alcohol by a person once labeled "alcoholic" does not necessarily initiate a physical need that in turn causes further drinking.

Corollary D. An individual may experience a strongly felt need to drink in certain situations and not in others, which may be exacerbated by the consumption of small amounts of alcohol.

Proposition 6. *Continued drinking of large doses of alcohol over an extended period of time is likely to initiate a process of physical dependence.*

Corollary A. The state of physical dependence is marked by increased tolerance to alcohol and may manifest the symptoms of an alcohol withdrawal syndrome of varying severity.

Corollary B. Any person who consumes a sufficient amount of alcohol over time eventually develops some degree of physical dependence. This varies over a wide continuum from the increased tolerance of the nonproblem light drinker, to the hangover of the occasional intoxicated drinker, to the severe withdrawal symptoms of the chronic heavy drinker.

Corollary C. The development of physical dependence is related primarily to amount and frequency of alcohol intake, not to a unique metabolic processing of alcohol.

Corollary D. A state of physical dependence may exist without any other adverse consequences of drinking, except the physiological sequelae.

Corollary E. There may be individual differences in biological sensitivity to the effects of alcohol, but such differences are neither necessary nor sufficient to establish physical dependence.

Corollary F. Physical dependence does not appear to be a permanent state but may vary with subsequent patterns of drinking once established. The degree of physical dependence appears to be reversible.

Proposition 7. *The population of individuals with alcohol problems is multivariant.*

Corollary A. While the range of types and severity of problems may be arbitrarily defined into categories for research or clinical utility, such typologies must be recognized as relatively arbitrary heuristic classifications.

Corollary B. Treatment intervention must be multivariant. Individual treatment plans need to address (1) the severity of the person's alcohol use, (2) the particular problems and consequences associated with the individual drinking pattern, and (3) the person's ability to achieve specific treatment goals.

Corollary C. Comprehensive rehabilitation requires a variety of services that range from information and education to intensive long-term care. Available services, methods, and goals should be flexible enough to meet individual needs and abilities to participate.

Proposition 8. *Alcohol problems are typically interrelated with other life problems, especially when alcohol dependence is long established.*

Corollary A. Rehabilitation should aim at specific changes in drinking behavior suitable to each individual.

Corollary B. Rehabilitation should aim at specific changes in problem areas of life function, in addition to efforts aimed at drinking behavior per se.

Corollary C. Rehabilitation must take into account individual preferences, goals, choice of treatment, degree of disability, and ability to attain goals.

Proposition 9. *Because of the documented strong relationship between drinking behavior and environmental influences, emphasis should be placed on treatment procedures that relate to the person's drinking environment.*

   Corollary A. The alcohol-dependent individual may require temporary removal from his environment (i.e., hospital or supportive residential facility) with a planned return to his natural environment.

   Corollary B. To avoid further problems and achieve some stable level of existence, some alcohol-dependent individuals may require a quasipermanent sheltered living environment.

   Corollary C. Rehabilitation is likely to require direct involvement in the environment. This should begin with an analysis of the alcohol-dependent person's interactions with his environment and proceed to planned environmental interventions with family, relatives, friends, and others in the social network.

Proposition 10. *Treatment and rehabilitation services should be designed to provide for continuity of care over an extended period of time.* This continuum of services should begin with effective identification, triage, and referral mechanisms, extend through acute and chronic phases of treatment, and provide follow-up aftercare.

Proposition 11. *Evaluative studies of treatment of alcohol dependence must take into account the initial degree of disability, the potential for change, and an inventory of dysfunctions in diverse life areas in addition to drinking behavior.* Assessment of improvement should include both drinking behavior and behavior in other areas of life function, consistent with presenting problems. Degrees of improvement must also be recognized. Change in all areas of life function should be assessed on an individual basis using pretreatment and post-treatment comparison measures of treatment outcome.

Uses of the Emergent Model

Relevant to the field of *primary prevention,* the new model suggests that all people who drink have some risk of developing alcohol problems. (If we speculate that only certain people are born "alcoholic," then it is merely a step away to conclude that it is futile to study the drinking habits of our total population, for drinking habits must not be related to the development of alcohol dependence.) The notion of "social drinking" also serves to mask much antisocial and dyssocial drinking behavior. By ignoring or encouraging dysfunctional uses of alcohol, we thereby increase the risk among those more vulnerable to the abuse of alcohol. The most visible casualty of dysfunctional use of alcohol is the labeled "alcoholic," yet many other people pay a high personal and social price as a result of their drinking behavior, which may not be severe or overt enough for them to be labeled "alcoholic." There is an urgent need to recognize the broad spectrum of alcohol problems in order to increase the likelihood that people will recognize and appropriately deal with drinking situations which are likely to be damaging to themselves and/or others.

In the field of *secondary prevention,* there has long been a recognized need to identify and offer intervention for persons who exhibit minimal or moderately self-damaging drinking behavior. Many experience serious consequences as a result of their drinking, yet never reach the stage of being labeled "alcoholic." These individuals often refuse or simply do not seek treatment because they do not view themselves as matching the stereotypic notion of an "alcoholic." Our current treatment methods, designed to deal with syndromes of alcohol dependence, may be neither appropriate nor effective for the mild to moderate problem drinker. It can be expected that a certain proportion of individuals identified as having mild to moderate drinking problems is likely to develop increasingly serious alcohol problems, including alcohol dependence. Early intervention, designed in accordance with individual patterns of alcohol use, may be effective in halting and reversing such patterns of unidentified alcohol abuse.

In the area of *comprehensive community services,* the new model emphasizes the need for a concurrent broad array of both programs and services. It is hoped that this emphasis will promote greater referral and cooperation between programs, so that clients can be directed to a treatment program which best meets their individual needs.

In the area of *treatment prescription,* the new model suggests that rather than focusing on drinking behavior per se, we must look at the functions which drinking serves in a person's total life. This should lead to treatment based on an assessment of individual needs. The treatment goal for alcohol-dependent individuals is not to be characterized by changes in drinking patterns as such but by changes in the consequences of drinking. In this sense, the goal of all treatment is a reduction in problems associated with drinking toward a nonproblem level. This criterion may be statisfied if the individual adopts either an abstinent or nonproblem drinking pattern.

In the area of *treatment evaluation,* the new model specifies the value of multiple, differential, quantitative, and well-defined evaluation. This should lead to more precise measures of treatment effectiveness and efficiency.

In terms of *empirical research,* the model sets forth distinct areas that require further laboratory and clinical research to resolve current ambiguities.

A *data-based orientation,* the emergent model is likely to promote a greater understanding and recognition of treatment progress by both service providers and the public.

This emergent model should be considered as a *set of working hypotheses,* to be tested and charged in accord with further empirical data. We need to develop systematic knowledge about both the causes and treatment of alcohol problems, a goal that can only be achieved if the new model is considered as a set of hypotheses and not facts.

Cautions about Misuse

The traditional model of alcoholism described in Part I was for many years highly utilitarian. It served to establish alcohol studies as a scientific field, generated a remarkable expansion of clinical resources, and sustained the development of positive public support for services for alcohol-dependent individuals.

However, as a result of our evaluation of the traditional model, we believe that the formulation of a new model of alcohol dependence is in order. The construction of a new model of alcohol dependence as a set of hypotheses is important not only for science and clinical practice but also has value for public policy. A new model can direct attention toward potential areas of fruitful research, provide working guidelines for clinical practice, and serve as justification for public policy.

Following the exemplary attitude of E. M. Jellinek, we would like to offer some explicit cautionary statements about the potential for misuse of the emergent model.

First, we do not offer our analysis of the issues as an ideological weapon for acrimonious and polarized debate among the various factions in the field of alcohol studies. Rather, we support continuing rigorous study in anticipation that open-minded inquiry will lead to an improved model of alcohol dependence to better serve all persons involved in the field.

Second, although in our analysis of the data we have sometimes taken issue with persons and organizations who have made magnificent and sometimes lonely contributions to the development of alcoholism rehabilitation, our criticisms are not intended to disparage their contributions.

Third, recognizing the inevitable differences between a scientific and a lay approach to alcohol problems, we suggest that more explicit attention be given to a rapprochement between professionals and lay persons involved in alcohol rehabilitation. The proposed new model is not addressed solely to a scientific audience, for its eventual utility will be measured by its relevance for all in the field.

Fourth, we do not propose a definitive new model of alcohol dependence but rather a tentative reformulation which may provide the basis for further conceptual refinement. We recognize the limitations of the data in each area we have examined.

Fifth, we do not propose the wholesale rejection of the disease concept of alcohol dependence, which is not only entrenched in our culture but also retains some utility. However, we do propose appropriate limitations in the application and use of the disease concept.

Sixth, the new model does not offer support to any unitary etiology of alcohol dependence. As we see it, the proposed model offers the opportunity to incorporate the contributions of genetic, biological, psychological, social, environmental, and cultural variables.

Seventh, the new model does not support any single method or theory of treatment. Since current treatment and evaluation are relatively imprecise, the model supports the empirical specification and assessment of all treatment approaches.

Finally, we wish to reiterate our cautions about drinking by alcohol-dependent individuals. We specifically do not advocate promiscuous experimentation with continued drinking. We do not find sufficient evidence at this time to accurately define the most desirable or feasible drinking goals in different treatment programs. We do advocate the planned development of treatment programs which are designed to meet client needs most efficiently and which are based on ethical procedures and careful systematic evaluation.

Clinical Applications

The treatment of alcohol dependence has typically been viewed with skepticism and pessimism, as there seem to be no effective long-term treatment methods or modalities. This pessimism has resulted in two major approaches to treatment: (1) the "shotgun" approach exposes individuals to a wide variety of different treatments, in anticipation that "something will work"; (2) the "competitive monolith" approach offers a particular type of treatment as the "proven best," asserting that all other methods are poor or unsuccessful.

Much of the pessimism about treatment has resulted from failure to appreciate individual differences among alcohol-dependent persons. For example, a skid-row alcohol-dependent population may have a very low potential for total rehabilitation, a goal achieved by perhaps only 5 percent of a treatment sample. Thus, any treatment method used with this population is likely to have dismal results, whereas a subpopulation of industrial employees, identified through an in-house occupational alcohol program, may have a much higher rehabilitation potential irrespective of the particular treatment modality.

Another long-standing issue has been the focus on abstinence as an evaluation of treatment effectiveness. Frequently other dimensions of life functioning and adjustment are seen as irrelevant if the "alcoholic" continues using alcohol. Consequently, many programs largely ignore the substantial degrees of improvement many of their clients achieve.

Other confounding issues in most treatment outcome studies are summarized by Miller et al. (1970): (1) the definition of alcoholism used by the facility, (2) the specification of the population enrolled, (3) the reputation of the program, (4) client's refusal of treatment referral, (5) rejection of applicants, (6) client's failure to report after acceptance, (7) exclusions from study protocols, (8) dropouts, (9) client's partial participation in treatment regimes, (10) deaths, (11) untraceable clients, and (12) clients uncooperative with follow-up. Failure to account for these variables has resulted in biased samples of treatment results that often do not reflect either the adequacy of the program or its differential suitability for potential clients.

Historically, the development of treatment methods has been based on the traditional model of alcoholism. Hence, it had been commonly deduced that there was one population of "alcoholics" with one problem—"alcoholism"—who needed to be treated in one way to achieve the one treatment outcome of abstinence.

Such oversimplification of alcohol-dependence treatment ignores the significant literature which indicates that there are major differences between subpopulations of persons with alcohol problems, major differences between types of treatment, and major differences in treatment outcome (Cahn, 1970; Einstein, Wolfson, and Gecht, 1970).

The proposed new model of alcohol dependence incorporates no assumption that there is only one population of individuals dependent on alcohol. Rather, we propose that there are a variety of ways in which such individuals can be classified into subpopulations which have clinical utility for treatment planning. The task then focuses on planning treatment programs capable of meeting the varied needs of specific individuals. This we term a "differential diagnostic and assessment" approach to treatment.

We further suggest that no one treatment program is suitable for all alcohol-dependent individuals. A more realistic and valuable alternative is to develop a variety of treatment services to serve different types of subpopulations. A comprehensive community alcohol program, therefore, is not necessarily an integrated multiple component program but more usually consists of a network of related rehabilitation services (see Pattison, 1974).

Although this is probably an oversimple typology, it is useful to consider the rehabilitation of alcohol-dependent individuals in terms of various areas of life health: (1) drinking health, (2) emotional health, (3) vocational health, (4) social/familial health, and (5) physical health.

Not all alcohol-dependent persons are impaired in each area of life health, nor does impairment in one area necessarily imply impairment in another. Thus, we may expect different profiles of impairment for different subpopulations. Clinically, individual profiles of impairment in each area of life health need to be established so we can ask what can be done to improve function in each area of impairment. Thus, differential assessment leads to differential prescriptions for treatment. Although we cannot examine differential diagnoses and treatment in detail here, we can review how one might proceed to determine treatment goals.

Determination of Treatment Goals

The use of a total abstinence criterion implies that if an alcohol-dependent individual achieves abstinence he will also demonstrate improvement in other areas of life health. However, Pattison et al. (1968) presented empirical and clinical data to illustrate the abstinent "alcoholics" often did not exhibit improvement in other areas of life health, and in fact some individuals actually showed deterioration in some areas. Similar instances of life deterioration as a concomitant of abstinence have been reported by Rossi et al. (1963), Wilby and Jones (1962), and Flaherty et al. (1955). The most significant study in this regard was by Gerard et al. (1962). In their evaluation of a group of totally abstinent "successes," they found 43% to be overtly disturbed, 24% inconspicuously inadequate, 12% "AA addict" successes, and only 10% independent successes. Thus, abstinence alone does not necessarily indicate rehabilitation.

> *Case example.* This 56-year-old white salesman had been a compulsive drinker since age 18. He had asthma and stuttered. He was plagued with guilt feelings and the inability to express himself in social situations. He was in treatment for five years. He had been abstinent for 2 years, yet he continually feared a relapse. He felt psychotherapy helped him understand his conflicts, but he ascribed his sobriety to intensive participation in AA. Although he enjoyed his sobriety, he had multiple neurotic complaints that interfered with social function, so that he stayed mostly at home where his wife sheltered him. He could not work effectively because of his inhibitions, and he was so dependent upon his wife that he could not assume any assertive role with her. Any anxiety or frustration would precipitate psychosomatic symptoms.

In this case, we see a man who is abstinent but who has major dysfunctions in the emotional, vocational, social/familial, and physical spheres of life.

Conversely, it has usually been assumed that alcohol-dependent persons who do drink cannot be considered to be functioning successfully. This assumption was not examined in most of the earlier evaluation studies, as they ignored other areas of life health. However, even some persons who have been physically dependent on alcohol have been able to change their drinking patterns and attain a successful life adjustment.

Total abstinence may be associated with improvement, no change, or deterioration in other critical areas of total life health. The singular and inappropriate concentration on abstinence as a criterion of successful treatment of alcohol dependence minimizes or obscures treatment methods which should focus on rehabilitation in other areas of life health. In a given case, abstinence may be neither a necessary nor a desirable goal in terms of drinking outcome.

Abstinence

Although we challenge the use of abstinence as the sole or primary criterion for evaluation of treatment, abstinence is a legitimate and feasible outcome goal. However, abstinence should only be considered a drinking goal and should not lead to any inference that beneficial change has occurred in any other area of life health. Second, since abstinence is only one of several possible drinking outcomes, there is no logical justification for assuming that it is a more desirable goal than any other. It seems more appropriate to determine the circumstances under which abstinence is a necessary or desirable drinking outcome, where it may be a less desirable outcome, and where it may be desirable but not achievable.

Social drinking

"Social drinking" is a vague and ambiguous term which merely states that one drinks among other people. It does not specify the meaning, function, amount, or consequences of drinking. Hayman (1966) calls this "the myth of social drinking," for the rubric of social drinking often serves only to obscure, justify, and rationalize many dysfunctional, dyssocial, and psychopathological forms of drinking. As the phrase "social drinking" does not seem to be appropriate or useful, we suggest that it no longer be used.

Attenuated drinking

Attenuated drinking defines a drinking goal in which pathological drinking is not immediately eliminated but is attenuated, perhaps leading to its eventual termination.

Recognition that continued drinking in and of itself does not indicate poor rehabilitation has occasioned research that differentiates between the drinking variable and other life health variables. For instance, Ludwig et al. (1970) found that although 80% to 90% of previously hospitalized patients returned to their former patterns of pathological drinking after discharge, many patients demonstrated sustained improvement in other areas of life health. They concluded: "return to drink need not be automatically equated with return to all the maladaptive behaviors which lead to mental hospitalization in the first place . . . most patients are able to carry on most of their other social tasks, at least at a higher level than that noted on hospital admission" (p. 187).

Following treatment for alcohol dependence, an individual who shows no change or only modest improvement in his drinking pattern may still profit from treatment, as evinced by better adjustment in other spheres of life health. Mayer and Meyerson (1971) reported cases where individuals achieved stability and drank less after treatment even though they still experienced episodes of insobriety. Gillis and Keet (1969) reported that 58% of their sample showed significant improvement in life adjustment although still drinking. At the same time, the extent of pathological drinking was reduced from 70% of drinking episodes to 20% of drinking episodes. In this same sample, some 47% had improved drinking health without deterioration, while 23% improved in drinking health but showed some deterioration of overall function. Fitzgerald et al. (1971) found that of a sample of persons treated for alcohol dependence, 22% with good adjustment were abstinent, 19% with good adjustment were drinking, and 18% with poor adjustment were drinking. In another study of treatment outcome, Kish and Hermann (1971) reported that 22% of those evaluated as improved were abstinent, while 26% of those evaluated as improved either occasionally or regularly engaged in self-damaging drinking. Belasco (1971) succinctly sums up this issue; behavioral and social adjustment do not have a high correlation with indices of drinking.

In these studies and others (Canter, 1968; Chandler, Hensman, & Edwards, 1971; Ludwig, 1973; Mindlin, 1959; Plaut, 1967; Thomas, Gliedman, Freund, Imber, & Stone, 1959), there is suggestive evidence that some moderation in the amount of alcohol intake, the frequency of drinking, and the degree of intoxication —all measures of increased control—do have a correlation with improvement in other areas of life health. We do not now know which particular measures of change in drinking may be more significant. However, the evidence continues to accumulate that continued pathological drinking may not be a dire indicator of total treatment failure. Especially as a short-term goal, reduction or attenuation of the degree of pathological drinking may in some cases be an acceptable goal, in conjunction with improvement in other areas of life health. While attenuated drinking may not be an ideal goal, it may suffice to return an individual to a degree of improved life functioning. It is possible in some cases to set an immediate treatment goal of reduction of the severity of drinking problems. The person continues to drink at a self-damaging level but in an attenuated fashion. The result may be a shift from a fully incapacitating state to a pattern of successful adaptation despite ongoing deleterious drinking.

If we ignore these facts, we may fail to help some persons achieve at least some degree of improvement in drinking health, or fail to help them see and utilize the real gains they may have made in other areas of life health. Successful treatment does not have to be an all-or-none affair; degrees of improvement are realistic goals.

> *Case example.* This 46-year-old single male lives with his widowed mother. For five years his drinking problems increased in severity. He drank daily, usually to intoxication, and often until he passed out. His job as a warehouseman was in jeopardy. He was "fed up" with his drinking, and his mother urged him to seek treatment. He had several interviews at an Alcoholism Information Center, but he refused any further treatment. His drinking subsequently subsided. He stated that the few interviews were enough for him to see his problems and alter his behavior. Now, four years later, he drinks only on specific occasions, but he no longer passes out. He is no longer absent from work and has no alcohol-related job impairment.

Controlled drinking

Behavior modification programs for alcoholics have focused attention on a drinking goal that is defined by the establishment of control over the drinking patterns and situations, the consequences of drinking, the frequency of drinking, and/or the amount of alcohol consumed. Such a "controlled drinking" pattern may involve changing the functions which drinking serves for an individual. The person may also learn to monitor and avoid high-risk circumstances where drinking is apt to have self-damaging consequences.

The various protocols usually involve an attempt to analyze the person's drinking patterns and the antecedents and consequences of that drinking. There is also an attempt to specify the changes to be made in behaviors, and the reinforcement contingencies to achieve and maintain the desired behavioral goals.

In some cases, behavior modification may not seek to change the individual's coping style that has led to impulsive and deleterious drinking but may simply modify his environment so that he no longer encounters circumstances conducive to deleterious drinking. Since alcohol problems typically result in manifold disruptions in a person's capacity to function, it may only be necessary to decrease drinking behavior in some instances in order to effect substantial rehabilitation.

The notion is unsubstantiated by recent research that persons who have been dependent on alcohol have a physical "craving" for drink that necessarily leads to continued and damaging drinking once drinking starts. Individuals who have been dependent on alcohol can and sometimes do control their drinking, and can be taught to increase that control. However, control of drinking per se, just like abstinence or moderation of drinking per se, does not necessarily imply that there is improvement in other areas of life health.

Case example. A 36-year-old machinist had drunk heavily since adolescence. Drinking became a compulsive daily routine that threatened to disrupt both his job and marriage. He was in therapy for two years, during which time he noticed a change in his pattern of drinking. He now drinks about once a week and does not experience a desire to drink more. However, when he feels depressed he feels an urge to go and get drunk, and he avoids drinking at bars because he would drink more in the company of his friends than he does now at home.

Case example. A 45-year-old musician had drunk compulsively for 20 years. He had been in psychoanalysis for five years, and his emotional adaptation improved, but his drinking worsened to the point that he could not perform in public. During the course of two years of therapy focused on drinking behavior change, he learned to limit himself to one drink before a performance and to avoid drinking at parties. He occasionally would drink to intoxication at home when severely depressed.

Case example. A 43-year-old married engineer drank heavily for two years, consuming a half gallon of wine daily, in addition to taking 50 mg of Valium per day. He entered treatment when his work performance was affected to such a degree that he believed his job was in jeopardy. The presentation of proposals at meetings was a major vocational component related to his drinking. He reported that the heavy drinking had begun as a purposeful behavior for relaxation. After his withdrawal from alcohol, a behavioral treatment sequence was directed at providing him with relaxation skills and an increased ability to function at work in front of groups of colleagues. A treatment goal of controlled drinking was supported by his wife. He now drinks a limited number of drinks (seldom more than two or three) when dining out or on camping trips with friends who drink moderately. This pattern has been maintained for over three years. Currently, he continues to monitor his drinking but feels no desire to drink in a self-damaging manner.

In the above cases, the individuals changed their overt pattern of drinking but continued to occasionally desire drinking as a coping behavior. Therefore, they had to monitor their drinking carefully and maintain specific limits on where and how much they drank. Although the meaning of drinking was only slightly changed, the actual drinking changed drastically. In the other cases, the functions of drinking were changed in addition to changes in the actual pattern of alcohol consumption.

Normal drinking

Many reports indicate that a certain proportion of formerly alcohol-dependent persons drink normally either after treatment or without treatment, if there have been changes in their life circumstances. Unfortunately, many of these reports do not provide enough clinical data to determine whether the change in drinking pattern was "attenuated," "controlled," or "normal" drinking. In the "attenuated" drinking outcome, the individual continues to use alcohol as a functional drug, although he is able to increase his control over its use. In some cases of "controlled" drinking, the person may occasionally feel like engaging in dysfunctional drinking. He has not necessarily changed his perception of the meaning (function) of drinking.

In contrast, normal drinking involves a change in the meaning of drinking (Bolman, 1965; Krystal, 1962). In this sense, the abstinent individual may not have changed the meaning of drinking and, although abstinent for 10 or 20 years, may still be vulnerable to the deleterious use of alcohol should he drink even small amounts. He has never learned how to drink in a limited fashion or without encountering serious consequences. Thus, the common observation is likely to be true that the abstinent person who was formerly dependent on alcohol cannot take a drink without risking loss of control and deleterious drinking.

The concept of normal drinking has been colorfully described by Eric Berne (1964) in terms of the "game of alcoholism": "The criterion of a true game cure is that the former alcoholic should be able to drink socially without putting himself into jeopardy . . . the psychological cure of an alcoholic also lies in getting him to stop playing the game altogether . . . the usual total abstinence cure will not satisfy the game analyst" (p. 56). Berne goes on to note that the abstinent "alcoholic" can continue the "game of alcoholism" as a "dry alcoholic." In similar vein, Arthur Cain (1965) observed that the recovered individual does not drink primarily because he does not want to drink, whereas the arrested individual still has the desire to drink but knows that he should not and avoids doing so. Cain states:

> The recovered alcoholic, by definition, does not care whether he can drink normally, and he definitely does not want to become intoxicated again. . . . Most alcoholics do not want to return to normal drinking: rather by normal drinking they (alcoholics) mean the intoxication they were once able to control—which is nothing like our definition of normal drinking . . . the arrested alcoholic never really loses his desire to become intoxicated with alcohol. He learns to control his desire, he learns to live with his disease but he never learns to transcend his desire. . . . The fact that normal drinking has been achieved is a dramatic indication of one's successful effort to attain social, intellectual, and religious maturity. (p. 234)

Some alcohol-dependent persons report that they have never been normal drinkers but drank in a self-damaging fashion from the time of their first drink. A great deal of American "social drinking" might well be characterized as psychopathological, that is, drinking which occurs in circumstances where there is a high probability that such behavior will result in deleterious consequences for the individual. Since American drinking practices exist without clear norms or constraining boundaries, the novitiate drinker is introduced to drinking practices that are potentially dependency producing. In our clinical interviews, individuals sometimes report that they engage in 20 years of "social drinking," after which they "suddenly" became dependent on alcohol. Careful analysis of their social drinking behavior sometimes reveals that they were actually engaged in self-damaging drinking for 20 years, but it was conducted in social settings where the drinking was not defined as aberrant.

Use of a drinking goal in treatment does not necessarily imply that an individual returns to a normal drinking pattern. Rather, he must learn normal drinking for the first time in his life. This involves changing the functions of drinking as well as changing the specific drinking behaviors. Most treatment programs have not made such goals explicit, so that the number of persons who develop attenuated, controlled, or normal drinking behaviors may not reflect what can be achieved in treatment. We may glean some indications from the literature, however. Gerard & Saenger (1966) report that the normal drinking outcome appears to vary with treatment philosophy and whether normal drinking is made a specific goal. DeMorsier & Feldmann (1952) followed 500 cases in which 15% achieved a social cure as a deliberate goal. A "social cure" was defined as avoiding the psychological bad effects of drinking, changing attitudes toward drinking, and drinking only in a family and social context. Mention should also be made of the Scandinavian Polar Bear Clubs, whose aim is to teach their members how to drink normally (Bruun, 1966).

> *Case example.* This 30-year-old mechanic had drunk heavily for 10 years. For six years he had been unable to work steadily because of his drinking. His marriage had been stormy and his wife had left him at the time he entered treatment. At that point he was depressed and suicidal. Individual and conjoint marital therapy resulted in resolution of marital conflict. He stopped drinking and obtained a steady job. He resumed drinking only at family gatherings with his wife's full acceptance. He experienced no compulsion to drink. He had no desire to get drunk, and he felt no need to drink as a way of coping with his life.

Life Health Variables

Whatever the nature of the drinking variable, there is no necessary correlation with the other variables of life health outcome. Change or no change in drinking status is not highly predictive of changes in these other variables, although there is a positive association between improvement in drinking and improvement in other areas of life health. However, one cannot necessarily ascribe a causal relation, since improvement in drinking may not cause improvement in other areas of life health. It is a reasonable clinical assumption that a person will be able to achieve better adaptation in other life areas if his drinking improves. However, there are two confounding sets of possible alternative outcomes: (1) drinking may not improve while there may be improvement in other aspects of life health, (2) drinking may improve while there may be no change or even deterioration in other areas of life health.

The most important issue for treatment, however, is the necessity to specify the target areas of deficit clearly. A differential assessment of life health functions made before treatment (pre-treatment assessment) shows that alcohol-dependent persons vary in their degree of dysfunction in various areas of life health, with good function in some areas and major deficits in others. In some areas of life health there is little need, and little room, for improvement. For example, some "high bottom" individuals show little dysfunction aside from their uncontrolled drinking (Blane &

Meyers, 1964). On the other hand, some "low bottom" individuals show across-the-board dysfunction in all areas of life health (Feeney, Mindlin, Minear, & Short, 1955; Miller, Pokorny, & Kanas, 1970; Myerson & Mayer, 1966).

To define the treatment goals, we must specify the target areas of life health, the degree of dysfunction, and the degree of improvement we can reasonably anticipate. This, in turn, leads to a differential assessment of predicted outcome for each area of life health and for each individual. Pattison et al. (1969) compared groups of clients who had been treated at three different facilities. Each of the three alcohol-dependent populations had different pretreatment profiles, and each of the three groups showed improvement. Most importantly, however, the pattern of improvement was different for each population.

Development of Differential Treatment Profiles

To illustrate how a differential approach may be utilized, we shall use data from the study by Pattison et al. (1973) which compared the client populations at four different facilities—an aversion-conditioning hospital (ACH), an alcoholism outpatient clinic (OPC), a halfway house (HWH), and a police work farm (PWF).

Table 1 illustrates that each of the four client populations has a different self-definition of "alcoholism" and a different self-specified treatment goal.

Table 2 presents a differential assessment of disability for each area of life health in each of the four populations. At the time of admission, the profile of each population showed a different pattern of dysfunction. Each population showed a different profile of expected change.

Although all the clients have serious alcohol problems, the ACH population might be considered "high bottom" individuals. They have little disability in most areas of life health, and hence fewer areas in which to demonstrate improvement. Their healthier pretreatment profile shows less opportunity for improvement than those whose pretreatment profile is much more dysfunctional. The major change expected for the ACH population is improvement in their drinking behavior per se.

The OPC population has more pretreatment dysfunction, and hence can be expected to show more improvement in several areas of life health. Yet their disabilities are not likely disabling, and their improvement will not likely be dramatic.

Table 1. Conceptual differences expressed between alcohol-dependent clients at four different treatment programs

Concept	Aversion-Conditioning Hospital	Alcoholism Outpatient Clinic	Halfway House	Police Work Farm
Self-definition of "alcoholism"	a medical allergy	a neurotic symptom	a life problem	a secondary nuisance
Self-specified treatment goal	abstinence	resolution of neurosis	learn to life a new life	stay dry, warm, and sober

Table 2. Differential disability and improvement profiles for four different groups of alcohol-dependent individuals

Target Health Area	Aversion-Conditioning Hospital		Alcoholism-Outpatient Clinic		Halfway House		Police Work Farm	
	Disability on Admission	Predicted Degree of Improvement	Disability on Admission	Predicted Degree of Improvement	Disability on Admission	Predicted Degree of Improvement	Disability on Admission	Predicted Degree of Improvement
Drinking	4	4	4	4	4	4	4	4
Interpersonal	1	1	2	2	4	4	4	1
Emotional	1	1	3	3	4	4	4	1
Vocational	0	0	1	1	4	4	4	1
Physical	1	1	0	0	2	2	4	3

Note. Disability ratings are on a scale of 0–4: 0 = no disability; 4 = highest disability. Degree of Improvement ratings are on a scale of 0–4: 0 = no improvement; 4 = greatest degree of improvement.

209

The HWH population has severe disability in almost every area but a high potential for rehabilitation as well. These are the classic "chronic alcoholics" whose prior successful lives have been disintegrated by "alcoholism." They can be expected to show the most dramatic change and improvement.

The PWF population are the skid-row or "low bottom" individuals. They, too, have great dysfunction in all areas of life health but, unlike the HWH population, no prior history of successful life adaptation, and hence little potential for rehabilitation and little change or improvement could be predicted.

This chart illustrates the necessity to carefully describe the precise disabilities for a specific subpopulation of alcohol-dependent individuals, and also the need to estimate the degree of potential improvement in each area of dysfunction.

Table 3 lists possible appropriate drinking goals for each of the four populations. Although several drinking goals may be possible for each population, there are not currently enough data to allow firm generalizations. Thus this chart is only offered as a preliminary frame of reference against which one can make empirical evaluations.

The case examples from these four populations are not intended as definitive population characteristics, nor does this one study cover all types of populations and treatment methods. Rather this oversimplified schemata drawn from one study is intended to illustrate the conceptual frame of reference, so that in the future we may plan and evaluate treatment programs with more precision and rigor.

The emerging model of alcohol dependence sets forth a basis for the development of rational treatment planning and programming. Programs can specify the types of individual they serve so that treatment plans can then be based on specific evaluations of pretreatment impairment in each area of life health. Specific goals of treatment can be logically linked to both impairment and potential for improvement. Treatment evaluation can be built into the program, with regular review of the client's progress toward specific goals in each area of impairment. We may thus avoid the prescription of inappropriate, ineffective, or harmful treatment regimes that are arbitrarily imposed on clients as part of global treatment programs that try to help everyone in every way, and may fail in all.

Table 3. Possible differential drinking goals for four different groups of alcohol-dependent individuals

Drinking Goal	Aversion-Conditioning Hospital	Alcoholism Outpatient Clinic	Halfway House	Police Work Farm
Abstinent Social	Primary X *	X *	Primary X *	Problematic X *
Attenuated Controlled	Problematic X?	Problematic X?	Problematic X?	Primary X
Normal		Primary X		

Primary X: Goal most likely to be achieved in terms of treatment offered.

Problematic X: Goal may be achieved but is unlikely or difficult to attain because of the psychosocial problems of that group.

X?: Goal may be achievable but sufficient data not yet available.

* Social drinking is listed here for completeness, but only to indicate that it is a vacuous goal that has no operational meaning, and hence is not achievable.

9. Selection of Treatment

The major problem now facing clinicians is how to determine quickly and accurately what types of treatment should be offered to an alcohol-dependent individual. Different individuals not only need different treatment but seek and accept treatment in accord with their personal predilections. Thus the problem is to offer the individual appropriate treatment whose methods and goals he will accept and work toward.

Heretofore, many "alcoholism" programs have only offered one treatment approach—*their* approach. The problem, of course, is that the one approach may fail to provide certain important elements for comprehensive rehabilitation; it may be unsuited or unacceptable to some individuals and detrimental to others.

The "multiple method" approach, which offers a little bit of everything to each client in the hope that "something will help," also has major liabilities: such programs may confuse the alcohol-dependent person with multiple contradictory messages about rehabilitation; the individual may be led to sample many methods yet fail to get engaged in a specific program of treatment; and random exposure to multiple methods fails to provide a precise analysis of the individual's problems and a specific program of exact treatment methods and goals suited to him.

There is an urgent need to develop multiple treatment approaches, that are complementary rather than competitive. This requires the implementation of initial differential diagnosis of the alcohol-dependent client to determine the areas and degree of disability and the individual's capacity for change in these areas. The next step involves matching the client's acceptance of treatment methods and goals with available resources.

Unfortunately, we have not yet reached the point in clinical practice where such differential diagnosis and selection of treatment can be accurately implemented. Although there are clinical programs where such differential selection of treatment is being developed on an empirical basis, we lack the precision of experimental and evaluative data to provide a general scientific base for selection of treatment.

The following readings focus on preliminary attempts to develop criteria for selection of treatment. Although the two papers use different criteria, they present a common conclusion: there are clinically useful criteria that do indicate subpopulations of alcohol-dependent individuals who choose, accept, and profit from different approaches to treatment. Although these papers must be considered as only illustrative attempts toward a scientific differential approach to treatment, they do show the promise of a rigorous approach to treatment selection.

E. Mansell Pattison,
Ronald Coe, and Hans O. Doerr

Population Variation among Alcoholism Treatment Facilities

Introduction

This report is part of a series of studies designed to assess the social system characteristics of alcoholism treatment programs in a community (Pattison, 1966, 1968; Pattison et al., 1968, 1969). Recent surveys of community planning programs have strongly recommended that communities establish multiple treatment programs that can provide a broad range of treatments based on population selectivity (Blum & Blum, 1967; Plaut, 1967). These recommendations are based on the assumption that the effectiveness of various treatment methods will be maximized by selecting the treatment approach most appropriate for specific types of alcoholics.

This concept of multiple treatment programs has been subject to a variety of misinterpretations, however. One misinterpretation has led to the "shotgun" approach, namely, providing a number of different treatment methods in one facility in the hope that "something will take." Another misinterpretation has resulted in the "competitive monolithic" approach, namely, multiple facilities in a community, each offering its treatment approach as "the" way to treat all alcoholics.

Neither of the above approaches to multiple treatment programs provides a sound conceptual and scientific base for comprehensive community planning. Our research is an attempt to define the characteristics of the total social system of alcoholism treatment in a

From *International Journal of Addictions*, 1973, 8, 199–229. Reprinted by courtesy of Marcel Dekker, Inc.

community. We have based our analysis on the interaction between three variables: (1) variation in the total population of alcoholics, (2) variation in treatment facilities, and (3) variation in treatment outcome. Historically, the analysis of alcoholism treatment programs was based on the assumption that there was minimal variation in these variables: there was *one* population of alcoholics, to be treated by *one* best method, which would produce *one* therapeutic outcome—abstinence. However, cumulative research has demonstrated that each of these variables is not uniform, but rather consists of subsets which are combined in different permutations. An examination of how these subsets of variables interact as a social system may indicate how we may make better use of the total social system of treatment in a community (Krause et al., 1968).

Alcoholic population variation

Although many attempts have been made to define subtypes of alcoholics, these typologies have not been of much aid in planning treatment programs. In fact, some clinicians have asserted that variations in alcoholic populations are irrelevant to the outcome of treatment. However, reviews by Pattison (1966), Hill and Blane (1967), and Pokorny et al. (1968) have cited numerous studies which demonstrate that population variables have been largely ignored in evaluating treatment programs. A recent research monograph by Schmidt et al. (1968) demonstrated that social class variation at one facility directly affected both diagnosis and treatment. Other clinical studies have supported the conclusion that differences in treatment response do relate to preexistent population differences (Blane et al., 1963; Mindlin, 1959; Sutherland et al., 1950; Tomsovic, 1968). What is lacking to date is a systematic method of linking population differences to treatment programs in clinically useful profiles.

Treatment facility variation

It is difficult to assess the effectiveness of many treatment programs because many methods are combined which may be additive, synergistic, antagonistic, or merely superfluous. Or multiple treatment methods may turn out to be antitherapeutic.

Many facilities have no clearly specified goals, or the explicit and overt goals may be countermanded by implicit and covert procedures that may be acted out without realization by the staff (Chafetz et al., 1962). Even when there is a supposedly uniform treatment method, there may be great variation (Moore & Buchanan, 1966). For example, Gerard and Saenger (1966) have shown that outpatient alcoholism clinics conduct widely variant programs, and that the "product" turned out varies with the philosophy and method of each facility. Thus far we have few parameters for defining the *relevance* of a treatment program or its treatment *potency*.

Treatment outcome variation

The traditional criterion of assessing successful treatment of alcoholics has been the attainment and maintenance of abstinence. A series of critiques of this concept suggest the inadequacy of this view (Baily & Stewart, 1967; Davies, 1962; Kendall, 1965). Abstinence is only one dimension in the rehabilitation of an alcoholic. Other dimensions include emotional function, social function, vocational function, and physical function (Clancy et al., 1965; Goldfried, 1969; Hurwitz & Lalos, 1968; Kissin et al., 1968; Negrete et al., 1966; Pokorny et al., 1967). Improvement in drinking may not result in improvement in these other areas of life function (Gerard et al., 1962). Concomitantly, improvement in these other dimensions of living may occur as a result of treatment, with only moderate or minimal improvement in drinking behavior. Changes in each of these life functions and changes in drinking are related by somewhat independent variables (Pattison et al., 1969).

Models for treatment programs

A simple unilinear model of treatment assumes that each of the three above categories is homogeneous. However, if we consider that each category may be heterogeneous, then several different models for relationships between these categories can be logically suggested. These are illustrated in Table 1.

Models I, II, III, IV all share the premise that the category of outcome does not vary, and hence these may be discarded.

Model V is illogical in that no variability can exist in outcome when no variability exists in either the patient population or in the treatment facility.

Model VI suggests that the variability in outcome is due only to the variability of the patient population which goes through nonvariant treatment facilities. But since facilities do vary, this model must be discarded.

Table 1. Postulated models of relationship between variables of alcoholism treatment evaluation

I	( )	( )	( )
	(P)	(F)	(O)
	( )	( )	( )
	Homogeneous patient population	Homogeneous facility	Homogeneous outcome
II	( )	F_1	( )
	(P)	F_2	(O)
	( )	F_3	( )
		Heterogeneous facilities	
III	P_1	( )	( )
	P_2	(F)	(O)
	P_3	( )	( )
	Heterogeneous patient population		
IV	P_1	F_1	( )
	P_2	F_2	(O)
	P_3	F_3	( )
	Heterogeneous patient population	Heterogeneous facilities	
V	( )	( )	O_1
	(P)	(F)	O_2
	( )	( )	O_3
			Heterogeneous outcome
VI	P_1	( )	O_1
	P_2	(F)	O_2
	P_3	( )	O_3
		Homogeneous facilities	
VII	( )	F_1	O_1
	(P)	F_2	O_2
	( )	F_3	O_3
	Homogeneous population		
VIII	P_1	F_1	O_1
	P_2	F_2	O_2
	P_3	F_3	O_3
		All heterogeneous	

Model VII suggests that the variability in outcome is due only to the differences in the treatment facilities and their methods. However, the research available provides evidence that there is a correlation between outcome variability and population variability. Hence this model is contradicted by the data.

Model VIII represents our view. It suggests that outcome variablity is due to both a variable patient population and a variable treatment program. If this model is correct, then several corollaries may be suggested: (1) it may be possible to match a certain type of patient with a certain type of treatment and facility to yield the most effective results; (2) outcome success rates could be maximized if the expectations of the patient and the facility could be matched; (3) treatment programs can maximize effectiveness by clearly specifying what population they propose to serve, what goals are feasible with that population, and what methods can be expected to best achieve those goals.

In this context, evaluation research could then clearly address the question of "potency" or effectiveness of a treatment program. Further, one can then compare different methods that deal with comparable populations with comparable treatment goals.

Rationale

A prior study in this series (Pattison et al., 1969) examined the relationships among population, facility, and outcome at three different alcoholism treatment facilities: an aversion-conditioning hospital, a half-way house, and an outpatient clinic. A patient sample from each facility was rated at the time of intake on scales of life health adaptation: Drinking Health, Interpersonal Health, Vocational Health, Physical Health. The ratings were repeated a minimum of one year after discharge from the facility. The characteristics of each facility were described in terms of their own philosophy on the etiology of alcoholism, their methods of treatment, and their criteria of successful treatment.

On each of the above scales, the populations at each facility were found to vary significantly between each other at intake. At follow-up the populations at each facility showed ratings of improvement, with all three populations *not* different from each other. However, an examination of relative change on each variable of health adaptation revealed a different picture. The three populations each entered treatment at a different level of adaptation and had different degrees of relative improvement on each variable of life adaptation. Each of the three populations improved in different ways that varied according to the role of alcoholism in their lives, their rehabilitation needs, and the methods and goals of the facility to which they went. The study suggested that each of the three facilities and the alcoholic populations they served were distinct social systems.

Although the first study produced informative and provocative results, there was a major methodological problem. We were able to demonstrate a significant variation and interaction among population, facility, and outcome, but we had selected a patient population from each facility that was composed of "successful" cases. Therefore, we could not conclude that the differences in patient population were preexistent. Indeed, the variation in patient population could be solely due to their "successful" experience at the treatment facility. Further, the relatively successful "match" between population needs and treatment methods which were found might not reflect the fact that the alcoholic found the right facility, but merely the fact that our sample only included those who were best suited to this facility—hence their successful outcome. We did not know whether the total population presenting at each facility consisted indeed of different populations, nor did we have data to determine how homogeneous each total population was that came to each facility.

The present study was undertaken to determine: (1) what variation, if any, might exist in alcoholic populations presenting at admission to each of four different alcoholism treatment facilities; (2) the degree of homogeneity of the population presenting to each facility; and (3) the degree of match between treatment needs of the population at admission and the treatment offered.

Experimental Method

This study compared the population characteristics of alcoholics admitted for treatment at four different alcoholism treatment facilities in Seattle, Washington, during 1968.

Facility 1 is an aversion-conditioning private medical hospital (abbreviated ACH). The major treatment modality is aversion-conditioning. Various psychotropic drugs are occasionally prescribed; patients live in a supportive milieu, and most patients have psychiatric interviews under thiopental (Pentothal). However, the main emphasis at this facility is on a biochemical etiology of alcoholism, and the goal of treatment is to achieve abstinence in the patient. Aversion treatment is conducted over a period of ten days to two weeks, with a variable number of follow-up interviews which may occasionally include additional reinforcement treatments of aversion-conditioning. Treatment costs may range over $1,000.

Facility 2 is a mental health outpatient clinic conducted exclusively for alcoholics (abbreviated OPC). It offers psychiatric and social work counseling on an individual and group basis for outpatients. Psychotropic drugs and disulfiram (Antabuse) are occasionally used. Although abstinence is seen as an important goal, it is not a requisite for continuing treatment, nor is failure to achieve abstinence defined as a treatment failure. The major focus of the psychotherapy is on the causes and consequences of drinking. Emphasis is placed on producing changes in psychological and social functioning. Fees from $1.00 to $15.00 per visit are charged on a sliding scale based on income, financial obligations, and type of treatment. Most patients are seen on a once-weekly basis.

Facility 3 is a half-way house (abbreviated HWH). It offers extended residence in order to achieve and maintain sobriety and to reestablish vocational stability. Abstinence is a requirement for remaining in the house. An active program of self-government is maintained in the facility. Some nonprofessional counseling is afforded families of residents, some vocational counseling is available, and attendance is required at Alcoholics Anonymous meetings at the house. Charges, at cost, are made for living in the house. These fees of about $30 per week are paid by the residents after they have obtained a job.

Facility 4 is a county police work rehabilitation center (abbreviated PWC). This is a facility established under the jurisdiction of the county sheriff's office. Persons convicted for public intoxication in the municipal court may request assignment to the work rehabilitation center in lieu of a jail sentence. Residents live for approximately 60 days at the center before discharge to the community. The center is located in an isolated rural area and residents typically spend their entire time at the center. The focus of the program is twofold: to assess the vocational capabilities of the resident so that he can be placed in a meaningful work experience at the center, and to provide an experience in self-responsible communal living in the small dormitories. Some psychological testing is conducted as an adjunct to discharge counseling. Alcoholics Anonymous meetings are conducted on the site, with required participation of all residents. Alcoholism is defined as a disease following the AA philosophy; however, the acquisition of practical skills in conducting one's life, both vocationally and socially, is the main emphasis.

Patient population selection

At each of the four facilities we sought to evaluate the total population admitted for treatment. At each of the four facilities during the same period of two months, July–August 1968, all consecutive admissions were evaluated. Because of different admission rates, and occasional incomplete protocols at each facility, the population number varies for each facility:

Aversion-Conditioning Hospital (ACH): $n = 30$
Outpatient Clinic (OPC): $n = 26$
Half-Way House (HWH): $n = 31$
Police Work Center (PWC): $n = 34$

There is a total $n = 121$, of which 18 are women. At the OPC, 13 of 26 subjects are women, and at the ACH, 5 of 30 subjects are women. The HWH and the PWC are male-only facilities.

Method

Each subject was interviewed upon admission by the same rater. An alcoholism assessment and interview schedule was employed, based on previous studies by Pattison et al. (1968). Details of methods and of scaling are reported in the earlier paper. Ordinal scales were used to rate physical health (PSS), interpersonal health (ISS), and vocational health (VSS). The sum of subscale scores yielded a total score in each of these areas for purposes of statistical analysis. A drinking scale (DSS) reflects drinking quantity, behavior, and sequelae. All the scores increase with pathology. The ranges for the scales are PSS (0–7), ISS (0–15), and VSS (0–10). On the DSS range (0–12), 0 indicates abstinence, 1–5 normal drinking, and 6–12 pathological drinking.

The Minnesota Multi-Phasic Personality Inventory (MMPI) was administered to each subject. In addition to the usual clinical scales, the MacAndrew Alcoholism Scale was scored. Routine demographic data were obtained for each subject.

In addition to the above standardized protocols, each subject was asked to respond to six open-ended questions:

1. What is your attitude toward treatment here?
2. What other methods and facilities have you previously sought for treatment of your alcoholism problem?

3. Why did you choose this facility for your treatment?
4. How do you anticipate that this treatment program will be different from the previous ones which you have tried?
5. What do you expect to obtain from your treatment in this program?
6. What other resources might you turn to?

The responses to these questions were rated in nominal categories for purposes of analysis and comparison.

Results

Table 2 presents the variation in demographic items among the four facilities. Although there is a statistically significant difference between mean age levels, all four populations fall in the fifth decade of life, which suggests that age difference does not primarily account for the variance found on other measures. There is statistically significant variation in educational level, as well as distinct modal differences (not statistically rated) on occupational level and marital status.

These demographic variables can be taken to reflect a general variable—social competence. In this light, the four populations range in a continuum from high social competence to low social competence: ACH–OPC–HWH–PWC.

The ACH population has the highest level of education, representing college-type people. These subjects have a high socioeconomic status and have retained intact marriages. This population reflects a high degree of social competence in several areas of life.

Table 2. Variation on demographic items for four facility populations

	Mean for Age [a]	Mean Grade Level [b]	Modal Occupational Level	Modal Marital Status
ACH	50.3	14.9	White collar professional	Married
OPC	42.2	12.5	White collar	Married, divorced
HWH	42.2	11.4	Skilled labor	Divorced
PWC	46.5	9.9	Unskilled labor	Single, divorced

[a] Means between each facility (except ACH × PWC; OPC × HWH) differ from each other at $p \leq 0.10$ (t-test).
[b] Means between each facility differ from each other at $p \leq 0.05$ (t-test).

The OPC population has completed a high school education and has held middle-level jobs in life. Most of these subjects have married, although almost half were divorced. This population reflects a fairly typical middle-class social competency with some breakdown in social competence reflected in the divorce rate.

The HWH population has not completed high school and generally has not attained other than skilled labor-type jobs. Almost all of this population who have married are divorced. These subjects represent a marginal level of overall social competence in our society.

The PWC population has attained only a grade school education, having held almost solely unskilled labor jobs. A majority have never married; those who did marry are divorced. This group demonstrates poor social competence in every area of life noted here.

Health scale scores

Table 3 presents the Health Scale scores for each of the facility populations. Each of the four populations has very high (pathological) drinking scale scores (DDS), as might be expected since the scale reflects the typical clinical parameters used to define overt

Table 3. Health score variation of four facility populations

Facility	Drinking Health Score (DSS)	Interpersonal Health Score (ISS)	Vocational Health Score (VSS)	Physical Health Score (PSS)
	Mean scale score for populations			
ACH	9.3	3.1	1.9	2.8
OPC	9.6	5.6	3.0	2.7
HWH	10.0	6.1	4.6	2.4
PWC	9.8	4.7	3.9	2.1
	Comparative difference between population p-values (for Duncan Multiple Range Test)			
ACH × OPC	n.s.	<0.01	<0.05	n.s.
ACH × HWH	n.s.	<0.01	<0.01	n.s.
ACH × PWC	n.s.	<0.05	<0.01	n.s.
OPC × HWH	n.s.	n.s.	<0.01	n.s.
OPC × PWC	n.s.	n.s.	n.s.	n.s.
HWH × PWC	n.s.	<0.05	n.s.	n.s.

alcoholism. In other words, all four populations are clinically alcoholic. The differences in scores are not statistically significant.

The scores on the physical health scale (PSS) are modest. No statistically significant difference was found among population scores. Since each of the four facilities was geared to the treatment of alcoholism per se, rather than physical concomitants of alcoholism, it is not surprising to find minimal variation on this scale. Although there may be differences in these four populations in terms of physical symptoms secondary to alcoholism, these physical problems would have received treatment before referral to any of the four facilities for treatment of the alcoholism per se.

On the interpersonal health scale (ISS) we do find graded differences between facilities. In rank order, healthy to unhealthy: ACH (3.1)–PWC (4.7)–OPC (5.6)–HWH (6.1). The differences are significant at both ends of the continuum, with the ACH population statistically significant in difference from all the other populations. Thus this scale correlates with the demographic data on social competence. The ACH population has sustained the least social disintegration. The PWC population has lived a relatively isolated existence and hence shows little deterioration, since these subjects have developed a style of life that does not involve others. The OPC population does have sustained interpersonal relations; however, they are marred by conflict. The HWH population represents those whose families have disintegrated secondary to their alcoholism.

On the vocational health scale (VSS) we find a comparable but not identical pattern. In rank order, from healthy to unhealthy: ACH (1.9)–OPC (3.0)–PWC (3.9)–HWH (4.6). Both in rank order comparison and statistical comparison, the ACH population has maintained high function. Here the OPC population shows greater continued function, as one might expect from an outpatient population. Both the PWC and HWH populations represent those who have no current vocational functional capacity. Again, the PWC population consists of those who have never had much vocational skill, while the HWH subjects have lost theirs.

A comparison of the profiles developed from the demographic data and the Health Scale scores presents similar pictures. The major difference lies in the fact that the Health Scale scores are sensitive to *change* in status. Hence, in terms of social competence, we find the ACH population has retained overall social competence in the face of alcoholism problems. The OPC population has lost competence in the area of interpersonal relations; the HWH population has lost competence in both interpersonal and vocational areas; while the PWC population never had a high degree of competence in any area, which shows up in our Health Scale scores as spuriously healthier scores than those populations which have lost competence.

MMPI scale scores

The first procedure with the MMPI data consisted of plotting mean MMPI profiles for each of the four facility populations. Each of these population profiles was then submitted for blind analysis by a rater uninvolved in data collection. These are presented in Figure 1.

The MMPI profile for the ACH population displays a negative F-K ratio approaching significance. People who score in this fashion would be intent to present themselves as "rational," socially acceptable people who would not be inclined to define difficulties in living as due to problems in themselves. Preferred psychological defenses would be those of externalization. There is a moderate use of somatization. Defenses are not quite adequate in preventing unawareness of a lingering, chronic moderate depressed state. In view of the accompanying elevation on the Mf scale, denoting passivity, few active steps would be taken to alleviate uncomfortable feelings. The rest of the profile is unremarkable, suggesting that one would not expect a great deal of traumatic change, either for better or for worse, in this population. The overall impression is that of a chronic, lingering dissatisfaction which, however, would not prevent a person from moving in social settings and being accepted there.

The MMPI profile for the OPC population is introduced by an elevation on the F scale exceeding one standard deviation. In the absence of a significant F-K ratio, it would appear that this population was quite willing to report openly about itself and, if anything, to take some pains in calling attention to difficulties. Significant peaks are on the depression and psychopathic deviant scales, with secondary peaks on the Pt and Sc scales. In the presence of the considerable elevated Mf scale, this profile would depict the population as a rather passive but angry group who would find it difficult to express aggression in a direct way. They would, in part, express this frustration in intrapsychic ways through depression. This group reports that they have a vague

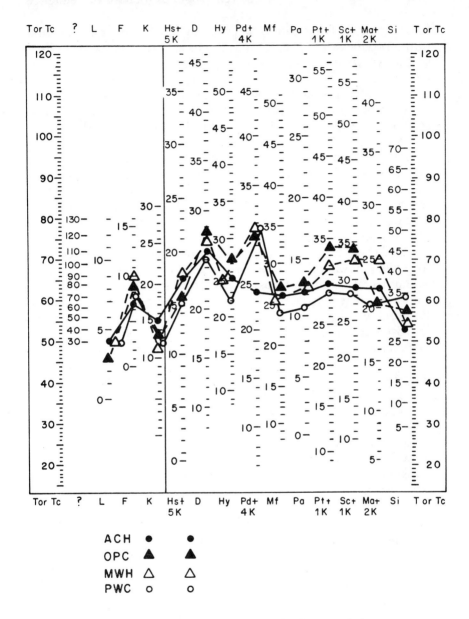

Figure 1. Composite MMPI profiles for four populations.

feeling of not having gotten their due in life. The overall elevation of the profile would suggest that things are still somewhat in flux, that most modes of defense have been tried out and found wanting. A basic triad of passivity, anger, and depression exists.

The MMPI profile for the HWH population is introduced by considerable elevation on the F scale, suggesting an intent to draw attention to their plight. There are peak elevations on the Pt, Sc, and Ma scales. A good deal of anger is present, but with a certain amount of passivity that would make a direct expression of feelings difficult. The overall elevation suggests a broad picture of some somatic complaints, a general feeling of dissatisfaction, indirect manipulations with a goal of being taken care of, but all in less than extreme proportions. In all, the demand of "being taken care of" is most prominently developed in this profile.

The MMPI profile for the PWC population is introduced by a somewhat elevated F scale, suggesting that these people are quite willing to talk about intrapsychic matters and might even call attention to their personal problems. There are peaks on the depression and psychopathic deviant scales with slight elevation, not approaching significance, on the Mf scale. This population appears to be an angry one that would act out their feelings of anger and nonconformity. Yet the presence of moderate depression indicates that even the acting out of conflict as a defense is not adequate to ward off discomfort.

A comparison of the MMPI profiles for each of the four populations does present significant differences in the clinical terms described above. It should be noted also that there are several uniform features. Most striking is the uniform elevation on the depression scale found in all four populations. This concurs with commonplace clinical observation of depression among alcoholics. Also, in all but the ACH population there is an elevation on the sociopathic deviant scale. Again, this is a commonplace observation: poor ego controls with antisocial behavior are part of the constellation of alcoholic behavior. However, the ACH alcoholics do not demonstrate this characteristic, in keeping with their overall high social competence. The second procedure with the MMPI data consisted of an analysis of variance of each set of scale scores. Statistically significant variance was found on scales F, K, Hy, Pd, Ma, Si, and the MacAndrew Alcoholism Scale. Since these scales represent more enduring characterological traits, not as subject to variation over time, we conclude that differences on these scales between populations may reasonably reflect intrinsic population differences. The scores on these scales were then analyzed between populations using the Duncan Multiple Range Test (Edwards, 1968). These data are presented in Table 4.

The F scale represents a collation of qualities including calling for help; seeking attention; demanding, yet with somewhat callous disregard for others; a degree of manipulativeness; and the appearance of dependency (in rank order, highest to lowest in these qualities: HWH–OPC–PWC–ACH). The polar extremes are statistically significant. In clinical terms, the HWH population must admit total defeat, ask for admission, and acquiesce to the communal living program of the half-way house. At the other extreme, the ACH population is allowed to maintain its pose of personal competency by the aversion-conditioning hospital. Both personality traits fit well with the character of the treatment institution.

The K scale is tabbed the "social desirability" scale, reflecting the disinclination to locate problems within oneself, to externalize, to somatize, to appear normal and conventional (in rank order, from highest to lowest ACH–OPC–PWC–HWH). Again the polar extremes are statistically significant. The findings here correlate nicely with the previous scale. The ACH population is more set toward social desirability, while the HWH population is

Table 4. MMPI score variation of four facility populations

Facility	F	K	Hy	Pd	Ma	Si	MacAndrew Alcoholism Scale
	Mean scale scores for populations						
ACH	59.4	55.0	66.4	67.1	61.9	53.2	25.3
OPC	64.1	52.0	67.1	74.5	60.1	59.0	26.3
HWH	67.1	49.2	64.8	76.8	69.9	54.9	30.6
PWC	62.9	49.6	61.1	75.1	60.8	60.2	28.3
	Comparative differences between populations p-values (for Duncan Multiple Range Test)						
ACH × OPC	n.s.	n.s.	n.s.	<0.01	n.s.	<0.05	n.s.
ACH × HWH	<0.01	<0.05	n.s.	<0.01	<0.01	n.s.	<0.01
ACH × PWC	n.s.	<0.05	<0.05	<0.01	n.s.	<0.05	n.s.
OPC × HWH	n.s.	n.s.	n.s.	n.s.	<0.01	n.s.	<0.01
OPC × PWC	n.s.	n.s.	<0.05	n.s.	n.s.	n.s.	<0.01
HWH × PWC	n.s.	n.s.	n.s.	n.s.	<0.01	n.s.	n.s.

made up of social undesirables, the more so because they have lost what they had once attained in terms of life function.

The Hy scale is a mixed scale. It reflects the use of repression and specific somatization of anxiety (in rank order, from highest to lowest: OPC–ACH–HWH–PWC). Again the polar extremes are statistically significant. The two populations with the highest overall competence, ACH and OPC, continue to function despite their alcoholism problems, whereas the other two populations experience more overt distress and disruption of their life. They do not exhibit as much capacity to defend against the conflicts concomitant to their alcoholism.

The Pd scale reflects the qualities of egotisticalism, disdain of social convention, anger, and the acting out of conflict (in rank order, from highest to lowest: HWH–PWC–OPC–ACH). Each of the four populations shows elevation on this scale, although the ACH population is statistically significantly lower, in keeping with the traits of this population observed on the prior scales, while the HWH population, with the highest score, has indeed acted out its anger and inability to adapt to social convention.

The Ma scale reflects action orientation and the amount of available energy for utilization by the person (in rank order, from highest to lowest: HWH–ACH–PWC–OPC). The HWH population differs significantly from the rest. This may reflect the lack of neurotic mechanisms found in the ACH and OPC populations which would bind energy, and the relatively low level of life style of the PWC population. The OPC population has the lowest rating of available energy, reflecting the neurotic internalization of energy.

The Si scale reflects the extroversion-introversion dimension of personality. Elevation on this scale indicates introversion (in rank order, from highest to lowest: PWC–OPC–HWH–ACH). Three of the populations demonstrate significant introversion, with ACH the lowest and statistically significant in difference. Again, the ACH population presents with a capacity for external social competence, whereas the other populations are more internally oriented.

The MacAndrew (1965) alcoholism scale was devised to differentiate alcoholism from general neurotic traits that might be associated with alcoholism. It does not contain items directly pertaining to alcohol use in its recommended 49-item inventory. A presumptive diagnosis of alcoholism is made with scores of 24 or above. All four populations scored above this cutoff point [in rank order, from highest to lowest: HWH (30.6); PWC (28.3); OPC (26.3); ACH (25.3)]. The polar extremes on this scale are statistically significant. The rank order is interesting, in that it seems to reflect the views of each population regarding alcoholism. The HWH population must admit to alcoholism in order to be admitted, the PWC population can hardly deny alcoholism since they were convicted, the OPC population finds alcohol a complication of their lives, while the ACH population can define alcoholism as an allergy which really does not involve them as persons. This variation seems to be reflected in the variation in scores on the MacAndrew scale. Nevertheless, all four populations are above the cutoff score for the definition of overt alcoholism.

Population orientation toward treatment and facility

This section examines the open-ended questions that were addressed to each subject. Our intent was to assess, if possible, factors in the social system that "matched" each population to a particular facility.

Table 5 presents the response to Question 1: What is your attitude toward treatment here? Although each population generally responded with a positive attitude toward treatment, there are some notable trends. The two populations with higher social competency (ACH, OPC) express more negativism toward treatment. The OPC population has a majority which is not positively oriented toward treatment. This may reflect the fact that this population consists of persons with an orientation toward emotional conflict as their major problem, rather than alcoholism per se. Further, the OPC facility does not demand a high degree of expressed positive motivation as a "card of admission," whereas at the other facilities a subject is likely not to be admitted if he does

Table 5. Question 1 – What is your attitude toward treatment here?

Facility	Want very much to be helped	Some desire to be helped	Neutral	Some disinclination to be helped	Protests attendance
ACH	5	15	7	3	0
OPC	4	7	6	8	1
HWH	5	24	1	1	0
PWC	4	20	6	4	0

not express himself positively (regardless of whether he actually feels positively or not). This becomes evident in subsequent questions which reveal a marked disparity between the subjects' personal feelings about treatment versus their public avowal to the facility personnel.

Table 6 presents the responses to Question 2: What other resources have you sought previously for treatment of your alcoholism? Aside from a rather typical scatter, several patterns stand out. The two populations with higher social competence (ACH, OPC) have tried medications that influence psychic function (narcotics, barbiturates, tranquilizers), whereas the other two populations (HWH, PWC) show a lower absolute and proportionate use rate. This may reflect the psychodynamic differences revealed by the MMPI profiles. The more socially competent populations try to change their internal function, while the other two populations turn toward change of external factors.

The use of Alcoholics Anonymous is quite striking. The ACH patients have not "hit bottom" and the AA route does not seem to have been a desirable choice, while a preponderance of the PWC population, the socially inept, have tried AA. The PWC population does not seem to be tied in to typical social institutions. These subjects have made less use of private physicians and mental health facilities, yet have had the most contact of all populations with Skid Row missions and half-way houses. In contrast, such

Table 6. Question 2 – What other resources have you sought previously for treatment of your alcoholism?

Resource	ACH	OPC	HWH	PWC
Antabuse	4	5	6	8
Narcotics	1	0	0	0
Barbiturates	2	3	1	1
Tranquilizers	11	11	7	0
Alcoholics Anonymous	10	18	19	26
Private physician	12	13	11	1
Mental health professional	9	9	10	7
Clergy	4	5	12	7
Medical hospitalization	2	3	4	4
Skid Row missions	0	0	2	3
Alcoholism information center	0	1	1	0
Half-way house	0	2	1	10
Nothing	7	4	6	5

Note. Multiple responses were recorded.

institutions of social support have not been much utilized by the socially competent populations (ACH, OPC). The HWH population is remarkable for its high use of clergy, which perhaps reflects the fact that this population has sustained marked disruption in their life patterns. Hence clergy might well be sought out by this population to help prevent their lives from breaking up.

Table 7 presents the data on Question 3: Why did you choose to come to this facility? Note that the two populations that are sensitive to social performance (ACH, OPC) ascribe their choice to the recommendation of high status social others (professionals). This dimension is totally lacking in the two other populations (HWH, PWC). The concept of seeking a treatment that had something specific to offer is represented in both the ACH and HWH populations, but surprisingly not in the OPC population. This may be a correlate of the general negativistic attitude on the part of the OPC population. It is noteworthy that the PWC population does not see its facility as a treatment opportunity, but merely the better of bad alternatives. In assembling this chart from the raw data, the authors were impressed by the lack of sense of choice and direction in seeking treatment. It is almost as if the subjects go where they are told or pushed, rather than from any internal incentive and personal selection of a preferable alternative.

This trend is emphasized in Table 8, which presents Question 4: If you anticipate that this treatment experience will be different from your prior treatment experience, how do you expect this to be different?

It is noteworthy how many subjects in each population antici-

Table 7. Question 3 – Why did you choose to come to this facility?

Reason	ACH	OPC	HWH	PWC
A preferable alternative to jail				21
Forced to come here by family			6	
Professional recommendation	17	22		
Good reputation of the facility for helping alcoholics	10	4	16	
Provides a better program than other facilities	3		4	3
Failure of treatment at other facilities			4	
Opportunity for isolation from life and alcohol			1	10

Table 8. Question 4 – If you anticipate that this treatment experience will be different from your prior treatment experiences, how do you expect this to be different?

Difference	ACH	OPC	HWH	PWC
My own attitude has changed	6	17	13	5
This facility has a better attitude toward alcoholics	4	0	4	5
This facility has a better treatment program	11	2	0	0
This program will provide isolation	0	0	0	7
No difference anticipated	9	7	14	18

pate no difference in this treatment setting—that is, failure. This is particularly noticeable for the PWC population, and to a lesser extent for the HWH population. Also, in both these populations there is little sense that the facility is different or better than others.

Likewise, the OPC population does not perceive the clinic as offering a better treatment experience, but rather indicates that their own attitude has changed toward treatment. Perhaps some other facility and method might work as well, in their view. Only in the ACH population is there a sense of having chosen a better and more effective program. In part this may reflect the fact that the ACH population has had less experience in other alcoholism treatment programs, and also the fact that the ACH facility actively sells its program as the definitive treatment of alcoholism.

Table 9 presents the data on Question 5: What do you expect to obtain from treatment at this facility? The population with highest

Table 9. Question 5 – What do you expect to obtain from treatment at this facility?

Expectation	ACH	OPC	HWH	PWC
Isolation from life and alcohol			4	25
Total rehabilitation of my life	12		25	1
Vocational rehabilitation			1	6
Emotional rehabilitation		20		
Abstinence	18	5		
Nothing		1	1	2

social competence (ACH) stands out with the goal of abstinence, or total rehabilitation. Those goals are within the realm of realistic expectation for them. The OPC subjects define their expectations in terms of emotional rehabilitation, with far less emphasis on abstinence. The HWH and PWC population do not even list abstinence as the primary goal. For the HWH, their goal is life rehabilitation, whereas the PWC population have very meager goals—just to stay away from alcohol for a short while. Although all four facilities treat "alcoholism," it is apparent that each of the four populations hopes to attain rather different gains, and that treatment for alcoholism means quite a different thing to each of the four populations.

Finally, Table 10 presents the responses to Question 6: What other resources are you aware of that might provide help for your alcoholism problems? The "nothing" response is striking in the HWH population, who are characterized in their MMPI profile as seeking to get others to take care of them. The PWC population in contrast looks for another external shelter (Skid Row mission or half-way house). The ACH population turns toward socially acceptable resources (hospitals, clinics), while the OPC population, interestingly, looks toward forms of therapy very different from the psychotherapy setting of their facility (namely, an aversion treatment or a half-way house). The OPC population attitude may reflect their indiscriminate attitude and general tone of negativism.

Table 10. Question 6 – What other resources are you aware of that might provide help for your alcoholism problems?

Resources	ACH	OPC	HWH	PWC
Alcoholics Anonymous	18	19	16	19
Aversion therapy	0	13	8	8
Medical hospitalization	10	1	3	5
Skid Row missions	0	0	3	5
Alcohol information center	3	8	4	4
Mental health clinics	4	4	3	2
Clergy	0	1	0	0
Private physicians	2	0	1	0
Half-way house	3	11	3	22
Nothing	5	2	9	3

Note. Multiple responses were recorded.

Data Analysis

We have obtained several classes of data for each of the four facility populations. There is relative congruence between the findings derived from the several classes of data that suggests internal validity for our findings. Hence, we suggest that our data support the hypothesis that each of the four alcoholism treatment facilities serves different populations of alcoholics.

In terms of homogeneity, there is an obvious range of variation within each population, as well as the variation between populations. Each population is not totally different from the other populations; in some instances there are shared characteristics, and there is some overlap of characteristics between populations. In conceptual terms it may be more accurate to view the four populations as arranged along a continuum, rather than as extremely distinct subsets. However, in most instances our data demonstrate a relative degree of within-population homogeneity, so that differences among the four populations can be posited to represent significant differences, rather than a random variation. This is supported by the statistical procedures with the MMPI data in which we employed the Duncan Multiple Range procedure. By that method we were able to account for within-population variation and still demonstrate significant differences among populations.

Working from the premise that we have data to support our contention that each of the four treatment facilities serves four different populations of alcoholics, we can take the next step of summarizing the characteristics of each population and examining the characteristics of the population vis-à-vis the treatment offered by each facility. The questions we wish to raise are: (1) Does the orientation of the facility match the orientation of the population it serves? (2) Are the treatment services appropriate to the orientation?

As suggested earlier, it appears congruent with our data to arrange the four populations along a continuum of social competence. Other research workers utilizing the construct of social competence have shown that essential alcoholics possess less social competence than reactive alcoholics; in addition, variation in social competence is related to treatment outcome (Goldfried, 1969; Rudie and McGaughran, 1961; Singer et al., 1964; Sugerman et al., 1965). The four populations range according to social competence, from highest to lowest: ACH–OPC–HWH–PWH.

The aversion-conditioning hospital population

This population has the highest education, has achieved the highest socioeconomic status, has maintained intact marriages, has the healthiest interpersonal and vocational health scores. These are all indicators of capacity for successful social competence. The MMPI data indicate a constellation of personality traits requisite for social skills, for they are oriented toward social acceptance, externalization of problems, somatization of anxiety. In other words, these people are able to successfully keep life conflict outside themselves, or at least out of conscious conflict. As a corollary, they have the lowest MacAndrew alcoholism score, seek a treatment program that will restore flagging social acceptance, are sensitive to social sanctions, and turn to appropriate social resources.

This population is relatively "less sick," hence has less need for, or room for, improvement in total life rehabilitation. Alcoholism is for them still an external problem. Alcoholism has not severely disrupted their social and vocational life. If these people feel that they have reached their most desperate point, that level is not nearly as low as for subjects at other facilities. These are the "high bottom" alcoholics. Further, being socially sensitive, they may seek treatment earlier in the career of alcoholism before disintegration has occurred, with more social and vocational pressures present to push them into treatment. (Their older average age may reflect greater capacity to defend against overt alcoholism for a longer period of life, for the ACH population had been drinking for as many years as the other populations.)

For this population, alcoholism is a disease, a medical problem akin to heart trouble or a broken leg, not a reflection of personal conflict. The medical view of alcoholism is a psychodynamic and sociodynamic stance that allows them to maintain their characteristic life style.

The facility in turn reflects the needs and perceptions of this population. The population is "high class" and the treatment is "high priced." The medical orientation of the hospital conveys the message that medical personnel will "do something" to the person to rid him of the unpleasant affliction—alcoholism. The aversion treatment philosophy allows the subjects to maintain their image of adequate, successful individuals. Further, this facility does little in the way of social and vocational rehabilitation, since little is needed in this area. Nor does it provide much psychological treatment. Overtly, this facility does not define alcoholism as a psychological problem. Yet, the facility would probably be less successful if it did attempt psychological treatment, for such would challenge the major defense systems of its population.

The outpatient clinic population

This population provides evidence of less social competence. The patients have a high school education, have more middle-class jobs, have married but experienced more divorces, have intermediate interpersonal and vocational health scores. The MMPI data indicate a capacity for moderate defenses against anxiety, but not sufficient enough to prevent the breakthrough of anger, depression, and feelings of inadequacy and passivity. The partial breakthrough is represented in the intermediate MacAndrew score. Thus, this population experiences conflict while still maintaining a reasonable degree of social competence. The subjects are still socially sensitive and look to socially respectable resources; however, they are more negativistic and pessimistic. They see alcoholism as a personal problem, yet fear that it will overwhelm their lives more than it has. The definition of alcoholism as an expression of neurotic conflict is an apt summation of their personal experience of being alcoholic. In this population there is less need to maintain status by using a medical rationalization such as the ACH population. On the other hand, alcoholism is disrupting their lives and, hence, undercuts their capacity to deny that alcoholism is a personal problem.

The outpatient clinic is the most eclectic of the facilities. It has a physician and nurse in attendance who can deal with withdrawal symptoms. Disulfiram and psychotropic drugs are prescribed, and patients are informed of and encouraged to attend Alcoholics Anonymous if they so desire. Yet the main modality is psychotherapy. Treatment is addressed to the personal conflicts that cause the patient to abuse alcohol, and it aims at dealing with the consequences of drinking in order to provide insight and strengthen ego adaptive skills. These subjects do not seek the dramatic life rehabilitation that is the goal of the HWH and PWC populations, yet they cannot afford the "closing over" of conflict that the ACH population can maneuver. The facility does not provide the shelter required of the HWH and PWC populations, for this population can still maintain social competence. Nor does this facility focus on abstinence as its treatment goal, since the supposition is that symptomatic alcoholism will disappear with the resolution of life conflict. This is a feasible treatment approach for this population. In contrast, abstinence must be a treatment goal for the ACH population since life conflict is maintained outside awareness; and in the HWH and PWC populations there is insufficient social competence to go ahead with the business of living life while simultaneously coping with drinking problems —abstinence must be a precursor to rehabilitation for them.

The half-way house population

This population demonstrates the effects of diminished social competence. The patients have only partial high school education, have held laboring and technical jobs, have mostly suffered marital disintegration, and show less healthy interpersonal and vocation scores. Their MMPI data show characterological traits of inability to cope adequately with conflict and stress. They seek succorance; anger is repressed in the service of getting others to help them; and manipulation of others to provide for them becomes a major coping style in life. Their MacAndrew score is high. They experience a breakdown of coping mechanisms and turn to others—the clergy, institutions—to rehabilitate them.

These are the "low bottom" alcoholics. They possessed enough social competence to achieve a degree of successful social adaptation before alcoholism caught up with them. But they have suffered huge steps downward from their previous jobs and family relationships. Although not on Skid Row they are close to it. Alcoholism in this population is not an isolated affliction, but a major disruption of their entire life. The use of the medical illness model of the ACH population is not a defense this population can use. Even if they stopped drinking immediately they would still face immense problems of social and vocational rehabilitation. Neither can they employ the model of emotional illness used by the OPC population, for alcoholism is a total life problem, not just the expression of "neurotic conflict." Further, the psychological "set" of this population would not fit them for the usual models of middle-class psychotherapy, for they are faced with real-life exigencies of just existing. Alcoholism is a problem of life; a need to start over, to achieve spiritual renewal; a destruction of self which means that a new style of life adaptation must be carved out.

The half-way house facility reflects the needs of the population in both philosophy and program. There is heavy reliance on Alcoholics Anonymous philosophy, including the need to surrender one's previous life style, to start over, to begin to live one day at a time, the quasireligious conversion to becoming a new man. The AA philosophy emphasizes the need to change one's whole orientation toward life and toward oneself, and this matches very well the fact that alcoholism has destroyed these subjects' lives and a major reconstruction of a pattern of living is needed. Similarly, the program does not emphasize denial, as with ACH, nor strengthening of already present ego skills, as with OPC, but rather starts by providing nurturance, gratification of daily needs and desires—and limit-setting and behavior-defining boundaries —very necessary for persons with limited ego skills and strengths. The facility provides opportunity for resocialization, and only secondarily any psychological enquiry into what has been the emotional style of life in the past.

The police work center

This population lies at the lowest end of the social competence scale. These subjects are the socially inept. They only completed grade school, have held transient laboring jobs, have usually never married. Their interpersonal and vocational health scores are the unhealthiest. Their MacAndrew alcoholism scale score is the highest. Their MMPI data reveal a lack of capacity to cope with stress. They show little capacity to deal with internal conflict save via direct action. Hence, they show psychopathic qualities, nonconformity, overt hostility, yet despair and depression. There is little strength in themselves which they can call upon; hence they can only look to external agencies and personnel to cope with life. Alcoholism is for them just another piece of problematic behavior with which they cannot cope. They see little difference between treatment methods or facilities. They have no hope that life can be different. Their only goal is to achieve some respite in life by living in an institution that will provide them with support and nurturance that they cannot give themselves. They will pass from one institution to the next. Within the institution that provides necessary supports they can function; outside a supportive institution, they cannot.

The facility provides a program that in actuality meets the immediate needs of this population, although the treatment goals of the facility may be much more ambitious than appropriate to the population. The subjects live in the facility for 60 days isolated from society and from liquor. The subjects are provided with guided and supervised living experiences, and some realistic work experience is provided. It is the type of facility which, if it were a long-term domiciliary, might provide a sheltered living base where this population might function at some level of effectiveness. The facility makes no major effort at gradual social reentry; it does not provide significant psychological counseling. It may perceive these areas as desirable additions to the program, but they would doubtless effect little change in this population. In contrast to the HWH population where the problem is "resocialization," the problem here is "socialization," which would also require significant augmentation of basic psychological coping skills. The facility provides a modest short-term "drying out" experience, which may be the appropriate level of intervention for this population.

Discussion

In overview, one can observe gross and subtle differences between each of the four populations: differences in basic social competency, in basic characterological styles, in patterns of coping with alcoholism. There are differences in how alcoholism is defined, how the subject comes to treatment, how the subject perceives treatment, what the subject expects from treatment, and how the subject will continue on in life thereafter.

One is struck by the relatively good "match" found between population needs and perceptions and the philosophies and methods of the facilities to which they go. The goals of treatment are basically different, whether defined by the population or by the facility. One would expect each of the four populations to improve in different ways, according to the role alcoholism plays in their life, their particular life style defenses, their rehabilitation needs, and the methods and goals of the facility to which they went. We have demonstrated the validity of this proposition in our earlier work (Pattison et al., 1969).

We still cannot answer how successful each facility is with its population, or whether each facility could increase its "successful" yield from treatment. However, that question may be more accurately studied by developing research procedures that evaluate successful outcome in terms of separate populations, instead of more global criteria.

Further, we cannot determine why we find such a high degree of congruence between population and facility. Since we examined the subjects immediately upon admission, it may not be sufficient to argue that the populations had already been successfully indoctrinated by the facility. Psychodynamic and sociodynamic characteristics may predetermine a type of self-selection. That is, the population that seeks admission to a facility may do so because the facility is perceived as congruent with the subject's psychodynamic and sociodynamic style of coping with alcoholism. This thesis is the subject of further research currently under way.

In terms of comprehensive community planning for alcoholism programs, the data raise several issues.

First, we may conclude that if a subject appropriate to one facility went instead to another of the facilities, the response to treatment might be poor. On the other hand, when a patient seeks treatment at a facility matching his situation, the likelihood of success appears much better. No facility can ever hope to attain a "complete match" with its clients. However, we would like to approximate an 80% match instead of perhaps a 20% match.

Second, the gross variation among populations suggests that a treatment facility should pay close attention to the characteristics of the population it seeks to serve. Commendable and useful treatment methods appropriate elsewhere may be inappropriate, redundant, or destructive for its population. Treatment philosophy and methods should be congruent with the anticipated population.

Further, changes in treatment methods should be undertaken with careful consideration of population variables. If the ACH were to add intensive psychotherapy to its program, that might well run counter to the prevailing perceptions and defenses of its clients as well as to the institution itself. Or if the OPC were to expand its population to other types of alcoholics, it would have to provide more assistance beyond once-a-week contact. Or if the HWH were to professionalize its program, that would run counter to the ethos of self-help and group help rather than professional help. Or if the PWC were to seriously attempt a strenuous rehabilitation program it might set up insuperable goals leading only to frustration for its subjects and its staff. In other words, one cannot change the population or methods without shifting the interplay of all the variables under consideration.

Third, our data strongly suggest that no one facility is in a position to provide a "comprehensive" treatment program for all types of alcoholic populations in a community. Or if such a comprehensive program were established, it might well have to consist of parallel-type programs. Many communities today have only one or another type of alcoholism treatment facility. Thus, they most likely provide treatment for only a particular subpopulation of alcoholics. In their recent books on comprehensive community treatment programs for alcoholics, Plaut (1967) and Blum and Blum (1967) recommend the use of multiple treatment approaches. However, multiple treatment approaches may best be construed as complementary facilities serving particular population needs rather than competitive facilities seeking to see who can "do it best."

Our data suggest that alcoholism treatment programs do not exist in isolation in a community. Rather they are part of a complex system of social regulation and social interaction. Our data suggest that we need to obtain further data on how and why subjects move into certain treatment facilities and where they go subsequently. The treatment of alcoholism in the community can then be analyzed in terms of larger social systems that provide the basis for more rational community planning and implementation.

References

Bailey, M. B. and Stewart, J. Normal drinking by persons reporting previous problem drinking. *Quart. J. Studies Alc.,* 1967, *28,* 305–315.

Blum, E. M., and Blum, R. H. *Alcoholism: modern psychological approaches to treatment.* San Francisco: Jossey-Bass, 1967.

Blane, H. T., Overton, W. F., and Chafetz, M. E. Social factors in the diagnosis of alcoholism, I. Characteristics of the patient. *Quart. J. Studies Alc.* 1963, *24,* 640–663.

Chafetz, M. E., Blane, H. T., Abram, H. S., Golner, J. G., Lacy, E., McCourt, W. F., Clark, E., and Meyers, W. Establishing treatment relations with alcoholics. *J. Nervous Mental Disease* 1962, *134,* 395–409.

Clancy, J., Vornbrock, R., and Vanderhoof, E. Treatment of alcoholics: a follow-up study. *Diseases Nervous System,* 1965, *26,* 555–561.

Cummings, E. *Systems of social regulation.* New York: Atherton Press, 1968.

Davies, D. L. Normal drinking in recovered alcohol addicts. *Quart. J. Studies Alc.,* 1962, *23,* 94–104.

Edwards, A. L. *Experimental design in psychological research,* 2d ed. New York: Holt, Rinehart, & Winston, 1968.

Edwards, G., Hensman, C., Hawker, A., and Williamson, V. Who goes to Alcoholics Anonymous? *Lancet,* 1966, *2,* 382–384.

Gerard, D. L., and Saenger, G. *Outpatient treatment of alcoholics: a study of outcome and determinants.* Toronto: University of Toronto Press, 1966.

Gerard, D. L., Saenger, G., and Wile, R. The abstinent alcoholic. *Arch. Gen. Psychiat.* 1962, *6,* 83–95.

Goldfried, M. R. Prediction of improvement in an alcoholism outpatient clinic. *Quart. J. Studies Alc.,* 1969, *30,* 129–139.

Hill, M. J., and Blane, H. T. Evaluation of psychotherapy with alcoholics. *Quart. J. Studies Alc.,* 1967, *28,* 76–104.

Hurwitz, J. I., and Lelos, D. A multilevel interpersonal profile of employed alcoholics. *Quart. J. Studies Alc.* 1968, *29,* 74–76.

Kendall, R. E. Normal drinking by former alcohol addicts. *Quart. J. Studies Alc.* 1965, *26,* 247–257.

Kissin, B., Rosenblatt, S., and Machover, S. M. Prognostic factors in alcoholism. *Psychiat. Res. Rept.,* 1968, *24,* 22–43.

Krause, M. S., Ransohoff, D. J., and Cohen, P. Promoting possible alcoholism referrals. *Comm. Mental Health,* 1968, *4,* 13–16.

MacAndrew, C. The differentiation of male alcoholic outpatients from nonalcoholic psychiatric outpatients by means of the MMPI. *Quart. J. Studies Alc.,* 1965, *26,* 238–245.

Mindlin, D. F. The characteristics of alcoholics as related to prediction of therapeutic outcome. *Quart. J. Studies Alc.,* 1959, *20,* 604–619.

Moore, R. A., and Buchanon, T. K. State hospitals and alcoholism: a nationwide survey of treatment techniques and results. *Quart. J. Studies Alc.,* 1966, *27,* 549–568.

Negrete, J. C., MacPherson, A. S., and Dancey, T. E. A comparative study of the emotional and social problems of active and arrested alcoholics. *Laval. Med.* 1966, *27,* 162–167.

Pattison, E. M. A critique of alcoholism treatment concepts: with special reference to abstinence. *Quart. J. Studies Alc.,* 1966, *27,* 49–71.

Pattison, E. M., Headley, E. B., Gleser, G. C., and Gottschalk, L. A. Abstinence and normal drinking: an assessment of changes in drinking patterns in alcoholics after treatment. *Quart. J. Studies Alc.,* 1968, *29,* 610–633.

Pattison, E. M. A critique of abstinence criteria in the treatment of alcoholics. *Intern. J. Soc. Psychiat.,* 1968, *14,* 268–276.

Pattison, E. M., Coe, R., and Rhodes, R.J. Evaluation of alcoholism treatment: a comparison of three facilities. *Arch. Gen. Psychiat.,* 1969, *20,* 478–488.

Plaut, T. F. A., *Alcohol problems; a report to the nation.* New York: Oxford, 1967.

Pokorny, A. D., Miller, B. A., and Cleveland, S. E. Response to the treatment of alcoholism: a follow-up study. *Quart. J. Studies Alc.,* 1968, *29,* 364–381.

Rudie, R. R., and McGaughran, L. S. Difference in developmental experience, defensiveness, and personality organization between two classes of problem drinkers. *J. Abnormal Social Psychol.*, 1961, *62*, 659–665.

Schmidt, W., Smart, R. G., and Moss, M. K. *Social class and the treatment of alcoholism.* Toronto: University of Toronto Press, 1968.

Singer, E., Blane, H. T., and Kasschau, R. Alcoholism and social isolation. *J. Abnormal Social Psychol.* 1964, *69*, 681–685.

Sugerman, A. A., Reilly, D., and Albahary, R. S. Social competence and the essential-reactive distinction in alcoholism. *Arch. Gen. Psychiat.* 1965, *12*, 552–556.

Sutherland, E. H., Schroeder, H. G., and Tordella, O. L. Personality traits and the alcoholic: critique of existing studies. *Quart. J. Studies Alc.,* 1950, *11*, 547–561.

Tomsovic, M. Hospitalized alcoholic patients. A two-year study of medical, social and psychological characteristics. *Hosp. Comm. Psychiat.* 1968, *19*, 197–204.

Trice, H. M., and Belasco, J. A. A selective approach to the improvement of treatment for alcoholics. Paper read at the annual meeting of the National Council of Alcoholism, New York, April, 13, 1966.

Zwerling, I., and Clifford, B. J. Administration and population consideration in outpatient clinics for treatment of alcoholics. *N. Y. Med. J.,* 1957, *57*, 3869–3875.

Reginald G. Smart,
Wolfgang Schmidt, and Marcia K. Moss

Social Class as a Determinant of the Type and Duration of Therapy Received by Alcoholics

The principles which should govern the treatment of alcoholics have never really been clarified. There is no established treatment which guarantees more than about 35% abstinence rates. Considering the lack of theoretical and empirical knowledge about the treatment of alcoholics, interest in these questions comes to reside in the principles *actually* governing current treatment.

Implicit in the operation of most treatment facilities is the as-

From *International Journal of Addictions,* 1969, *4,* 543–556. Reprinted by courtesy of Marcel Dekker, Inc.

sumption that treatment is offered "to each according to his needs." If treatment is to be given wisely and fairly to all alcoholic patients there must be an assessment of their present drinking and personality status and an estimate of their abilities to benefit from therapy. A further requirement is that the selection of treatment depend upon the patient's diagnosis and prognosis or on other knowledge about the nature of his illness and its development. Ideally, factors extraneous to the patient's personality and disease process should have no bearing on the type or duration of the treatment offered to him, especially in state-supported facilities.

The burden of the argument presented here is that these ideals do not receive adequate expression in the treatment of alcoholics. This argument will be based upon empirical observations which show that numerous factors completely extraneous to the diagnosis and prognosis of patients determine the choice of treatment offered them. Chief among these factors is the patient's social class. Attempts will be made to investigate the importance of this variable in determining treatment as compared to the importance of variables associated with the diagnosis, presenting problems, or personalities of the patients.

Social Class as a Determinant of Treatment among Alcoholics

Most of what is known about social class and treatment for alcoholism comes from Hollingshead and Redlich's (1958) psychiatric census of New Haven in 1950. This census uncovered 91 alcoholics who were being treated by psychiatrists, but several considerations lead one to doubt this figure as an accurate estimate of alcoholics in treatment. For example, this figure includes only alcoholics being treated by psychiatrists, mental health facilities, and alcoholism clinics, but it does not include those attending Alcoholics Anonymous. Just how one would classify AA treatment is problematic, of course, but it should likely be considered a form of group psychotherapy.

Another concern about Hollingshead and Redlich's alcoholics relates to the very large proportion (51%) being treated in mental hospitals. This tends to suggest an underreporting of cases being seen as outpatients or private cases. A related point is that 46% of the alcoholics in the census were diagnosed as "chronic alcoholism with psychosis," although the percentage of alcoholics ever having any psychosis is usually taken to be much smaller (Jellinek, 1960). (The breakdown of the alcoholic population into "With" and

"Without psychosis" was not published by Hollingshead and Redich but they graciously made it available to J. R. Seeley for more extended analyses [Seeley, 1960a, 1960b].)

Exclusive of Hollingshead and Redlich's study, only fragmentary information on social class and the treatment of alcoholics is available. Zax, Marsey, and Biggs (1961) found no relationship between education or occupation and length of stay of alcoholics in psychotherapy, using a rough categorization of cases above and below the median number of therapeutic contacts. Social class variables were not specifically investigated, but education and occupation correlate highly with them. Blane and Meyers (1964) did find that lower-class alcoholics had fewer therapeutic contacts than did lower-middle-class alcoholics. There were no differences among upper-middle-class and lower-class alcoholics in number of contacts. There is, as yet, no reliable information on the ways in which social class determines type of treatment for *outpatient alcoholics*—no indications as to whether lower-class patients get mainly organic, nonpsychotherapeutic treatment interventions.

There are some compelling reasons for predicting that an alcoholic's social class would *not* relate closely to the type of therapy he receives. Treatment for psychiatric disorders with important components of physical illness such as organic and senile psychoses have been shown to be relatively free of social class determinants (Hollingshead & Redlich, 1958). Many alcoholics present problems of physical illness such as gastric ulcers, organic brain damage, and cardiovascular ailments and it may be that their physical condition reduces the therapists' choice of treatment so markedly that the patient's social class is an unimportant determinant.

It can also be argued (Hollingshead & Redlich, 1958) that the availability of a cheap and effective treatment for psychiatric disorders (such as ECT for affective psychoses) would reduce the influence of social class on choice of treatment. There are several sets of drugs in common use as cheap but effective therapies for alcoholism—the protective drugs (disulfiram and Temposil) and the tranquilizers and antidepressants. These drugs form an important part of most outpatient therapies for alcoholism but their effect in reducing social class influence is completely unknown.

On the other hand, there is at least suggestive evidence, however suspect, from Hollingshead and Redlich's work that social class *is* an important determinant of treatment choice. There are also indications from studies of neurotics that social class determines source of referral, length of therapy, and the relative experience of the therapist assigned. The present study was designed to investigate fully the relationships between the social class of alcoholic patients and their therapeutic experience, including the areas suggested above.

A further addition to the relevant literature is attempted by making detailed breakdowns of the type of therapy used. Most earlier studies have been comparisons of psychotherapy with "custodial" or "organic" therapy with almost no indication of the procedures actually employed in them. Also, psychotherapy has rarely been differentiated from supportive case work therapies, or even from group psychotherapy. A further consideration is that there is no knowledge of how various drug therapies are administered to various social classes. Indeed, most of the relevant papers in this area, including those by Hollingshead and his associates (1958) completely predate the introduction of tranquilizing and antidepressive drugs for psychiatric patients. In addition, the protective drugs in alcoholism may be a therapy which might be applied equitably to patients of all classes. The present study examines the variables of social class as determinants of all aspects of treatment for alcoholics.

The Treatment Setting

To test hypotheses about social class and treatment the program of treatment for alcoholism in the Toronto Addiction Foundation clinic was studied. The treatment services provided by the Foundation are designed primarily for those alcoholics who acknowledge a need for assistance—regardless of which pressures and events conspired to bring about the expression of such a need. For patients who come with acute physiological disturbances, treatment is provided in one of three general hospitals. Here, the aim is to restore patients to physical well-being as quickly as possible.

Most patients arrive sober at the clinic, usually at a scheduled appointment time. Patients, no matter how they are referred, are seen by a physician or a social worker for an intake interview which is basically diagnostic. The patient's expectation of therapy is determined, and the patient, with the help of the therapist, decides whether to move directly into the Foundation's inpatient facilities (16-bed hospital) or to use only the outpatient facilities. Ideally, this decision is based on the patient's physical and psychological condition; however, at times, fear of losing a job, or lack of hospital space are also important determinants. Inpatients are expected to remain in the hospital for about two to three weeks and here their treatment centers around "group learning," which consists of didactic presentations on various aspects of the alcoholism problem and films, followed by group discussion. These group experiences are highly structured and attendance is expected. Concurrently, the patient also receives individual attention from a social worker, psychiatrist, or physician; however, the main emphasis is on group processes.

It is not unusual that one of these three professions carries a case from intake to termination of treatment, and therapists are largely free to choose those patients whom they wish to see on a continuous basis. In general, it may be said that the therapists enjoy a large measure of autonomy with respect to *all* aspects of individual treatment. While in the hospital a patient may begin to use a protective drug (Antabuse or Temposil) or he may receive other forms of medication such as tranquilizers and antidepressants.

Alcoholics on an outpatient basis may have formal regular weekly meetings with one of the treatment staff, or their contacts may be as informal as occasional visits to the hospital lounge. They may also participate in group psychotherapy conducted for outpatients. These groups are not limited in numbers of participants nor are there rigid demands made on frequency and regularity of attendance. As in the case with inpatients, extensive use is made of medication as an adjunct to group and individual treatment. (The present description applies to the operation of these facilities during the study years. Since the clinic's orientation is essentially experimental, major changes have been made over the last four years. To mention only a few, a day care program and certain concepts of the therapeutic community have been introduced. This has resulted in more patient participation in disciplinary and social functions and in the breakdown of some traditional clinical formalities.)

The Alcoholic Sample

The alcoholic sample investigated was selected from all patients whose initial contact with the clinic was in the years 1958, 1959, and 1960. A one-third sample of all these "initial contact" patients was randomly chosen. This made a total of 520 patients, from which 108 were excluded because insufficient information was available to determine their social class; thus the number actually studied was 402.

Social class determination

In accordance with previous research in this area (Hollingshead & Redlich, 1958) a three-factor index of social class was used for each of the 402 alcoholic patients. The three items of information required to determine an individual's position in the class structure are (1) residential characteristics, (2) occupational level, and (3) educational achievement. Essentially, the Hollingshead and Redlich method of scoring was employed; this method involves seven-point ratings on these three factors and multiplying each rating by a factor weight determined by a regression equation (Hollingshead & Redlich, 1958).

The Residential Scale. On the basis of the housing and other demographic data reported in the 1961 Census of Metropolitan Toronto, the city was mapped according to its ecological characteristics. The Census divides the city into relatively homogeneous regions (census tracts); for each of these regions a series of ratios was devised which provided an estimate of the socioeconomic level of the residents in a particular region. These ratios took into account the education, occupation, and income of the residents as well as the characteristics of their dwellings.

The Occupational Scale. The occupation of a patient was taken to be the one he had held most of his life, in other words, his main occupation and not his most recent. These were ranked on a seven-point scale which was adapted to the occupational distribution of the patient population from which the sample was drawn.

The Educational Scale. Education was ranked according to the number of years an individual completed in an educational institution. Thus, only formal education was taken into consideration in this scale.

The three scaled items were combined in the following equation: $X = 6a + 9b + 5c$, *where x* = the social class score, *a* = the residential scale value, b = the occupational scale value; and c = the educational scale value; and the three constants (6, 9, and 5) are factor weights derived empirically by Hollingshead and Redlich (1958).

Since each of the three factors was ranked on a seven-point scale, the theoretical range of the scores was from 20 to 160. Following, again, the method of Hollingshead and Redlich (1958), the inference was made that "the index of social position scores should cut at the point of most heterogeneity between raw scores and weighted scores." On this basis the range of scores for each class was decided as shown in Table 1.

Table 1. Social class levels

Class Level	Class Score Range	Percentage of Cases
Class I	20–40	10.6
Class II	55–86	53.8
Class III	110–139	35.6

Class I comprises patients who, for the most part, hold college degrees, are professionals, or hold medium-level managerial positions. They typically own and live in medium-priced, one-family urban or suburban homes, with a small minority in rented apartments.

Class II includes mainly small proprietors, salesmen, and white collar workers. They are frequently high school graduates or hold similar degrees from technical schools. None in this group attended college. They usually live in newer suburban developments of the lower-price range, but rarely own a house within the city proper.

Class III consists mainly of unskilled and occasional workers, educated to the primary level or less, and living in the lowest rental transitional areas of the inner city. It also includes a small number of semiskilled factory hands but with educational and residential characteristics similar to the unskilled groups.

Collection of Diagostic and Treatment Data

A schedule was developed to record all the data relevant to the questions being investigated. The data on treatment were separated into:

1. Inpatient treatment
2. Outpatient treatment
3. Recommendations for therapy
4. Individual therapy
5. Group therapy
6. Medication for nonphysical disorders
7. Medication for physical disorders
8. Prognosis

It must be emphasized that the findings to be reported are all derived from a study of the patient files of a single agency for the treatment of alcoholism. Because of this limitation there are questions. They typically own and live in medium-priced, one-family patient population studied seems to be similar to other alcoholic populations at alcoholism clinics, at least in terms of social characteristics.

Control of factors associated with diagnosis and treatment

Prior to investigation of social class and treatment it was thought that the three classes might differ in characteristics which could influence the alcoholic's treatment. Some of these are marital status (Gibbins & Armstrong, 1957), ethnicity (Popham, 1959), sex (Lisansky, 1957; Bronetto, 1965), age (Jellinek, 1946), and alcoholic symptoms. Consequently, consideration of these factors was necessary in order to clarify the direct relationship between treatment and social class.

Statistical analyses showed no class differences between ethnicity, race, or sex; hence it was unnecessary to control these factors in the present analyses.

More striking class differences in age necessitated routine control of the age factor in all analyses where the numbers were large enough to accommodate a third factor. This is controlled in all analyses by founding class comparisons on data from which age differences were removed. It consisted, first, of a categorization of cases above and below the median age. Second, a three-dimensional chi-square design (Winer, 1962) was employed. This design permits analyses of three factors simultaneously and also analysis of the association between any two factors with the third controlled. All analyses performed involved social class and age, and one of the diagnostic or treatment variables. This analysis also yields an interaction term, the size of which indicates the independence of any two factors from the third.

Results and discussion

Therapies which were actually received were analyzed. The first question concerned possible class differences in the *number* of treatment contacts, and the three classes did not differ in this measure.

A breakdown of contacts by the professions of the therapists showed that Class I patients are most often treated by psychiatrists and Class III patients by physicians. Class II had an intermediate position between the higher and lower classes. Social workers treat similar proportions in all three socioeconomic groups. These class-related treatment patterns could not be fully explained by differences in diagnosis or age, thus confirming the earlier impression that treatment tends to follow social class lines.

Two important findings should be emphasized. First, there is no evidence that it is *more difficult* for a Class III person to be admitted to treatment than it is for persons in the other two classes. Second, the three classes do not differ in their *respective number* of treatment contacts. Thus, the inequalities in treatment which were found related solely to the profession of the therapist. Perhaps it is an oversimplification to expect that the choice of therapy should be solely related to a patient's psychological or physical condition. One has to consider that the use of many psychiatric techniques presupposes certain characteristics in the patient. For example, insight therapy relies heavily on verbal communication, and it can be assumed that persons in the lower social classes are less likely to have the capacity for verbalization than the better educated classes. Furthermore, "talking therapy" runs counter to the expectations of many lower-class patients. Hollingshead and Redlich (1958) comment that "the need and value of insight therapy is not appreciated by lower-class patients. They seek material help in the form of pills, needles, obscure rays, and ritual; some actually seek support and sympathy." Further, they reported that lower-class psychiatric patients present mostly somatic symptoms when they enter psychiatric treatment and, accordingly, ask their therapists for organic treatments. Under such circumstances, it is not surprising that, in the present sample, lower-class patients show less therapy by psychiatrists and more by physicians than patients in the upper classes.

Physicians in the present clinic do not employ uncovering techniques, and, aside from medication, their approach consists mainly in giving support and advice. This form of therapy probably best meets the demands of many lower-class patients for an authoritarian attitude on the part of the physician. Whether such methods are the most successful ones among those available in this clinic cannot be answered. Nevertheless, they apparently prevent lower-class patients from ceasing contact with the clinic at a higher rate than patients of other classes. Clinics which offer only therapy by psychiatrists frequently report (Hollingshead & Redlich, 1958) that patients in the lower classes drop out of treatment much faster than those in the higher classes. It will be recalled that in the present population the three classes did not differ in their overall number of treatment contacts. This may have occurred because more than one psychiatric technique was made available to the patients. A lower-class patient who is not "psychologically oriented" and does not respond to insight therapy might discontinue treatment if no alternative technique were made available to him. Similarly, a psychologically oriented patient may find the supportive techniques and the advice given by physicians insufficient. Although it does not appear to be an explicit policy of the present clinic to assign patients according to such criteria, the distribution of contacts with psychiatrist and physician nevertheless suggests a selective process of that nature.

The absence of class differences in the case loads of social workers is probably due to the adaptiveness of this profession to the needs of their patients. The records indicate that case workers in this clinic provide insight therapy as well as supportive therapy. In some cases they concentrate on social and other environmental problems, in others on emotional problems. The overall impression is that the varying approaches of case workers are largely determined by the problems a patient presents. If a person does not comprehend a psychogenic explanation of his problems, case workers apparently accept this difficulty and apply another approach. This versatility is probably the most significant single factor explaining the absence of class differences among patients treated by social workers. It should be added here that the two classes which are commonly referred to as upper- and lower-upper-class are not represented in the present sample. Members of this social strata have been known to resent being treated by social workers. There were no indications of such attitudes detectable in this study material.

Group therapy is most widely participated in by Class II patients, but among those patients who do attend the group sessions, there are no class differences in the respective number of contacts. From the distribution of recommendations for therapy, one would have expected Class I to rank lowest in receiving this therapy. Yet, it was found that Class III least often received group therapy. It is felt that these results reflect, first, the extensive pretreatment exposure of Class II patients to group processes in Alcoholics Anonymous. For many of these patients, the group therapy offered by the clinic may constitute in some respects a continuation of an earlier and familiar form of treatment experience. Second, the low rate of participation of Class III patients is probably related to their difficulties in engaging in group interaction.

Prior to this study, little attention had been devoted to the relationships between social class and the administration of drugs to alcoholics. The largest and most comprehensive study of social class and mental illness, reported by Hollingshead and Redlich (1958), was completed before the introduction of psychoactive drugs. Nevertheless, these authors expressed the belief that therapy with a cheap and effective drug might minimize the effects of social class and treatment. The use of psychoactive and protective drugs for alcoholics would appear to fall into this category. However, these drugs do not seem to have done away with class influences on therapy. Drug therapy relates to social class in ways similar to other therapies. A number of factors unconnected with the patient's illness contribute to the drug therapy received.

Other considerations which require further discussion are that drug therapy is *rarely recommended* but *frequently prescribed* and that medication for physical disorders does not seem to follow physical diagnoses.

It was found that physical diagnoses do not relate to the prescriptions of medications for physical disorders. Class I had the highest proportion of physical disorders and Class III the lowest, but Class II patients received the most medication. This has been explained by the collateral finding that physicians prescribe many drugs in the absence of a stated diagnosis—especially drugs for gastric disorders. It has not been taken to indicate some overall inefficiency in prescribing medication but merely a fault of the recording system. This system allows drugs to be prescribed without a recorded physical diagnosis, and for diagnoses with no prescription following. It would be most interesting to know whether prescriptions ordinarily do relate to social class or solely to physical pathology, but these questions could only be answered with data from more complete files than were available here.

Difficulties in understanding current therapy are even greater when prescription patterns for psychoactive drugs are studied. These psychoactive drugs include tranquilizers, antidepressants, and sedatives. Although they constitute one of the most common therapies (more than 50% of all patients receive them), they are never part of the official "recommendation for therapy." It may be that this reflects the therapist's concern about the efficacy of the psychoactive drugs or perhaps concern about the alcoholic's addictive liability. Alcoholics, after all, are persons who have demonstrated an inability to use a drug—alcohol—moderately, and there are numerous reports of the tendency of alcoholics to shift their dependency to other drugs (Westling, 1958; Chessick, Looff, & Price, 1961).

Many of the psychoactive drugs administered could, of course, be a stopgap therapy for patients who cannot be offered any psychotherapy, although prescriptions for these drugs are concentrated in the classes already receiving the most group and psychotherapy. These drugs appear, then, to be an adjunct to therapy rather than a substitute for it. They do not represent a cheap and inexpensive therapy which is applicable to patients of all social classes, and the same nondiagnostic considerations are involved with their prescription as with other therapies.

It was demonstrated that psychoactive drugs tend to be more often prescribed for Class I and II patients than for Class III. However, there were no class differences in the frequency of nonalcoholic psychoses or neuroses which would require more psychoactive drugs in Class I and II patients. In addition, Class III showed more alcohol psychoses than the other two classes and the same number of personality disorders as in Class I. Little rationale for the class differences in prescriptions can be found among the formal diagnoses given. Social class seems to be the best predictor of whether a patient will receive a psychoactive drug.

When personality descriptions are considered, still no meaningful pattern emerges. Class III patients are least often described as neurotic, as self-dissatisfied, or as having guilt feelings. Patients in Classes I and II were not described as more depressed, or as more worried, tense, nervous or anxious, although they were described as more discontented. It might be expected that tranquilizers would be widely used to overcome these personality defects in Class I and II patients. However, tranquilizers were not more often prescribed for Class I and II patients than for Class III. There were large class differences in the prescribing of sedatives and antidepressants, with Class III getting far fewer than the other two classes. However, there were no class differences in formal diagnoses of depression which would naturally lead to more sedative and antidepressive medication in Classes I and II. In general, then, very little correspondence can be found between formal and informal diagnoses and the type of drug therapy offered. Again, social class seems to outweigh diagnostic considerations and the therapist's stated evaluation of personality.

Protective drugs are rarely recommended as therapy but are frequently prescribed. However, there are no social class differences in the actual use of protective drugs. It is widely held that protective drugs are the most useful adjunctive agents to other forms of therapy. They have only very limited counterindications and form a simple, inexpensive form of treatment. From the literature it would appear (Hollingshead & Redlich, 1958) that organic treatments which meet these requirements are least likely to be differentially distributed over the social classes. Thus, the absence of class differences in this form of medication in the present sample apparently confirms the validity of the above statement.

However, the relative importance of social class in the recommendations for protective drug therapy runs counter to the expectations derived on this basis. Explanation of this class pattern has to be sought in the clinical practice concerning medication with disulfiram and Temposil. The use of the two drugs is extensively discussed with all patients and, with rare exceptions, medication is made available to them. But unlike other medication, it is not prescribed without a patient's expressed desire to submit to this treatment. In fact, prior to receiving a prescription, a patient has to sign a form indicating that the action of the drug has been explained to him. Although no pressure is exerted on a patient to take protective drugs, the treatment policy apparently contains an implicit expectation for patients to avail themselves of this therapy, and as the data indicate, about one-half of them, in all three classes, actually do so. In addition, protective drugs are at times explicitly recommended as a therapy of choice. The impression gained from the study of the latter instances is that by and large this is done when intensive individual therapy is not indicated. Thus, such a recommendation is very rarely combined with a recommendation to receive psychotherapy and quite frequently made in conjunction with group therapy. One may conclude that a formal recommendation of protective drugs usually implies that individual treatment is not warranted rather than that protective drugs will bring about a desired change.

Summary

The social class of an alcoholic is closely associated with many aspects of treatment. In fact, it is often a better predictor of type of therapy than is physical or psychiatric diagnosis. It would be well, of course, to determine the generality of these findings. We have some indications that the main relationships hold, but individual findings may vary from one facility to another.

References

Blane T., and Meyers, W. R. Social class and establishment of treatment relations by alcoholics. *J. Clin. Psychol.*, 1964, *20*, 287–290.

Bronetto, J. A preliminary examination of the double standard hypothesis of differences in certain characteristics between male and female alcoholic patients. ARF Substudy, 4-8-65, 1965.

Chessick, R. D., Looff, D. H., and Price, H. G. The alcoholic narcotic addict. *Quart. J. Stud. Alc.* 1961, *22*, 261–268.

Gibbons, R. J., and Armstrong, J. D. Effects of clinical treatment on behavior of alcoholic patients. *Quart. J. Stud. Alc.*, 1957, *18*, 429–450.

Hollingshead, A. B., and Redlich, F. C. *Social class and mental illness.* New York: Wiley, 1958.

Jellinek, E. M. Phases in the drinking history of alcoholics. *Quart. J. Stud. Alc.* 1946, *7*, 1–88.

Jellinek, E. M. *The disease concept of alcoholism.* New Haven: Hillhouse Press, 1960.

Lisansky, Edith. Alcoholism in women: social and psychological concomitants. I: Social history data. *Quart. J. Stud. Alc.*, 1957, *18*, 588–623.

Popham, R. E. Some social and cultural aspects of alcoholism. *Canad. Psychiat. Assoc. J.*, 1959, *4*, 222–229.

Seeley, J. R. Treated chronic alcoholism and social class. ARF Substudy. 21-2-60, 1960a.

Seeley, J. R. Social class risk rates for being in treatment for alcoholism. ARF Substudy 22. 1-1-60, 1960b.

Westling, A. Drug addicts and alcohol. *Duodecim*, 1958, *74*, 411–422.

Winer, B. J. *Statistical principles in experimental design.* New York: McGraw-Hill, 1962.

Zax, M., Marsey, R., and Biggs, C. F., Demographic characteristics of alcoholic outpatients and the tendency to remain in treatment. *Quart. J. Stud. Alc.*, 1961, *22*, 98–105.

10. Outcome of Treatment

35% abstinent rate today

In accord with the principles set forth in this discussion, differential selection of treatment leads to differential outcome in treatment. That is, there is no uniform single outcome of alcohol rehabilitation; rather there are different patterns of outcome.

Much of the traditional pessimism about the treatment of alcohol-dependent individuals has come from the indiscriminate mix of individuals with poor prognosis with those having a good prognosis, resulting in a mediocre overall picture of treatment efficacy. Further, the failure to define specific treatment goals has perhaps led to ineffective, inappropriate, unachievable, or overlooked treatment goals. We propose that treatment outcomes of alcohol-dependent individuals can range from very modest changes in total life style to dramatic rehabilitation. Since individual differences are profound, we must assess individual progress in terms of each individual case. Within different subgroups of alcohol-dependent individuals, we believe that different treatment outcomes can be developed as general guidelines for treatment.

In this section we shall focus on multivariant outcomes of treatment. In our view, treatment should aim to change, and hopefully improve, function in each life health area where the alcohol-dependent individual may demonstrate dysfunction. Thus, the outcome of treatment is really multiple outcomes, for we must examine the degree of change in dysfunction in each area of life health.

In the first paper, Pattison presents one of the early published studies on multivariant outcome. He not only sets forth the rationale for multiple outcome criteria but reviews the empirical data that support the validity for this approach to treatment.

The intriguing study by Orford shows how client choice is an important determinant of the successful achievement of treatment goals. His study also demonstrates that drinking behavior alone does not indicate what changes are going on in other areas of a client's life.

In the final reading, Sobell and Sobell present the results for multiple areas of life health of a unique experimental individualized behavioral treatment program. The study was a controlled experiment using 70 male state hospital patients as voluntary subjects. All subjects had been diagnosed as "alcoholic," had experienced al-

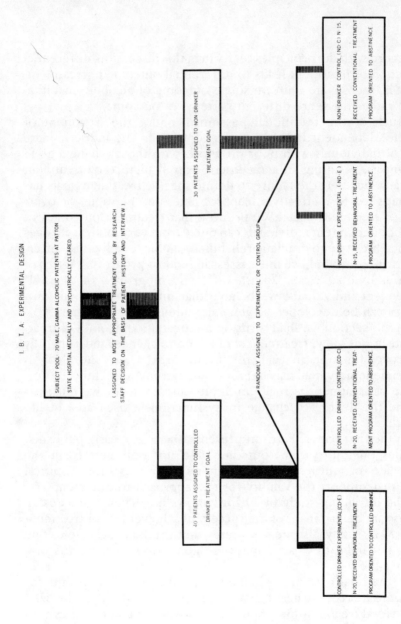

Figure 1. Experimental design used in study of individualized behavior therapy for alcoholics (IBTA). Reprinted from *Behavior Therapy*, 1973, 4, 49–72. Copyright © 1973 by Academic Press, Inc.

I. B. T. A. EXPERIMENTAL DESIGN

SUBJECT POOL: 70 MALE GAMMA ALCOHOLIC PATIENTS AT PATTON STATE HOSPITAL MEDICALLY AND PSYCHIATRICALLY CLEARED

(ASSIGNED TO MOST APPROPRIATE TREATMENT GOAL BY RESEARCH STAFF DECISION ON THE BASIS OF PATIENT HISTORY AND INTERVIEW)

40 PATIENTS ASSIGNED TO CONTROLLED DRINKER TREATMENT GOAL

30 PATIENTS ASSIGNED TO NON DRINKER TREATMENT GOAL

RANDOMLY ASSIGNED TO EXPERIMENTAL OR CONTROL GROUP

CONTROLLED DRINKER EXPERIMENTAL (CD E) N-20, RECEIVED BEHAVIORAL TREATMENT PROGRAM ORIENTED TO CONTROLLED DRINKING

CONTROLLED DRINKER CONTROL (CD-C) N-20, RECEIVED CONVENTIONAL TREATMENT PROGRAM ORIENTED TO ABSTINENCE

NON DRINKER EXPERIMENTAL (ND E) N-15, RECEIVED BEHAVIORAL TREATMENT PROGRAM ORIENTED TO ABSTINENCE

NON DRINKER CONTROL (ND C) N 15, RECEIVED CONVENTIONAL TREATMENT PROGRAM ORIENTED TO ABSTINENCE cohol withdrawal symptoms, and were participating in an alcoholism treatment program. The experimental design is shown in Figure 1. The experimental treatment was based on a rationale that self-damaging drinking can be conceptualized as a discriminated, operant behavior (i.e., situation-specific and a function of its consequences), and that treatment procedures should be tailored whenever possible to meet the individual's specific needs. Prior to random assignment to either experimental or control treatment, each subject was carefully screened to determine his most appropriate drinking treatment goal—nondrinking (abstinence) or controlled drinking.

The experimental treatment procedures were extremely complex and can only be briefly summarized here. A complete description of the rationale for the study, its procedures, and earlier outcome findings are available in other publications (Sobell & Sobell, 1972, 1973a, b, 1977). Procedures included videotaping intoxicated subjects under experimental conditions, providing sober subjects with videotaped self-confrontation of their own drunken behaviors, and shaping of appropriate controlled drinking or nondrinking behaviors respective to treatment goal (alcohol was available throughout the program). The experimental program also included training in problem-solving skills, which involved a four-stage procedure concentrating on (1) problem identification —determining setting events (discriminative situations) for each subject's drinking, (2) training the subject to generate a series of alternative responses (behavioral options) applicable to those situations, (3) training the subject to evaluate the delineated alternatives in terms of potential immediate and delayed consequences, and (4) preparing the subject to employ the alternative(s) which could be expected to incur the best probable total outcome.

Control subjects received conventional treatment procedures which included group therapy, chemotherapy, Alcoholics Anonymous, physiotherapy, and other traditional services. At 6 months and 1 year following hospital discharge, follow-up evaluations found that experimental subjects functioned significantly better than control subjects, irrespective of treatment goal. This reading reports the findings of continued follow-up of the study.

E. Mansell Pattison

A Critique
of Alcoholism Treatment Concepts,
with Special Reference to Abstinence

Professional interest in the treatment of alcoholism has increased remarkably in the past 20 years. During this time, evaluative reports have gradually changed from empirical clinical impressions to control-designed follow-up studies. But the wide range of follow-up studies has been so heterogeneous that few reliable conclusions can be drawn about either treatment methods or results. Recent reviews of research on psychotherapy have indicated variables in both treatment process and outcome which are relevant to alcoholism (77). In the present paper these critiques will be applied to evaluations of the treatment of alcoholism.

Reviews of treatment up to 1942 reported improvement rates of 35 to 40% (99). At the time, Bowman and Jellinek (7) found only 7 adequately designed studies. A review of 20 follow-up studies available in English in the next 20 years has similarly yielded few reports sufficiently similar in methodology to be comparable (9, 14, 17, 22, 25, 26, 27, 34, 56, 61, 64, 72, 74, 79, 92, 94, 99, 100, 101, 106). Improvement rates range widely; many report 30 to 40% and a few report 70 to 80%. Moore and Buchanan (60) in a large sample of American state hospitals found a 1-year rate of about 33%.

Critical workers have repeatedly pointed out that neither treatment process nor outcome is a unitary phenomenon. In alcoholism, evaluation of treatment process has dealt with so many variables that it has been difficult to decide which therapeutic processes were being evaluated. Evaluation of treatment outcome has mainly focused on one variable—abstinence, which in isolation may be a grossly misleading criterion of improvement.

Cultural values also exert an influence on the criteria employed. The change in acceptance of alcoholism as a disease has affected case finding, treatment goals, and often the whole milieu of diagnosis and therapy.

Duhl (19) has noted that therapeutic progress is dependent upon

Reprinted by permission from *Quarterly Journal of Studies on Alcohol,* 1966, *27,* 49–71. Copyright by Journal of Studies on Alcohol, Inc., New Brunswick, N.J. 08903.

the development of new models of illness. In the field of alcoholism the models have been loosely structured and the epidemiological definitions ill formed. Follow-up studies, however, are an epidemiological problem and, as such, the relevance of the research depends upon the manner in which the problem is defined (29, 41, 48). This paper will explore some necessary refinements of definition suggested by clinical experience, cultural value conflicts, and recent research on abstinence.

Epidemiological criteria

Zubin et al. (108) have described a basic model for epidemiological research which I shall follow: "What clinical syndromes at which stage of their development and in what kinds of patients respond under what conditions in what short- and long-range ways to which measures administered by whom?"

"What clinical syndromes . . ."

Attempts to classify alcoholism have ranged from Knight's (40) classic divisions of essential and reactive to Jellinek's (38) recent fivefold typology. In actual clinical practice, however, no one classification has been satisfactory.

The heuristic cultural need to define alcoholism as a disease has sprung from a medical pathophysiological model which defines disease as an alteration in body physiology and which requires the demonstration of a pathophysiological process such as an allergic, endocrine, or appetite disorder. For alcoholism to qualify as a disease it would be necessary to demonstrate a physiological habituation, addiction, or compulsion to drink.

Talcott Parsons (67), however, has pointed out that disease is a multilevel concept. A strictly physiological concept (such as a "silent" cancer) pertains neither to personal discomfort nor to any social role. An intermediary concept combines physiological, personal, and social factors (laryngitis as a disease for an opera singer versus nondisease for a riveter). A social concept of disease has no necessary physiological aspect at all (whether a dental appointment is creditable sick leave).

All three concepts share a functional definition of sickness. In our western society the sick person is relieved of responsibility, afforded care, and expected to make efforts toward recovery. Society, in turn, neither demands continued function from the sick person nor blames him for his condition, but provides help for his recovery.

The conceptual level employed to define alcoholism has not been clear (51). Historically, alcoholism was defined solely at the level of physiology, following the model of disease most universally accepted (52). The recent World Health Organization definition is more nearly a social one, in keeping with the greater acceptance of socially dysfunctional roles within the compass of "ill roles" by our society (39, 80).

Blane, Overton, and Chafetz (6) have demonstrated that the diagnosis of alcoholism is a function of social perceptions, dependent upon both cultural and personal biases. In their study of physician referrals the doctors tended not to nominate a patient as alcoholic if he was working and retained his social and economic standard—they elected a physical diagnosis rather than the "alcoholic" label.

Diagnostic categories vary according to their purpose: treatment, prognosis, etiology, or some other. Confusion of purpose has occurred in the nomenclature of alcoholism with the result that the accuracy and usefulness of current diagnostic schema are minimal. Actually, alcoholism may be defined as a disease at multiple conceptual levels; some syndromes are primarily physiological, some primarily social. Recognition of this can avert futile efforts to conceptualize all problems related to alcohol at only one level. It seems more cogent to develop a classification of alcoholism syndromes based upon a multilevel schema of disease.

"At which stages of their development . . ."

What is the life stage of the patient, the psychodynamic stage of the personality, or the developmental stage of the alcoholism syndrome?

The age at which alcoholism becomes manifest may indicate both the type of syndrome and the prognosis. Alcoholism in a young person would indicate a more severe character pathology, while a similar problem in older persons suggests temporary recourse to immature behavior traits. While therapeutic potential may be greater in a young person during early stages of alcoholism, the older person may be more motivated for treatment after long experience with his alcoholism.

Psychodynamically there may be important distinctions between fixated and regressed alcoholics (1). In terms of the psychosexual phases of human development, they may remain fixated at an infantile mode of personality function, or, when the more advanced modes fail to cope adequately with life situations, regress to immature ones. The prognosis for a regressed alcoholic is frequently better than that for a fixated one. Treatment of alcoholics with orally fixated character disorders might well be different in terms of techniques, goals, and prognosis from treatment of alcoholics manifesting oral behavior but with a history of more mature behavior.

The stages of the alcoholism syndrome were described by Jellinek (37) in his survey of Alcoholics Anonymous members. His well-known chart on the progression of alcoholism has given rise to the popular idea of an inexorable progression of alcoholism to its florid stages. In his original article, however, Jellinek pointed out that many people "stuck," remaining at a given level of alcoholismic behavior.

Further popular misconception has arisen from Tiebout's (95) description of "hitting bottom." This has been taken to mean that treatment is futile until the alcoholic has progressed to the most florid stages of decompensation, overlooking the therapeutic intervention which can be made by confronting the patient with his situation and effecting successful treatment. (Round table discussion on alcoholism at the meetings of the American Psychiatric Association. St. Louis; May 1963.)

Previous evaluations of treatment concerned patients with long-standing, severe alcoholism. Today many reports indicate the presence of latent, hidden, or early problem drinkers who do not have florid alcoholism but who do demonstrate a pathological drinking pattern (35, 89). The prognosis for cases treated at this stage would be expected to be more favorable than in the advanced stages.

An example of stage-specific effects is "crisis intervention" therapy (66, 76). Therapeutic intervention in the patient faced with an acute life crisis is planned to assist in the healthful resolution of the conflict and avert the use of pathological modes, such as alcoholism (69). When alcoholism is triggered by crisis, immediate treatment may prevent the development of what might become a fixed problem.

The stage of illness is most important in assessing the effects of treatment. Those who are "sickest" may improve much, yet remain incapacitated; while those with minimal pathology may have little room for change and show no dramatic improvement—the "ceiling effect" (50).

To date we do not know the natural history of specific alcoholism syndromes. It would be helpful to know whether reactive alcoholics become essential alcoholics, or vice versa, what the remission rate is for specific syndromes, and whether treatment significantly augments the spontaneous rate of improvement.

Finally, we can consider stages in terms of Caplan's (10) three levels of treatment. Primary treatment is aimed at preventing development of the disease, secondary treatment at earlier and more effective case finding, and tertiary treatment at more effective treatment of overt pathology. Discussion of therapy in alcoholism has been characteristically limited to tertiary phase treatment alone. We are beginning to see some developments in secondary phase treatment, which I have suggested is affecting the definition and outcome of treatment programs, but little has really been done in terms of primary treatment (8, 62).

"In what kind of patients . . ."

Much evidence indicates that there are various personality types among alcoholics (36), and the idea of the alcoholic as a unique personality type has not been proven; not because it is untrue but, rather, too simple. Alcoholics Anonymous members, hospitalized alcoholics, outpatients, industrial employees, workhouse inmates and other categories are not homogeneous in either personality or alcoholism. Yet clinical experience indicates that there might be characteristic personalities for specific alcoholism syndromes if these could be defined. Zwerling (109) has described a schizoid personality common to his clinic; Seiden (81) has noted the type of successful AA member; and others have described the workhouse alcoholic and the Skid Row "wino" (20). In Cincinnati we have seen a specific personality in the Southern Appalachian migrant alcoholic (5).

It has been suggested that specific alcoholic syndromes may be characteristic of specific cultures (3). From our clinic data we have come to anticipate compulsive binge drinking in an oral-masochistic character structure from the Jewish or Catholic urban groups, whereas a Southern Appalachian would probably be a regular, intensive drinker with little proclivity for binge behavior and with an anal-sadistic character structure.

Such models are oversimplified, but they may have clinical usefulness in planning treatment programs. For example, Stone's (88) study suggests the effect of social migrancy upon successful AA affiliation. In our experience, the Southern Appalachian migrant has rarely found AA a useful resource, nor does he respond to the usual psychotherapy procedures. Survey of a local industrial plant revealed that a successful disulfiram-oriented program was treating a different socioeconomic class from any seen in either the local AA or our alcoholism clinic. (Personal communications from Edward Buyniski, M.D., Medical Director, General Electric Plant, Cincinnati.) The City Hospital sees many recidivistic alcoholics who are rarely referred anywhere for treatment after hospitalization.

One of the outstanding problems, then, in comparing follow-up studies of treatment programs is that the patient populations are so variable in composition (57). The evidence all suggests that rather than being uniform, the population of alcoholics is a complex, heterogeneous one.

"Respond under what conditions . . ."

Little attention has been paid to the effects of the treatment milieu. The patient treated in a setting where he cannot obtain alcohol is being subjected to an entirely different set of stimuli from the outpatient alcoholic involved in the ongoing stresses of job, home, and spouse.

The treatment milieu may be the most determinative factor in therapy. Some of the studies on aversion therapy during the 1940's pointed out that the results appeared to be predicated more on the therapeutic milieu than on the aversion treatment itself (11, 45, 91). Wallerstein (102) has demonstrated that the specific benefit of milieu approximated that of allegedly specific therapies. Mechanic (54) has also documented the therapeusis of milieu.

As an example of the variability of the milieu, the patient who attends a clinic under probation requirements may be compared with the voluntary patient (55), or with the different type of alcoholic, seen at an earlier stage, who is treated in his factory under the auspices, encouragement and support of his employer.

Another important variable is the patient's family (32). Studies of mental patients report that successful rehabilitation in the community has been primarily related to the therapeutic support of the family (18, 68, 86). The neurotic interaction of the alcoholic and his wife has been amply documented and exemplifies the effect of the social setting on the perpetuation of the alcoholism despite therapeutic efforts (69, 70).

The treatment setting, the influence of therapist-patient expectations (28), and the social context of the patient (3) have all been erratically controlled variables in most evaluative studies.

"In what short- and long-range ways . . ."

An immediate goal of halting drinking may be readily obtained; hospitalization will suffice to ensure abstinence. But it is common knowledge that this usually does not halt the alcoholism for more than a few months.

Short-range response to situational treatment needs to be distinguished from long-range reconstructive goals. Alcoholics may temporarily abstain and demonstrate better psychosocial functioning as a "flight into health" from treatment. Particularly in binge drinkers, the psychodynamic motivation for lengthy periods of abstinence leads to falsely encouraging success. A minimum of 6 months and an optimum of at least 1 year after treatment termination seems necessary to assure the presence of more than transitory benefits (24).

But is short-range abstinence always necessary for successful treatment? May it ever be contraindicated in terms of long-range goals of personality reconstruction?

It is also relevant to ask whether marked overall improvement, despite some continued drinking difficulty, may not be an appropriate goal. Total social, vocational, and psychological rehabilitation may be only idealistic goals. In both physical and psychological syndromes one cannot often eradicate fundamental pathology. Too idealistic a therapeutic aim on the part of both therapist and patient may lead to mutual frustration and failure to accomplish anything therapeutically. In alcoholism, the establishment of reasonable goals that can be achieved by a patient may be necessary and may not include total abstinence or total psychosocial rehabilitation.

Similarly, evaluation studies in which criteria of success are too unrealistic may give a falsely poor notion of the efficacy of treatment.

"To which measures . . ."

Multiple methods applied simultaneously have been employed in shotgun fashion on the thesis that perhaps something will "catch on." But the characteristic poor-treatment-risk alcoholic will not necessarily show improvement despite a massive load of therapeutics: he is hospitalized, followed as an outpatient, given disulfiram, sent to AA, given socioeconomic rehabilitation; he or his wife or both are seen in group, individual, or conjoint therapy; he writes letters, returns for more aversive conditioning, and is visited in his home; he is placed on probation, must attend programs in his factory, or may voluntarily seek help. With the wide variety of alcoholic syndromes, the stages of illness, and types of personalities, there seems to be no good reason to assume that all or most alcoholics will benefit universally from such a regimen. The prescription of multiple methods of treatment makes it difficult to assign significance to any one method.

In the most complete research design to date, Wallerstein's group at the Menninger Clinic (102) compared the effectiveness of disulfiram, conditioned reflex, group hypnotherapy, and milieu therapy and found roughly similar results, with disulfiram somewhat more effective than the others. Hoff (34) reported an increased improvement rate of about 40% by the addition of disulfiram or methaminodiazepoxide to the usual psychotherapy regimen.

Hospital treatment has varied from routine medical admissions to specifically structured milieu wards, and psychotherapy from brief superficial contacts to psychoanalytically oriented treatment. The use of disulfiram, tranquilizers, and placebos further complicates treatment evaluation. Moore and Buchanan (60) surveyed results in 103 state hospitals and found that rates of improvement varied little, no matter what the treatment program—most had about 33% improvement a year after therapy.

Rarely have multiple treatment variables been controlled. It is assumed that multiple treatment is synergistic, but to date no one has investigated the possibility that two treatments may be antagonistic. A suggestive study by Titchener, Sheldon, and Ross (96) found that group psychotherapy mobilized anxiety which counteracted the effects of prescribed tranquilizers. Other reports indicate that mobilization of anxiety, aggression, or fear in exploratory psychotherapy may serve to impede overall treatment rather than augment it. Similarly, reports on disulfiram therapy indicate that some patients fear a reaction and flee treatment if compelled to take the drug (12, 13, 53, 97).

I suggest that treatment be based on a diagnostic evaluation of the alcoholic syndrome, the personality structure, and the social and cultural determinants of this alcoholic syndrome, the phase of its development, and the patient's attitude. The poor statistics for the treatment of alcoholism may not reflect on the intrinsic value of the treatment modalities; it may only reflect poor matching of treatment for the appropriate syndrome.

"Administered by whom"

The sine qua non of psychotherapy is the therapist's fundamental respect for the patient, and yet it is obvious that in many instances the alcoholic is viewed begrudgingly. One man refused to return to AA because "they don't like 'flunk-outs' "; a psychiatrist "never wanted to see an alcoholic again"; a counselor "can't stand to have alcoholics dependent on me."

A negative response to disulfiram can be predicted when given by a hostile, deprecating clinician or under the watchful eye of a demeaning wife; or perhaps positively when dispensed by a factory medical department to workers accepted as problem drinkers by their company. Thus the effects of this particular treatment are largely determined by interpersonal relationships (30, 107).

Reports on psychotherapy with the alcoholic suggest the negative therapeutic effect of the hostile or overly permissive therapist (59). The effect of treatment with moral overtones by religious personnel is unexplored, as is the fact that many professional executives and helpers in the field of alcoholism are recovered alcoholics.

It is not known how treatment outcome is affected by the great variety of therapists, who range from the frankly hostile or reactively permissive personnel, to temperance and beverage industry groups with vested interests, to recovered alcoholics with personal involvement in the problem themselves, and to those with various degrees of professional involvement in the problem of alcoholism.

Recently Krystal and Moore (43) discussed various criteria for employing treatment personnel. One conclusion was that alcoholism programs have yet to define the roles of various therapists. Various people may appropriately play therapeutic roles, but this will affect the type of improvement and expected success. For example, the family doctor may be expected to achieve a remission of drinking through his supportive role and the judicious prescription of drugs, whereas a psychotherapist might aim for more enduring personality changes. On the other hand, both might have the same goals and use fairly much the same methods for certain patients. Whether their improvement rates would be the same we do not know, but one suspects that the therapist does affect treatment outcome (28, 65).

Cultural Criteria

The cultural determinants of alcoholism are too well known to require review here. In America the ascetic Protestant tradition has been a dominant force whose crucial dynamic is the ambivalence to hedonism (31, 63, 93). In essence, self-gratification is glorification of the body at the expense of soul; man must conquer the earth through frugality and hard work; pleasure is a distraction from that end. To hew to such an ethic has become increasingly difficult in our affluent society. Nevertheless, it is difficult to reject built-in emotional attitudes which still influence cultural mores.

The ambivalence is manifest in the social or professional rejection of the alcoholic who indulges in pleasurable, self-gratifying behavior. Selzer (83) describes the ambivalent hostility observed in the therapist who cannot tolerate the alcoholic's pleasurable drinking and hence becomes overly permissive, encouraging the alcoholic to act out vicariously the therapist's own desires for such unacceptable pleasure. Even when alcohol is treated as a food the same problem obtains, for the ascetic Protestant perceives food in utilitarian terms. We should eat to live, not live to eat.

The ambivalence is expressed in the psychodynamics of Alcoholics Anonymous. In the Twelfth Step the AA member engages in active assistance of other alcoholics. This rescue operation psychologically represents a vicarious self-rescue by the AA member; that is, he is rescuing himself in this alterego alcoholic. Consequently, the AA member cannot allow the other alcoholic to drink at all, for that would represent allowing himself to drink—the forbidden pleasure (46).

The ambivalence can be seen in the comments on Davies' article reporting return to normal drinking by a few previously addicted drinkers (16). The responses to this report appear to be a mixture of scientific comments and cultural reactions. The scientific responses were concerned with the validity and reliability of the data. Here the question is one of assessing whether abstinence is a necessary contingency of therapy, whether it is an adequate criterion of successful treatment, or a healthful sequel to alcoholism. Such questions must be answered according to operational scientific criteria.

Confusion between scientific and cultural criteria has been a recurring problem in alcoholism. Frank (23) has tersely noted our reluctance to examine value-laden behavior by scientific criteria alone without immediately involving cultural criteria. An example is Selzer's (16) anecdote on the "embarrassing" results of his research, which he was asked to squelch. Davies (15) points out that scientific research criteria must be rigorously separated from cultural criteria.

In this sense, cultural criteria are irrelevant in those responses to Davies which argued for arbitrary abstinence lest drinking harm more people, undercut interest in therapy, contradict educational efforts, or disconcert current theories about alcoholism. These are all questions which must first be answered with scientific assessment of data. It is in the second stage, determination of public and professional policy, that cultural criteria are relevant.

The contemporary American ambivalence toward alcoholism is reflected in our hesitancy to explore the scientific evidence which would evaluate the question of abstinence as a desirable condition of therapy or as a desirable outcome of therapy. Cultural criteria have been so dominant in alcoholism that they have obscured the scientific data and tended to preclude posing appropriate research questions. Cultural criteria are indispensable—but within the province to which they are relevant.

Criteria of Successful Treatment: Abstinence and Health

The usual criterion of successful treatment has been unqualified abstinence. But there are several qualifications:

1. Is abstinence a valid or reliable criterion of successful treatment? It is suggested that abstinence may result in poorer health or that successful treatment may be achieved without abstinence.

2. Are abstinence and mental health parallel phenomena? It is suggested that the problem of alcoholism may be resolved in the face of continuing mental health problems. Similarly, mental health problems may be significantly improved despite no improvement in the alcoholism.

3. Is abstinence a necessary condition to the conduct of successful therapy? It is suggested that the condition of abstinence may be contraindicated, unnecessary, or impossible to achieve in therapy.

First let us look at abstinence as a reliable criterion of successful outcome.

Davies (14) reported that 7 of 93 alcohol addicts returned to normal drinking after a period of abstinence. Several of these men had been treated with disulfiram or had attended AA sporadically since treatment. Davies himself notes that none of these men received a thoroughgoing psychodynamic reconstruction of the "core" personality conflict, having had only routine supportive hospital therapy for several months. Fox and Smith (22), comparing first- and second-year follow-ups, reported that 24% of the total group had shown improvement in the second follow-up, albeit with some drinking. Moore and Ramseur (61) found that 5 of 14 most improved patients were well-controlled social drinkers, whereas 6 of 15 abstinent patients were only slightly improved. Norvig and Nielsen (64) reported that 74% of 57 patients with temporary indulgence were doing well, and they therefore questioned the dictum of no social drinking. Pfeffer and Berger (72) found that 7 of 60 patients had changed patterns of drinking, 3 of whom were free of psychological symptoms. They remarked on the need for follow-up on this group in a larger sample. Selzer and Holloway (82) reported that 16% of 83 patients had returned to successful social drinking, suggesting the need for re-examination of the hypothesis of never drinking again. Lemere (44) reported that 3% of problem drinkers returned to normal drinking. Shea (84) reported a psychoanalytic case of an addictive compulsive alcohlic who returned to normal drinking.

It is more difficult to document partial improvement in either psychosocial functioning or in drinking behavior. If successful treatment is to be defined as total rehabilitation then probably most medical and psychological syndromes would have very low rates of effective treatment. But willingness to accept a partial improvement in some areas of total life adaptation seems to be not unreasonable and perhaps is realistically the most feasible for many alcoholics. In almost all follow-up studies the patients have been divided into gradations of improvement. If symptomatic relief, partial amelioration of psychosocial problems, or amelioration of drinking behavior are feasible goals, the improvement rates in most follow-up studies would jump to twice the reported values.

Examining abstinence in terms of overall life adaptation suggests that it may be followed by deterioration of total health rather than improvement. The most obvious example is the borderline psychotic who uses alcohol to maintain ego integration, diminish hallucinations, or allay overwhelming anxiety. Such persons become frankly psychotic when abstinent. This is so common an observation that it needs no documentation.

Rossi, Stach, and Bradley (79) comment that the effect of abstinence on unconscious feelings may mobilize psychological reactions which then threaten the maintenance of abstinence. Wilby and Jones (106) reported that while abstinence increased, overall improvement decreased when their group was assessed at 18- and 24-month intervals. Pfeffer and Berger (72) found that about 30% of their abstinent patients still had significant psychological symptoms and difficulty. Flaherty, McGuire, and Gatsky (21) observed the symptoms of depression and anxiety occurring after many months of abstinence, a syndrome also described by Wellman (104). Wallerstein (101) summed up the problem of disulfiram treatment by noting that enforced sobriety could be disastrous to personality integration.

The most significant study to date has been that of Gerard, Saenger, and Wile (25). Evaluating a group of totally abstinent "successes," they found 43% overtly disturbed, 24% inconspicuously inadequate, 12% AA successes, and 10% independent successes. They pointed to the normalizing effect of alcohol for some people which, when removed, permitted deterioration of personality function.

Their data on AA successes suggest a further problem with abstinence in that it may be maintained only at the expense of effective functioning in other areas. The abstinent AA member may not drink, but it may cost him a total investment of time, interest, and energy which Shea (84) has called an obsessional or fetishistic devotion. Gerard, Saenger, and Wile note that the patients in their sample with continued dependence on AA had constricted social and psychological functioning, involving what Pittman and Snyder (73) called the "dysfunctional" aspects of AA. Other reports suggest that continued therapeutic contact is necessary for the maintenance of abstinence. Hayman (33) suggested that alcoholics would need lifelong maintenance. Fox and Smith (22) reported continued sporadic outpatient and AA contacts with patients discharged several years previously. Pfeffer and Berger (72) had patients still in intensive therapy, although abstinent for several years. Rossi, Stach, and Bradley (79) found that their patients made "slips" and would return for further help. Many studies report sporadic contact via letters and telephone, and in person. Additionally many attend AA sporadically, take disulfiram in times of stress, or seek help from other sources, such as pastors, relatives, and employers.

This suggests that the maintenance of abstinence may not represent a reintegration but rather a condition maintained by continued "treatment." Follow-up studies do not discriminate between patients who remain abstinent because of structural personality changes and those who require continued treatment, in some sense, to maintain their abstinence. These studies of abstinence suggest that this criterion alone is misleading. Abstinence may, but does not necessarily, indicate degrees of rehabilitation, or it may be responsible for the deterioration of personality functioning.

Next, the relationship of improvement in drinking behavior to social, vocational, and psychological adjustment will be considered.

Thomas et al. (92) found that drinking behavior did not correlate with three other areas of life adaptation. Bruun (9) defined being cured as either abstinent or engaging in nondeviant drinking; being changed was defined as social or psychological change in the person. He suggested that drinking variables be considered apart from the other variables of improvement.

Mindlin (57) found a high correlation between drinking and other parameters of health, although they did not parallel the drinking problem. Others have found that the covert types of alcoholics display few dysfunctional social and psychological problems during the early stages of their abnormal drinking (6).

The World Health Organization definition of alcoholism in terms of the drug effect on social and psychological functioning unfortunately tends to fuse these parameters (80). Clinically it seems warranted to consider drinking deviancy apart from general adaptations in social, vocational, and psychological areas, and from physical health. A study by Blane, Overton, and Chafetz (6) indicates the diagnostic and therapeutic confusion which arises from assuming that alcoholism implies a total life pattern of deterioration.

 No necessary relationship between abstinence and the successful conduct of therapy has been demonstrated. Lorand (49) reported theoretical differences among psychoanalysts about the necessity for abstinence in therapy. Moore (58) and Krystal (42) concluded that the prescription of abstinence must depend upon understanding the role of alcoholism in a given patient's life. Weinstein (103) pointed out that alcohol is a symbol whose meaning in therapy is highly variable and must be understood in individual terms.

It has usually been assumed that abstinence is a requisite for the conduct of therapy, a carry-over from the AA philosophy and the legal treatment of narcotic addiction. But clinically some patients never are abstinent during treatment or only achieve abstinence subsequently. While much lip-service is given to the idea that drinking cannot be tolerated if therapy is to be successful, no systematic studies have demonstrated this.

This is not a recommendation for the abandonment of abstinence as a condition and goal in the treatment of alcoholism. That would be unwarranted. But there is a need to define the prescription of abstinence. For some patients, immediate and lifelong abstinence appears imperative, but that does not apply to all of the alcoholism syndromes. Other patients cannot and do not achieve abstinence and therapeutic opportunity may be obstructed by demanding that they do so.

There seems to be no specific relationship between therapy and abstinence. Gibbins and Armstrong (26), finding no correlation between length of therapy and maintenance of abstinence, concluded that whatever treatment was given served as a facilitative measure to whatever internal changes were occurring in the patient. Gerard, Saenger, and Wile (25) found that the patients often came to the hospital already abstinent, which was reinforced by the hospital treatment. Davies (14) noted that his successful cases had not had extensive rehabilitative therapy. Bruun (9) concluded that the same general approaches would achieve the same general results with most patients. Wallerstein (101) concurred that probably the patient's own attitude and motivation rather than extensive therapy were the important requisites. Moore and Ramseur (61) questioned the necessity of high-powered therapy in terms of therapeutic efficacy. Zwerling and Clifford (110) suggest that brief contact therapy was often decisively therapeutic, a point Lolli (47) has made and which we have reported from our Cincinnati Clinic (69, 71).

In the light of Davies' article and other reports on the change to nondeviant drinking, we need to reassess concepts of therapeutic intervention in terms of the psychodynamic shifts which occur in some alcoholics despite minimal therapy.

It seems true that the visible alcoholic of 20 years ago with frank addictive drinking learned to avoid drinking. Every clinic has frequently seen cases of binge drinking, following several years of abstinence, ostensibly triggered by one drink. Hence, it is usually advised that the alcoholic should be treated for a lifetime; yet many of the improved patients in the follow-up studies reviewed never did stop drinking or only did so for brief periods of time.

A consideration of the importance of individual responses to pharmacological agents, as extensively documented in recent research, should be included in any discussion of continued drinking versus abstinence. Addiction is not purely a physiological mechanism, nor is the compulsion to drink. The apocryphal stories of alcoholics being set on binges by rum in the pudding as representing a physiological event should certainly be questioned. An opposite example reported by Snyder (87) is that of Catholic and Episcopal priests who are members of AA yet can partake of sacramental wine without threat to their abstinence.

In psychopharmacological terms there is no normal physiological response to a drug. One cannot discuss the drug effect on the person without discussing personality effect on the physiological action of the drug. Variability of positive and negative placebo responses within the same person points to the importance of the sociopsychological conditions influencing the person's response to that drug (4, 78).

This suggests that the addictive response to alcohol does not depend upon the physiological response alone or primarily (75, 85, 90). Personality factors may contribute to addictive drinking or effectively oppose or override whatever physiological component to impulsion that exists.

Since the addictive drinker seems often to represent the oral phase of psychosexual development, addictive drinking would be expected to occur in persons who had regressed to an oral level from a previously more mature level of functioning. This parallels Lolli's (47) statement that he often found little psychopathology preceding the onset of alcoholism. Addictive drinking in the regressed patient might well yield to therapy and the patient be able to return to normal drinking, whereas the orally fixated patient would present a continuing problem of impulsive drinking. At this point this is speculative because no research has been reported on patients who have gone through phases of nonaddictive to addictive to nonaddictive drinking (1).

Finally, our Cincinnati research group has reported a study in which we specifically tested, among other questions, the hypothesis that some successfully treated alcoholics do engage in normal drinking and are as healthy as abstinent alcoholics (71). The mental, interpersonal, physical, and vocational health of 32 patients were rated before therapy and 20 months after discharge. They were also rated on an alcoholism scale. According to criteria of drinking behavior previously defined, the scores on the alcoholism scale at follow-up separated the sample into 3 groups: abstinent ($n = 11$), normal drinkers ($n = 11$), and pathological drinkers ($n = 10$). At intake the 3 groups were homogeneous in the severity of alcohol addiction and overall ill-health. At follow-up all 3 groups had improved but the abstinent and normal drinkers had virtually identical low scores (healthy), while the pathological drinkers scored as high (unhealthy) as before treatment. Our findings indicate that abstinence and "life health" are related but separate variables. Also, our clinical observations on the "normal" drinkers revealed that they had undergone no enduring character changes and had had relatively brief therapy (12 to 35 sessions). One way of understanding this phenomenon may be to see alcohol addiction as the result of family and personal disequilibrium. Relatively superficial intervention in the disequilibrium may allow the alcoholic to re-equilibrate with different defenses and relationships which eliminate the personal and social forces that perpetuated the addictive pattern of drinking.

The studies examined in this section suggest that abstinence is an inadequate criterion of health or of successful treatment in alcoholism. It is not to be disregarded but should be placed in appropriate perspective along with other parameters of health and adaptation.

Bibliography

1. Alcohol Clinic of the State University of New York. Annual Report. Brooklyn, N.Y.; Downstate Medical Center, 1963.
2. Bahn, A. K., Anderson, C. L., and Norman, V. B. Outpatient psychiatric clinic services to alcoholics, 1959. *Quart. J. Stud. Alc.* 1963, *24*, 213–226.
3. Bales, R. F. Cultural differences in rates of alcoholism. *Quart. J. Stud. Alc.*, 1946, *6*, 480–499.
4. Beecher, H. K. *Measurement of subjective responses.* New York: Oxford, 1959.
5. Bewley, T. H. *Effects of certain social and cultural factors on the development and progress of alcoholism.* [Research Monograph.] Cincinnati: University of Cincinnati, 1957.
6. Blane, H. T., Overton, W. F., and Chafetz, M. E. Social factors in the diagnosis of alcoholism. I. Characteristics of the patient. *Quart. J. Stud. Alc.,* 1963, *24*, 640–663.
7. Bowman, K. M., and Jellinek, E. M. Alcohol addiction and its treatment. *Quart. J. Stud. Alc.,* 1941, *2*, 98–176.
8. Brightman, I. J. The future of alcoholism programs. *Publ. Hlth. Rep., Wash.,* 1960, *75*, 775–777.
9. Bruun, K. Outcome of different types of treatment of alcoholics. *Quart. J. Stud Alc.,* 1963, *24*, 280–288.

10. Caplan, G. *Principles of preventive psychiatry.* New York: Basic Books, 1964.
11. Carlson, A. J. The conditional-reflex therapy of alcohol addiction. *Quart. J. Stud. Alc.,* 1944, *5,* 212–215.
12. Child, G. P., Osinski, W., Bennett, R. E., and Davidoff, E. Therapeutic results and clinical manifestations following the use of tetraethylthiuram disulfide (Antabuse). *Amer. J. Psychiat.,* 1951, *107,* 774–780.
13. Dale, P. W., and Ebaugh, F. G. Personality structure in relation to tetraethylthiuramdisulfide (Antabuse) therapy of alcoholics. *J. Amer. Med. Ass.,* 1951, *146,* 314–319.
14. Davies, D. L. Normal drinking in recovered alcohol addicts. *Quart. J. Stud. Alc.,* 1962, *23,* 94–104.
15. Davies, D. L. Normal drinking in recovered alcohol addicts; response by Dr. D. L. Davies. *Quart. J. Stud. Alc.,* 1963, *24,* 330–332.
16. Davies, D. L. Normal drinking in recovered alcohol addicts. (Comment by various correspondents.) *Quart. J. Stud. Alc.,* 1963, *24,* 109–121, 321–332.
17. Davies, D. L., Shepherd, M., and Myers, E. The two-years' prognosis of 50 alcohol addicts after treatment in hospital. *Quart. J. Stud. Alc.,* 1956, *17,* 485–502.
18. Davies, J. A., Freeman, H. E., and Simmons, O. G. Rehospitalization and performance level among former mental patients. *Social Probl.,* 1957, *5,* 37–44.
19. Duhl, L. J. Alcoholism: the public health approach; a new look from the viewpoint of human ecology. *Quart. J. Stud. Alc.,* 1959, *20,* 112–125.
20. Feeney, F. E., Mindlin, D. F., Minear, V. H., and Short, E. E. The challenge of the Skid Row alcoholic; a social, psychological and psychiatric comparison of chronically jailed alcoholics and cooperative alcoholic clinic patients. *Quart. J. Stud. Alc.,* 1955, *16,* 645–667.
21. Flaherty, J. A., McGuire, H. T., and Gatski, R. L. The psychodynamics of the "dry drunk." *Amer. J. Psychiat.,* 1955, *112,* 460–464.
22. Fox, V., and Smith, M. A. Evaluation of a chemopsychotherapeutic program for the rehabilitation of alcoholics; observations over a two-year period. *Quart. J. Stud. Alc.,* 1959, *20,* 767–780.
23. Frank, J. D., The role of cognitions in illness and healing. In: Strupp, H. H., and Luborsky, L. (eds.), *Research in psychotherapy,* vol. II. Washington, D.C.: American Psychological Association, 1962.
24. Gerard, D. L., and Saenger, G. Interval between intake and follow-up as a factor in the evaluation of patients with a drinking problem. *Quart. J. Stud. Alc.,* 1959, *20,* 620–630.
25. Gerard, D. L., Saenger, G., and Wile, R. The abstinent alcoholic. *A.M.A. Arch. Gen. Psychiat.,* 1962, *6,* 83–95.
26. Gibbins, R. J., and Armstrong, J. D. Effects of clinical treatment on

behavior of alcoholic patients; an exploratory methodological investigation. *Quart. J. Stud. Alc.,* 1959, *18,* 429–450.

27. Glatt, M. M. Treatment results in an English mental hospital alcoholic unit. *Acta. Psychiat. Scand.* 1961, *37,* 143–168.

28. Goldstein, A. P. *Therapist-patient expectations in psychotherapy.* New York: Pergamon, 1962.

29. Gordon, J. E. The epidemiology of alcoholism. In: Kruse, H. D. (ed.), *Alcoholism as a medical problem,* ch. 1. New York: Hoeber-Harper, 1956.

30. Gottesfeld, B. H., Lasser, L. M., Conway, E. J., and Mann, N. M. Psychiatric implications of the treatment of alcoholism with tetraethylthiuram disulfide. *Quart. J. Stud. Alc.,* 1951, *12,* 184–205.

31. Gusfield, J. R. Status conflicts and the changing ideologies of the American temperance movement. In: Pittman, D. J., and Snyder, C. R. (eds.) *Society, culture, and drinking patterns,* ch. 6, pp. 101–120. New York: Wiley, 1962.

32. Guze, S. B., Tuason, V. B., Stewart, M. A., and Picken, B. The drinking history; a comparison of reports by subjects and their relatives. *Quart. J. Stud. Alc.,* 1963, *24,* 249–260.

33. Hayman, M. Current attitudes to alcoholism of psychiatrists in southern California. *Amer. J. Psychiat.,* 1956, *112,* 485–493.

34. Hoff, E. C. The use of pharmacological adjuncts in the psychotherapy of alcoholics. *Quart. J. Stud. Alc.,* 1961, Suppl. No. 1, pp. 138–150.

35. Hunter, G. Alcoholism and the family agency; with particular reference to early phase and hidden types. *Quart. J. Stud. Alc.,* 1963, *24,* 61–79.

36. Jackson, J. K. Types of drinking patterns of male alcoholics. *Quart. J. Stud. Alc.,* 1958, *19,* 269–302.

37. Jellinek, E. M. Phases of alcohol addiction. *Quart. J. Stud. Alc.,* 1952, *13,* 673–684.

38. Jellinek, E. M. *The disease concept of alcoholism.* Highland Park, N.J.: Hillhouse Press, 1960.

39. Keller, M. Definition of alcoholism. *Quart. J. Stud. Alc.,* 1960, *21,* 125–134.

40. Knight, R. P. The dynamics and treatment of chronic alcohol addiction. *Bull. Menninger Clin.,* 1937, *1,* 233–250.

41. Kramer, M. A discussion of the concepts of incidence and prevalence as related to epidemiologic studies of mental disorders. *Amer. J. Publ. Hlth.,* 1957, *47,* 826–840.

42. Krystal, H. The problem of abstinence by the patient as a requisite for the psychotherapy of alcoholism. II. The evaluation of the meaning of drinking in determining the requirement of abstinence by alcoholics during treatment. *Quart. J. Stud. Alc.,* 1962, *23,* 112–121.

43. Krystal, H., and Moore, R. A. Who is qualified to treat the alcoholic? A discussion. *Quart. J. Stud. Alc.,* 1963, *24,* 705–720.

44. Lemere, F. What happens to alcoholics. *Amer. J. Psychiat.* 1953, *109, 674–676.*

45. Lemere, F. Psychological factors in the conditioned-reflex treatment of alcoholism. *Quart. J. Stud. Alc.,* 1947, *8,* 261–264.

46. Lindt, H. The "rescue fantasy" in group treatment of alcoholics. *Int. J. Group Psychother.,* 1959, *9,* 43–52.

47. Lolli, G. On "therapeutic" success in alcoholism. *Quart. J. Stud. Alc.,* 1953, *14,* 238–246.

48. Lipscomb, W. R. Epidemiological methods in the study of alcoholism. *Amer. J. Publ. Hlth.,* 1959, *49,* 327–333.

49. Lorand, S. A survey of psychoanalytic literature in problems of alcohol: bibliography. In: Lorand, S., *The yearbook of psychoanalysis,* vol. I. New York: International Universities Press, 1945.

50. Luborsky, L. The patient's personality and psychotherapeutic change. In: Strupp, H. H., and Luborsky, L. (eds.), *Research in psychotherapy,* vol. II. Washington, D.C.; American Psychological Association, 1962.

51. Marconi, J. T. The concept of alcoholism. *Quart. J. Stud. Alc.,* 1959, *20,* 216–235.

52. Martin, C. G. Use of "disease" for chronic alcoholism. *J. Amer. Med. Ass.,* 1962, *179,* 742.

53. May, P. R. A., and Ebaugh, F. G. Pathological intoxication, alcoholic hallucinosis, and other reactions to alcohol; a clinical study. *Quart. J. Stud. Alc.,* 1953, *14,* 200–227.

54. Mechanic, D. Relevance of group atmosphere and attitudes for the rehabilitation of alcoholics; a pilot study. *Quart. J. Stud. Alc.,* 1961, *22,* 634–645.

55. Mills, R. B., and Hetrick, E. S. Treating the unmotivated alcoholic; a co-ordinated program in a municipal court. *Crime & Delinqu.,* 1963, *9,* 46–59.

56. Mindlin, D. F. Evaluation of therapy for alcoholics in a workhouse setting. *Quart. J. Stud. Alc.,* 1960, *21,* 90–112.

57. Mindlin, D. F. The characteristics of alcoholics as related to prediction of therapeutic outcome. *Quart. J. Stud. Alc.,* 1959, *20,* 604–619.

58. Moore, R.A. The problem of abstinence by the patient as a requisite for the psychotherapy of alcoholism. I. The need for abstinence by the alcoholic patient during treatment. *Quart. J. Stud. Alc.,* 1962, *23,* 105–111.

59. Moore, R. A. Reaction formation as a counter-transference phenomenon in the treatment of alcoholism. *Quart. J. Stud. Alc.,* 1961, *22,* 481–486.

60. Moore, R. A., and Buchanan, T. K. State hospitals and alcoholism; a nationwide survey of treatment techniques and results. *Quart. J. Stud. Alc.,* [In press.]

61. Moore, R. A., and Ramseur, F. Effects of psychotherapy in an open-ward hospital on patients with alcoholism. *Quart. J. Stud. Alc.,* 1960, *21,* 233–252.

62. Muench, H. Education in the treatment of alcoholism. In: Kruse, H. D. (ed.), *Alcoholism as a medical problem.* New York: Hoeber-Harper, 1956.

63. Myerson, A. Alcohol: a study of social ambivalence. *Quart. J. Stud. Alc.,* 1940, *1,* 13–20.

64. Norvig, J., and Nielsen, B. A follow-up study of 221 alcohol addicts in Denmark. *Quart. J. Stud. Alc.,* 1956, *17,* 633–642.

65. Parloff, M. B. Therapist-patient relationships and outcome of psychotherapy. *J. Consult. Psychol.,* 1961, *25,* 29–38.

66. Parad, H. J., and Caplan, G. A framework for studying families in crisis. *Social Work,* 1960, *5,* 3–15.

67. Parsons, T. Definitions of health and illness in the light of American values and social structure. In: Jaco, E. G. (ed.), *Patients, physicians, and illness.* New York: Free Press, 1958.

68. Pasamanick, B., and Ristine, L. Differential assessment of post-hospital psychological functioning: evaluations by psychiatrists and relatives. *Amer. J. Psychiat.,* 1961, *118,* 40–46.

69. Pattison, E. M. Treatment of alcoholic families with nurse home visits. *Family Process,* 1965, *4,* 75–94.

70. Pattison, E. M., Courlas, P., Patti, R., Mann, B., and Mullen, D. Diagnostic–therapeutic intake groups for wives of alcoholics. *Quart. J. Stud. Alc.,* 1965, *26,* 605–616.

71. Pattison, E. M., Headley, E. B., Gleser, G. C., and Gottschalk, L. A. The relation of drinking patterns to over-all health in successfully treated alcoholics. Read at the 121st Annual Meeting of the American Psychiatric Association, New York, May 1965.

72. Pfeffer, A. Z., and Berger, S. A follow-up study of treated alcoholics. *Quart. J. Stud. Alc.,* 1957, *18,* 624–648.

73. Pittman, D. J., and Snyder, C. R. Responsive movements and systems of control. In: Pittman, D. J., and Snyder, C. R. (eds.), *Society, culture and drinking patterns,* pp. 547–552. New York: Wiley, 1962.

74. Prout, C. T., Strongin, E. I., and White, M. A. A study of results in hospital treatment of alcoholism in males. *Amer. J. Psychiat.,* 1950, *107,* 14–19.

75. Rado, S. The psychoanalysis of pharmacothymia (drug addiction). *Psychoanal. Quart.,* 1933, *2,* 1–23.

76. Rapaport, R. Normal crises, family structure, and mental health. *Family Process,* 1963, *2,* 68–84.

77. Reznikoff, M., and Toomey, L. A. *Evaluation of changes associated with psychiatric treatment.* Springfield, Ill.: Thomas, 1959.

78. Rinkel, M. (ed.), *Specific and non-specific factors in psychopharmacology.* New York: Philosophical Library, 1963.

79. Rossi, J. J., Stach, A., and Bradley, N. J. Effects of treatment of male alcoholics in a mental hospital; a follow-up study. *Quart. J. Stud. Alc.,* 1963, *24,* 91–108.

80. Seeley, J. R. The W.H.O. definition of alcoholism. *Quart. J. Stud. Alc.*, 1959, *20*, 352–356.
81. Seiden, R. H. The use of Alcoholics Anonymous members in research on alcoholism. *Quart. J. Stud. Alc.*, 1960, *21*, 506–509.
82. Selzer, M. L., and Holloway, W. H. A follow-up of alcoholics committed to a state hospital. *Quart. J. Stud. Alc.*, 1957, *18*, 98–120.
83. Selzer, M. L. Hostility as a barrier to therapy in alcoholism. *Psychiat. Quart.*, 1957, *31*, 301–305.
84. Shea, J. E. Psychoanalytic therapy and alcoholism. *Quart. J. Stud. Alc.*, 1954, *15*, 595–605.
85. Simmel, E. Alcoholism and addiction. *Psychoanal. Quart.*, 1948, *17*, 6–31.
86. Simmons, O. G., and Freeman, H. E. Familial expectations and post-hospital performance of mental patients. *Hum. Relat.*, 1959, *12*, 233–242.
87. Snyder, C. R. *Alcohol and the Jews.* New Brunswick, N.J.: Publications Division, Rutgers Center of Alcohol Studies, 1958.
88. Stone, G. P. Drinking styles and status arrangements. In: Pittman, D. J., and Snyder, C. R. (eds.), *Society, culture and drinking patterns*, ch. 7, pp. 121–140. New York: Wiley, 1962.
89. Straus, R., and Bacon, S. D. Alcoholism and social stability; a study of occupational integration in 2,023 male clinic patients. *Quart. J. Stud. Alc.*, 1951, *12*, 231–260.
90. Szasz, T. S. Role of counterphobic mechanisms in addiction. *J. Amer. Psychoanal. Ass.*, 1958, *6*, 309–325.
91. Thimann, J. Conditional-reflex treatment of alcoholism. *New Engl. J. Med.*, 1959, *241*, 406–410.
92. Thomas, R. E., Gliedman, L. H., Freund, J., Imber, S. D., and Stone, A. R. Favorable response in the clinical treatment of chronic alcoholism. *J. Amer. Med. Ass.*, 1959, *169*, 1994–1997.
93. Thorner, I. Ascetic Protestantism and alcoholism. *Psychiatry*, 1953, *16*, 167–176.
94. Thorpe, J. J., and Perret, J. T. Problem drinking: a follow-up study. *A.M.A. Arch. Industr. Hlth.*, 1959, *19*, 24–32.
95. Tiebout, H. M. The act of surrender in the therapeutic process; with special reference to alcoholism. *Quart. J. Stud. Alc.*, 1949, *10*, 48–58.
96. Titchener, J. L., Sheldon, M. B., and Ross, W. D. Changes in blood pressure of hypertensive patients with and without group therapy. *J. Psychosom. Res.*, 1959, *4*, 10–12.
97. Usdin, G. L., Rond, P. C., Hinchliffe, J. A., and Ross, W. D. The meaning of disulfiram to alcoholics in group psychotherapy. *Quart. J. Stud. Alc.*, 1952, *13*, 590–595.
98. Voegtlin, W. L., and Broz, W. R. The conditioned reflex treatment of chronic alcoholism. *Ann. Intern. Med.*, 1949, *30*, 580–597.
99. Voegtlin, W. L., and Lemere, F. The treatment of alcohol addiction: a review of the literature. *Quart. J. Stud. Alc.*, 1942, *2*, 717–803.

100. Wall, J. H., and Allen, E. B. Results of hospital treatment of alcoholism. *Amer. J. Psychiat.,* 1944, *100,* 474–479.
101. Wallerstein, R. S. Comparative study of treatment methods for chronic alcoholism. *Amer. J. Psychiat.,* 1956, *113,* 228–233.
102. Wallerstein, R. S. *Hospital treatment of alcoholism.* New York: Basic Books, 1957.
103. Weinstein, E. Discussion of symbolism of alcoholism. In: Kruse, H. D. (ed.), *Alcoholism as a medical problem.* New York: Hoeber-Harper, 1956.
104. Wellman, M. Fatigue during the second six months of abstinence. *Canad. Med. Ass. J.,* 1955, *72,* 338–342.
105. Wellman, W. M., Maxwell, M. A., and O'Hollaren, P. Private hospital alcoholic patients and the changing conception of the "typical" alcoholic. *Quart. J. Stud. Alc.,* 1957, *18,* 388–404.
106. Wilby, W. E., and Jones, R. W. Assessing patient response following treatment. *Quart. J. Stud. Alc.,* 1962, *23,* 325.
107. Winship, G. M. Disulfiram as an aid to psychotherapy in the case of an impulsive drinker. *Quart. J. Stud. Alc.,* 1957, *18,* 666–672.
108. Zubin, J., Burdock, E. I., Sutton, S., and Cheek, F. Epidemiological aspects of prognosis in mental illness. In: Pasamanick, B. (ed.), *Epidemiology of mental disorder.* Washington, D.C.: American Association for the Advancement of Science, 1959.
109. Zwerling, I., Psychiatric findings in an interdisciplinary study of forty-six alcoholic patients. *Quart. J. Stud. Alc.,* 1959, *20,* 543–554.
110. Zwerling, I., and Clifford, B. J. Administration and population considerations in outpatient clinics for the treatment of chronic alcoholics. *N.Y. Med. J.,* 1957, *57,* 3869–3875.

Jim Orford

A Comparison of Alcoholics Whose Drinking Is Totally Uncontrolled and Those Whose Drinking Is Mainly Controlled

Introduction

In a recent article Bigelow et al. (1972) raised the possibility of the alcoholic's having a choice between abstinence and moderation.

Reprinted by permission from *Behaviour Research and Therapy,* 1973, *11,* 565–576. Copyright by Pergamon Press, Inc., Elmsford, N.Y. 10523.

The possibility of treatment programs, either singly or collectively, offering such a choice is to be welcomed. Abstinence has predominated as the official goal of treatment to the virtual exclusion of alternatives although the inflexibility of this approach has recently provoked criticism. Pattison (1966) has criticized the use of abstinence as the sole or major criterion of successful outcome of alcoholism treatment and Canter (1968) has discussed the disadvantages of the requirement that the symptom, drinking, is not displayed at all during treatment. Bigelow et al. (1972) suggest that the abstinence goal in many cases delays the seeking of treatment until a relatively chronic stage at which treatment is more difficult. The most telling criticism, however, is the unsatisfactory outcome of treatment oriented toward the conventional abstinence goal. The findings of McCance and McCance (1969), concerning the outcome of treatment at two hospitals in Scotland, are fairly representative. The rate of "good" outcome (improved social functioning associated with abstinence or isolated relapses only) appears to vary between approximately one-quarter and one-half of the total number treated, depending upon the degree to which the treated sample is selected but depending very little upon the nature of the treatment given. The McCances found group psychotherapy and aversion therapy to be equally, and modestly, effective, but neither was obviously more effective than simple ward routine.

Hope of an alternative goal for alcoholism treatment has been encouraged by a series of reports, reviewed by Caddy (1968) and by Litman (1973), that a proportion of alcoholics treated conventionally are found upon follow-up to have returned to a pattern of drinking judged to be "normal," "social," or "controlled." The exact proportions reported mostly lie between 5 and 15%, but this is the percentage of treated cases, not of successfully treated cases. As a proportion of cases with good outcome, this group represents at least 10–30%, which must be considered a sizable proportion particularly as most were probably advised to abstain. Even more recently there have appeared a number of reports of procedures which have been successful in bringing about controlled drinking in alcoholics. These include the administration of aversive stimulation contingent upon drinking beyond a certain blood alcohol level (Lovibond & Caddy, 1970); or contingent upon drinking too much, too fast, or in too large sips (Mills et al., 1971); the provision of an enriched ward environment contingent upon abstinence or moderate drinking (Bigelow et al., 1972); and the provision of opportunities to decide whether or not to drink at fixed intervals (Gottheil et al., 1972, 1973). In at least one instance (Sobell & Sobell,

1972, 1973), the results of 12 months follow-up demonstrate that behavioral treatment aimed at controlled drinking can be successful.

If the alcoholic is to have a choice in the matter, then there will almost certainly continue to be those who prefer the target of abstinence, and one of the most important questions in this area which research must attempt to answer is whether the frequency of favorable treatment outcome can be maximized by matching individual cases with treatment goal on more than a haphazard or ideological basis. Alcoholics presenting for treatment differ among themselves in terms of many social and behavioral variables, any of which might successfully predict differential success under treatments oriented toward abstinence and moderation. One might reasonably predict, for example, that greater age, chronicity, and severity of alcoholism symptomatology would predispose to a relatively greater chance of success under treatment oriented toward an abstinence goal.

However, on the basis of the principle that past behavior is likely to be the best predictor of future behavior, the strongest candidate seems likely to be the presence or absence of controlled drinking in the recent past. Jellinek's (1960) is perhaps the best known of suggested typologies of alcoholic drinking patterns. However, it makes no reference to variability in the uniformity with which an alcoholic's drinking is uncontrolled. A number of alternative types of alcoholism are contrasted by Jellinek with the *gamma*, "loss-of-control," type, but none of them suggests the possibility that some alcoholics may drink in a controlled fashion some, or even most, of the time. The *delta*, or "inability-to-abstain," type, for example, is said to drink relatively steadily, but reference is made to his "high intake" and the assumption appears to be that his drinking is constantly excessive. The *alpha* type is said to drink for psychological reason, not to be addicted, but to drink in an "undisciplined" fashion. But the possibility of his drinking in this way only part of the time is not raised. The *epsilon* type is said to drink uncontrollably only during infrequent bouts, but the nature of his drinking between bouts is not discussed.

The variability-uniformity of absence of control in the drinking of alcoholics appears therefore to be a much neglected variable. The collection of follow-up data for a controlled trial of two types of alcoholism treatment, which differed in intensity, provided the opportunity to examine this variable through the reports of male alcoholics and their wives. As alcoholics in this sample were found to differ from one another considerably in terms of this variable, two extreme groups, those whose drinking was totally uncontrolled ($n = 22$) and those whose drinking was predominantly controlled ($n = 14$), were compared in terms of a number of social, behavioral, and motivational variables.

Method

Overall design

The study from which data for this report were drawn concerns 100 men who at intake to the study were married and living with their wives, and for whom a diagnosis of alcoholism was confirmed on initial assessment. Patients over 60 years of age were excluded as were patients with severe or chronic physical disorder or those suffering from an organic or severe functional mental disorder. Otherwise the cases represented consecutive outpatient referrals to one consultant of the Maudsley Hospital who specializes in the treatment of alcoholism. Following an intake assessment of each case, which involved both the patient and his wife, cases were assigned on a random basis to a maximum- or a minimum-intensity treatment group, the latter receiving no further treatment other than a single counseling session immediately following the initial assessment. Regular psychiatric consultations for the patient and regular contact with a social worker for the wife constituted the main ingredients of treatment for the maximum-intensity group, and treatment for this group continued for up to 1 year but in most cases was of much briefer duration. The division of subjects into these two groups will not be referred to again here as a comparison of the outcome for these two groups will be the subject of a later report.

The intake assessment involved separate interviews of the alcoholic patient by a psychiatrist, the patient by a psychologist, and the patient's wife by a social worker. Data obtained during this first assessment will be identified by the term *intake*. All patients in both groups were reassessed 12 months later, the same pattern of independent interviews being repeated. Data obtained from these interviews will be identified by the expression, *12 months after intake.* A further 12 months later the assessment was repeated, but on this occasion the majority of interviews took place in the patient's own home and the same interviewer attempted to interview the patient and his wife independently. Data obtained from those interviews will be identified by the expression *24 months after intake.*

Drinking behavior data

Twelve months after intake, and again 24 months after intake, patients and wives were independently asked to reconstruct as carefully as possible the broad outline of the patient's drinking behavior over the preceding 12 months. Each informant was asked to apportion the 52 weeks of the previous year into three categories as accurately as possible. Patients were asked to estimate how many weeks they had been *totally abstinent* from alcohol, how many weeks there had been at least one drinking occasion but *never amounting to 5 pints of beer* or its equivalent per day (interviewers were provided with a conversion table to estimate the equivalence of different quantities of different types of alcoholic beverage, 5 pints of beer being taken as roughly equivalent to 8-10 oz. of 86-proof liquor) and how many weeks drinking had *exceeded that limit* on at least 1 day. Similarly, wives were asked to apportion the weeks into abstinent weeks, weeks involving at least one drinking episode but not involving any drinking which was "unacceptable" to her or created a "problem" for her, and weeks containing at least one episode of unacceptable or problem drinking.

The operational definition of "controlled drinking" adopted here is, therefore, drinking which by the patient's account does not exceed 5 pints of beer or its equivalent on any 1 day over a period of 1 week, and which by the wife's account does not constitute unacceptable or problem drinking to her over the same period of time. The criterion is therefore a fairly conservative one. Drinking must be light according to the patient and must give the patient's wife no cause for complaint in order to qualify as controlled. The independent criteria used by patient and wife are quite different, the one in terms of quantity, the other in terms of acceptability, and this of course leaves much room for disagreement. Some light drinking will be unacceptable to some wives and in some cases much heavier drinking will not constitute a problem. However, other cutoff points have been examined (e.g., a 10-pint cutoff as opposed to a 5-pint cutoff for the patient) but it appears that on average wives are likely to find drinking unacceptable when patients report that it amounts to 5 pints of beer or the equivalent per day.

The total number of cases upon which this report is based is 77. In 10 cases of the original 100, either one informant or both reported total abstinence from alcohol throughout the first 52-week period following intake, and, as the concern of this report is with variations in the degree to which drinking is controlled or uncontrolled, these cases are of no relevance to this report and are excluded from consideration. Two patients died during this same period, and in a further 11 cases data collected 12 months after intake were not complete from one or other informant. In some of these cases both patient and wife were lost to follow-up; in other cases the patient and his wife had separated during the intervening period and the wife was unable to provide corroborative information.

Additional variables

The degree of association between variability–uniformity of absence of control and each of a number of additional variables was examined. These additional variables were as follows:

a. Patient's age.

b. Chronicity of the patient's alcoholism independently estimated by patient and wife. Both informants were asked to estimate the patient's age at which drinking first "became a problem" and in each case replies were converted to the number of years elapsing between that time and the present.

c. Severity of alcoholism symptomatology reported by the patient at intake. An internally consistent 10-item scale was derived from a larger number of yes/no items referring to signs and symptoms of alcoholism. Items covered psychophysiological symptoms (e.g., tremors), drinking behavior (e.g., secret drinking) as well as social complications of drinking (e.g., getting into debt and losing time at work). In each case the patient was asked whether the sign or symptom had occurred at any time during the previous 12 months.

d. Family consequences of drinking reported by wives at intake. An internally consistent 10-item scale was similar derived from a larger pool of items. Items were again presented in a yes/no format and referred to the previous 12 months. They referred to such matters as failure of the patient to join in family activities, quarrels, threats, and physical violence. This collection of items was always referred to by the research team as the "beastliness scale."

e. History of offenses other than for drunkenness and of treatment for mental illness reported by the patient at intake.

f. The occurrence of imprisonment and mental hospital admission during the subsequent year, reported by the patient 12 months after intake.

g. Positive and negative sentiments toward drinking expressed by patients at intake. Two 6-item sentence completion tests of drinking sentiments were constructed. Items constituting the test for negative sentiments included sentence stems such as: "One of the worst things about my drinking has been . . .," "My drinking was responsible for . . . ." Items constituting the positive sentiments test included stems such as: "If I gave up drinking altogether I might miss . . . ." "For me one of the best things about drinking was . . . ." Each item was scored by assigning a score of 2 for any sentence completion expressing a sentiment of the type (positive or negative) which the stem was designed to encourage and by assigning a score of 0 if the sentence was not completed or if it was completed in such a way that the sentiment finally expressed was opposite to that which the item was designed to encourage (for example, in many cases patients "denied" the stem by writing such things as ". . . there has been *nothing* good about my drinking" in reply to the stem, "For me one of the best things about drinking was . . ."). A score of 0 or 2 was assigned to the vast majority of replies but a score of 1 was assigned in the event of an ambiguous reply or a reply which expressed both a positive and negative sentiment. Scores assigned by two independent judges were compared and the level of agreement found to be 92%, scores differing by two points for less than 1% of items. (The expected chance level of agreement was 56%.)

h. Self-definition of patient as alcoholic or excessive drinker at intake and again at 12 months after intake. Patients were asked whether they considered themselves to be, or to have been, an alcoholic and replies were categorized as "Yes," "Uncertain," or "No." Patients who did not define themselves as alcoholics or who were uncertain were further asked whether they considered that they drank, or recently had drunk, more than was good for them. Replies to this second question were categorized in the same way.

i. Patient's preferred future drinking target reported at intake and again at 12 months after intake. Patients were asked what they ". . . hoped to do about their drinking in the future?" and replies were placed in one of the four following categories: no change in drinking felt to be necessary; more moderate drinking hoped for; uncertain or ambiguous (this category included replies suggesting that abstinence was hoped for in the distant future but not immediately, abstinence would be aimed for if it were suggested by the clinic, or the patient would aim for abstinence but didn't like it, or was not convinced it was necessary); preference for abstinence unequivocally expressed. Data on drinking sentiments, self-definition, and preferences for future drinking targets were obtained during the course of an interview with a psychologist who was not a member of the treatment team.

Results

Husband and wife reports of controlled drinking during 12 months following intake

Table 1 shows a comparison of husband and wife reports of the balance of controlled and uncontrolled drinking during the first 12-month period following intake. For each informant the data have been expressed as the percentage of drinking (non-totally-abstinent) weeks during which drinking was on no day uncontrolled (more than 5 pints of beer or equivalent in the case of patient informants and "unacceptable" in the case of wife informants). Figures presented in the table display an overall concordance between the judgments of the two sets of informants. Dichotomizing both distributions at the 24/25% mark yields a significant chi-squared value (chi-squared = 10.4, d.f. = 1, p <0.01). On the other hand the number of apparent disagreements is high. Even when both sets of judgments are collapsed to dichotomies (as in calculating the chi-squared value quoted), the overall concordance rate is only 70% compared with an expected chance concordance rate of 51%. However, it must be borne in mind that the two informants concerned were asked to operate with rather different criteria for "contolled drinking," and the "disagreements" apparent from Table 1 may or may not constitute real differences of opinion.

Nearly half of both patients and wives reported no controlled drinking weeks and in 22 cases patients and wives were in agreement on this. This extreme group of 22 cases will be referred to as "totally uncontrolled" drinkers. It should of course be borne in mind that a unit time period of 1 week has been adopted here and variations in the degree of control exercised over drinking during the course of any 1 week are therefore ignored. Some of the cases called "totally uncontrolled" here may indeed exercise control on many individual days.

At the other extreme, 8 patients and 5 wives report that drinking has been 100% controlled. These figures correspond very well with the 5–15% rate of "return to normal drinking" reported in follow-up studies, but it is of some interest that total control is only agreed upon by husbands and wives in 3 of these cases. In 2 cases in

Table 1. A comparison of the reports of patients and wives concerning the proportion of drinking weeks during which drinking was controlled

Proportion of drinking weeks during which drinking did not exceed 5 pints of beer or equivalent in any one day (reported by patient) (%)	Proportion of drinking weeks during which drinking was acceptable (reported by wife) (%)					
	0	1–24	25–49	50–74	75–99	100
0	22 (Totally uncontrolled)	4	6	1	2	1
1–24	3	3	0	0	0	0
25–49	4	0	1	2	0	1
50–74	2	2	1	2	1	0
75–99	2	1	2	2	4 (Mainly controlled)	0
100	2	0	1	0	2	3

which the wife reports 100% control the patient admits to some drinking beyond the 5 pint level, and in the majority of cases in which the patient reports drinking that never exceeds that level wives report at least some "unacceptable" drinking.

However, there are no fewer than 28 cases for whom patient and wife agree that there have been some weeks during which drinking was controlled. In 14 of these cases patient and wife are agreed that controlled drinking weeks constitute 50% or more of total drinking weeks, and these cases are referred to here as "mainly controlled."

The remainder of the results section of this paper is concerned with a comparison of the two extreme groups identified in Table 1, namely totally uncontrolled and mainly controlled drinkers.

Weeks of abstinence in the 12 months following intake

The figures presented in Table 1 are based on percentages with total drinking weeks as the base. However, this base varies in individual cases from a high of 52 drinking weeks out of a possible 52, which was reported by both patient and wife in 3 of the extreme cases (2 totally uncontrolled cases and 1 mainly controlled case), to a low of 2–3 drinking weeks reported by patient and wife in one mainly controlled case. The total number of abstinent weeks therefore varies widely, and it seemed important to ascertain whether totally uncontrolled drinkers and mainly controlled drinkers differed in this regard. Patients in the totally uncontrolled group report an average of 17.8 abstinent weeks, and their wives report an average of 15.1 abstinent weeks. Patients in the mainly controlled group report an average of 19.3 abstinent weeks and their wives report an average of 13.6. The differences between the two groups do not approach statistical significance for either set of informants.

Age and chronicity

The mean age of totally uncontrolled drinkers at intake was 41.6 and that of mainly controlled drinkers 38.7. Five out of 14 mainly controlled drinkers were aged under 30 at intake as opposed to only 2 out of 22 totally uncontrolled drinkers. Neither the difference in means nor the difference in proportions is statistically significant.

There are, however, differences in problem chronicity, at least as estimated by patients. At intake 9 out of 14 mainly controlled drinkers, but only 6 out of 22 uncontrolled drinkers, considered that they had no drinking problem or that their problem started less than 2 years previously. The median estimated chronicity for patients in the totally uncontrolled group is 3 years, while that for the mainly controlled group is 1 year. A comparison of the two groups using the Mann-Whitney U-test reveals a significant difference ($z = 1.7, p = 0.04$, 1-tailed test). The corresponding median wife estimates lie between 9 and 10 years for the totally uncontrolled group and between 5 and 10 years for the mainly controlled group. The difference between the groups in terms of wife estimates is not significant ($z = 0.38, p > 0.10$).

It is interesting to note here the highly significant difference which exists for both groups between estimates of chronicity given by patients and those given by their wives. The overall patient median is 3 years, while the overall wife median lies between 9 and 10 years. The wife's estimate is greater than the patient's estimate in no fewer than 29 out of 36 cases, while the reverse is true in only 2 cases.

Severity of alcoholism symptomatology and family consequences reported at intake

Mean scores on the 10-item symptom scale were 6.0 for the totally uncontrolled group and 4.0 for the mainly controlled group, and this difference is significant ($t = 2.41, p < 0.05$). When items are examined individually, 4 items out of the 10 yield significant chi-squared values: morning drinking, tremors, hallucinations, and time lost from work.

Mean scores on the family consequences scale were 6.8 for the totally uncontrolled group and 5.4 for the mainly controlled group. The difference is only of borderline significance ($t = 1.67, p < 0.10$).

Criminal and mental illness history; imprisonment and hospitalization during the 12 months following intake

At intake the majority of patients in both groups gave a history of either offenses other than drunkenness or of mental hospital admission, and there was no significant difference in frequencies. However, the fate of the two groups in terms of institutionalization during the 12 months following intake differed dramatically. Thirteen of the totally uncontrolled group were imprisoned or hospitalized in a mental hospital at some time during the year (2 imprisoned, 10 hospitalized, and 1 both) whereas only one of the mainly controlled drinkers was hospitalized in a mental hospital and none was imprisoned during the same period. The difference is significant (chi-squared = 7.65, df = 1, $p < 0.01$).

Drinking sentiments

At intake members of the totally uncontrolled group expressed slightly more negative sentiments toward drinking in comparison with members of the mainly controlled group (means of 9.8 and 9.6 respectively) and expressed slightly fewer positve sentiments (means of 7.9 and 8.9 respectively). In neither case was the difference statistically significant. However, the impression was formed that a more detailed content analysis might reveal considerable differences between the groups. Whereas themes of ruin, misery, family breakup, and death predominated in the negative drinking sentiments expressed by totally uncontrolled drinkers, mainly controlled drinkers were more likely to express negative sentiments in terms of future predictions of harm or deterioration. These remain as impressions at the moment, though.

Self-definitions at intake and at 12 months after intake

Figure 1 shows the distribution of members of the two groups in three self-definition categories, those who think of themselves as alcoholics, those who don't think of themselves as alcoholics or who are unsure about it but who do think of themselves as excessive drinkers, and finally those who do not consider themselves to be excessive drinkers or alcoholics. Both at intake (Fig. 1a) and at 12 months after intake (Fig. 1b) there is an excess of totally uncontrolled drinkers among those who think of themselves as alcoholics and an excess of mainly controlled drinkers who think of themselves as neither alcoholics nor excessive drinkers. A comparison of those who define themselves as alcoholics with the remainder yields a significant difference for intake data (chi-squared = 5.34, df = 1, $p < 0.05$) and a nonsignificant trend for data obtained 12 months after intake (chi-square = 2.46, df, = 1, $p < 0.20$).

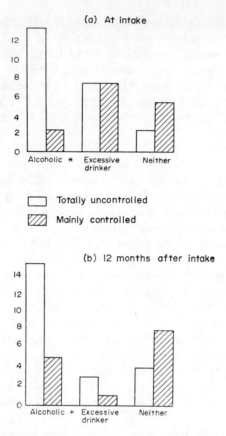

Figure 1. Self-definitions of totally uncontrolled and mainly controlled drinkers.

Preferences for future drinking targets

Table 2 shows the frequencies of replies in four categories given by members of the two groups to the question regarding preference for future drinking at intake and again at 12 months after intake. At both times, members of the totally uncontrolled group are more likely to make an unequivocal statement of preference for future abstinence, and combining the other three reply categories yields a significant difference between the groups both at intake (chi-squared = 4.26, df = 1, $p < 0.05$) and at 12 months after intake (chi-squared = 6.41, df = 1, $p < 0.05$).

Table 2. Preferred future drinking target of totally uncontrolled and mainly controlled drinkers

Target	At intake		12 months after intake	
	Totally uncontrolled	Mainly controlled	Totally uncontrolled	Mainly controlled
No change	1	0	3	7
More moderate drinking	1	5	4	2
Uncertain or ambiguous	8	7	3	4
Abstinence*	12	2	12	1
Total	22	14	22	14

*A comparison of the frequency of replies in the abstinence category versus the remaining three categories combined yields a significant difference (df = 1, $p < 0.05$) between TU and MC both at intake (chi-squared = 4.26) and 12 months after intake (chi-squared = 6.41).

The stability of control or lack of control over a 2-year period

On the basis of information provided 24 months after intake, an attempt was made to categorize the drinking of each of the 36 extreme patients in the same manner for the second 12-month period. It was possible to do this for 22 out of the 36 cases. In 3 cases information at 24 months after intake was not available, in 3 further cases the patient was abstinent throughout the second 12-month period, in 6 cases patients and their wives disagreed about drinking to the extent that a categorization could not be made, and in a further 2 cases (1 in each group) patient and wife agreed that drinking had been mainly, but not totally uncontrolled. Of the 22 cases who could be categorized, 15 had been in the totally uncontrolled group on the basis of their drinking during the first 12-month period and 7 had been in the mainly controlled group. Of the former, all 15 were categorized as totally uncontrolled during the second 12-month period, and of the latter, 6 out of 7 were categorized as mainly controlled. The difference is clearly significant ($p < 0.005$, Fisher exact probability test).

Discussion

The method of obtaining drinking pattern data

The method of reporting on drinking patterns over a 12-month period which this report relies upon is admittedly crude and open to a variety of biases. However, it has been cautiously used here. Patient and spouse reports have been compared and found to show at least a moderate degree of concordance. Thereafter, only cases which are extreme on the basis of *both* patient and spouse reports have been included in the analysis. In view of the evidence that cases placed in one of these two extreme groups are likely to be placed in the same group one year later, again on the basis of both patient and spouse reports, it is concluded that the method employed is sufficiently sound to allow a reliable division between such extreme groups.

The two extreme groups

How should the difference between the two groups extracted from Table 1 and subsequently termed "totally uncontrolled" (TU) and "mainly controlled" (MC) be interpreted? The absence of a significant difference in terms of total drinking weeks is important. Both TU and MC drinkers continue to drink. In both groups there are men who mostly abstain and men who scarcely ever abstain for more than a few days at a time. However, while TU drinkers apparently never drink for as long as a week without exceeding both the 5 pints of beer or equivalent per day quantity and their wives' "acceptability" limit, MC drinkers mostly do. The latter, still "drinking alcoholics" in terms of official treatment goals and expectations, can go for several weeks without exceeding this fairly modest quantity limit and without giving their wives much cause for complaint.

Differences at intake

This difference would appear to be fundamental. What is the extent of the evidence that these two groups come from separate populations in other respects? First there is considerable evidence that the groups were already very different at "intake" (i.e., at the *beginning* of the period which provided the drinking patterns on the basis of which the groups were identified). At that time drinkers subsequently classified as TU reported more symptoms, reported having had a drinking problem for longer, and were more likely to view themselves as alcoholics and to unequivocally prefer abstinence as a future goal.

Symptomatology

In view of the nature of the individual symptoms which differentiate the two groups (including "tremors," "morning drinking," and "hallucinations"), it is possible that TU drinkers may be showing a greater degree of "physical dependence" or addiction to alcohol than are MC drinkers, and the TU/MC division may therefore roughly correspond to Jellinek's (1960) distinction between *gamma* and *delta* alcoholism on the one hand and *alpha* alcoholism on the other. This may explain the merely borderline degree of the difference on the scale of marital effects, which, it might be supposed, are increased by addiction but are affected in addition by psychological dependence as well as personality factors. Differences in degree of physical addiction could also explain the highly discrepant patient and wife reports of chronicity and the fact that the former, but not the latter, differentiates TU and MC drinkers. It seems likely that husband and wife thresholds for perception of the husband's drinking as a problem depend on quite different "effects" of drinking. Whereas the wife's threshold may be reached with the onset of financial or interactional effects, the husband's threshold may in many cases not be reached until much later, when signs of addiction appear. Wives of TU and MC drinkers are likely to have been above their threshold for a number of years, but the MC drinkers themselves may only recently, if at all, have reached the higher husband threshold. If this analysis is correct, it would be of some interest to know whether the higher threshold is more a function of being the male member of a household or is more a function of being the one whose drinking is "up for redefinition."

Self-definitions and choice of drinking goal

That TU drinkers are more likely to think of themselves as alcoholics and to prefer abstinence as a future goal is of the greatest importance if alcoholics are to be offered a choice of goal (Bigelow et al., 1972) and is central to the theme of this paper.

Conventional treatment approaches require self-definition as "alcoholic" and orientation toward abstinence. The failure of many patients, who are then likely to be called "unmotivated," to define and orient themselves in accordance with these expectations provides one of the main themes of the alcoholism treatment literature (e.g., Tiebout, 1953; Mindlin, 1959; Sterne & Pittman, 1965) and is undoubtedly responsible for much breakdown in therapist-patient relationships. That the expression "unmotivated" is typically used in the very limited sense of "agreement with fashionable treatment goals" is supported by the lack of significant differences between groups in amounts of expressed pro- and antidrinking sentiments. Although MC drinkers are less well motivated to accept the requirements of abstinence-oriented treatment, they seem nonetheless almost as ready to admit the personal disadvantages of their past drinking behavior and are in this sense "motivated."

Subsequent differences

As well as differences already apparent at intake, TU and MC drinkers show a number of subsequent differences. The difference in rates of institutionalization (prison or mental hospital) during the first 12-month period following intake validates the division into the criterion groups which was made on the basis of reported drinking pattern. A TU drinking pattern is more likely than not to be associated with imprisonment or psychiatric hospitalization while a MC pattern is very unlikely to be.

Differences in self-perceptions and choices of drinking goal which were apparent at intake were still apparent 12 months later, and in the majority of cases for whom an extreme categorization could be made, TU and MC drinking patterns reported 24 months after intake were in all but one case the same as those reported 12 months after intake. The differences in drinking patterns and attitudes focused on here seem, therefore, to be at least moderately stable over a period of 1–2 years.

However, some consideration must be given to the role of conventional treatment or advice in the origin of the MC pattern which has only been clearly described for these cases *following* treatment contact. It is possible that the MC pattern can be partly attributed to the applications of treatment or advice and that this pattern would not be so commonly encountered in "new cases" presenting for treatment for the first time. Although detailed reports of drinking patterns prior to treatment contact are not available for this sample, the stability of these patterns over the subsequent 1–2 years and the differentiation of the two groups in terms of self-definition and preferred goal at *intake* strongly suggest that TU–MC differences are "natural" occurrences not solely the products of treatment intervention.

Conclusion

In conclusion, one can speculate that the drinking pattern dimension revealed here offers the possibility of discovering a rational basis for deciding on the best course of alcoholism treatment in individual cases. It seems logical to expect that the potential for "normal" or "totally controlled" drinking is greater for those alcoholics whose drinking is already "mainly controlled." In such cases the desired target behavior, limited or controlled drinking, already exists in the patient's behavioral repertoire and in many cases is displayed with considerable frequency. Research should now be directed toward testing the prediction that patient characteristics, such as the one focused upon here, can serve as differential predictors of success following abstinence-oriented and controlled drinking–oriented treatment.

References

Bigelow, G., Cohen, M., Liebson, I., and Faillace, L. Abstinence or moderation? Choice by alcoholics. *Behav. Res. and Therapy,* 1972, *10,* 209–214.

Caddy, G. Abstinence or cure: a re-evaluation of the nature of alcoholism and implications for treatment. Mimeographed paper, 1968.

Canter, F. M. The requirement of abstinence as a problem in institutional treatment of alcoholics. *Psychiat. Quart.,* 1968, *42,* 217–231.

Gottheil, E., Murphy, B. F., Skoloda, T. E., and Corbett, L. O. Fixed interval drinking decisions. II. Drinking and discomfort in 25 alcoholics. *Quart. J. Stud. Alc.,* 1972, *33,* 325–340.

Gottheil, E., Alterman, A. I., Skoloda, T. E., and Murphy, B. F. Alcoholics' patterns of controlled drinking. *Amer. J. Psychiat.,* 1973, *130,* 418–422.

Jellinek, E. M. *The disease concept of alcoholism.* New Haven, Conn: College and University Press, 1960.

Litman, G. Return to moderate drinking as a byproduct of treatment aimed at abstinence (in preparation).

Lovibond, S. H., and Caddy, G. Discriminated aversion control in the moderation of alcoholic drinking behavior. *Behav. Therapy,* 1970, *1,* 437–444.

McCance, C., and McCance, P. F. Alocholism in North East Scotland: its treatment and outcome. *Brit. J. Psychiat.,* 1969, *115,* 189–198.

Mills, K. C., Sobell, M. B., and Schaefer, H. H. Training social drinking as an alternative to abstinence for alcoholics. *Behav. Therapy*, 1971, *2*, 18–27.

Mindlin, D. The characteristics of alcoholics as related to prediction of therapeutic outcome. *Quart. J. Stud. Alc.*, 1959, *20*, 604–619.

Pattison, E. M. A critique of alcoholism treatment concepts; with special reference to abstinence. *Quart. J. Stud. Alc.*, 1966, *27*, 49–71.

Sobell, M. B., and Sobell, L. C. Individualized behavior therapy for alcoholics: rationale, procedures, preliminary results and appendix. *Calif. Dept. Ment. Hyg., Calif. Ment. Health Res. Mon.*, 1972, no. 13.

Sobell, M. B., and Sobell, L. C. Individualized behavior therapy for alcoholics. *Behav. Therapy*, 1973, *4*, 49–72.

Sterne, M. W., and Pittman, D. J. The concept of motivation: a source of institutional and professional blockage in the treatment of alcoholics. *Quart. J. Stud. Alc.*, 1965, *26*, 41–57.

Tiebout, H. M. Surrender versus compliance in therapy: with special reference to alcoholism. *Quart. J. Stud. Alc.*, 1953, *14*, 58–68.

Mark B. Sobell and Linda C. Sobell

Second-Year Treatment Outcome of Alcoholics Treated by Individualized Behavior Therapy: Results

This paper reports second-year treatment outcome results for subjects who participated in an individualized behavior therapy program for alcoholics (IBTA) (Sobell & Sobell, 1972, 1973a). The rationale, design, treatment procedures, and first-year outcome results of this treatment experiment have been reported in detail elsewhere (Sobell & Sobell, 1972, 1973a, b). Briefly, the experiment investigated a behavior modification treatment for alcoholics which was based on the assumption that heavy, abusive drinking of alcoholic beverages could be considered as a discriminated, operant behavior, and that experimental treatment procedures should be tailored whenever possible to each individual's learning history.

Seventy male, *gamma* (Jellinek, 1960) alcoholics who were inpatients at Patton (CA) State Hospital volunteered to serve as subjects in the experiment. Subjects were interviewed by the research

Reprinted by permission from *Behaviour Research and Therapy*, 1976, *14*, 195–215. Copyright by Pergamon Press, Inc., Elmsford, N.Y. 10523.

staff and then assigned by staff decision to one of two treatment goals—nondrinking (abstinence) or controlled drinking (for assignment criteria, see Sobell & Sobell, 1972, 1973a). Thirty Ss were assigned to the nondrinking treatment goal group, and the remaining 40 Ss were assigned to the controlled drinking treatment goal group. Within each of these two groups, Ss were randomly assigned to either an experimental group receiving 17 experimental treatment sessions or a control group receiving conventional state hospital treatment (oriented toward abstinence). Thus, the two experimental treatment conditions—nondrinking and controlled drinking—each had an appropriate control group. In all, there were four experimental conditions: (1) Controlled Drinker Experimental (CD-E), $n = 20$; (2) Controlled Drinker Control (CD-C), $n = 20$; (3) Nondrinker Experimental (ND-E), $n = 15$; and (4) Nondrinker Control (ND-C), $n = 15$.

Previous follow-up results reporting 6- and 12-month data for 69 of the 70 total Ss found that experimental Ss had functioned significantly better than control Ss, irrespective of treatment goal. This paper reports characteristics of Ss' functioning during the second year following their discharge from the hospital.

Method

Tracking procedures

The extensive tracking procedures used to follow Ss throughout the 2-year follow-up interval have been discussed in detail in earlier publications (Sobell & Sobell, 1972, 1973a, b). Subjects and respective multiple "Collateral Information Sources" (CIS) were contacted for follow-up every 3–4 weeks for a period of 2 years. CISs included individuals and/or agencies who had had any contact with the Ss. Subjects and CISs were unaware of the exact dates and times when they would be contacted. Official driver's records and arrest records for each S were routinely obtained, and incarcerations and deaths were always verified. A plethora of cooperating agencies and individuals provided invaluable assistance in tracking Ss.

Measures of treatment outcome

Follow-up contacts with Ss and CISs were structured so that specific data were always obtained regarding the S's functioning since the time of the last follow-up contact. Most of the primary dependent variable measures of treatment outcome used in this study have been operationally defined in detail elsewhere (Sobell & Sobell, 1973b), and complete defintions will not be reiterated here. In summary fashion, the dependent variable measures of treatment outcome included:

(1) *Daily Drinking Disposition*—alcohol consumption on each day was coded into one of five mutually exclusive categories: (a) *drunk days*—usually consumption of greater than 6 oz. of 86-proof liquor or its equivalent in alcohol; (b) *controlled drinking days*—usually consumption of 6 oz. or less of 86-proof liquor or its equivalent in alcohol content; (c) *abstinent days*—no consumption of alcohol; (d) *incarcerated days, jail*—for alcohol-related arrests; (e) *incarcerated days, hospital*—hospitalized for an alcohol-related health problem, usually detoxification.

(2) *General Adjustment*—rated by a CIS who had had frequent contact with the S as either "Improved," "Same," or "Worse," as compared to the year preceding the S's hospitalization.

(3) *Vocational Status*—S's evaluation of his vocational satisfaction as either "Improved," "Same," or "Worse," as compared to the year preceding his hospitalization. Evaluations could be based on changes in types of duties, hours worked, supervision, etc.

(4) *Occupational Status*—an objective indicator of each S's vocational activities during the majority of each 6-month interval.

(5) *Residential Status and Stability Index (RSSI)*—an evaluation of both the S's type of residence and duration at a single location. The RSSI has a range from 1.0 (highest possible residential status and stability) to approaching 0.0 (as residential status and stability near total impairment). See Sobell and Sobell (1973b) for a description of computational procedures used to obtain RSSI values.

(6) *Valid Driver's Licence Status*—the number of Ss possessing valid driver's licenses at the end of the 2-year follow-up interval compared to those possessing valid driver's licenses at the time of hospital discharge.

(7) *Marital Status*—a comparison of Ss' marital status at the end of the 2-year follow-up interval with their marital status at the time of hospital discharge.

(8) *Use of Therapeutic Supports*—an evaluation of whether or not Ss used any outpatient therapeutic supports during each 6-month follow-up interval.

(9) *Possession of Research Program Do's and Do Not's Card*—asked only of both groups of experimental Ss.

(10) *Physical Health Evaluation*—at the end of the second year of follow-up, each S was asked to evaluate whether, in his opinion, his physical health was "Improved," "Same," or "Worse" compared with his physical condition the year or two before he entered the hospital.

At the end of their 2-year follow-up interval, Ss were interviewed concerning their evaluation of various elements of the treatment program in which they had participated, their attitudes toward the utility of follow-up, and their general postdischarge functioning. All interviews were audio tape-recorded. With minor exceptions, results from those interviews will be published as a separate report.

Discrepancies between reports of Ss and their CISs, between reports of different CISs, or between Ss or CISs and official records were always probed, with final data being determined by the most verifiable information source.

Finally, we have developed two general measures of treatment outcome which summarize results using multiple measures. At this time, these general measures should be viewed as preliminary and suggestive, with their validity being undetermined. The first suggested general measure of outcome, a *Factor Success* method, incorporates the second year follow-up variables of drinking behavior, general adjustment as evaluated by a CIS, and vocational status as evaluated by the S. With respect to selecting criteria for success, we somewhat arbitrarily proposed the following: (a) successful drinking behavior, defined as greater than or equal to at least 75% of all days either abstinent and/or controlled drinking, (b) an evaluation of "Improved" general adjustment, and (c) an evaluation of "Improved" vocational status. Thus, a S evaluated as successful on all three of these criterion variables could be considered a three-factor success, a S evaluated as successful on two variables would be a two-factor success, and single-factor successes were also possible. This method of combining factors equally weights outcomes on drinking, general adjustment, and vocational adjustment dimensions, and can only be statistically analyzed using nonparametric tests.

The single general indicator of treatment outcome involves the development of a single parametric index of success to compare individual outcomes. Incorporating the same three dependent variable measures as used in the first general measures of outcome, a *General Index of Outcome (GIO)* was calculated, having a range from

0.00, representing the poorest possible outcome, to 1.00, representing the highest attainable outcome. The computational formula for calculating the GIO is as follow:

$$GIO = \frac{\left[\begin{array}{l}\text{(proportion of days abstinent + proportion of days controlled drinking)} \\ \text{+ general adjustment weight (1.0 = Improved, 0.5 = Same, 0.0 = Worse)} \\ \text{+ vocational status weight (1.0 = Improved, 0.5 = Same, 0.0 = Worse)}\end{array}\right]}{3}$$

Results

Sources of data

Complete second-year outcome data were obtained for 69 of the 70 total Ss, and at least two CISs were interviewed for each S found. Table 1 indicates the number of Ss in each experimental condition who were followed throughout each of the third (mos. 13–18) and fourth (mos. 19–24) 6 months of follow-up, and the mean number

Table 1. Number of subjects located for follow-up and the mean number of collateral information sources (CISs) interviewed per subject for each experimental group during the third (mos. 13–18) and fourth (mos. 19–24) 6-month (183-day) follow-up intervals

Experimental condition [a]		Follow-up months 13–18		Follow-up months 19–24	
	N	Number of subjects found	Mean number of CISs interviewed	Number of subjects found	Mean number of CISs interviewed
CD-E	20	20	3.65	20	3.80
CD-C	20	19	4.79	19	5.00
ND-E	15	15 [b]	5.64 [b]	15 [b]	7.36 [b]
ND-C	15	15 [b]	4.79 [b]	15 [b]	4.64 [b]
All	70	69	4.63 [b]	69	5.06 [b]

[a] Experimental conditions were controlled drinker experimental (CD-E), controlled drinker control (CD-C), nondrinker experimental (ND-E), and nondrinker control (ND-C).

[b] Subjects located include one deceased subject in each of the nondrinker groups. See text for details. These subjects were not included in the computation of mean number of collaterals interviewed.

of CISs interviewed per subject for each experimental group. Tape-recorded interviews were conducted with 67 Ss at the end of the 24-month follow-up period. Two Ss died before the end of their follow-up period. It continued to be the case that follow-up information could not be gathered for one CD-C subject. During the second, and even a third year of follow-up, this individual has not been reported as arrested or imprisoned in the United States, nor reported deceased by any state he had frequented or by the Social Security Administration. Further, the Social Security Administration has no record of his having been employed during this time interval.

Drinking behavior measures

Daily drinking disposition was the primary measure used to evaluate treatment outcome for this study. For purposes of statistical comparisons, daily drinking dispositions of abstinent and controlled drinking were combined and operationally defined as days "functioning well," as compared to days "not functioning well," which were operationally defined as the sum of drunk days and days incarcerated in a hospital or jail as a result of drinking. Using these measures for each S's second-year follow-up data (366 days), the 20 CD-E Ss "functioned well" for a mean of 85.17% of all days, compared to the 19 CD-C Ss who "functioned well" for a mean of 42.27% of all days during the same interval. This difference is statistically significant ($t_{37} = +4.73, p < 0.001$). During the same interval, the 14 living ND-E Ss "functioned well" for a mean of 64.15% of all days, as compared to the 14 living ND-C Ss who "functioned well" for a mean of 43.23% of all days. This difference is not statistically significant ($t_{26} = +1.55, 0.10 < p < 0.05$). As had been previously reported (Sobell & Sobell, 1972, 1973a), one ND-C S died from barbiturate-related causes within 2 months after his discharge from the hospital. One ND-E S died a few days after the completion of his first-year follow-up. In this case, the coroner's autopsy report stated that death was caused by a subdural hematoma as the result of a fall. The autopsy report found no evidence of any alcohol or drugs in the S's bloodstream.

The percentage of days that each individual S "functioned well" during the third and fourth 6-month (183 days each) follow-up intervals are graphically presented in Figure 1 for controlled drinker Ss, and Figure 2 for nondrinker Ss. During the fourth 6

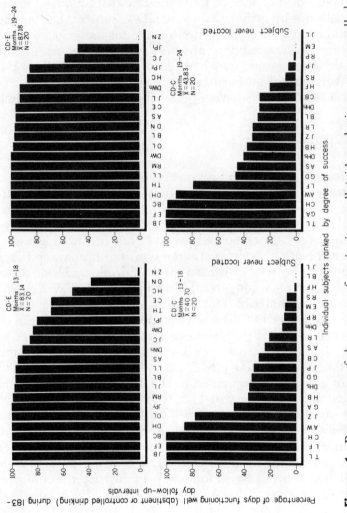

Figure 1. Percentage of days spent functioning well (either abstinent or controlled drinking) by individual controlled drinker experimental and control subjects during third and fourth 6-month (183-day) follow-up intervals.

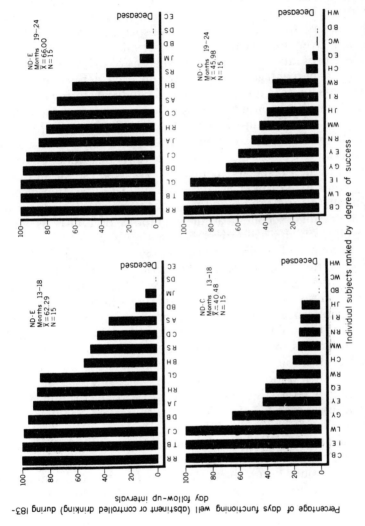

Figure 2. Percentage of days spent functioning well (either abstinent or controlled drinking) by individual nondrinker experimental and control subjects during third and fourth 6-month (183-day) follow-up intervals.

months of follow-up, 17 of the 20 total CD-E Ss "functioned well" for more than 85% of all days. Only 4 of the 19 CD-C Ss met this criterion, and only 5 of the CD-C Ss "functioned well" for even the majority of that follow-up period. It is of interest that all of the groups, except the ND-E condition, displayed a pattern of improvement over the 2-year follow-up period.

Table 2 presents a more detailed analysis of drinking behavior —the mean percentage of days spent in each defined drinking disposition—for Ss in each experimental condition during both the third and fourth 6-month follow-up intervals, and over the entire second year of follow-up. During the second year of follow-up, both CD-E and ND-E Ss not only experienced fewer drunk days but also evinced a considerably greater number of abstinent days as compared to their respective control Ss. Total days spent incarcerated by controlled drinker Ss, and especially CD-E Ss, diminished substantially during the second year of follow-up. In contrast to first-year results, second-year incarcerations of ND-E Ss were more frequently in a jail rather than in a hospital.

The incidence of controlled drinking by Ss in all but the CD-E group was rather minimal during the second year of follow-up. As has been discussed previously (Sobell & Sobell, 1973b), a more detailed analysis of the controlled drinking which did occur has clinical significance. Table 3 relates functioning throughout the second year interval to controlled drinking practices by Ss in each group. It displays the mean percentages of days spent in various drinking dispositions by Ss in each experimental condition for the third and fourth 6-month follow-up intervals, with Ss categorized according to whether they engaged in no controlled drinking days, some but fewer than 5% (9 or less days) controlled drinking days, or greater than 5% controlled drinking days during each interval. In general, Ss from all groups who were able to successfully engage in 5% or greater controlled drinking days during the follow-up interval functioned better than other Ss in their respective groups. Similar to the first year follow-up findings, those Ss who never engaged in controlled drinking during the follow-up interval usually functioned considerably less well than other Ss in their respective groups. The findings for Ss who practiced controlled drinking for fewer than 5% of all days of the follow-up interval are equivocal, because of the small number of Ss in this category.

An analysis regarding the type of controlled drinking which our Ss engaged in has been suggested by Madsen (Doherty, 1974). This

Table 2. Mean percentage of days spent in different drinking dispositions by subjects in each experimental group during both the third (mos. 13–18) and fourth (mos. 19–24) 6-month (183-day) follow-up intervals, and over the entire second year (mos. 13–24) of follow-up

Drinking Disposition	Experimental condition[a]			
	CD-E	CD-C	ND-E[b]	ND-C[b]
Follow-up months 13–18				
Controlled drinking	21.58	4.03	2.89	1.13
Abstinent, not incarcerated	61.56	36.67	59.40	39.35
Drunk	12.81	51.77	19.67	36.85
Incarcerated, alcohol-related:				
hospital	2.71	2.59	6.48[c]	11.59[c]
jail	1.34	4.94	11.56[c]	11.08[c]
Total	100.00	100.00	100.00	100.00
Follow-up months 19–24				
Controlled drinking	23.55	7.59	4.41	1.99
Abstinent, not incarcerated	63.64	36.24	61.59	43.99
Drunk	11.72	46.73	21.08	38.09
Incarcerated, alcohol-related:				
hospital	0.46	2.39	5.78[c]	6.05[c]
jail	0.63	7.05	7.14[c]	9.88[c]
Total	100.00	100.00	100.00	100.00
Follow-up year 2 (months 13–24)				
Controlled drinking	22.57	5.81	3.65	1.56
Abstinent, not incarcerated	62.60	36.46	60.50	41.67
Drunk	12.27	49.25	20.37	37.47
Incarcerated, alcohol-related:				
hospital	1.58	2.49	6.13[c]	8.82[c]
jail	0.98	5.99	9.35[c]	10.48[c]
Total	100.00	100.00	100.00	100.00

[a] Experimental conditions were controlled drinker experimental (CD-E), $n=20$; controlled drinker control (CD-C), $n=19$; nondrinker experimental (ND-E), $n=14$; and, nondrinker control (ND-C), $n=14$.

[b] Does not include data for one deceased subject in each of the nondrinker groups.

[c] Nondrinker group incarceration data tend to reflect extreme scores of a few individual subjects.

Table 3. Mean percentage of days spent in various drinking dispositions during the third and fourth 6-month (183-day) follow-up intervals by subjects in each experimental group*

Drinking Disposition	Experimental Condition[a]							
	No CD days		<5% CD days		≥5% CD days		All Ss	
	n	%	n	%	n	%	n	%
Follow-up months 13–18								
CD-E								
Functioning well[b]	7[c]	69.79	2	80.87	11[d]	92.05	20	83.14
Incarcerated		4.45		7.65		3.13		4.05
Drunk		25.76		11.48		4.82		12.81
Total	7	100.0	2	100.00	11	100.00	20	100.00
CD-C								
Functioning well	13[e]	42.08	3	18.58	3[f]	56.83	19	40.70
Incarcerated		8.87		9.29		0.00		7.53
Drunk		49.05		72.13		43.17		51.77
Total	13	100.00	3	100.00	3	100.00	19	100.00
ND-E								
Functioning well	10	54.70	2	70.48	2	92.08	14[g]	62.29
Incarcerated		24.92		1.10		0.55		18.04
Drunk		20.38		28.42		7.37		19.67
Total	10	100.00	2	100.00	2	100.00	14	100.00
ND-C								
Functioning well	12	37.61	0		2	57.65	14[g]	40.48
Incarcerated		26.28				1.10		22.67
Drunk		36.11				41.25		36.85
Total	12	100.00	0		2	100.00	14	100.00

Table 3. *(continued)*

Drinking Disposition	Experimental Condition[a]							
	No CD days		*<5% CD days*		*≥5% CD days*		*All Ss*	
	n	%	n	%	n	%	n	%
Follow-up months 19–24								
CD-E								
Functioning well	3[b]	66.67	2	96.72	15[i]	90.02	20	87.19
Incarcerated		0.00		0.00		1.46		1.09
Drunk		33.33		3.28		8.52		11.72
Total	3	100.00	2	100.00	15	100.00	20	100.00
CD-C								
Functioning well	11	45.35	2	17.77	6	49.72	19	43.83
Incarcerated		8.45		41.80		0.46		9.44
Drunk		46.20		40.43		49.82		46.73
Total	11	100.00	2	100.00	6	100.00	19	100.00
ND-E								
Functioning well	9	55.31	1	97.81	4	82.11	14[g]	66.00
Incarcerated		18.52		0.55		3.41		12.92
Drunk		26.17		1.64		1₄.48		21.08
Total	9	100.00	1	100.00	4	100.00	14	100.00
ND-C								
Functioning well	9	34.73	2	69.40	3	64.12	14[g]	45.98
Incarcerated		20.70		0.27		12.02		15.93
Drunk		44.57		30.33		23.86		38.09
Total	9	100.00	2	100.00	3	100.00	14	100.00

*Categorized according to whether they had no controlled drinking (CD) days during the follow-up intervals, some but less than 5% CD days during the interval, or greater than 5% CD days during the interval.

[a] Experimental conditions were controlled drinker experimental (CD-E); controlled drinker control (CD-C); nondrinker experimental (ND-E); and nondrinker control (ND-C).

[b] "Functioning well" was operationally defined as the algebraic sum of the percentage of days abstinent plus percentage of days controlled drinking.

[c] Two of these 7 subjects were totally abstinent throughout this interval.

[d] Nine of these 11 subjects functioned well in excess of 95% of all days composing this interval.

[e] Two of these 13 subjects functioned well in excess of 87% of all days composing this interval.

[f] One of these 3 subjects functioned well throughout this entire interval.

[g] Data are not reported for deceased subjects: 1 ND-E and 1 ND-C subject.

[h] Two of these 3 subjects were totally abstinent and the other totally drunk throughout this interval.

[i] Eleven of these 15 subjects functioned well in excess of 95% of all days composing this interval.

311

indicator, which we shall refer to as a Drinking Control Index (DCI), is computed for individual Ss and consists of the proportion of all drinking days during which a S engaged in controlled drinking. Thus, for each S who engaged in any drinking during the follow-up interval, an index ranging from 1.00 (totally controlled drinking) to 0.00 (totally uncontrolled drinking) was computed. However, as opposed to Madsen's preference for computing a single index for each group of Ss based on combined group data, this index is only meaningfully considered when individual S's indices are calculated. Group data would obviously be greatly influenced by extreme scores from a small number of Ss. For controlled drinker Ss, differences in DCIs between the experimental and control groups for both the third and fourth 6-month intervals were found to be statistically significant (mos. 13–18, t_{32} = +4.11, $p < 0.001$; mos. 19–24, t_{33} = +6.06, $p < 0.001$). Differences between nondrinker experimental and control Ss for each interval were not statistically significant (mos. 13–18, t_{22} = +1.01; mos. 19–24, t_{22} = +0.63). These data support Orford's (1973) assertion that some alcoholics are capable of controlling their drinking nearly all of the time (approximately 11 to 13 of the CD-E Ss, 1 of the DC-C Ss, 1 or 2 of the ND-E Ss, and 1 of the ND-C Ss), others are capable of controlling their drinking on some or most drinking occasions, and still others appear to never engage in drinking without drinking large amounts.

Individual subject data, on which the DCI analysis was based, are included in Table 4, which presents detailed drinking profiles for each of the 69 Ss found. This method of presenting results is preferable to descriptive summaries of group data because it provides a more complete portrayal of each S's functioning. From these profiles it appears the Ss who successfully engaged in controlled drinking typically did not initiate extended periods of drunk days as a result of this type of drinking. For example, only CD-E Ss displayed a high incidence of isolated drunk days, as compared to the predominant pattern by other Ss of extended periods of continuous drunk days. The profiles also suggest that: (a) only one S (a CD-C) engaged in controlled drinking days which involved the consumption of straight drinks, (b) controlled drinking days were evinced more in a social context and at the S's own residence compared to when the Ss drank alone and away from home, and (c) no CD-E Ss spent time in an explicitly abstinence-oriented environment (e.g., a halfway house, Twelfth Step House, Salvation Army, or similar residential settings) during the second year of follow-up, while several Ss in the other groups lived in such an environment for a substantial number of days during that period.

Adjunctive measures of treatment outcome

It has been repeatedly demonstrated that changes in drinking behavior do not necessarily imply or reflect that an individual has therefore improved his life functioning in other respects (Gerard & Saenger, 1966; Pattison et al., 1968; Belasco, 1971; Emrick, 1974), although these variables are often highly correlated, especially when group data are considered. For this reason, treatment outcome data were also collected for various adjunctive measures of life functioning. Table 5 presents second-year results for several adjunctive measures of treatment outcome. Data for all variables are presented separately for the third and fourth 6-month follow-up intervals, with the exception of the measures concerning residential status and stability, driving status, and marital status, which were computed for the entire second-year interval.

Group differences for the variable of general adjustment were statistically significant between CD-E and CD-C groups for each 6-month follow-up interval (mos. 13–18, $p < 0.01$; mos. 19–24, $p < 0.01$). Fisher-Yates Exact Probability Tests (McNemar, 1962) were used to analyze these results from two-by-two contingency tables formed by comparing the number of Ss in each group who were rated "Improved" for that interval with pooled Ss rated as either "Same" or "Worse." The differences between these groups for this measure had also been statistically significant throughout the first year of follow-up. However, while the differences between ND-E and ND-C groups for this variable were statistically significant throughout the entire first year of follow-up, they did not remain so for either of the 6-month intervals in the second year. This measure is of particular interest, as the method of treatment used with both groups of experimental Ss (CD-E and ND-E) emphasized their learning to respond to problem situations more constructively than they had in the past.

Two different measures of vocational functioning were obtained. Vocational status was a S's own evaluation of his own job satisfaction. For this measure, differences were statistically analyzed by a Fisher-Yates Exact Probability Test in the same manner as the general adjustment variable. Again, differences between the CD-E and CD-C groups were found to be significant at each of the 6-month intervals (mos. 13–18, $p < 0.02$; mos. 19–24,

Table 4. Individual drinking profiles summarizing subjects' predominant drinking patterns during the second year (366 days) of follow-up

Group[a] and Ss initials	Abstinent days total no.	Controlled drinking days total no.	type drinks[b]	no. drinks	days/wk.	soc. env.[c]	where[d]	Drinking Days total no.	style[e]	max. binge[f]	Drunk days type drinks[b]	no. drinks	soc. env.[c]	where[d]	No. of days in abstin. orient. env.[g]
Controlled Drinker–Experimental															
J.B.	162	204	W	1-2	4	S	R	0	—	—	—	—	—	—	0
E.F.	252	112	M	3-5	2-3	S	R,O	2	I	—	M	10	S	R,O	0
D.H.	363	3	B	2-3	<1	S	R	0	—	—	—	—	—	—	0
O.L.	236	127	B	3-4	2-3	S	R,O	3	I	—	B	10-16	S	O	0
L.L.	164	197	B	2-4	3-5	S,A	R,O	5	I	—	B,M	10-12	A	R	0
B.C.	99	258	B	3-5	5	S,A	R	9	C	3	B	9	S	R	0
B.L.	302	55	B	3-5	5-6	S	R	9	I	—	B	10-15	S	R	0
J.L.	295	58	M	4-5	1	S	R,O	13	I	—	B	12	S	R,O	0
A.S.	255	97	B,M	1-4	2	S	R	14	I	—	B,M	10	S	R	0
J.Pr.	282	57	B,M	2-3	2	S	R,O	27	C	7	H	>20	S	R,O	0
D.Wn.	327	12	M	2-3	<1	S	R,O	27	C	3	W	12	S	R,O	0
D.Wr.	336	0	—	—	—	—	—	0	—	—	—	—	—	—	0
R.M.	175	140	M	2	4-5	S	R	1	I	—	M	10	A	R	0
T.H.	311	0	—	—	—	—	—	48	C	48	H	16	S	O	0
C.E.	272	33	B	5-6	<1	A	R	29	C	14	B	12-15	A	O	0

J.C.	0	R	S	8->20	H	85	C	89	R	S,A	3-4	4	B	93	170
H.C.	0	R	A	12->20	B,W	2	C	104	R	A	<1	3-4	B	211	44
D.N.	0	R	A	>20	W	64	C	69	R	S	C^b	4-6	B	208	38
J.Pl.	0	O	A	12	W	34	C	96	R	S	<1	2-3	B	221	12
Z.N.	0	O	S	>20	H,W	351	C	351	—	—	—	—	—	3	0

Controlled Drinker–Control

T.L.	0	—	—	—	—	—	—	0	—	—	—	—	—	366	0
C.H.	0	R	S	16	H	—	I	1	R	S	1-2	3-4	M	292	73
L.F.	291	R	A	12	W	29	C	35	—	—	—	—	—	329	0
A.W.	143	O	A	>20	H	8	C	23	—	—	—	—	—	329	0
G.A.	0	O	S	>20	H	91	C	91	—	—	—	—	—	271	0
J.Z.	171	R,O	A	12	B,W	49	C	150	—	—	—	—	—	206	0
C.B.	68	O	S	>20	H,B,W	67	C	211	R	S	—	—	—	172	0
G.D.	0	R	S	7-12	B	21	C	217	O	S	2	3-4	B	43	105
D.Ms.	0	O	S	9-16	H,B	92	C	226	R	S	2	3-4	B	26	114
H.B.	93	R	A	8-10	H	60	C	230	R	A	<1	6	H	93	43
A.S.	0	R	S	8-12	H	5	C	236	R	S	1	1-3	B,W	80	48
L.R.	3	R,O	A	>20	H,B	39	C	157	O	A	<1	1-4	B,M	98	2
D.Hn.	19	R,O	A,S	>20	H	42	C	63	—	—	—	—	—	82	0
J.P.	0	O	S	>20	B	70	C	248	—	A	—	—	—	71	0
B.L.	0	O	A	>20	W	116	C	285	O	—	<1	2-6	B	38	16
H.F.	0	R	A	8-10	H	45	C	316	—	A	—	—	—	43	0
R.S.	0	R,O	A	>16	H	16	C	337	—	—	—	—	—	29	0
R.P.	0	R,O	A	15-20	B	49	C	249	R	A	<1	5	B	19	3
E.M.	0	R,O	A	8-16	H	350	C	350	—	—	—	—	—	16	0
J.L.							(never located)								

315

Table 4 (*continued*)

Group[a] and Ss initials	Abstinent days total no.	Controlled drinking days — total no.	type drinks[b]	no. drinks	days/wk.	soc. env.[c]	where[d]	Drinking Days — total no.	style[e]	max. binge[f]	Drunk days — type drinks[b]	no. drinks	soc. env.[c]	where[d]	No. of days in abstin. orient. env.[g]
T.B.	366	0	—	—	—	—	—	0	—	—	—	—	—	—	0
R.R.	366	0	—	—	—	—	—	0	—	—	—	—	—	—	0
D.B.	344	11	M	8	<1	S	R	8	I	—	H	10	A	R	0
C.J.	284	67	B,M,W	2-7	1	S	O	15	C	6	W,B	8	S	R	60
G.L.	285	57	B	2-3	1	S	R	22	C	20	H	16	S	O	0
J.A.	327	0	—	—	—	—	—	21	C	21	H	>20	A	R	0
R.H.	311	0	—	—	—	—	—	45	C	19	H	>20	A	R	150
C.D.	221	3	B	1	C[b]	A	R	140	C	28	H	>20	A	R	0
B.H.	184	29	B	2	<1	S	R	149	C	28	W,H	>20	S	S	0
A.S.	179	20	B	6	<1	S	O	56	C	21	H,B	>20	S	O	68
R.S.	158	0	—	—	—	—	—	153	C	28	W	>20	A	R	44
J.M.	107	0	—	—	—	—	—	82	C	16	W	12[i]	S,A	O	25
B.D.	39	0	—	—	—	—	—	51	C	7	W,B	9-12	A	O	0
D.S.	0	0	—	—	—	—	—	304	C	163	H	>20	S	R	0
E.C.							(deceased—not alcohol-related)								

Nondrinker–Experimental

Nondrinker–Control [a]

	[b]		[f]		[c]	[d]		[e]		[b]	[f]	[c]	[d]	[g]
C.B.	341	25	B	2-3	<1	S	R	0	—	—	—	—	—	—	0
L.W.	366	0	—	1	<1	A	R	0	—	—	—	—	—	—	0
I.E.	350	7	B	—	—	—	—	8	I	7	B	12-18	A	R	0
G.Y.	246	0	—	1-2	<1	S	O	61	C	21	H	>20 [i]	A	O	230
E.Y.	187	0	B	—	—	—	—	103	C	36	H	>20	A	O	93
R.N.	114	17	—	2	—	A	R	53	C	97	B	9-12	S	R	0
R.W.	122	0	B	1-2	<1	A	R,O	241	C	30	H	>20	A	R	0
W.M.	110	1	B	—	—	—	—	186	C	49	W	18	A	R,O	0
R.I.	66	30	O	—	—	—	—	266	C	22	B	14-18	A	O	0
J.H.	95	0	—	—	—	—	—	113	C	173	W	18	S	R	95
E.Q.	82	0	—	—	—	—	—	254	C	91	H,W	>20	A	O	0
C.H.	54	0	—	—	—	—	—	285	C	4	W,B	18	S	R	39
W.C.	2	0	—	—	—	—	—	4	C	190	H,B	>10	A	O	0
B.D.	0	0	—	—	—	—	—	346	C	—	H,W	>20	A	R	0
W.H.	(deceased—barbiturate-related)														

a Subjects within groups are ranked according to the percentage of days they "functioned well" (operationally defined as the algebraic sum of abstinent and controlled drinking days) during the second year of follow-up.

b Type of beverage typically consumed was coded as: H=straight whiskey or other high-proof (i.e., over 40% alcohol) beverage, M=mixed drink consisting of hard liquor plus a nonalcoholic mixer, W=wine with 12% alcohol content, and B=beer with 4% alcohol content.

c The nature of the social environment where drinking typically occurred was coded as: A=drinking alone, or S=drinking in the presence of others.

d The location where drinking typically occurred was coded as: R=in the subject's own residence, or O=in a location other than the subject's residence.

e Drunk days which occurred in a continuous (i.e., daily drinking) fashion were coded as C, whereas drunk days which occurred in isolation were coded as I.

f When drunk days were continuous for a subject, the entry in this column indicates the length of the longest drinking binge recorded for that subject.

g Days spent in an explicitly abstinence-oriented environment included any days when a subject was living at a halfway house, Twelfth Step house, Salvation Army, or other similar residential programs.

h In these cases, use of the code C indicates that the controlled drinking days consisted of continuous daily drinking.

i In these cases, concurrent use of barbiturates and alcohol was reported by subjects.

Table 5. Adjunctive measures of treatment outcome for subjects in each experimental group for the follow-up intervals indicated

Adjunctive Measure	Experimental Condition [a]			
	CD-E (%)	CD-C (%)	ND-E (%)	ND-C (%)
Follow-up months 13–18				
Evaluation of general adjustment by collaterals:				
Improved	90.00	47.37	50.00	50.00
Same	5.00	15.79	35.72	28.57
Worse	5.00	36.84	14.28	21.43
Vocational status:				
Improved	70.00	31.58	50.00	28.57
Same	25.00	31.58	35.72	57.15
Worse	5.00	36.84	14.28	14.28
Occupational status:				
Full-time work	65.00	36.84	50.00	28.57
Part-time work	10.00	15.79	0.00	14.28
Retired	5.00	5.26	0.00	0.00
Student	0.00	0.00	7.14	0.00
Disabled	5.00	0.00	0.00	0.00
Unemployed	15.00	42.11	42.86	57.15
Used therapeutic supports: Yes	35.00	26.32	64.29	35.72
Retained research program card: Yes	65.00	n.a.	78.54	n.a.
Follow-up months 19–24				
Evaluation of general adjustment by collaterals:				
Improved	85.00	42.11	64.29	35.72
Same	5.00	26.32	14.28	42.85
Worse	10.00	31.57	21.43	21.43
Vocational status:				
Improved	70.00	26.32	50.00	28.57
Same	25.00	36.84	35.72	57.15
Worse	5.00	36.84	14.28	14.28
Occupational status:				
Full-time work	55.00	36.84	35.72	35.72
Part-time work	20.00	15.79	7.14	7.14
Retired	5.00	5.26	0.00	0.00
Student	5.00	0.00	14.28	0.00
Disabled	10.00	0.00	0.00	7.14
Unemployed	5.00	42.11	42.86	50.00
Used therapeutic supports: Yes	35.00	31.57	71.44	42.86
Retained research program card: Yes	65.00	n.a.	78.54	n.a.

Table 5. *(continued)*

Adjunctive Measure	Experimental Condition[a]			
	CD-E (%)	CD-C (%)	ND-E (%)	ND-C (%)
Follow-up year 2 (months 13–24)				
Mean residential stability and status index (RSSI) (1.0=ideal):	0.4233	0.3819	0.2181	0.2401
Median RSSI:	0.1479	0.0896	0.0487	0.0623
Initials of subjects with reported alcohol-related traffic violations (number of violations incurred):	T.H. (1)	G.D. (1)	G.L. (1)	C.H. (1)
	Z.N. (1)	H.F. (1)	D.S. (1)	R.N. (1)
		R.P. (2)		E.Y. (1)
Two-year follow-up interval (months 1–24)				
Possessed valid driver's license:				
At discharge	70.00	60.00	80.00	53.33
End year 2	60.00	36.82	50.00[b]	28.56[b]
Marital status, at discharge:				
Married	30.00	20.00	20.00	40.00
Single	20.00	25.00	20.00	13.33
Divorced, separated or annulled	50.00	55.00	60.00	40.00
Widower	0.00	0.00	0.00	6.67
Marital status, end year 2:[c]				
Married	50.00	21.05	46.67	26.67
Single	20.00	26.32	6.66	13.33
Divorced, separated or annulled				
Widower	30.00	52.63	46.67	60.00
	0.00	0.00	0.00	0.00

[a] Experimental conditions were controlled drinker experimental (CD-E), $n=20$; controlled drinker control (CD-C), $n=19$; nondrinker experimental (ND-E), $n=14$; and nondrinker control (ND-C), $n=14$. Data not included for deceased subjects (1 ND-E and 1 ND-C) unless otherwise noted.

[b] Data are not included in these values for the two subjects (1 ND-E and 1 ND-C) who died prior to the end of their second year of follow-up. Each had a valid driver's license at the beginning of year 1 and at the time of their deaths.

[c] Figures given do not include marital status for the CD-C subject who was never located, as this status was indeterminate. The ND-E and ND-C group data do include the marital status at the time of death for the two subjects who died prior to the end of their second year of follow-up.

$p < 0.01$), while ND-E and ND-C group differences were not statistically significant for either interval. The measure of occupational status refers to the actual type of employment, nonemployment (retired, disabled, student), or unemployment Ss were engaged in during the majority of each follow-up interval. This variable provides a more objective measure of vocational functioning. For this variable, a Fisher-Yates Exact Probability Test was performed by pooling employed and other categories versus unemployed in each group for each of the 6-month follow-up periods. Employment rate differences between CD-E and CD-C groups approached significance for months 13–18 ($p < 0.09$) and were statistically significant during the final 6 months of follow-up ($p < 0.01$). Again, differences between the ND-E and ND-C groups were not statistically significant for either 6-month interval. During the first year of follow-up, no statistically significant differences in vocational functioning had been found between any of the groups.

A final variable used to compare respective experimental and control Ss over the third and fourth 6-month follow-up intervals measured the Ss' use of therapeutic supports. Since this measure is subject to varying interpretations, all lacking foundation in the literature, no statistical analyses were attempted for these data. A more detailed consideration of the problems surrounding this variable is included in an earlier report (Sobell & Sobell, 1973b). Seven of the 20 CD-E Ss utilized therapeutic supports during each of the second-year intervals. One of these Ss attended AA meetings, two Ss attended outpatient therapy or counseling sessions, one received services from a private therapist, two used other self-help organizations (e.g., Neurotics Anonymous), and one S used multiple supports. Five and six of the 19 CD-C Ss used therapeutic supports during the third and fourth 6-month follow-up intervals, respectively. Three of these Ss attended AA meetings, one used Antabuse, and one S received religious counseling throughout the second year of follow-up. During the fourth 6 months of follow-up, an additional S in this group joined a self-help group. A greater proportion of Ss in each of the nondrinker groups used therapeutic supports during the second year of follow-up than did Ss in the controlled drinker groups. Of the nine ND-E Ss who used therapeutic supports throughout the second year of follow-up, three Ss attended AA meetings, two participated in outpatient therapy or counseling, two received the services of private therapists, and two used multiple supports. During the fourth 6 months of follow-up, one additional ND-E S used multiple supports. Five of the ND-C Ss used therapeutic supports throughout the second year of follow-up. Four of these Ss attended AA meetings, while one used the services of another self-help group. During the fourth 6 months of follow-up, an additional ND-C S attended AA meetings. Thus, during the second year of follow-up, 28.6% of the ND-E Ss, 35.7% of the ND-C Ss, 5.0% of the CD-E Ss, and 15.79% of the CD-C Ss made use of AA. It should be recalled that all controlled Ss received a conventional treatment oriented toward abstinence regardless of their judged suitability for the controlled drinking or nondrinking treatment goals. Furthermore, Ss in all but the CD-E group were advised that it would be in their best interest to try and maintain abstinence. The finding that Ss selected for the controlled drinking groups made only slight use of AA is consistent with the fact that one of the major criteria for their having been assigned to the controlled drinking goal was an expressed dissatisfaction with traditional treatment modalities, including AA. The relatively low level of participation in AA by Ss in the nondrinker groups, however, was unexpected.

Residential status and stability were evaluated as an adjunctive index of treatment outcome for the entire second year of follow-up using individual subject indices. Since the calculated index values for individual Ss tended to be distributed as a bimodal distribution, differences between groups were analyzed using the Mann-Whitney U-Test. In order to ease comparison of these data with previously reported first-year results (Sobell & Sobell, 1973b), both mean and median values for the RSSI are included in Table 4. This analysis indicated that the difference between CD-E and CD-C groups approached but did not attain statistical significance ($p < 0.09$). The difference between nondrinker groups was not significant and, in fact, reversed the trend found during the first year of follow-up. At this time, it is equivocal whether or not this particular index is a valid measure of treatment outcome, and, if valid, whether it is sufficiently sensitive for general use. However, considering the paucity of available quantifiable indicants to assess alcoholism treatment outcome, continued investigation of this variable appears warranted. For instance, if only residential status were considered and Ss were grouped according to whether they had spent the majority of the interval in a permanent as opposed to nonpermanent residence, the controlled drinker group differences would have been statistically significant by a Fisher-Yates Exact Probability Test.

Another adjunctive measure of treatment outcome concerned the ratio of alcohol-related driving violations (e.g., drunk driving, open container in car) per driver. As only a few Ss were cited for an alcohol-related driving violation during the second year of follow-up, statistical analysis of those data would lack meaning. Table 5 identifies by initials those Ss in each group who were cited for violations and the number of times such events occurred.

Another use of driving status as a measure of degree of successful functioning concerns the number of Ss in each group who possessed valid driver's licenses at the end of their 2-year follow-up interval, as compared to the number who possessed valid licenses at their time of hospital discharge. As is evident in Table 5, the number of Ss possessing valid driver's licenses at the end of follow-up was less for all groups than at the time of their hospital discharge, although CD-E Ss were proportionally less affected than Ss in the other three groups. This variable is again difficult to interpret, as Ss could lose their driving privileges for a variety of reasons not necessarily related to drinking, such as being cited for driving on an already suspended or revoked license. Using a Fisher-Yates Exact Probability Test, neither of the group differences was statistically significant for this variable.

Marital status at the time of hospital discharge and at the end of the 2-year follow-up period is similarly difficult to interpret. As shown in Table 5, the frequency of married Ss increased over this interval for both experimental groups, and the frequency of divorced, separated, or annulled relationships concurrently decreased. Still, to speculate that such differences were in the Ss' best interests would constitute a value judgment which we are not prepared to make at this time.

An additional indicator of treatment outcome, physical health status, was added to the existing battery of measures for the second year of follow-up. This measure was derived from the interviews conducted with Ss at the end of the 2-year follow-up period. Subjects were asked to evaluate their present physical health status retrospectively compared to their physical health during the year or two preceding their hospitalization, as either "Improved," "Same," or "Worse." Fisher-Yates Exact Probability Tests were performed with this data by pooling the categories of "Same" and "Worse" versus "Improved." Differences between CD-E and CD-C Ss approached statistical significance (< 0.08) in the direction of experimental Ss having a greater frequency of reported improved physical health. Differences between nondrinker groups were not statistically significant.

A final variable of interest concerned whether experimental Ss retained their research program card (*Do's* and *Do Not's* card) after discharge from the hopital. A majority of the experimentally treated Ss—65.00% of the CD-E Ss and 78.54% of the ND-E Ss—still retained their cards at the end of the 2-year follow-up interval. This variable cannot be used for comparison between experimental and control Ss, as control Ss did not receive program cards. The high incidence of retained program cards among experimental Ss after 2 years may possibly be indicative of the value of the cards for the Ss.

General measures of treatment outcome

Thus far, this report has only considered the results from a number of single dependent variable measures. Table 6 presents results obtained using two indicators of general treatment outcome. Computational procedures for these measures were presented in the Method section of this paper. Each summary measure has various advantages and disadvantages.

Statistical analyses of "Factor Success" outcomes were performed using a Fisher-Yates Exact Probability Test to compare the number of three-factor successes in each respective experimental and control group with the pooled remaining Ss in each of those groups. Thus categorized, CD-E Ss had a significantly greater incidence of three-factor successes than CD-C Ss at each 6-month interval ($p < 0.01$), while nondrinker groups were not significantly different for either interval. This measure demonstrates the distribution of individual subject success profiles within each group of Ss.

The second general indicator of treatment outcome, "General Index of Outcome" (GIO), provides a single parametric index ranging from 0.00 to 1.00, with 1.00 representing the highest attainable outcome. Differences between respective experimental and control groups were analyzed by performing t tests using individual subject GIO's as raw data. Consistent with the majority of results, CD-E Ss were found to differ significantly from CD-C Ss for both the third and fourth 6-month follow-up intervals (mos. 13–18, $t_{37} = +4.30$, $p < 0.001$; mos. 19–24, $t_{37} = +4.25$, $p < 0.001$). Again, the ND-E and ND-C groups did not differ significantly in GIO at either interval.

Additional results

As was mentioned in the 1-year follow-up report (Sobell & Sobell, 1973b), some Ss have experienced personal problems and tragedies which are not reflected in the quantitative outcome data.

Table 6. Results of two different general summary measures of treatment outcome which indicate general degree of successful outcome for second-year follow-up intervals

Method and Follow-up Interval	Experimental Condition [a]			
	CD-E	CD-C	ND-E	ND-C
Follow-up months 13–18				
Factor Success method:				
Percentage of *three*-factor successes	60.00	10.52	42.86	21.43
Percentage of *two*-factor successes	25.00	26.32	7.14	7.14
Percentage of *single*-factor successes	5.00	21.05	7.14	21.43
Percentage totally unsuccessful	10.00	42.11	42.86	50.00
General Index of Outcome (GIO) method:				
Mean GIO	0.8605	0.4778	0.6600	0.5397
Follow-up months 19–24				
Factor Success method:				
Percentage of *three*-factor successes	60.00	10.52	35.72	21.43
Percentage of *two*-factor successes	25.00	26.32	28.57	7.14
Percentage of *single*-factor successes	10.00	10.52	7.14	7.14
Percentage totally unsuccessful	5.00	52.64	28.57	64.29
General Index of Outcome (GIO) method:				
Mean GIO	0.8573	0.4794	0.6843	0.5342

Note: Each measure combines results from drinking, general adjustment, and vocational status dependent measures.

[a] Experimental conditions were controlled drinker experimental (CD-E), $n = 20$; controlled drinker control (CD-C), $n = 19$; nondrinker experimental (ND-E), $n = 14$; and nondrinker control (ND-C), $n = 14$.

Events of this type that have already been reported will not be reiterated here. However, the following anectodal outcome data have not been reported elsewhere. Subject A.W., a CD-C, died 33 months after hospital discharge. His death was a result of thermal burns over 50% of his body. Apparently, a fire started in his boardinghouse room when he fell asleep while smoking in bed. The autopsy found that his blood alcohol concentration was 0.28%. Nondrinker experimental subject D.S also died 33 months after hospital discharge. His causes of death were listed on the death certificate as : (1) bronchopneumonia, terminal; (2) hepatic coma; and (3) cirrhosis of the liver, severe. During the first year of follow-up, subject J.H., a ND-C, fell off a two-story building while drunk and broke his neck, causing a temporary paralysis which necessitated his being hospitalized for 3 months. Finally, ND-C subject R.I., near the end of his first follow-up year, was involved in a single-car traffic accident and injured himself and his passenger as a result of colliding with a telephone pole. As a result, he was hospitalized for 11 days with a broken jaw. He was reported to have been drinking on the day of the accident. Therefore, over the entire extended follow-up period for which information is available, a total of seven control Ss and only one experimental Ss suffered serious alcohol-related physical damage.

Discussion

An evaluation of Ss functioning, using both drinking behavior measures and adjunctive measures of outcome, supports the conclusion that hospitalized male alcoholic Ss who received the program of individualized behavior therapy with a treatment goal of controlled drinking functioned significantly better during the second year following their discharge from treatment than did their respective control Ss who received only conventional treatment oriented toward abstinence. Furthermore, evidence is presented that many of the CD-E Ss engaged in limited, nonproblem drinking during that interval. These findings are consistent with previously reported first-year outcome data for these Ss (Sobell & Sobell, 1973b) and with over 60 studies in the alcoholism literature which demonstrate that such nonproblem drinking by *some* former alcoholics is possible and does occur (reviewed by Sobell & Sobell, 1975d). Since these findings have typically been reported as follow-up of abstinence-oriented treatment programs, it is hardly surprising that a treatment program with an explicit goal of limited drinking should also evince success.

Although substantial differences exist between ND-E and ND-C Ss for the variable of drinking behavior, differences for this and other treatment outcome measures were not statistically significant during the second year of follow-up. Differences between these groups on the drinking and general adjustment measures had been significant over the first year of follow-up (Sobell & Sobell, 1973b).

From the results of this study, it might appear that the treatment goal of controlled drinking contributed more to successful outcomes than did the method of individualized behavior therapy. However, it must be recalled that Ss were selectively assigned to drinking treatment goals, although assignment to experimental or control groups within each goal condition was randomly determined. Thus, subject variables, rather than treatment or goal variables, may account for the lack of continued significant differences between ND-E and ND-C Ss.

The result of this study and a great many others suggest that controlled drinking can now be appropriately considered as alternative treatment goals to abstinence for *some* alcoholics. However, legitimizing alternatives to abstinence as viable treatment objectives for some alcoholics does not imply that this is appropriate for all or even most alcoholics. Similarly, it should be recognized that not all or even most persons currently working in the alcoholism treatment field are presently skilled to pursue alternatives to abstinence with clients. As with any kind of therapeutic procedure, this treatment modality should only be used by trained individuals aware of the methodology, benefits, dangers, and limitations involved in such an approach. A further caveat is that just as the feasibility of this goal has been too easily dismissed by many in the past (Sobell & Sobell, 1975d), so it is possible to erroneously accept a controlled drinking goal as a panacea.

At this time, arguments can be made that either abstinence or controlled drinking might be easier behavior to maintain over the long run. While individuals seldom become permanently abstinent simply as a result of treatment (Paredes et al., 1973), we should also expect that some individuals treated with controlled drinking objectives may at times reacquire excessive drinking patterns. In this regard, when abstinence is the treatment goal and the client experiences a "slip" (reacquires an excessive drinking pattern), this does not imply that the treatment goal of abstinence should be discarded. In such cases, treatment is typically reinitiated with the objective of reacquiring an abstinent pattern. Similarly, if a client who has demonstrated an ability to moderate his drinking experiences a "slip," such an event does not necessarily indicate changing treatment goals.

Currently, it is not known what proportion of alcoholics, under appropriate low risk conditions and as a result of a specifically designed treatment program, could engage in limited nonproblem drinking. Edwards (1970) has suggested that perhaps the best candidates for controlled drinking goals may, in fact, be the very individuals who are also excellent candidates for abstinence. Long-term abstinence is a difficult goal to achieve, as documented in the alcoholism treatment literature. Paredes et al. (1973), for instance, have reviewed studies indicating that approximately 86% of treated alcoholics return to some type of drinking within 1 year of discharge from a treatment program. Also, Gillies et al. (1974) recently reported that an average of only 12.7% of alcoholics admitted to any of six alcohlism treatment units "became abstinent during the one year after treatment begins" (p. 133). In one of the few reported studies designed to gather information on subject variables and limited drinking outcomes, Orford (1973) evaluated 100 alcoholics who had participated in a conventional abstinence-oriented treatment program. Of the 100 subjects, only 10% (10) had maintained total abstinence for a full year, two had died, and incomplete data were reported for 11 cases. The remaining 77 subjects were found to have demonstrated a pattern of drinking which ranged from fully controlled to fully uncontrolled, with the majority fitting neither extreme. Differences in the degree of control exhibited by subjects over their drinking were significantly related to treatment goal preferences, with the totally uncontrolled subjects expressing a greater preference for an abstinence objective.

It seems reasonable to speculate that fully controlled drinking can be expected as a treatment outcome for only a portion of the population of persons who have serious drinking problems. On the other hand, for a large number of that total population, substantially reduced drinking might be a more realistic treatment outcome objective than either controlled drinking or total abstinence. Indeed, our findings appear to indicate that for a few of the subjects—for instance, CD-E subjects J.D., H.C., and J. Pr., CD-C subjects G.D. and D.H.s, ND-E subjects C.J. and G.L., and ND-C subject H.N.—such a portrayal of treatment outcome would more accurately describe their posttreatment drinking behavior.

Drinking outcomes demonstrating various degrees of control over drinking appear to be a frequent and consistent finding in well-designed alcoholism treatment evaluation studies. At this time, it appears that traditional views, regardless of how lacking in empirical support, present a significant threat to scientific inquiry and treatment innovation in this area, especially with respect to reporting drinking outcome data for alcoholics. For example, the National Council on Alcoholism recently issued a press release stating the following: (1) "Abstinence from alcohol is necessary for recovery from the disease of alcoholism"; (2) "there can be no relaxation from the stated position that no alcoholic may return with safety to any use of alcohol"; and (3) "claims that alcoholics can drink again" are "misleading and dangerous" (NCA, 1974). Additionally, a highly prominent and influential lay alcohologist in the United States has recently speculated that such research "might indeed expose them (alcoholics) to an inability *ever* to stop or to recover, and to eventual death or insanity" (Mann, 1974, italics added). Finally, in a recent review of *progress* in the research and treatment of alcoholism it has been suggested that: "we must now question the motives of those who would strip the alcoholic of his 'disease' label," and "we must return the challenge to those lay or medical critics with the demand that they resolve their own personal conflicts regarding the use of alcohol" (Gitlow, 1973, pp. 6–7). Irrespective of the arguments presented thus far, these are not heuristic questions and certainly are not going to be resolved by polemics. However, these questions can be adequately tested using sound scientific methodology. Fortunately, empirical research in this area continues to proliferate and, taken in concert, suggests that there is now an urgent need for changed conceptions of the nature of alcohol dependence as a phenomenon (Pattison, 1966). In the final analysis, the relative efficacy of various treatment objectives will only be determined by clinical research and will, very probably, be found to be highly dependent upon individual case circumstances.

A number of other issues relevant to the results presented in this paper have been considered in earlier publications (Sobell & Sobell, 1972, 1972a, 1973b), and readers are referred to these sources for detailed discussions of these issues.

Differences from first-year results

The most important difference between the first-and second-year follow-up data is that none of the differences between the ND-E and ND-C groups was statistically significant during the second year of follow-up. Possible explanations for this finding were discussed earlier. Another major difference was that for most subjects the adjunctive measures of treatment outcome paralleled the drinking behavior measure more in the second follow-up year than in the first. A similar finding has been reported by Gillis and Keet (1969), who found alcoholics' improvement on adjunctive measures of outcome to follow their improvement on drinking behavior variables.

The relatively low rates of complete abstinence reported for subjects in this study are of some interest (Emrick, 1974). Comparison of this study with other studies in the literature can, in part, account for such differences. For example, there is reason to question the validity of the majority of alcoholism treatment outcome studies which have been reported to date (Hill & Blane, 1967; Miller et al., 1970; Crawford & Chalupsky, 1973). Further, the follow-up procedures and measures used in this study differed substantially from traditional techniques, particularly in the proportion of subjects located for follow-up, the use of frequent follow-up contacts, gathering of daily drinking data, and wording of follow-up questions so as to be relatively free of demand characteristics. Additional research also suggests that the outcome results for our control groups were not atypical for state hospitalized alcoholics. In an unpublished pilot study performed at the Orange County (CA) Alcoholism Services, we undertook a 6-month post-discharge evaluation of 52 alcoholics who had been treated in rehabilitation programs at three nearby private alcoholism hospitals. Nearly all of these subjects qualified as *gamma* alcoholics (Jellinek, 1960), and they were generally less physically and socially deteriorated than the subjects who served in the study reported in this paper. Complete 6-month follow-up data were obtained from 46 (88.46%) of the 52 subjects and from collateral information sources for 51 (98.08%) of the subjects. Drinking disposition questions were phrased similarly to the present study (i.e., "How many days during the past 180 days have you consumed any alcoholic beverages?"). In the 46 cases where both the subject and a collateral were interviewed, only 7 (15.22%) subjects had been totally free of alcohol over the 6 months since their hospital discharge. However, not all patients who had consumed alcohol during this interval did so to the point of drunkenness.

Further consideration on the nature of adequate follow-up procedures and measures

Recent evidence suggests that unless outcome data are gathered for a large proportion of subjects in a given study, the results might be biased in a positive direction. Typically, studies in the alcoholism literature report complete outcome data for only 40 to 60% of all subjects in a study. In a recent treatment follow-up study, Barr et al.

(1973) found some level of information for 81% (407 of 503) of their subjects. Unsatisfied with this retrieval rate, they implemented a second wave of follow-up to obtain a more complete subject sample. This second effort located an additional 10% of the subjects for whom no data had previously been collected, and "virtually none of this group was doing well" (p. 6). Bowen and Androes (1968) have reported similar observations. Data from the present study also support the conclusion that subjects who cannot be easily located are typically functioning less well than other subjects. Five of the 69 subjects found were extremely difficult to locate for follow-up. Final data for these subjects were completed long after their designated follow-up intervals had expired. Two of these subjects were found to have functioned worse than all other subjects in their respective groups during the second year of follow-up (Z.N., CE-E, 0.81% days functioned well; B.D., ND-C, 0.000% days functioned well); two functioned considerably less well than their respective group averages (R.V., CD-C, 7.92% days functioned well; C.B., CD-C, 28.42% days functioned well); and the remaining subject functioned slightly below the average for his group (R.H., ND-E, 58.20% days functioned well). This kind of evidence stands in direct contradiction to investigators who would use the criterion of "no news is good news" as evidence of successful adjustment (Knox, 1972, p. 108).

The use of daily drinking dispositions in this study represented an attempt to develop more sensitive and quantifiable treatment outcome measures. In the future, it is suggested that this approach be modified to simply report the number of ounces, if any, of pure ethanol consumed per day per subject. Similarly, Hunt and Azrin (1973) have used the percent of time subjects were unemployed and the percent of time subjects were away from home as adjunctive outcome measures. Such continuous and quantifiable parameters are more representative of the entire follow-up interval and are preferable to probe day or majority disposition measures. The use of more sensitive outcome measures might, however, make it necessary to conduct more frequent follow-up contacts with subjects than has been the case in the past (Sobell & Sobell, 1975a, d). Finally, objective indicants of subjects' blood alcohol concentrations can be obtained on a probe day basis by using infield portable breath tests (Miller et al., 1973; Sobell & Sobell, 1975c).

Regardless of the measures used, self-reports by subjects and their collaterals will probably continue to be the primary source from which both drinking and other life functioning data will be obtained. Unfortunately, despite the frequent and extensive use of self-reports in the alcoholism field, only a few studies have investigated the reliability and validity of such reports (Guze et al., 1963; Summers, 1970; Sobell & Sobell, 1975c). A comparison of offical records with the self-reports of prior alcohol-related arrests given by subjects who served *in the present study* found that their self-reports were surprisingly accurate and acceptable for use as a primary information source (Sobell et al., 1974). The existing limited evidence suggests that self-reports by alcoholics, at least concerning alcohol-related events, are adequate for use as outcome data, especially when corroborated by official record information and interviews with collateral information sources.

Finally, it is possible that the present study incorporated some interview reactivity as a result of our using frequent follow-up contacts and a single follow-up interviewer (Sobell & Sobell, 1973b). However, there is little evidence in the experimental literature to document either the presence or absence of such effects in the natural environment or when an experimenter conscientiously attempts to be objective (Silver, 1973). Additionally, the results of the 2-year recorded interviews with subjects suggest that besides serving a data-gathering function, frequent follow-up contacts also seemed to often provide some type of "continuing care" for both experimental and control subjects (Sobell & Sobell, 1975a). This alternative conceptualization of follow-up as continued care is not novel. In 1965, Blake suggested that "follow-up interviews supply a kind of aftercare function" (p. 80). More recently, Gallen (1974) reported that 55% of his 48 alcoholic subjects explicitly acknowledged that frequent follow-up contacts played an important role in their posthospital discharge functioning. Furthermore, 65% of the collateral informants also felt that the continued contacts had contributed positively to the subjects' adjustment.

In an effort to determine the extent to which such factors influenced the results of the present study, an independent, double blind third-year follow-up investigation was jointly conducted by two investigators. This independent study interviewed subjects on or about the date of their third year of discharge from the hospital. Interviewers were totally blind regarding the nature of the original experiment, the experimental hypotheses and groups, and academically naive to traditional or radical beliefs about the syndrome commonly known as "alcoholism." Interviews with subjects and CISs were tape-recorded. The recordings were then scored by independent judges, equally blind to the hypotheses. That study, which has now been completed, had four basic objectives: (1) to determine how subjects functioned during their third year of follow-up; (2) to assess whether there were any indications from the third-year follow-up data that the continuous 2-year follow-up contacts may have functioned as a "continuing care" process; (3) to generally determine the validity of the 2-year follow-up results already reported; and (4) to determine whether conclusions about the degree of successful alcoholism treatment outcome are significantly influenced by the nature of outcome measures used (the third-year project assessed treatment outcome using many of the measures used in the present study, along with some entirely different evaluation measures).

Final considerations

The results of the research reported here, taken collectively with other proliferating evidence also contradictive of traditional beliefs, have major implications for the design of alcoholism treatment and prevention programs. A multivariant approach to the treatment of alcoholics has received increasing attention in recent years (Pattison, 1966; Gillis & Keet, 1969; Wanberg & Knapp, 1970; Wanberg & Horn, 1973; Wanberg et al., 1973; Pattison et al., 1968) and appears likely to be a major influence on future program development. Such an orientation emphasizes determining what kinds of services are most appropriate for different individuals. Further studies such as the one reported in this paper are needed to provide an empirical basis for the design of individualized treatment plans.

References

Barr, H. L., Rosen, A., Antes, D. E., and Ottenberg, D. K. Two-year follow-up study of 724 drug and alcohol addicts treated together in an abstinence therapeutic community. Paper presented at the 81st American Psychological Association, Annual Convention, Montreal, Canada, 1973.

Belasco, J. A. The criterion question revisited. *Br. J. Addictions,* 1971, 66, 39–44.

Blake, B. G. The application of behavior therapy to the treatment of alcoholism. *Behav. Res. & Therapy,* 1965, 3, 75–85.

Bowen, W. T., and Androes, W. A follow-up study of 79 alcoholic patients: 1963–1968. *Bull. Menninger Clinic.* 1968, 32, 26–34.

Crawford, J. J., and Chalupsky, A. B. Evaluation strategies used in current alcoholism rehabilitation programs: problems and specifications for improvement. In *Proc. 81st annual convention of the American Psychological Assocation,* Montreal, Canada, 1973, *8,* 795–796.

Doherty, J. Controlled drinking: valid approach or deadly snare? *Alcohol and Health Res. World,* 1974, Fall, 2–8.

Edwards, G. The status of alcoholism as a disease. In *Modern trends in drug dependence and alcoholism* (ed. R. V. Phillipson), pp. 140–163. New York: Appleton-Century-Crofts, 1970.

Emrick, C. D. A review of psychologically oriented treatment of alcoholism. *Q. J. Stud. Alc.,* 1974, *35,* 523–549.

Gallen, M. Toward an understanding of follow-up research with alcoholics. *Psychol. Rep.,* 1974, *34,* 877–878.

Gerard, D. L., and Saenger, G. *Out-patient treatment of alcoholism.* Toronto: University of Toronto Press, 1966.

Gillies, M., Laverty, S. G., Smart, R. G., and Aharan, C. H. Outcomes in treated alcoholics. *J. Alcoholism,* 1974, *9,* 125–134.

Gillis, L. S., and Keet, M. Prognostic factors and treatment results in hospitalized alcoholics. *Q. J. Stud. Alc.,* 1969, *30,* 426–437.

Gitlow, S. E. Alcoholism: a disease. In *Alcoholism–progress in research and treatment* (eds. P. G. Bourne and R. Fox). New York: Academic Press, 1973.

Guze, S. B., Tuason, V. B., Stewart, M. A., and Picken, B. The drinking history: a comparison of reports by subjects and their relatives. *Q. J. Stud. Alc.,* 1963, *24,* 249–260.

Hill, M. J., and Blane, H. T. Evaluation of psychotherapy with alcoholics: a critical review. *Q. J. Stud. Alc.,* 1967, *28,* 76–104.

Hunt, G. M., and Azrin, N. H. A community-reinforcement approach to alcoholism. *Behav. Res. & Therapy,* 1973, *11,* 91–104.

Jellinek, E. M. *The disease concept of alcoholism.* New Haven: Hillhouse Press, 1960.

Knox, W. J. Four-year follow-up of veterans treated on a small alcoholism ward. *Q. J. Stud. Alc.,* 1972, *33,* 105–110.

Mann, M. Presentation as part of panel discussion "Human Subjects for Alcoholism Research: Ethical and Legal Considerations." 25th Annual Meeting of the Alcohol and Drug Problems Assoc., San Francisco, December, 1974.

McNemar, Q. *Psychological statistics.* New York: Wiley, 1962.

Miller, B. A., Pokorny, A. D., Valles, J., and Cleveland, S. E. Biased sampling in alcoholism treatment research. *Q. J. Stud. Alc.,* 1970, *31,* 97–107.

National Council on Alcoholism. Press release, July 19, 1974.

Orford, J. A comparison of alcoholics whose drinking is totally uncontrolled and those whose drinking is mainly controlled. *Behav. Res. & Therapy,* 1973, *11,* 565–576.

Paredes, A., Hood, W. R., Seymour, H., and Gollob, M. Loss of control in alcoholism: an investigation of the hypotheses, with experimental findings. *Q. J. Stud. Alc.*, 1973, *34,* 1146–1161.

Pattison, E. M. A critique of alcoholism treatment concepts; with special reference to abstinence. *Q. J. Stud. Alc.*, 1966, *27,* 49–71.

Pattison, E. M., Headley, E. B., Gleser, G. C., and Gottschalk, L. A. Abstinence and normal drinking: an assessment of changes in drinking patterns in alcoholics after treatment. *Q. J. Stud. Alc.*, 1968, *29,* 610–633.

Silver, M. J. Investigator effects, experimenter effects, and experimenter bias: a taxonomy and a clarification. *J. Suppl. Abstract Serv.*, 1973, *3,* ms. no. 335.

Sobell, L. C., and Sobell, M. B. Frequent follow-up interviews as a dual process: data gathering and "continued care." Paper presented at the Southeastern Psychological Convention, Atlanta, March 27, 1975(a).

Sobell, L. C., and Sobell, M. B. Outpatient alcoholics give valid self-reports. *J. Nerv. Ment. Dis.*, 1975(b), *161,* 32–42.

Sobell, M. B., and Sobell, L. C. A brief technical report on the Mobat: an inexpensive portable test for determining blood alcohol concentration. *J. Appl. Behav. Anal.*, 1975(c), *8,* 117–120.

Sobell, M. B., and Sobell, L. C. The need for realism, relevance and operational assumptions in the study of substance dependence. In *Biological and behavioral approaches to drug dependence* (eds. H. D. Cappell and A. E. LeBlanc), pp. 133–168. Toronto. Addiction Research Foundation, 1975(d).

Sobell, M. B., and Sobell, L. C. Alcoholics treated by individualized behavior therapy: one-year treatment outcome. *Behav. Res. & Therapy,* 1973(a), *11,* 599–618.

Sobell, M. B., and Sobell, L. C. Individualized behavior therapy for alcoholics. *Behav. Therapy,* 1973 (b), *4,* 49–72.

Sobell, M. B., and Sobell, L. C. Individualized behavior therapy for alcoholics: rationale, procedures, preliminary results, and appendix. Sacramento: California Mental Health Research Monograph, No. 13, 1972.

Sobell, M. B., Sobell, L. C., and Samuels, F. H. The validity of self-reports of prior alcohol-related arrests by alcoholics. *Q. J. Stud. Alc.*, 1974, *35,* 276–280.

Summers, T. Validity of alcoholics' self-reported drinking history. *Q. J. Stud. Alc.*, 1970, *31,* 972–974.

Wanberg, K. W., and Horn, J. K. Alcoholism syndromes related to sociological classifications. *Int. J. Addictions,* 1973, *8,* 99–120.

Wanberg, K. W., Horn, J. L., and Foster, F. M. A differential model for the diagnosis of alcoholism: scales of the alcohol use questionnaire. Paper presented at the 24th Annual Meeting of the Alcohol and

Drug Problems Association of North America, Bloomington, Mn. Sept. 23–28, 1973.

Wanberg, K. W., and Knapp, J. A. A multidimensional model for the treatment and research of alcoholism. *Int. J. Addictions,* 1970, *5,* 69–98.

References

Allman, L. R. Group drinking during stress: effects on alcohol intake and group process. *The International Journal of the Addictions*, 1973, *8*, 475–488.

Allman, L. R., Taylor, H. A., and Nathan, P. E. Group drinking during stress: effects on drinking behavior, affect, and psychopathology. *American Journal of Psychiatry*, 1972, *129*, 669–678.

Alterman, A. I., Gottheil, E., Skoloda T. E., and Grasberger, J. C. Social modification of drinking by alcoholics. *Quarterly Journal of Studies on Alcohol*, 1974, *35*, 917–924.

American Medical Association. *Manual on alcoholism*, 1968.

Anant, S. S. Former alcoholics and social drinking: an unexpected finding. *The Canadian Psychologist*, 1968, *9*, 35.

Anonymous. *Alcoholics Anonymous comes of age.* New York: Alcoholics Anonymous Publishing, 1957.

Anonymous. *Alcoholics Anonymous: the story of how thousands of men and women have recovered from alcoholism*, 2d ed. New York: Alcoholics Anonymous World Service, 1955.

Anonymous, *Alcoholics Anonymous.* New York: Works Publishing, Inc., 1939.

Archibald, W. P. Alternative explanations for self-fulfilling prophecy. *Psychological Bulletin*, 1974, *81*, 74–84.

Arikawa, K., Kotorii, M., and Mukasa, H. The therapeutic effect of cyanamide on the alcoholic addicts in out-patient clinic. *Clinical Psychiatry (Jap.)*, 1972, *14*, 219–227.

Armstrong, J. D. The search for the alcoholic personality. *Annals of the American Academy of Political and Social Science*, 1958, *315*, 40–47.

Bacon, S. D. The problems of alcoholism in American society. In *Social disability*, D. Malikin (ed.). New York: New York University Press, 1973. Pp. 8–30.

Bailey, M. B., and Stewart, J. Normal drinking by persons reporting previous problem drinking. *Quarterly Journal of Studies on Alcohol*, 1967, *28*, 305–315.

Baker, T. B., Udin, H., and Vogler, R. E. A short-term alcoholism treatment program using videotape and self-confrontation techniques. Paper delivered at the 80th Annual Convention of the American Psychological Association, Honolulu, 1972.

Barchha, R., Stewart, M. A., and Guze, S. B. The prevalence of alcoholism among general hospital ward patients. *American Journal of Psychiatry*, 1968, *125*, 681–684.

Barr, H. L., Rosen, A., Antes, D. E., and Ottenberg, D. J. Two year follow-up study of 724 drug and alcohol addicts treated together in an abstinence therapeutic community. Paper presented at the 81st

Annual Convention of the American Psychological Association, Montreal, Canada. Washington, D.C.: American Psychological Association, 1973.

Barry, H. B., III. Psychological factors in alcoholism. In *The biology of alcoholism,* Volume 3: *Clinical pathology,* B. Kissin and H. Begleiter (eds.). New York: Plenum Press, 1974. Pp. 53–107.

Belasco, J. A. The criterion question revisited. *The British Journal of the Addictions,* 1971, *66,* 39–44.

Berne, E. *Games people play.* New York: Grove Press, 1964.

Bhakta, M. Clinical applications of behavior therapy in the treatment of alcoholism. *The Journal of Alcoholism,* 1971, *6,* 75–83.

Bigelow, G., Cohen, M., Liebson, I., and Faillace, L. A. Abstinence or moderation? Choice by alcoholics. *Behaviour Research and Therapy,* 1972, *10,* 209–214.

Bigelow, G., and Liebson, I. Cost factors controlling alcoholic drinking. *Psychological Record,* 1972, *22,* 305–314.

Bigelow, G., Liebson, I., and Griffiths, R. Alcoholic drinking: suppression by a behavioral time-out procedure. *Behaviour Research and Therapy,* 1974, *12,* 107–115.

Blake, B. G. The application of behaviour therapy to the treatment of alcoholism. *Behaviour Research and Therapy,* 1965, *3,* 75–85.

Blane, H. T. *The personality of the alcoholic: guises of dependency.* New York: Harper & Row, 1968.

Blane, H. T., and Meyers, W. R. Social class and the establishment of treatment relations by alcoholics. *Journal of Clinical Psychology,* 1964, *20,* 287–290.

Bolman, W. M. Abstinence versus permissiveness in the psychotherapy of alcoholism. *Archives of General Psychiatry,* 1965, *12,* 456–463.

Brush, S. G. Should the history of science be rated X? *Science,* 1974, *183,* 1164–1172.

Bruun, K. The polar bear approach to alcoholism. *Proceedings, 12th Institute on the Prevention and Treatment of Alcoholism.* Prague, 1966.

Caddy, G. R. Behaviour modification in the management of alcoholism. Unpublished doctoral dissertation. University of New South Wales, Australia, 1972.

Caddy, G. R. and Lovibond, S. H. Self-regulation and discriminated aversive conditioning in the modification of alcoholics' drinking behavior. *Behavior Therapy,* 1976, *7,* 223–230.

Cahalan, D. *Problem drinkers: a national survey.* San Francisco: Jossey-Bass, 1970.

Cahalan, D., Cisin, I. H., and Crossley, H. M. *American drinking practices: a national survey of behavior and attitudes,* Monograph No. 6. New Brunswick, N.J.: Rutgers Center for Alcohol Studies, 1969.

Cahalan, D., and Room, R. *Problem drinkers among American men.* New Brunswick, N.J.: Rutgers Center for Alcohol Studies, 1974.

Cahn, S. *The treatment of alcoholics: an evaluation study.* New York: Oxford University Press, 1970.

Cain, A. H. *The cured alcoholic.* New York: John Day, 1964.

Cannon, D., Ross, S. M., and Snyder, E. The reinforcing effects of alcohol as measured by a progressive ratio schedule. Paper presented at the 53rd Annual Meeting of the Western Psychological Association, Anaheim, California, 1973.

Canter, F. M. The requirement of abstinence as a problem in institutional treatment of alcoholics. *Psychiatric Quarterly,* 1968, *42,* 217–231.

Cappell, H., and Herman, C. P. Alcohol and tension reduction: a review. *Quarterly Journal of Studies on Alcohol,* 1972, *33,* 33–64.

Chandler, J., Hensman, C., and Edwards, G. Determinants of what happens to alcoholics. *Quarterly Journal of Studies on Alcohol,* 1971, *32,* 349–363.

Clark, W. B., and Cahalan, D. Changes in problem drinking over a four-year span. *Addictive Behaviors,* 1976, *1,* 251–259.

Cohen, M., Liebson, I. A., and Faillace, L. A. Case histories and shorter communications—the role of reinforcement contingencies in chronic alcoholism: an experimental analysis of one case. *Behaviour Research and Therapy,* 1971(a), *9,* 1–5.

Cohen, M., Liebson, I., and Faillace, L. Controlled drinking by chronic alcoholics over extended periods of free access. *Psychological Reports,* 1973, *32,* 1107–1110.

Cohen, M., Liebson, I. A., and Faillace, L. A. The modification of drinking in chronic alcoholics. In *Recent advances in studies of alcoholism,* N. Mello and J. H. Mendelson (eds.). Washington, D.C.: U.S. Government Printing Office, 1971(b). Pp. 745–766.

Cohen, M., Liebson, I. A., Faillace, L. A., and Allen, R. P. Moderate drinking by chronic alcoholics: a schedule-dependent phenomenon. *Journal of Nervous and Mental Disease,* 1971, *153,* 434–444.

Cohen, M., Liebson, I. A., Faillace, L. A., and Speers, W. Alcoholism: controlled drinking and incentives for abstinence. *Psychological Reports,* 1971, *28,* 575–580.

Conger, J. J. Reinforcement theory and the dynamics of alcoholism. *Quarterly Journal of Studies on Alcohol,* 1956, *17,* 296–305.

Crawford, J. J., and Chalupsky, A. B. Evaluation strategies used in current alcoholism rehabilitation programs: problems and specifications for improvement. In *Proceedings of the 81st Annual Convention of the American Psychological Association,* Montreal, Canada. Washington, D.C.: American Psychological Association, 1973, *8,* 745–746.

Crawford, J. J., Chalupsky, A. B., and Hurley, M. M. *The evaluation of psychological approaches to alcoholism treatments: a methodological review.* Final Report AIR-96502-3/73-FR. Palo Alto, Calif.: American Institutes for Research, 1973.

Curlee, J. Attitudes that facilitate or hinder the treatment of alcoholism. *Psychotherapy: Theory, Research and Practice,* 1971, *8,* 68–70.

Cutter, H. S. G., Schwaab, E. L. Jr., and Nathan, P. E. Effects of alcohol on its utility for alcoholics and nonalcoholics. *Quarterly Journal of Studies on Alcohol,* 1970, *31,* 369–378.

Davies, D. L. Normal drinking in recovered alcohol addicts (Comment by various correspondents). *Quarterly Journal of Studies on Alcohol,* 1963, *24,* 109–121, 321–332.

Davies, D. L. Normal drinking in recovered alcohol addicts. *Quarterly Journal of Studies on Alcohol,* 1962, *23,* 94–104.

Davies, D. L., Scott, D. F., and Malherbe, M. E. L. Resumed normal drinking in recovered psychotic alcoholics. *The International Journal of the Addictions,* 1969, *4,* 187–194.

Davies, D. L., Shepard, M., and Myers, E. The two-years' prognosis of 50 alcohol addicts after treatment in hospital. *Quarterly Journal of Studies on Alcohol,* 1956, *17,* 485–502.

de Morsier, G., and Feldman, H. Le traitement de l'alcoolisme par l'apmorphine: étude de 500 cas. *Schweiz. Archives Neurologic Psychiatrie,* 1952, *70,* 434–440.

Dubourg, G. O. After care for alcoholics—a follow-up study. *The British Journal of Addictions,* 1969, *64,* 155–163.

Edwards, G. Drugs: drug dependence and the concept of plasticity. *Quarterly Journal of Studies on Alcohol,* 1974, *35,* 176–195.

Einstein. S., Wolfson, E., and Gecht, P. What matters in treatment: relevant variables in alcoholism. *International Journal of the Addictions,* 1970, *5,* 43–67.

Emrick, C. D. A review of psychologically oriented treatment of alcoholism. I. The use and interrelationships of outcome criteria and drinking behavior following treatment. *Quarterly Journal of Studies on Alcohol,* 1974, *35,* 523–549.

Engle, K. B., and Williams, T. K. Effect of an ounce of vodka on alcoholics' desire for alcohol. *Quarterly Journal of Studies on Alcohol,* 1972, *33,* 1099–1105.

English, G. E., and Curtin, M. E. Personality difference in patients at three alcoholism treatment agencies. *Journal of Studies on Alcohol,* 1975, *36,* 52–61.

Evans, I. M. Classical conditioning. In *The theoretical and experimental basis of behavior therapy,* M. P. Feldmann and A. Broadhurst (eds.). London: John Wiley & Sons, 1976.

Evans, M. The Cardiff Plan and the Welsh Unit. *The British Journal of the Addictions,* 1967, *62,* 29–34.

Faillace, L. A., Flamer, R. N., Imber, S. D., and Ward, R. F. Giving alcohol to alcoholics: an evaluation. *Quarterly Journal of Studies on Alcohol,* 1972, *33,* 85–90.

Feeney, F. E., Mindlin, D. F., Minear, V. H., and Short, E. E. The challenge of the skid-row alcoholic: a social, psychological and psychiatric comparison of chronically jailed alcoholics and cooperative alcohol clinic patients. *Quarterly Journal of Studies on Alcohol,* 1955, *16,* 465–477.

Fillmore, K. Drinking and problem drinking in early adulthood and middle age. *Quarterly Journal of Studies on Alcohol,* 1974, *35,* 819–840.

Fingarette, H. The perils of Powell: in search of a factual foundation for the "disease" concept of alcoholism. *Harvard Law Review,* 1970, *83,* 793–812.

Fitzgerald, B. J., Pasework, R. A., and Clark, R. Four-year follow-up of alcoholics treated in a rural state hospital. *Quarterly Journal of Studies on Alcohol,* 1971, *32,* 636–642.

Fletcher, C. R. Perceived personal causation as a predictor of punitive vs. psychiatric recommendations for deviants. *Criminologica,* 1966, *4,* 12–24.

Fox, R. Treatment of alcoholism. In *Alcoholism: basic aspects and treatment,* H. E. Himwich (ed.). Washington, D.C.: American Association for the Advancement of Science, 1957. Pp. 163–172.

Freedman, A. M., and Wilson, A. E. Childhood and adolescent addictive disorders. *Pediatrics,* 1964, *34,* 425–430.

Gallen, M., Williams, B., Cleveland, S. E., O'Connell, W. E., and Sands, P. A short-term follow-up of two contrasting alcoholic treatment programs: a preliminary report. *Newsletter for Research in Mental Health and Behavioral Science,* 1973, *15,* 36–37.

Gerard, D. L., and Saenger, G. *Out-patient treatment of alcoholism.* Toronto: University of Toronto Press, 1966.

Gerard, D. L., Saenger, G., and Wile, R. The abstinent alcoholic. *Archives of General Psychiatry,* 1962, *6,* 83–95.

Gibbins, R. J., and Armstrong, J. D. Effects of clinical treatment on behavior of alcoholic patients: an exploratory methodological investigation. *Quarterly Journal of Studies on Alcohol,* 1957, *18,* 429–450.

Gillis, L. S., and Keet, M. Prognostic factors and treatment results in hospitalized alcoholics. *Quarterly Journal of Studies on Alcohol,* 1969, *30,* 426–437.

Gitlow, S. E. Alcoholism: a disease. In *Alcoholism—progress in research and treatment,* P. B. Bourne and R. Fox (eds.). New York: Academic Press, 1973. Pp. 1–9.

Gitlow, S. E. The pharmacological approach to alcoholism. In *Alcoholism and family casework, theory and practice,* M. B. Bailey (ed.). New York: The Community Council of Greater New York, 1968. Pp. 31–42.

Glatt, M. M. *Drugs, society and man: a guide to addiction and its treatment.* New York: Halsted Press (Wiley), 1974.

Glatt, M. M. *The alcoholic and the help he needs.* London: Priory Press, 1970.

Glatt, M. M. The question of moderate drinking despite "loss of control." *The British Journal of the Addictions,* 1967, *62,* 267–274.

Glock, C. Y. Images of man and public opinion. *Public Opinion Quarterly,* 1964, *28,* 539–547.

Goldman, M. S. Drink or not to drink—experimental analysis of group drinking decisions by 4 alcoholics. *American Journal of Psychiatry,* 1974, *131,* 1123–1130.

Goodwin, D. W. The muse and the martini. *The Journal of the American Medical Association,* 1973, *224,* 35–38.

Goodwin, D. W., Crane, J. B., and Guze, S. B. Felons who drink: an 8-year follow-up. *Quarterly Journal of Studies on Alcohol,* 1971, *32,* 136–147.

Goodwin, D. W., David, D. H., and Robins, L. N. Drinking amid abundant illicit drugs: the Vietnam case. *Archives of General Psychiatry,* 1975, *32,* 230–233.

Goodwin, D. W., and Guze, S. B. Heredity and alcoholism. In *The biology of alcoholism,* Volume 3: *Clinical pathology,* B. Kissin and H. Begleiter (eds.). New York: Plenum Press, 1974. Pp. 37–52.

Gottheil, E., Alterman, A., Skoloda, T., and Murphy, B. Alcoholics' patterns of controlled drinking. *American Journal of Psychiatry,* 1973, *130,* 418–422.

Gottheil, E., Corbett, L. O., Grasberger, J. C., and Cornelison, F. S. Fixed interval drinking decisions. I. A research and treatment model. *Quarterly Journal of Studies on Alcohol,* 1972, *33,* 311–324.

Gottheil, E., Corbett, L. O., Grasberger, J. C., and Cornelison, F. S. Treating the alcoholic in the presence of alcohol. *American Journal of Psychiatry,* 1971, *128,* 107–112.

Gottheil, E., Crawford, H. D., and Cornelison, F. S. The alcoholic's ability to resist available alcohol. *Diseases of the Nervous System,* 1974, *34,* 80–82.

Gottheil, E., Murphy, B. F., Skoloda, T. E., and Corbett, L. O. Fixed interval drinking decisions. II. Drinking and discomfort in 25 alcoholics. *Quarterly Journal of Studies on Alcohol,* 1972, *33,* 325–340.

Griffith, R. Assessment of effects of ethanol self-administration on social interactions in alcoholics. *Psychopharmacologia,* 1974, *38,* 105–110.

Griffith, R., Bigelow, G., and Liebson, I. Effect of ethanol self-administration on choice behavior—money vs. socializing. *Pharmacology, Biology and Behavior,* 1975, *3,* 443–446.

Griffith, R., Bigelow, G., and Liebson, I. Suppression of ethanol self-administration in alcoholics by contingent time-out from social interactions. *Behaviour Research and Therapy,* 1974, *12,* 327–334.

Gross, M. M. (ed.). *Advances in experimental medicine and biology–alcohol intoxication and withdrawal: experimental studies II,* Volume 59. New York: Plenum Press, 1975.

Gross, M. M. (ed.). *Advances in experimental medicine and biology–alcohol intoxication and withdrawal: experimental studies II,* Volume 59. New York: Plenum Press, 1975.

Hacquard, M., Beaudoin, M., Derby, G., and Berger, H. Contribution à l'étude des resultats eloignes des cures de desintoxication ethylique. *Revue d'Hygiene et de Medicine Sociale,* 1960, *8,* 686–709.

Harper, J., and Hickson, B. The results of hospital treatment of chronic alcoholism. *Lancet,* 1951, *261,* 1057–1059.

Hayman, M. The myth of social drinking. *American Journal of Psychiatry,* 1967, *124,* 585–592.

Hedberg, A. G., and Campbell, L., III. A comparison of four behavioral treatments of alcoholism. *Journal of Behavior Therapy and Experimental Psychiatry,* 1974, *5,* 251–256.

Higgins, R. L., and Marlatt, G. A. The effects of anxiety arousal on the consumption of alcohol by alcoholics and social drinkers. *Journal of Consulting and Clinical Psychology,* 1973, *41,* 426–433.

Hill, M. J., and Blane, H. T. Evaluation of psychotherapy with alcoholics: a critical review. *Quarterly Journal of Studies on Alcohol,* 1967, *28,* 76–104.

Hurwitz, J. I., and Lelos, D. A multilevel interpersonal profile of employed alcoholics. *Quarterly Journal of Studies on Alcohol,* 1968, *29,* 64–76.

Hyman, M. M. Alcoholics 15 years later. Presented at the 6th Annual Medical Scientific Session, National Council on Alcoholism, Milwaukee, Wisc., 1975.

James, J. E., and Goldman, M. Behavior trends of wives of alcoholics. *Quarterly Journal of Studies on Alcohol,* 1971, *32,* 373–381.

Jellinek, E. M. *The disease concept of alcoholism.* New Haven, Conn.: Hillhouse Press, 1960.

Jellinek, E. M., Isbell, H., Lundquist, G., Tiebout, H. M., Duchene, H., Mardones, J., and MacLeod, L. D. The craving for alcohol: a symposium by members of the WHO Expert Committees on Mental Health and on Alcohol. *Quarterly Journal of Studies on Alcohol,* 1955, *16,* 34–66.

Jellinek, E. M. Phases of alcohol addiction. *Quarterly Journal of Studies on Alcohol,* 1952, *13,* 673–684.

Jellinek, E. M. Phases in the drinking history of alcoholics. Analysis of a survey conducted by the official organ of Alcoholics Anonymous. *Quarterly Journal of Studies on Alcohol,* 1946, *7,* 1–88.

Johnson, V. E. *I'll quit tomorrow.* New York: Harper & Row, 1973.

Keller, M. On the loss-of-control phenomenon in alcoholism. *The British Journal of the Addictions,* 1972(a), *67* 153–166.

Keller, M. The oddities of alcoholics. *Quarterly Journal of Studies on Alcohol,* 1972(b), *33,* 1147–1148.

Kendall, R. E. Normal drinking by former alcohol addicts. *Quarterly Journal of Studies on Alcohol,* 1965, *26,* 247–257.

Kendall, R. E., and Staton, M. C. The fate of untreated alcoholics. *Quarterly Journal of Studies on Alcohol,* 1966, *27,* 30–41.

Kessel, J. *The road back, a report on Alcoholics Anonymous.* New York: Alfred A. Knopf, 1962.

Kish, G. B., and Hermann, H. T. The Fort Meade alcohol treatment program: a follow-up study. *Quarterly Journal of Studies on Alcohol,* 1971, *32,* 628–635.

Kissin, B., and Begleiter, H. (eds.). *The biology of alcoholism,* Volume 2, *Physiology and behavior.* New York: Plenum Press, 1972.

Kissin, B., and Begleiter, H. (eds.). *The biology of alcoholism,* Volume 1, *Biochemistry.* New York: Plenum Press, 1971.

Kissin, B., Platz, A., and Su, W. H. Social and psychological factors in the treatment of chronic alcoholism. *Journal of Psychiatric Research,* 1970, *8,* 13–27.

Kissin, B., Rosenblatt, S. M., and Machover, S. Prognostic factors in alcoholism. Part I. *Psychiatric Research Report,* 1968(a), *24,* 22–43.

Kissin, B., Rosenblatt, S. M., and Machover, S. Prognostic factors in alcoholism. Part II. *Psychiatric Research Report,* 1968(b), *24,* 44–60.

Knox, W. J. Attitudes of social workers and other professional groups toward alcoholism. *Quarterly Journal of Studies on Alcohol,* 1973, *34,* 1270–1278.

Knox, W. J. Attitudes of psychiatrists and psychologists toward alcoholism. *American Journal of Psychiatry,* 1971, *127,* 1675–1679.

Kohrs, E. V. Behavioral approaches to problem drinkers in a rural community. *Behavioral Engineering,* 1973, *1,* 1–10.

Kraft, T., and Al-Issa, I. Desensitization and the treatment of alcohol addiction. *The British Journal of the Addictions,* 1968, *63,* 19–23.

Kraft, T., and Al-Issa, I. Alcoholism treated by desensitization: a case report. *Behaviour Research and Therapy,* 1967, *5,* 69–70.

Krystal, H. The problem of abstinence by the patient as a requisite for the psychotherapy of alcoholism. II. The evaluation of the meaning of drinking in determining the requirement of abstinence by alcoholics during treatment. *Quarterly Journal of Studies on Alcohol,* 1962, *23,* 112–122.

Kuhn, T. S. *The structure of scientific revolutions,* 2d ed. Chicago: University of Chicago Press, 1970.

Lambert, B. E. V. "Social" alkoholkonsumtion hos alkoholskadade? *Svenska Lakartidningen,* 1964, *61,* 315–318.

Lazarus, A. A. Towards the understanding and effective treatment of alcoholism. *South African Medical Journal,* 1965, *39,* 736–741.

Lemere, F. What happens to alcoholics. *American Journal of Psychiatry,* 1953, *109,* 674–676.

Levinson, T. The Donwood Institute—a five year follow-up study. Presented at the 31st International Congress on Alcoholism and Drug Dependence, 1975.

Linsky, A. S. Theories of behavior and the social control of alcoholism. *Social Psychiatry,* 1972, *7,* 47–52.

Lovibond, S. H., and Caddy, G. Discriminated aversive control in the moderation of alcoholics' drinking behavior. *Behavior Therapy,* 1970, *1,* 437–444.

Ludwig, A. M. The first drink—psychobiological aspects of craving. *Archives of General Psychiatry,* 1974, *30,* 539–547.

Ludwig, A. M. On and off the wagon. *Quarterly Journal of Studies on Alcohol,* 1972, *33,* 91–96.

Ludwig, A. M., Levine, J., and Stark, L. H. *LSD and alcoholism: a clinical study of treatment efficacy.* Springfield, Ill.: C.C. Thomas, 1970.

Ludwig, A. M., and Wikler, A. "Craving" and relapse to drink. *Quarterly Journal of Studies on Alcohol,* 1974, *35,* 108–130.

Lundquist, G. A. R. Alcohol dependence. *Acta Psychiatrica Scandinavica,* 1973, *49,* 332–340.

MacAndrew, C., and Edgerton, R. B. *Drunken comportment: a social explanation.* Chicago: Aldine Publishing Company, 1969.

Madsen, W. *The American alcoholic: the nature-nurture controversies in alcoholic research and therapy.* Springfield, Ill.: C.C. Thomas, 1974.

Mann, M. *New primer on alcoholism,* 2d ed. New York: Holt, Rinehart and Winston, 1968.

Mann, M. *Primer on alcoholism.* New York: Holt, Rinehart and Winston, 1958.

Marconi, J. The concept of alcoholism. *Quarterly Journal of Studies on Alcohol,* 1959, *20,* 216–235.

Marconi, J., Fink, K., and Moya, L. Experimental study on alcoholics with an inability to stop! *British Journal of Psychiatry,* 1967, *113,* 543–545.

Mardones, R. J. On the relationship between deficiency of B vitamins and alcohol intake in rats. *Quarterly Journal of Studies on Alcohol,* 1951, *12,* 563–575.

Mardones, R. J., and Onfray, B. E. Influencia de una substancia de la levadura (elementa del complejo vitaminico B?) sobre el consumo de alcohol en ratas en experimentos de autoselecction. *Revista Medica Ailment, Chile,* 1942, *5,* 148–149.

Marlatt, G. A. A comparison of aversive conditioning procedures in the treatment of alcoholism. Presented at the meeting of the Western Psychological Association, Anaheim, California, 1973.

Marlatt, G. A., Demming, B., and Reid, J. B. Loss of control drinking in alcoholics: an experimental analogue. *Journal of Abnormal Psychology,* 1973, *81,* 233–241.

Martorano, R. D. Mood and social perception in four alcoholics, effects of drinking and assertion training. *Quarterly Journal of Studies on Alcohol,* 1974, *35,* 445–457.

Mayer, J., and Myerson, D. J. Outpatient treatment of alcoholics: effects of status stability and nature of treatment. *Quarterly Journal of Studies on Alcohol,* 1971, *32,* 620–627.

McNamee, H. B., Mello, N. K., and Mendelson, J. H. Experimental analysis of drinking patterns of alcoholics: concurrent psychiatric observations. *American Journal of Psychiatry,* 1968, *124,* 81–87.

Mello, N. K. Behavioral studies of alcoholism. In *The biology of alcoholism,* Volume 2: *Physiology and behavior,* B. Kissin and H. Begleiter (eds.). New York: Plenum Press, 1972.

Mello, N. K., McNamee, H. B., and Mendelson, J. H. Drinking patterns of chronic alcoholics: gambling and motivations for alcohol. *Psychiatric Research Report,* 1968, *24,* 83–118.

Mello, N. K., and Mendelson, J. H. Drinking patterns during work —contingent and noncontingent alcohol acquisition. *Psychosomatic Medicine,* 1972, *34,* 139–164.

Mello, N. K., and Mendelson, J. H. A quantitative analysis of drinking patterns in alcoholics. *Archives of General Psychiatry,* 1971, *25,* 527–539.

Mello, N. K., and Mendelson, J. H. Experimentally induced intoxication in alcoholics: a comparison between programmed and spontaneous drinking. *The Journal of Pharmacology and Experimental Therapeutics,* 1970, *173,* 101–116.

Mello, N. K., and Mendelson, J. H. Operant analysis of drinking patterns of chronic alcoholics. *Nature,* 1965, *206,* 43–46.

Mendelson, J. H. (ed.) Experimentally induced chronic intoxication and withdrawal in alcoholics. *Quarterly Journal of Studies on Alcohol,* Supplement No. 2, 1964.

Mendelson, J. H., LaDou, J., and Solomon, P. Experimentally induced chronic intoxication and withdrawal in alcoholics, Part 3. Psychiatric Findings. *Quarterly Journal of Studies on Alcohol,* Supplement No. 2, 1964, 40–52.

Mendelson, J. H., and Mello, N. K. Experimental analysis of drinking behavior of chronic alcoholics. *Annals of the New York Academy of Sciences,* 1966, *133,* 828–845.

Merry, J. The "loss of control" myth. *Lancet,* 1966, *1,* 1257–1258.

Miller, B. A., Pokorny, A. D., and Kanas, T. E. Problems in treating homeless, jobless alcoholics. *Hospital and Community Psychiatry,* 1971, *21,* 98–99.

Miller, B. A., Pokorny, A. D., Valles, J., and Cleveland, S. E. Biased sampling in alcoholism treatment research. *Quarterly Journal of Studies on Alcohol,* 1970, *31,* 97–107.

Miller, P. M. The use of behavioral contracting in the treatment of alcoholism: a case report. *Behavior Therapy,* 1972, *3,* 593–596.

Miller, P. M., Hersen, M., and Eisler, R. M. Relative effecriveness of instructions, agreements, and reinforcements in behavioral contracts with alcoholics. *Journal of Abnormal Psychology,* 1974, *83,* 548–553.

Miller, P. M., Hersen, M., Eisler, R. M., Epstein, L. H., and Wooten, L. S. Relationship of alcohol cues to the drinking behavior of alcoholics and social drinkers: an analogue study. *The Psychological Record,* 1974, *24,* 61–66.

Miller, P. M., Hersen, M., Eisler, R. M., and Hemphill, D. P. Electrical aversion therapy with alcoholics: an analogue study. *Behaviour Research and Therapy,* 1973, *11,* 491–497

Miller, P. M., Hersen, M., Eisler, R. M., and Hilsman, C. Effects of social stress on operant drinking of alcoholics and social drinkers. *Behaviour Research and Therapy,* 1974, *12,* 67–72.

Mills, K. C., Sobell, M. B., and Schaefer, H. H. Training social drinking as an alternative to abstinence for alcoholics. *Behavior Therapy,* 1971, *2,* 18–27.

Mindlin, D. F. The characteristics of alcoholics as related to prediction outcome. *Quarterly Journal of Studies on Alcohol,* 1959, *20,* 604–609.

Mogar, R. E., Wilson, W. M., and Helm, S. T. Personality subtypes of male and female alcoholic patients. *International Journal of the Addictions,* 1970, *5,* 99–113.

Monnerot, E. Cure hospitaliere psychiatrique de l'alcoolomanie: reflexions therapeutiques sur un bilan, une enquete, unessai particulier. *Revue de l'alcoolisme,* 1963, *9,* 114–128.

Moore, R. A., and Ramseur, F. Effects of psychotherapy in an open-ward hospital on patients with alcoholism. *Quarterly Journal of Studies on Alcohol,* 1960, *21,* 233–252.

Mukasa, H., and Arikawa, K. A new double medication method for the treatment of alcoholism using the drug cyanamide. *The Kurume Medical Journal,* 1968, *15,* 137–143.

Mukasa, H., Ichihara, T., and Eto, A. A new treatment of alcoholism with cyanamide (H_2NCN). *The Kurume Medical Journal,* 1964, *11,* 96–101.

Myerson, D. J., and Mayer, J. Origins, treatment and destiny of skid-row alcoholic men. *New England Journal of Medicine,* 1966, *275,* 419–424.

Nathan, P. E., Goldman, M. S., Lisman, S. A., and Taylor, H. A. Alcohol and alcoholics: a behavioral approach. *Transactions of the New York Academy of Sciences,* 1972, *34,* 602–627.

Nathan, P. E., and O'Brien, J. S. An experimental analysis of the behavior of alcoholics and nonalcoholics during prolonged experimental drinking: a necessary precursor of behavior therapy? *Behavior Therapy,* 1971, *2,* 455–476.

Nathan, P. E., O'Brien, J. S., and Norton, D. Comparative studies of the interpersonal and affective behavior of alcoholics and nonalcoholics during prolonged experimental drinking. In *Recent advances in studies of alcoholism,* N. K. Mello and J. H. Mendelson (eds.). Washington, D.C.: U.S. Government Printing Office, 1971. Pp. 619–646.

Nathan, P. E., Silverstein, S. J., and Taylor, H. A. Blood alcohol level estimation and controlled drinking by chronic alcoholics. Presented at the 81st Annual Meeting of the American Psychological Association, Montreal, 1973.

Nathan, P. E., Titler, N. A., Lowenstein, L. M., Solomon, P., and Rossi, A. M. Behavioral analysis of chronic alcoholism. *Archives of General Psychiatry,* 1970, *22,* 419–430.

Nathan, P. E., Wilson, G. T., Steffen, J. J., and Silverstein, S. J. An objective look at three behavioral treatment approaches to alcoholism. In *Biological and behavioral approaches to drug dependence,*

H. D. Cappell and A. E. LeBlanc (eds.). Toronto: Addiction Research Foundation, 1975. Pp. 89–114.

Nørvig, J., and Neilsen, B. A follow-up of 221 alcohol addicts in Denmark. *Quarterly Journal of Studies on Alcohol*, 1956, *17*, 633–642.

O'Brien, J. S. Operant behavior of a chronic alcoholic under fixed ratio and fixed interval schedules of reinforcement using alcohol as a reinforcer. *The British Journal of the Addictions*, 1972, *67*, 167–176.

Oki, G. Alcohol use by skid row alcoholics: Part 1. Drinking at Bon Acord. Substudy No. 612. Toronto: Addiction Research Foundation, 1974.

Orford, J. Note on ordering of onset of symptoms in alcohol dependence. *Psychological Medicine*, 1974, *4*, 281–288.

Orford, J. A comparison of alcoholics whose drinking is totally uncontrolled and those whose drinking is mainly controlled. *Behaviour Research and Therapy*, 1973, *11*, 565–576.

Orford, J., and Hawker, A. Investigation of an alcoholism rehabilitation halfway house, 2. Complex question of client motivation. *The British Journal of the Addictions*, 1974, *69*, 315–323.

Paredes, A., Hood, W. R., Seymour, H., and Gollob, M. Loss of control in alcoholism; an investigation of the hypothesis, with experimental findings. *Quarterly Journal of Studies on Alcohol*, 1973, *34*, 1146–1161.

Paredes, A., Jones, B., and Gregory, D. An exercise to assist alcoholics to maintain prescribed levels of intoxication. *Oklahoma Alcohol Technical Reports*, 1974, *11*, 24–36.

Paredes, A., Ludwig, K. D., Hassenfeld, I. M., and Cornelison, F. S., Jr. Filmed representations of behavior and responses to self-observation in alcoholics. In *Recent advances in studies of alcoholism*, N. K. Mello and J. H. Mendelson (eds.). Washington, D.C.: U.S. Government Printing Office, 1971. Pp. 709–729.

Park, P. Developmental ordering of experiences in alcoholism. *Quarterly Journal of Studies on Alcohol*, 1973, *34*, 473–488.

Park, P. Drinking experiences of 805 Finnish alcoholics in comparison with similar experiences of 192 English alcoholics. *Acta Psychiatrica Scandinavica*, 1962, *38*, 227–246.

Pattison, E. M. The rehabilitation of the chronic alcoholic. In *The biology of alcoholism*. Volume III, *Clinical pathology*, B. Kissin and H. Begleiter (eds.). New York: Plenum Press, 1974.

Pattison, E. M. Trends in treatment of alcoholism. Second Special Report to Congress. *Alcohol and Health*, 1974, 145–167.

Pattison, E. M. The differential utilization of manpower. In *The paraprofessional in the treatment of alcoholism: a new profession*, G. E. Staub and L. Kent (eds.). Springfield, Ill.: C.C. Thomas, 1973. Pp. 9–31.

Pattison, E. M. Morality and the treatment of character disorders. *Journal of Religion and Health*, 1967, *4*, 290–316.

Pattison, E. M., Coe, R., and Doerr, H. D. Population variation between alcoholism treatment facilities. *International Journal of the Addictions*, 1973, *8*, 199–229.

Pattison, E. M., Coe, R., and Rhodes, R. A. Evaluation of alcoholism treatment: comparison of three facilities. *Archives of General Psychiatry*, 1969, *20*, 478–488.

Pattison, E. M., Headley, E. B., Gleser, G. C., and Gottschalk, L. A. Abstinence and normal drinking: an assessment of changes in drinking patterns in alcoholics after treatment. *Quarterly Journal of Studies on Alcohol*, 1968, *29*, 610–633.

Pfeffer, A. Z., and Berger, S. A follow-up of treated alcoholics. *Quarterly Journal of Studies on Alcohol*, 1957, *18*, 624–648.

Pickens, R., Bigelow, G., and Griffiths, R. Case histories and shorter communications. *Behaviour Research and Therapy*, 1973, *11*, 321–325.

Pittman, D. J., and Gordon, C. W. *The revolving door.* New York: Free Press, 1958.

Plaut, T. F. A. *Alcohol problems: a report to the nation.* New York: Oxford University Press, 1967.

Pokorny, A. D., Miller, B. A., and Cleveland, S. E. Response to treatment of alcoholism: a follow-up study. *Quarterly Journal of Studies on Alcohol*, 1968, *29*, 364–381.

Popham, R. E., and Schmidt, W. *A decade of alcoholism research.* Toronto: University of Toronto Press, 1962.

Quinn, J. T., and Henbest, R. Partial failure of generalization in alcoholics following aversion therapy. *Quarterly Journal of Studies on Alcohol*, 1967, *28*, 70–75.

Quirk, D. A. Former alcoholics and social drinking: an additional observation. *The Canadian Psychologist*, 1968, *9*, 498–499.

Rakkolainen, V., and Turunen, S. From unrestrained to moderate drinking. *Acta Psychiatrica Scandinavica*, 1969, *45*, 47–52.

Ravetz, J. *Scientific knowledge and its social problems.* New York: Oxford University Press, 1971.

Reilly, H. (pseud.) *Easy does it, the story of Mac.* New York: P.J. Kennedy & Sons, 1950.

Reinert, R. E., and Bowen, W. T. Social drinking following treatment for alcoholism. *Bulletin of the Menninger Clinic*, 1968, *32*, 280–290.

Robinson, D. The alcohologist's addiction—some implications of having lost control over the disease concept of alcoholism. *Quarterly Journal of Studies on Alcohol*, 1972, *33*, 1028–1042.

Robinson, L., and Podnoe, B. Resistance of psychiatrists in treatment of alcoholism. *Journal of Nervous and Mental Diseases*, 1966, *143*, 220–225.

Robson, R. A., Paulus, I., and Clarke, G. G. An evaluation of the effect of a clinic treatment program on the rehabilitation of alcoholic patients. *Quarterly Journal of Studies on Alcohol*, 1965, *26*, 264–278.

Rohan, W. P. A follow-up study of hospitalized problem drinkers. *Diseases of the Nervous System,* 1970, *31,* 259–265.

Roman, P. M., and Trice, H. M. The sick role, labelling theory and the deviant drinker. *The International Journal of Social Psychiatry,* 1968, *14,* 245–251.

Room, R. Assumptions and implications of disease concepts of alcoholism. Paper delivered at 29th International Congress on Alcoholism and Drug Dependence, Sydney, Australia, 1970.

Rosengren, E. Behandling av alkoholister med amtriptylin. *Svenska Lakartingningen,* 1966, *63,* 231–238.

Rossi, J. J., Stach, A., and Bradley, N. J. Effects of treatment of male alcoholics in a mental hospital. *Quarterly Journal of Studies on Alcohol,* 1963, *24,* 99–108.

Schaefer, H. H. Twelve-month follow-up of behaviorally trained ex-alcoholic social drinkers. *Behavior Therapy,* 1972, *3,* 286–289.

Schaefer, H. H., Sobell, M. B., and Mills, K. C. Some sobering data on the use of self-confrontation with alcoholics. *Behavior Therapy,* 1971(a), *2,* 28–39.

Schaefer, H. H., Sobell, M. B., and Mills, K. C. Baseline drinking in alcoholics and social drinkers: kinds of drink and sip magnitude. *Behaviour Research and Therapy,* 1971(b), *9,* 23–27.

Schaefer, H. H., Sobell, M. B., and Sobell, L. C. Twelve-month follow-up of hospitalized alcoholics given self-confrontation experiences by videotape. *Behavior Therapy,* 1972, *3,* 283–285.

Scheff, T. J. *On being mentally ill.* Chicago: Aldine Publishing Company, 1966.

Schuckit, M. A., and Winokur, G. A short-term follow-up of women alcoholics. *Diseases of the Nervous System,* 1972, *33,* 672–678.

Selzer, M. L., and Holloway, W. H. A follow-up of alcoholics committed to a state hospital. *Quarterly Journal of Studies on Alcohol,* 1957, *18,* 98–120.

Shapiro, D. *Neurotic styles.* New York: Basic Books, 1965.

Shea, J. E. Psychoanalytic therapy and alcoholism. *Quarterly Journal of Studies on Alcohol,* 1954, *15,* 595–605.

Silverstein, S. J., Nathan, P. E., and Taylor, H. A. Blood alcohol level estimation and controlled drinking by chronic alcoholics. *Behavior Therapy,* 1974, *5,* 1–15.

Skoloda, T. E., Alterman, A. I., Cornelison, F. S., and Gottheil, E. Treatment outcome in a drinking-decisions program. *Journal of Studies on Alcohol,* 1975, *36,* 365–380.

Smith, D. H., Reddy, R. D., and Baldwin, B. R. *Voluntary action research, 1972.* Lexington, Mass.: Lexington Books, 1972.

Smith, J. A. The choice of treatment procedure in the alcoholic. In *Alcoholism: basic aspects and treatment,* H. E. Himwich (ed.). Washington, D.C.: American Association for the Advancement of Science, 1957. Pp. 173–180.

Sobell, L. C., and Sobell, M. B. A self-feedback technique to monitor drinking behavior in alcoholics. *Behaviour Research and Therapy,* 1973, *11,* 237–238.

Sobell, M. B., Schaefer, H. H., and Mills, K. C. Differences in baseline drinking behaviors between alcoholics and normal drinkers. *Behaviour Research and Therapy,* 1972, *10,* 257–268.

Sobell, M. B., and Sobell, L. C. *Individualized behavioral treatment of alcohol problems.* New York: Plenum Press, 1977.

Sobell, M. B., and Sobell, L. C. Second-year treatment outcome of alcholics treated by individualized behavior therapy: results. *Behaviour Research and Therapy,* 1976, *14,* 195–215.

Sobell, M. B., and Sobell, L. C. The need for realism, relevance, and operational assumptions in the study of substance dependence. In *Biological and behavioral approaches to drug dependence,* H. D. Cappell and A. E. LeBlanc (eds.). Toronto: Addiction Research Foundation, 1975. Pp. 133–167.

Sobell, M. B., and Sobell, L. C. Individualized behavior therapy for alcoholics. *Behavior Therapy,* 1973(a), *4,* 49–72.

Sobell, M. B., and Sobell, L. C. Alcoholics treated by individualized behavior therapy: one year treatment outcome. *Behaviour Research and Therapy,* 1973(b), *11,* 599–618.

Sobell, M. B., and Sobell, L. C. Individualized behavior therapy for alcoholics: rationale, procedures, preliminary results and appendix. *California Mental Health Research Monograph,* No. 13. Sacramento, Calif., 1972.

Steffen, J. J. Electromyographically induced relaxation in the treatment of chronic alcohol abuse. *Journal of Consulting and Clinical Psychology,* 1975, *43,* 275.

Steffen, J. J., Nathan, P. E., and Taylor, H. A. Tension-reducing effects of alcohol: further evidence and some methodological considerations. *Journal of Abnormal Psychology,* 1974, *83,* 542–547.

Steiner, C. M. *Games alcoholics play: the analysis of self scripts.* New York: Grove Press, 1971.

Sterne, M. W., and Pittman, D. J. The concept of motivation: a source of institutional and professional blockage in the treatment of alcoholism. *Quarterly Journal of Studies on Alcohol,* 1965, *26,* 41–57.

Straus, R., and Bacon, S. D. *Drinking in college.* New Haven: Yale University Press, 1953.

Sutherland, E. H., Schroeder, H. G., and Tordella, O. L. Personality traits and the alcoholic: critique of existing studies. *Quarterly Journal of Studies on Alcohol,* 1950, *11,* 547–561.

Syme, L. Personality characteristics of the alcoholic. *Quarterly Journal of Studies on Alcohol,* 1957, *18,* 288–301.

Tamerin, J. S., and Mendelson, J. H. The psychodynamics of chronic inebriation: observations of alcoholics during the process of drinking in an experimental group setting. *American Journal of Psychiatry,* 1969, *125,* 886–899.

Tamerin, J. S., Weiner, S., and Mendelson, J. H. Alcoholics' expectancies and recall of experiences during intoxication. *The American Journal of Psychiatry*, 1970, *126*, 1697–1704.

Thomas, R. E., Gliedman, L. H., Freund, J., Imber, S. D., and Stone, A. R. Favorable response in the clinical treatment of chronic alcoholism. *Journal of the American Medical Association*, 1959, *169*, 1994–1997.

Toch, H. *The social psychology of social movements*. Indianapolis: Bobbs-Merrill, 1965.

Tomsovic, M. A follow-up study of discharged alcoholics. *Hospital and Community Psychiatry*, 1970, *21*, 38–41.

Tracey, D. A., Karlin, R. B., and Nathan, P. E. An experimental analysis of the behavior of female alcoholics. Presented at the 8th Annual Meeting of the Association for Advancement of Behavior Therapy, Chicago, 1974.

Trice, H. M., and Roman, P. M. Sociopsychological predictors of affiliation with Alcoholics Anonymous: a longitudinal study of "treatment success." *Social Psychiatry*, 1970, *5*, 51–59.

Trice, H. M., Roman, P. M., and Belasco, J. T. Selection for treatment: a predictive evaluation of an alcoholism treatment regimen. *International Journal of the Addictions*, 1969, *4*, 303–317.

Trice, H. M., and Wahl, J. R. A rank order analysis of the symptoms of alcoholism. *Quarterly Journal of Studies on Alcohol*, 1958, *19*, 636–648.

van Dijk, W. K. and van Dijk-Koffeman, A. A follow-up study of 211 treated male alcoholic addicts. *The British Journal of the Addictions*, 1973, *68*, 3–24.

Voegtlin, W. L., and Lemere, F. The treatment of alcohol addiction: a review of the literature. *Quarterly Journal of Studies on Alcohol*, 1942, *2*, 717–803.

Vogler, R. E., Compton, J. V., and Weissbach, T. A. Integrated behavior change techniques for alcoholics. *Journal of Consulting and Clinical Psychology*, 1975, *43*, 233–243.

Vogler, R. E., Lunde, S. E., Johnson, G. R., and Martin, P. L. Electrical aversion conditioning with chronic alcoholics. *Journal of Consulting and Clinical Psychology*, 1970, *34*, 302–307.

Walton, H. J., Ritson, E. B., and Kennedy, R. I. Response of alcoholics to clinic treatment. *British Medical Journal*, 1966, *2*, 1171–1174.

Warren, C. A. The use of stigmatizing social labels in conventionalizing deviant behavior. *Sociology and Social Research*, 1974, *58*, 303–311.

Wilby, W. E., and Jones, R. W. Assessing patient response following treatment. *Quarterly Journal of Studies on Alcohol*, 1962, *23*, 325–334.

Wilkinson, R. *The prevention of drinking problems: alcohol control and cultural influences*. New York: Oxford University Press, 1970.

Williams, R. J. *Alcoholism: the nutritional approach*. Austin: University of Texas Press, 1959.

Williams, R. J. Alcoholics and metabolism. *Scientific American*, 1948, *179*, 50–53.

Williams, R. J., and Brown, R. A. Differences in baseline drinking behavior between New Zealand alcoholics and normal drinkers. *Behaviour Research and Therapy,* 1974, *12,* 287–294.

Wilson, G. T., Leaf, R. C., and Nathan, P. E. Aversive control of excessive alcohol consumption by chronic alcoholics in laboratory settings. *Journal of Applied Behavior Analysis,* 1975, *8,* 13–26.

World Health Organization Expert Committee on Drugs. Drug dependence: its significance and characteristics. *Bulletin World Health Organization,* 1965, *32,* 721–733.

Name Index

Subject Index